AMERICAN EYES ON THE NETHERLANDS

AMERICAN EYES ON THE NETHERLANDS
Film, Public Diplomacy, and Dutch Identity, 1943–74

Including an Historical Survey of Dutch Visual Media in America

Henk Aay

Van Raalte Press

A. C. Van Raalte Institute, Hope College
Van Raalte Press is a division of Hope College Publishing

Theil-Nyenhuis Research Center
9 East 10th Street
Holland, MI 49423

PO Box 9000
Holland, MI 49422-9000

616.395.7678
vanraalte@hope.edu

Printed in the United States of America
Library of Congress Control Number: 2024933908

Jacob E. Nyenhuis, PhD, LittD
        Editor-in-Chief and Publisher Emeritus
JoHannah M. Smith
        Project Editor
Russell L. Gasero, Archivist, Reformed Church in America
        Layout and Design

In 2022 the digitized NIB/NIS films, along with the entire NIB/NIS archive, were moved from the Holland Museum to the Hope College Archives and Special Collections (HCASC), formerly the Joint Archives of Holland.

The design and production of all the maps and graphs were directed by the author and executed by students and graduates of Calvin University's geography program and its Center for Social Research, in particular, Megumu Jansen, Brianna Marshall, Nathan Mosurinjohn, Traci Montgomery, and Owen Selles.

Although many photos reproduced in this work are in the public domain, the author has done due diligence to satisfy the requirements of the photos with intellectual property rights.

For Christine

Synthetic material (geotextiles) rolled out on a giant spool and weighed down by rocks has replaced the time-honored woven willow matting to protect the sea bottom along the dike and its underwater outer slope (Holland Today, *1962*) (*NIS archive, HCASC*)

Contents

Preface and Acknowledgments

American Eyes on the Netherlands has been more than a decade in the making, and many institutions and individuals have played a key role in its completion. I learned about the Netherlands Information Bureau/Service (NIB/NIS) archive, including its 16 mm films, and hatched a research plan long before this project had even begun. At the reception for my installation as Meijer Chair in Dutch Language and Culture at Calvin College on September 26, 2006, David Zwart, history professor at Grand Valley State University, asked if I was aware of this archive at the Holland Museum in Michigan; he had recently used its materials for his own research. I confessed I was not. He spoke about the nature of this information agency and told me that its archive included a large collection of 16 mm films. That got my attention.

I was interested in the role of Dutch visual media in American perceptions of the Netherlands.

Three years later, an upcoming sabbatical leave window for the spring of 2011 gave me an opportunity to write one successful research proposal to Fulbright and another to Calvin University for a sabbatical in the Netherlands to study this program of Dutch film diplomacy. During the run-up to this research leave, I regularly visited the Holland Museum archive to collect materials related to the film diplomacy and ferry the films themselves in batches to Calvin College for digitizing. For all this necessary groundwork, I received unstinting support from the museum archivist Catherine (Caz) Jung. From 2010 to 2013, more than 230 films were digitized by students from Calvin's video production unit; funding for the digitization was provided by the Netherland America Foundation (NAF), the Meijer Chair in Dutch Language and Culture at Calvin College, and the Holland Museum. I owe a debt of gratitude to these funders, the Calvin students who digitized the films, and video producer Steven Niedzielski who supervised their work.

Students working for Calvin's Center for Social Research (CSR) entered the information from the films' eleven thousand-plus borrowing records into an Excel spreadsheet. Once that task was complete, geography students at the CSR, Nathan Mosurinjohn, Traci Montgomery, Brianna Marshall, and Owen Selles, from 2010 to 2015, in turn, (re)mapped and (re)graphed these data. A significant portion of their work is present as figures in this book. I am grateful to Neil Carlson, director of the CSR, for his support and supervision of this very important phase of the research. Toward the end of the project, Megumu Jansen, Calvin geography graduate and architecture student at the University of Minnesota, produced new maps and graphs for the final chapter and edited for publication several of the maps and graphs made earlier. To each of these students, a heartfelt thanks.

When the time came for the Fulbright (March to July 2011) at the Roosevelt Study Center (RSC) in Middelburg, Zeeland, the Netherlands, enough of the films had been digitized and data entered, mapped, and graphed for me to organize and analyze the circulation data. I zeroed in especially on the films of the 1940s, the history of documentary filmmaking in the Netherlands, the field of film studies, and the geography of film. Those four months flew by much too fast. I am extremely grateful to the Fulbright program and Dow Benelux BV for funding my research and to the RSC for their superb personal support and interest in my work. RSC director Kees van Minnen, scholars in residence Hans Krabbendam and Giles Scott-Smith, office manager Leontien Joosse, and other staff and interns all made Christine's and my stay both rewarding and memorable.

On September 1, 2012, I retired from Calvin and my six-year appointment as Meijer Chair in Dutch Language and Culture. Aside from the digitization of the films, I had not made much progress on the Dutch film diplomacy project since our return from the Netherlands in July 2011. Determined to move ahead on several incomplete tasks within that research project, I applied early in 2012 and was accepted into the visiting research fellow program at the Van Raalte Institute at Hope College. During the 2012–13 academic year, I divided my time between Hope and Calvin College and, with the support of Calvin student workers, moved further ahead with the index of films, digitization, mapping, and content analysis of the films. Much more significant, however, for the realization of what turned out to be an expanded project, was the Van Raalte Institute's decision in 2013—for which I will be forever grateful— to appoint me as a senior research fellow. The VRI and my wheelhouse are closely aligned, including Netherlands-United States relations and Dutch American history. My hoped-for descriptions of the outcomes of the film diplomacy project had been shorter pieces—several scholarly articles and a monograph. Now I had the chance to also do a close reading of many of the films and weave these into the changing and diverse American perceptions of the Netherlands that had been promoted by these documentaries. Now I could write a book.

I remain deeply appreciative of the VRI and my colleagues there for their steadfast support for this project in the form of advice, encouragement, and finances. The institute, among others, covered my expenses for the continuing services of the Calvin Center for Social Research, mapping work by students, and conferences at which I presented the results of my research. I have divided my time here at the VRI between completing this book and other research and writing projects. Now that writing this volume is finally finished, I must give a

huge thanks to Jacob E. Nyenhuis, director and editor-in-chief emeritus, for his careful and critical reading of the manuscript and to JoHannah Smith, our project editor, for the copy editing that caught errors and improved my writing and for seeing the entire publication process through to the book on the shelf. Finally, a very special thanks is owed to media historian Bert Hogenkamp, whose books have given me a thorough grounding in the history of Dutch documentary film, something essential for this film diplomacy project. He also read an advance digital copy and graciously wrote a testimonial for the cover.

Introduction

As I write this, the Israel-Hamas War is more than a month old; like all modern wars, it is not only a ground and aerial combat but also an (dis)information battle between the belligerents and their allies in which video and photographs play an essential part. Instant visuals of atrocities, bombed civilian residential apartment blocks and hospitals, and of the many stretchered wounded and dead—daily scenes such as these move the needle of regional and global public outcry, protest, and support and may help lay the groundwork for recalibrated and redirected policies and prosecution of the war on both sides.

More than eighty years earlier, the Dutch film diplomacy in the United States was also born as part of a—much tamer—war-time propaganda campaign to con-vince Americans to join the war against the Axis powers and to document, for sympathy and aid, the murderous, brutal, and ruinous rule of Germany and Japan in, respectively, the Netherlands and the Dutch East Indies. Additionally, the Dutch WWII propaganda campaign sought to persuade the American public that its colonies qualified the Netherlands as a reliable geostrategic and well-resourced partner in the global fight against the Axis states. It was christened the Netherlands Information Bureau (NIB); several other Allied and occupied countries ran similar programs.

The foreign-policy propaganda films distributed by the Dutch government in the United States during WWII, of course, were completely unlike today's nearly instantaneous and real-time news videos and pictures fed to our phones and social media and immediately available on television and the internet all day, every day. Nor were they newsreels, a documentary genre that had already been used for propaganda in theaters for decades. As an occupied country, the Netherlands could not produce newsreels, and further, such films were quickly outdated. Rather, the Dutch authorities, from their government in exile in London, produced compilation propaganda films, made and edited from earlier Dutch films. Led and integrated by authoritative voice-overs, these films made, visualized, and repeated highly generalized and basic claims and aspirations for America's and the Netherlands' own place in this global conflict; such films had more staying power.

From the beginning, the more aggressive propaganda side of this film campaign was coupled with an easygoing cultural side. Travelogues about captivating premodern Dutch places and exotic Dutch colonial islands were also made available to every kind of organization and address throughout the United States, essentially for postage only. Although such films were American-made during most of the 1940s, the NIB opened the door in the United States, for the first time, to Dutch-made documentaries about the Netherlands and its overseas territories; this expanded the suite of visual media with Dutch content from paintings, drawings, and photographs to films. Were it not for this wartime crisis for the Netherlands, a Dutch government entity such as the NIB would not have been created, and Dutch documentaries would not have been screened for a broad American public.

Once the lobbying for American support of the Dutch colonies—the remaining foreign policy issue for the NIB after WWII—ended in 1949, its propaganda arm was terminated. Motivated by threats from the United States to cut off aid to the Netherlands, the former Dutch East Indies became the independent state of Indonesia in that year. Rather than close the NIB for good, an outcome not unexpected because the propaganda side was regarded as its main priority, the Dutch government decided to repurpose it as a promotional information agency and keep its film diplomacy intact. For more than two decades, the now "Netherlands Information Service" (NIS) brought more than 150 Dutch-made documentaries to a large viewership throughout the country. When it was finally shuttered in 1974, the availability of Dutch documentaries in the United States went to zero. An international market for national documentaries did not materialize until the turn of the century and, even then, offered very few titles. Without an agency like the NIS, only the Dutch diplomatic circuit, through embassies and consulates, would have screened a very limited number of Dutch films to a select audience in a few locations.

The NIB/NIS service center in Holland, Michigan, served a twenty-state area in the midsection of the country. After the NIS was closed in 1974, it kept and archived its NIS film and book library, as well as office records and correspondence, for the thirty-four-year lifespan of the agency. The films and their circulation records were the most important sources for this study. A content analysis and close reading of the films made it possible to construct the changing knowledge palette about the Netherlands and its overseas territories on offer to Americans by way of these documentaries. Inventories and maps of the places shown in the films about the Netherlands were used to measure how well the entire country was represented. The circulation records documented viewership and screening locations: the former measured the cultural impact of the film diplomacy program, of groups of films and individual titles, the latter, their geographic coverage.

During the Covid shutdown, when my colleagues and I worked from home from March 2020 to June 2021, I finished chapter 7, the last chapter—I thought—about the film diplomacy of the 1960s and early 1970s. But during a careful review of that chapter, it began to dawn on me that, although this manuscript was a specialized and primary historical inquiry that indeed had needed to be done and deserved a place in film studies and in the field of Netherlands-United States relations, it would be far more fulsome, useful, and meaningful if placed into the history of Dutch visual media in the United States. What's more, I had the time and opportunity for further research: In what other ways had Americans throughout their history learned what the Netherlands looked like? What were this film diplomacy's antecedents, concurrent offerings, and subsequent developments? And what might the future of Dutch films in America look like?

These questions led to wide-ranging secondary research and surveys of Dutch art in New Netherland, British America, and the United States, including Dutch American painters; Dutch photographs in American magazines and newspapers, including those from the Dutch-American press; Dutch fiction (feature) films and documentaries (other than those in NIB/NIS library) about the Netherlands, marketed in the United States by way of direct sales, Dutch television broadcasting, and video on demand services. That history spanned all the visual media technolo-

gies: paint and charcoal on canvas; prints from engravings; photographs, wire photos, and slides; films in changing physical media—35 and 16 mm film, videotape, and DVD; and transmission of all digitized visual media over the internet (video on demand). This is all contained in chapter 8.

Today, much Dutch art and countless, high-resolution, Dutch photographs are just a few clicks away. Dutch feature films and documentaries, however, are another story. Although watching Dutch TV in the United States has become easier with different international streaming services and virtual private networks (VPN) that give access to Dutch streaming sites, they are principally for expats and immigrants who know Dutch, not for Americans or those of Dutch ancestry. The body of post-WWII Dutch feature films and documentaries is not (yet) available to American and other non-Dutch viewers by means of streaming with English subtitles. Dutch feature films on DVD more commonly include English subtitles; Dutch documentaries rarely do. But DVDs are on a rapid decline, increasingly replaced by streaming services. The final section of chapter 8 suggests ways forward for the Netherlands to stream films with English (and other) subtitles to the American public and other international audiences. That way, via film, the Netherlands can readily share its geography and its many and varied looks, personalities, life worlds, and stories with Americans and the entire world. People everywhere can then increase their knowledge about this country, much as they did by watching the NIB/NIS documentaries nearly eighty years ago.

CHAPTER 1

Discovering the World Outside as It Reaches In

People have always had a need to know about and an interest in countries, regions, and places outside of their own. For much of human history, and for most people, such knowledge came through lore—the stories of explorers, travelers, and outsiders—as well as written accounts. The ruling class and economic elites of every period have always traveled more and possessed superior knowledge about outside areas through their access to written records, chronicles, charts, drawings, paintings, and maps, and even living authorities. Such intelligence was an ingredient of their power.

What is outside of one geographical area is, of course, inside another, and in this way, for every place, region, or country, there is both discovering and learning about the world outside of itself and being

discovered by the outside world, thereby making itself known. Places, regions, and countries may not be content to simply be discovered; rather, for different reasons, they may prefer to be proactive and, in a wide variety of ways, direct specific information about themselves to the outside world or even to one specific area. This book is about one such campaign.

The acquisition of knowledge about the outside world has taken many forms. In preindustrial, preliterate peasant societies, almost everyone spent their entire life in the orbit of a small area, focused on a village or a local market center. People knew little about the world outside except what was told by those traveling through their area—peddlers and pilgrims—or by the resident literate and educated upper class—nobility, clergy, teachers—who had more extensive geographical experience and wider social networks. The indigent in any culture have always been more tied to local settings than other socioeconomic groups and, generally, have had much less opportunity to experience and learn about their outside world. Further along the mobility spectrum are displaced persons, refugees, and immigrants. Deported or forced to flee their homes, refugees the world over have had to come to grips with new and distant places in order to survive and make new lives for themselves. In the process, they have carried their culture to these places and passed it on to long-time residents. Other migrants and immigrants have relocated more willingly to outside regions and countries, either temporarily or permanently, and have come to know and adapt to new environments, cultures, and languages. All such migrants have carried their own material and immaterial worlds with them, making them accessible to the residents of these new places. Pilgrims, sailors, traders, soldiers, explorers, missionaries, and emissaries have always ventured far from home; they unselfconsciously spread their own culture en route and at their destinations and upon their return have shared with their home populations their new knowledge about the places they had visited and lived in. Each of these kinds of migrants and travelers, to varying degrees, has brought their world to the outside and/or carried the outside world in.

The growth of newspaper publishing, beginning in Europe in the early seventeenth century, revolutionized opportunities to learn about the outside world both near and far.[1] Newspapers, whose circula-

tion was at first restricted to large cities and the upper classes, over time, reached all corners of their potential market areas and with increasing revenue from advertising became affordable to a large cross section of the reading public. In time, in addition to the national and metropolitan dailies, regional, city, and local newspapers made their appearance, increasing still further one's ability to acquire knowledge of the outside world at every scale. Where public libraries arose, beginning in the mid-nineteenth century, selections of newspapers both from within a country and abroad, as well as books about and from other countries, regions, and cities, became available to the public, increasing yet again the local availability of regional, national, and international news, information, and opinions.

Before commercial tourism, few people participated in visitor travel. Relatively recently, however, such travel to experience and learn about the world beyond one's home region and country has become more commercialized and democratized, at least for those not living in poverty. The religious pilgrimages of the devout in the Middle Ages and the grand tours reserved for upper-class young men in early modern Europe began, in the nineteenth century, to give way to organized group and individual leisure travel at home and abroad for the middle classes, made possible by railway and steamship. For better-educated citizens, armchair visits by way of travel writing, regional literature, fiction set in places far and near, and regional and national newspapers both enriched and substituted for travel. And, as elementary and later secondary education became more widespread during the nineteenth and early twentieth centuries in economically advanced countries, a growing cross section

[1] Anthony Smith, *The Newspaper: An International History* (Thames and Hudson, 1979).

of their national populations began to learn more about the outside world through language, history, geography, current events, social studies, and literature classes. In the early decades of the twentieth century, films and filmstrips were added to the mix of educational textbooks, stories, literature from other lands, maps, photos, and posters. Much of people's knowledge about other countries came from their formal education, which taught material to students in a more systematic way, via a curriculum. This produced more of a gestalt of their own and other regions and countries, rather than snippets of information gleaned from various sources. Outside of formal education, documentary films in the form of travelogues and newsreels also became part of the repertoire of movie theaters, beginning early in the twentieth century. Such shorts mixed entertainment with information about the larger world.

Even though formal education has a great capacity to enhance international knowledge among students, the results are often very mixed and fall short, as studies of global geographic literacy—one proxy for international knowledge—show. Students from various countries achieve very different scores on geographic literacy surveys, with American students usually at the bottom.[2] Clearly, an overall international societal orientation and study programs and courses that are intentionally international and transnational are required for formal education to deliver its promise in this regard.

Today, primarily in the more economically developed countries, the acquisition of international knowledge has undergone other qualitative transformations when compared to the middle decades of the last century, the time period of this study. An even wider variety of intersecting activities, media, and technologies make possible and promote international knowledge (as well as misinformation, inadvertent or deliberate) as never before. The United Nations World Tourism Organization reported that cross-border tourist travel has exploded since the 1950s, from virtually no international tourists following WWII to more than 1.3 billion in 2018.[3] Tourist destinations, much dominated by Europe and the Americas until the 1990s, have become significantly more diversified, especially into Asia and the Pacific, with a 24 percent share in 2018. The split between advanced and emerging economies as destinations among international tourists is getting close to even. Although different types of organized travel, such as cruise ships, cultural tourism, and ecotourism, provide greater (sometimes fewer) opportunities for acquiring international knowledge, the rapid growth of people actually visiting other countries certainly has transformed the acquisition of such knowledge.

Since the mid-1990s, for those in the world with regular and unfettered access to it, the internet has allowed the amount of readily available information about other countries to grow exponentially. Various media (print, news, video, etc.) and content from unnumbered sources are assimilated via web browsers, the Google search engine, Wikipedia, and so forth. The internet itself has added some of its own capabilities to enhance international knowledge and understanding,

---

[2] For example, Final Report, National Geographic-Roper Public Affairs, *2006 Geographic Literacy Study* (GFK NOP, 2006).

[3] World Tourism Organization, *UNWTO Tourism Highlights 2018 edition* (WTO, 2018).

such as blogs, social media, and online education, as well as streaming radio, TV programs, and films.[4] The internet has provided a push to make much more information (and misinformation) about countries available in world languages, especially English. Online information about any country comes not only from its own institutions and people but also from international agencies and educational, travel, cultural, and scholarly organizations around the world.

The extent and depth of international knowledge, of course, depends on many factors. For an individual, as well as a country, that information will range from low to high conversance. Countries in the neighborhood—those with a similar or familiar language and economic development—are often more well known. A person or group's ancestry, knowledge of the language(s), family ties, visits, and particular interests will favor certain countries and foster a continuing pursuit of knowledge and staying current. Virtual visits (pen pals, social media, etc.) and cultural exchange programs (for students, scholars, athletes, musicians, and artists) nurture and often sustain knowledge about other countries. At the same time, knowledge about other countries may remain very rudimentary or nonexistent. Knowledge of a country's language(s) is a prerequisite for high conversance. The information about a country in a different language (commonly English) is usually abridged, oversimplified, and uncritical, lacking the cultural nuance and context of the country itself. More specialized subject matter is often unavailable.

---

4   C. Beaudoin, "The Internet's Impact on International Knowledge," *New Media and Society* 10, no. 3 (2003): 455–74.

International knowledge and constructed national identities

For the general public, the international knowledge applied to individual countries or regions of the world has often been drawn and consolidated from both the content of and advertising in diverse mass media: traditionally, print (newspapers, magazines, tourist brochures), broadcast (radio, television), and film (fiction and documentary) but today, the juggernaut of all mass media—the internet (all the previous forms, plus blogs, podcasts, social media, and streaming services). An article, a photo spread, a particular movie, or a podcast about a country or place can encode an identity among those in its audience. For instance, the record-grossing movie, *Crocodile Dundee* (1986) constructed for the world an outback image of Australia—a remote, vast, and sparsely populated continental interior of aboriginal people, deserts, mountains, and monsoon lands. Tourist brochures and videos of the Caribbean have cemented into place for North Americans and Europeans a one-dimensional image of private, get-away playgrounds and love nests on sun-drenched tropical islands, ringed by white beaches. The identity of the Netherlands, the subject of this book, has as its mass-media, ur-personality a tiny country below the sea. Although the internet does scale-up and energize traditional mass media, at the same time, it also narrowcasts to users with specialized interests. Anyone with an interest in a particular country or place has instant access to a surfeit of information to build and keep up-to-date a multifaceted or specialized topical understanding (e.g., bicycle infrastructure), leaving mass-media-constructed identities far behind.

Neighboring countries and others with intertwined histories have invested more effort to describe and explain to their own populations the identity of their neighbors and other influential partners, competitors, and antagonists. The national identities of those outside countries constructed by writers and artists in their own countries then become essential content of their public knowledge. The educated English public (and those from New England) of the seventeenth and eighteenth centuries, for example, worked for a time with an elaborate anti-Dutch narrative, born of their maritime wars over trade. The narrative portrayed the Netherlands as a watery marsh, its people fat and often drunk, and developed a series of insults, such as "Dutch courage" (bravery fueled by alcohol) and "Dutch wife" (a prostitute).[5]

Early Americans had to navigate between the Knickerbocker image of the American Dutch and the perception of the Dutch of the Netherlands.[6] The first was a negative and comic caricature of the Dutch of the Hudson Valley and northern New Jersey, much influenced by author Washington Irving.[7] It was also nurtured by a carryover to America of the earlier harsh and disagreeable British attitudes toward the Dutch. Writers and illustrators depicted the American Dutch as "portly, pipe smoking, gin-swilling Dutchmen sleeping in the shade, measuring land by laying

trousers end to end, and making absurd political pronouncements."[8] In the minds of many British Americans, Dutch ineptitude led to the loss of their colony.

The second image was much more positive; it came from attention—largely by Americans of non-Dutch backgrounds—accorded to the Dutch in the Netherlands. And, as with Irving's history of New York, it was historian John Lothrop Motley who, beginning in the mid-nineteenth century, laid the foundation of this alternate image of Dutchness, one that ultimately prevailed and became the dominant American view by the end of the century.[9] Motley drew favorable parallels between the rise of the Dutch and the American republics; it was the courageous and successful, eighty-year Dutch revolt against the Spanish Empire that brought democracy and freedom to the Dutch already in 1581 and laid the groundwork for Americans (and others) to resist tyranny and establish democratic rule nearly two centuries later. The Dutch and the American people became ideological confreres and the Netherlands a motherland of the United States; from that bond emerged an overall positive American at-

---

5   Jaap Verheul, "In Foreign Eyes," in *Discovering the Dutch; On Culture and Society of the Netherlands*, ed. Emmeline Besamusca and Jaap Verheul (Amsterdam University Press, 2010), 268–69.

6   Annette Stott, "Images of Dutchness in the United States," in *Four Centuries of Dutch-American Relations*, ed. Hans Krabbendam, Cornelis A. Van Minnen, Giles Scott Smith (SUNY Press, 2009), 238–49.

7   Irving Washington, *History of New York from the Beginning of the World to the End of the Dutch Dynasty* (G. P. Putnam's Sons, 1880).

8   Stott, "Images of Dutchness," 239.

9   John Lothrop Motley, *The Rise of the Dutch Republic. A History* (Harper and Bros., 1856). See also, Peter D. Van Cleave, "Remembering the Knickerbockers: A Lifetime of Scholarship on the Dutch American Atlantic," in *Sharing Pasts, Dutch Americans through Four Centuries*, ed. Henk Aay, Janny Venema, and Dennis Voskuil (Van Raalte Press, 2017), 237–58; Babs Boter, "Contemplating, Complicating, and Comparing Scenes: Elkanah Watson and William Elliot Griffis Connect Dutch America to the Netherlands," in *Sharing Pasts*, 259–77. A fine thesis by a Dutch researcher discussing the positive writings about the Dutch by John Lothrop Motley, Douglas Campbell, and William Elliot Griffis in mid- to late nineteenth-century America is G. H. Joost Baarssen, "Just Like US: The Dutch Image in Late Nineteenth–Century America (master's thesis, Radbout University, 2010).

Fig. 1.1. William Henry Howe, *Early Start for Market*, ca. 1888[11]

titude that was transferred to a cultural affection for especially the preindustrial Netherlands during the Dutch Republic (1649–1784) and its nineteenth-century counterparts. This also served as a nostalgic alternative and a sharp contrast to the rapid industrialization and urbanization that the United States was experiencing at this time.

Author Annette Stott describes the forty-year period (1880–1920) in which Americans put their interest and admiration for the Netherlands into practice.[10] Wealthy Americans bought Dutch paintings, and the middle classes decorated their homes and offices with reproductions. American artists visited Dutch towns, spent time in Dutch art colonies, and produced Dutch-themed paintings to sell in America (fig. 1.1). Dutch travel books were popular and featured the country's premodern locales as preferred destinations; those of means traveled to Holland—to the western coastal provinces (not to the rest of the Netherlands)—and visited quaint fishing villages, windmills in the polders, and historic towns and city centers. American residential construction copied Dutch and Flemish architectural styles.

It is this positive, American, home-grown kaleidoscope of Dutchness that

---

[10]   Annette Stott, *Holland Mania. The Unknown Dutch Period in American Art and Culture* (Overlook Press, 1998).

[11]   Ibid., 53–54. William Henry Howe (1846–1929), an American cattle painter, spent time in the Dutch artist colony of Laren, Noord-Holland, close to the Zuiderzee. *Early Start for Market* (fig. 1.1) depicts a premodern rural scene of a farmer driving a small number of his cattle to a nearby market; it contrasts sharply with the mass production of the American cattle industry at the time.

provided a favorable opening to and fertile ground for the Dutch public diplomacy initiative by film in the United States during WWII and the postwar period that is the subject of this study. In that regard, and as detailed in chapter 5, it is instructive to note that most of the earliest films about the Netherlands distributed in the United States by the Dutch government were actually American-made travelogues that embodied the content of these positive and preferred nostalgic and premodern American perceptions of the Netherlands.

Cultural nationalism and cultural diplomacy

Government agencies at all levels produce and disseminate information about their territories to the outside world. When national governments represent their country to people and institutions in other countries, they invariably employ promotional, advocatory, and persuasive rhetoric. They put their country in the best possible light to stimulate cooperation, tourism, investment, and exchange and trade and to showcase its cultural achievements. Or, by contrast, they report dire and difficult circumstances in their country to garner sympathy and financial, military, material, and other kinds of aid. Most commonly, it is the diplomatic mission in embassies and consulates abroad that, upon request and of its own initiative, makes relevant information and programs about its home country available to the general public and to particular organizations and opinion makers in the realms of education, commerce, and culture, among others. It regularly facilitates and supports theater, music, and the visual arts, as well as scholarship from the home country in the host country. The professional diplomatic corps

also initiates, negotiates, interprets, and implements bilateral and multilateral relations and agreements between the host and home countries.

A nongovernmental avenue for a country to use to foster knowledge about itself abroad is that of cultural institutes, such as the Goethe Institut, the Alliance française, the Italian Institute, and the British Council. These have complex European origins in the nineteenth century, related to nation building, colonialism, geopolitics, and ethnic diasporas.[12] These institutes established branches in many different countries around the world; the Alliance française, for example, has a presence in nearly every country, many with multiple locations. More recently, other countries, for example, Japan and China, have established such organizations. The nineteenth-century European cultural institutes served to project their national cultural and civilizing power into other countries, especially into their colonial and geopolitical spheres, as well as into their ethnic communities living outside their borders.

Today, a cultural institute's focus is centered on cultural understanding and appreciation. They share their own country's distinctive cultural achievements with their host country, showcasing art, music, film, literature, and scholarship on their own premises and at schools, libraries, galleries, and concert halls in major centers. They offer language courses and run cultural exchange programs. Many cultural institutes receive state subsidies, but they also raise money via tuition from their language courses and private donors, foundations, and firms. Because cultural

[12]　G. Paschalidis, "Exporting National Culture: Histories of Cultural Institutes Abroad," *International Journal of Cultural Policy* 15, no. 3 (2009): 275–89.

institutes are not government entities, they are regarded as having a more independent voice, representing the country at large, and are not as easily associated with the narrower interests and propaganda objectives of a central government. Others, such as the Japan Foundation, the United States Information Agency, and the Confucius Institute, are separate government agencies. With such initiatives, governments regard the projection of soft power important enough to reach beyond their diplomatic mission and establish and fund separate information and cultural institutes with branches in designated countries that reach out to a broad public rather than to decision makers. In so doing, they disguise and neutralize the more overt connections with the apparatus of the state.

When the primary purpose of such state agencies is to share the culture of the home country through literature, art, music, dance, cuisine, design, and fashion, they contribute to a celebration of the many-sided culture of the home country. By and large, cultural institutes present a pervasively positive image of their own home country. More activist campaigns defending contested policies and actions at home or lobbying against particular policies of the host country are typically not part of these cultural institutes; they are left to the diplomatic corps and native and expatriate leaders and scholars.

The institutional arrangements for cultural nationalism and diplomacy have taken other forms under different historical circumstances. This study examines one such institution established at the start of WWII, the Netherlands Information Bureau (NIB), later renamed the Netherlands Information Service (NIS), and provides a close reading of the films it distributed.

When it was founded, the NIB combined into one organization an activist, foreign-policy-directed campaign in the press and political arena and a demand-driven service providing information (including films) about the Netherlands and its colonies in response to inquiries and requests by letter and phone. The NIB was not a cultural institute as these operate today. It did not offer Dutch-language courses nor—given the German occupation of the Netherlands and its aftermath—could it do very much initially to share Dutch culture with the American public through performances and exhibits. Unlike cultural institutes, the NIB's bread and butter, at first, was political propaganda, but those foreign-policy priorities ended by the late 1940s, and the information service continued for more than twenty years. With the exception of the Institut Néerlandais in Paris, which opened its doors in 1957 and closed them in 2013, the Netherlands has not followed the cultural-institute model in its public diplomacy. This has to do with its small size in area and population, the relatively small number of Dutch speakers, the negligible place of Dutch in foreign-language education, and the relatively modest role of the Netherlands in global affairs. Cultural diplomacy today is housed largely in the Dutch diplomatic service. For example, Dutch Culture United States is a program of the government of the Netherlands centered in the Dutch Consulate in New York City and headed by the cultural attaché of the Netherlands to the United States. It facilitates, sponsors, and publicizes Dutch culture and heritage in the United States.[13]

[13] See www.dutchcultureusa.com.

CHAPTER 2

The Netherlands Information Bureau/Service

Founding

There are situations in which a national government regards its relationship with another country so decisive to its own future welfare and existence that it reaches beyond its diplomatic mission to establish a special and separate information and lobbying agency. Its mission is to reach out to a broad public, as well as to decision makers and other elites, with the aim of influencing opinions and policy. Britain, the Netherlands, and several other countries created such organizations in the United States and elsewhere at the beginning of WWII—Britain, the British Information Services (BIS), and the Netherlands, the Netherlands Information Bureau (NIB).

Hitler, unable to achieve air superiority over Britain, had decided by the autumn of 1940 not to invade the island

nation. Even with Britain spared from invasion, Nazi Germany went on to conquer almost all of the rest of Europe, as well as parts of Asia and North Africa. The conviction became widespread that Germany would be stopped and the tide turned only if the United States entered the conflict. Britain was the only remaining European Allied power with a fully functioning, independent, and well-resourced national government; it also enjoyed a special historical relationship with the United States.

At the time, Britain was one of only a few countries permitted and able to pursue an active propaganda campaign in the United States to convince the American government and the public that it was necessary for them to enter the war. And so, in 1940, the British Foreign Office established the British Information Services

(BIS), with headquarters in New York City (Rockefeller Center) and branch offices in Chicago, San Francisco, and Los Angeles.[1] It quickly began pressing the case—in the political corridors, in the press, in broadcasting, and on the lecture circuit—for American involvement; this required, among other things, taking on American isolationism, strongly represented especially in the United States' midsection, as well as a disinformation campaign in the United States by Nazi Germany, together with political maneuvering by other fascist leaders in the United States.[2] The BIS produced and assembled print, photographic, and film materials for distribution from its headquarters and branches not only to make the case for American involvement but also to provide information of all kinds about the United Kingdom.

The Dutch royal family and government leaders had managed to escape to Britain during the German invasion in 1940. Queen Wilhelmina and the Dutch government established themselves as the duly sanctioned rulers and leaders in exile in London. They rejected the idea of returning to the Netherlands and collaborating with Hitler as the Vichy French government had done and as De Geer, the prime minister of the Netherlands, had favored. Under newly appointed prime minister Pieter Gerbrandy, the Dutch cabinet allied itself with the British policy of influencing the United States to join the war effort.

Beginning with the German occupation of the Netherlands on May 15, 1940, and ending with the Japanese occupation of the Dutch East Indies by March 1942, the Netherlands lost all international military and economic power. The Dutch government in exile in London quickly realized that public diplomacy and information campaigns were the only influence it could still wield. It immediately established the Rijksvoorlichtingsdienst (RVD), the government information service. Although earlier Dutch administrations had provided information to the press, an agency providing information directly to the public at home and abroad was new and unexplored territory for the government.[3] For the occupied Netherlands, the RVD established information channels in the form of daily radio broadcasts (*Radio Oranje*) and communication ties to the clandestine Dutch press. In European and other cities outside the war zone, the RVD set up press offices and commissioned agents to distribute the magazine, *Vrij Nederland*. It placed and presented Dutch accounts and points of view in the foreign press and radio, challenging the versions of events and propaganda of the Axis powers. For communicating Dutch viewpoints and information

---

[1]   Consult, Nicholas John Cull, *The British Propaganda Campaign against American "Neutrality" in World War II* (Oxford University Press, 1995), and Thomas E. Mahl, *Desperate Deception: British Covert Operations in the United States, 1939–44* (Brassey's, 1998). Under the heading of BIS, WikiSpooks.com sketches a rather disapproving digest of the history of the agency with particular attention to its leaders and propaganda efforts in relation to contentious British foreign policy issues at home and abroad ("British Information Services," WikiSpooks, 25 March 2020, https://wikispooks.com/wiki/British_Information_Services).

[2]   Rachel Maddow, *Prequel; An American Fight against Fascism* (Crown, 2023).

[3]   This transition from a government press agency to an information agency is described in the Marja Roholl, "To Put Holland on the Map: Voorlichting als Instrument van Buitenlands Beleid van Nederland, 1900–1950," paper presented to the conference, Media en Sociaal-Culturele Veranderingen, International Institute for Social History, Amsterdam (24 May 1991), 1–4.

to the countries of the Western Hemisphere (principally, the United States), the RVD established the NIB in March of 1941, with headquarters in Rockefeller Center in New York City, the broadcast and cultural center of the nation; the BIS had located there earlier. Other occupied countries and Allied powers also established information bureaus near Rockefeller Center and elsewhere in Manhattan, as well as in Washington, DC, and Australia, Czechoslovakia, New Zealand, Norway, the Philippines, and Poland.[4] Like the NIB and BIS, some wanted to draw attention to their plight, counter the propaganda of the Axis powers, and appeal to the American public and decision makers, but others wanted to communicate their solidarity with the Allied cause.

N.A.C. Slotemaker de Bruine, head of the Dutch East Indies newswire service, was appointed director of the NIB, signaling the importance of the Dutch colonies in the Netherlands' relations with the United States. He established a special Dutch East Indies Department within the agency.[5] The rising world hegemony of the United States; its hoped-for, favorable future impact on the prosecution of the war; and its influence on the postwar world made this arm of the RVD the most important for pressing Dutch national objectives.[6]

Subsidiary NIB service centers were established later in Washington, DC; Boston; Holland, Michigan; San Francisco; and (later) Montreal, Canada, and Buenos Aires, Argentina. With one important exception, the service centers in the United States were in large, financial, cultural, and broadcasting capitals that also housed Dutch consulates. Although some of these places included significant populations with Dutch ancestry, they were not in any way Dutch American cities. Holland, Michigan, however—at that time, a very small and overwhelmingly Dutch American city—met none of these considerations. Chicago was a more natural choice for the middle of the country—the largest city in the region; a cultural, economic, and broadcasting powerhouse; a metropolitan area with a Dutch consulate; and home to a significant population of Dutch Americans. Nevertheless, Holland, Michigan, was chosen largely because of the lobbying by and qualifications of Willard "Bill" Wichers, a Holland, Michigan, native with tremendous energy, a promoter of all things Dutch and Dutch American, and someone who would also be able to enlist Dutch Americans as ambassadors for the NIB mission.[7] Wichers was also director of the Netherlands [now, Holland] Museum, founded in 1937, at that time supported with municipal funds and private donations.

New York, Boston, and Washington, DC, served a seventeen-state area, plus the Capital District along the East Coast; Holland, Michigan, served a twenty-state area in the midsection of the country; and San Francisco served a thirteen-state, western region (fig. 2.2). For a time, the Holland

---

4   "Directory of Producers and Distributors," in *Educational Film Guide, 1945 Edition*, comp. Dorothy E. Cook and Eva Rahbek-Smith (H. W. Wilson Co., 1945), 481–90. See Internet Archive, at archive.org. Information bureaus from these countries are listed here because they distributed films. See ch. 8 in this volume.

5   David J. Snyder, "Dutch Cultural Policy in the United States," in *Four Centuries of Dutch-American Relations* (SUNY Press, 2009), 970–81, esp. p. 971.

6   See endnote 2:5, p. 397.

7   See endnote 2:6, p. 397.

Fig. 2.1. Willard C. Wichers, director of the NIB/NIS, 1942-74 (*NIS archive, HCASC*)

NIB also had a representative in Dallas who organized activities in that state and reported to Wichers; the activities there became part of Wichers' regular reports to the head office in New York City. The Holland office called itself the Midwestern Division of the NIB, even though it included seven Southern states.

The establishment and features of the NIB in the United States followed the British pattern, albeit on a much smaller scale. Both were born of political necessity in wartime conditions. Both were government agencies, directed by and responsible to their ministries of foreign affairs and cabinet. Both were set up to especially reach out to the American people and influence public opinion to favor American participation in the war in the face of strong isolationism in the country, and similarly, both were determined to make a case for the rightness and difference in their colonial rule to counter the commitment to self-determination of colonial territories held by the American public and leadership. More generally, both worked hard to promote and build upon the positive American public perceptions of their countries. They set up branch offices (fig. 2.3) to facilitate the distribution of and access to materials, to program events in their service areas, and to engage and contribute to the national and regional press. Both were to be somewhat independent from their diplomatic missions, although, in practice, the embassies and consulates exercised a lot of control, especially when it came to the more activist side associated with politics, broadcasting, and the press. Because both were agencies of a foreign government in the

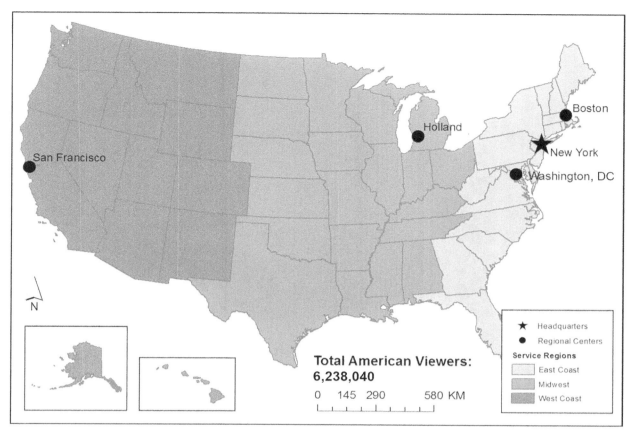

Fig. 2.2. NIB/NIS service regions and centers, including the estimated national viewership of NIB/NIS films, 1943-74

United States they were required to submit regular reports of their activities to the Justice Department. The very detailed monthly and later semiannual activity reports that Willard Wichers sent to the director of the NIB in New York were also sent to the Justice Department.[8] From the beginning, the regional directors sent activity reports to the NIB/NIS director in New York City. At first, these were monthly reports, but soon they were biannual. These activity reports gave a statistical summary of the work at the branch office, listing, among other things, telephone calls, letters written, packages of materials sent out, and film showings, including average attendance (fig. 2.4).[9]

The British propaganda campaign in the United States could be far more full-bodied than the Dutch one. Britain had a much larger place on the world stage, with more international standing and greater financial resources. The ties of a common language and heritage, special friendship with the United States, and loyalties of Anglo-American elites all made for a more effective, intense, and far-reaching propaganda campaign than the Dutch information agency was capable of prosecuting. But one can certainly argue that

8   Snyder, "The Problem of Power," 62.

9   "Monthly Reports to the Bureau," and "Activity Reports," box 3, NIS archive, HCASC.

Fig. 2.3. Reading room of the NIB and the Netherlands Museum during WWII. Photos of Queen Wilhelmina; Crown Princess Juliana and her two daughters, Princesses Beatrix and Irene; and a map of the Dutch East Indies grace the wall in front of the staff desk (*NIS archive, HCASC*).

the Dutch campaign—colored by its own political objectives—added yet another voice to counter and reverse American isolationism and prepare the way for American involvement in the war.

Culture- and foreign-policy-directed public diplomacy

The everyday busyness of the regional offices of the NIB showed up in the routines of a comprehensive information and promotion agency: answering specific questions and furnishing information about the Netherlands to individuals, schools, libraries, and businesses, in person and by phone and letter, as well as planning and promoting a wide range of cultural exhibits and events. Yet, such culture-directed activities, although contributing to improving American public understanding of the country, masked the core work of the NIB during the 1940s. Issues related to the war, making the case for American involvement in it, the management of the

CABLE ADDRESS: NETHINFORM

TELEPHONE: EXPORT 2-3129

THE NETHERLANDS INFORMATION SERVICE
(A Government Agency of The Netherlands)
MIDWESTERN DIVISION
NETHERLANDS MUSEUM, HOLLAND, MICHIGAN

WILLARD C. WICHERS, DIRECTOR

REF. NO.

July 6, 1959

MEMORANDUM TO: Mr. J. A. van Houten
FROM: Willard C. Wichers
SUBJECT: Activity Report for January - June, 1959

Statistical Survey Covering Part of Activities Report

Telephone calls received	1,140
Persons coming into office	325
Letters written	2,465
Packages of literature sent out	4,986
Number of films booked	90
Number of film showings	784
Number of film showings reported	758
Attendance reported	18,965
Average attendance	23+

PUBLIC SERVICE

713 letters

This category reports requests by letter and in person for general information on the Netherlands.

Literature on geography, culture, economics, history, was sent to:

3,946 schools   230 libraries   810 individuals

SERVICE PROJECTS

580 letters

This category reports projects requiring research, specific attention and development.

Fig. 2.4. Page 1 of the activity report for January to June 1959; Willard Wichers, director, Holland NIB, to J. A. van Houten, director, NIS, New York City (*NIS archive, HCASC*)

information about the Netherlands and its colonies circulating in the United States, postwar Dutch reconstruction, and the future of the Dutch colonies all made up a carefully planned NIB foreign-policy-directed public diplomacy. Generally, such diplomacy relates to very specific political and foreign-policy issues and has a more activist orientation. It is muscular, aggressive, and given to arm-twisting of varying kinds (e.g., lobbying, reacting to newspaper opinion pieces, and speeches by surrogates). When the *Chicago Tribune* in 1945 made the case that the Dutch monopoly of broadcasting from the Dutch East Indies made it impossible for Indonesian accounts and opinions to be heard abroad, it was attacked as a lie by the NIB.[10]

Culture-directed public diplomacy covers everything else and aims to improve understanding and appreciation of one country—its accomplishments, distinctives, history, and way of life—among the people of another country. The culture of a country encompasses all its distinctives in every area, by themselves and together, all the way from its natural environment to its economy, society, and religious life. It includes both high culture and popular culture. It may be planned—the Netherlands Bach Society on tour in the United States—or consumer driven—the public library in Amarillo, Texas, borrowing a film from the Holland, Michigan, branch of the NIB. Foreign-policy-directed public diplomacy is always propaganda; culture-directed public diplomacy may be propaganda but is always promotion. Both aim to put their country in a positive light.

The NIB was forged by the extraordinary conditions the Dutch government in exile faced beginning in May of 1940 and by the close cooperation and consensus of the British government and the Dutch government in exile in London. It was created as an agency of the Dutch government, first and foremost, to bend relevant American foreign policy in directions championed by the Dutch government in exile. Foreign-policy-directed diplomacy was its core business, although culture-directed diplomacy was conducted alongside and as part of and cover for this campaign. The latter was the more traditional and expected form of public diplomacy.

Given its wartime challenges, the Dutch government understandably would not have been at all interested in creating an agency to promote only Dutch culture. The foreign-policy-directed public diplomacy was a media and tactical campaign to change American public opinion and, from that base, American foreign policy. Its aims were to bring the United States into the war, generate a favorable outlook for keeping not only the Dutch East Indies but also other Dutch colonies, and win sympathy for the Netherlands as an occupied and war-torn land. Although there was no lack of American commiseration for the Netherlands, as well as other German (and Japanese) occupied countries, the campaign failed in its principal objectives. David Snyder considers this to have been a naïve undertaking by the Dutch government in exile. He puts the activist work of the NIB into a larger perspective in international relations and argues that the failure of the NIB to achieve its foreign policy objectives—that is, to bring the United States into the war and keep the East Indies—was due to a mismatch between its informational campaigns (soft power) and

---

[10] Snyder, "Dutch Cultural Policy," 973.

Dutch military and economic might (hard power).[11]

Despite its largely unsuccessful activist foreign policy campaign, the NIB, through its branch offices, did disseminate a great deal of highly diverse material about the Netherlands and its colonies to a large and broad American public throughout the entire country during the 1940s. And the foreign policy campaign did bring some success—it planted in the hearts and minds of Americans an image of a small, courageous, war-torn country that deserved American help.

From bureau to service

As the foreign policy issues related to the war and the Dutch colonies passed into history, and the Netherlands and the United States looked ahead in the Atlantic Charter and the Cold War to a more parallel foreign policy, the foreign-policy-directed diplomacy of the NIB came to an end, and the agency became defined principally by culture-directed diplomacy, and trade and investment between the Netherlands and the United States served as subsidiary objectives. In 1951, under its new director, Jerome Heldring, the NIB was renamed the Netherlands Information Service (NIS).

Governments rightly lead foreign-policy-directed diplomacy, but culture-directed diplomacy is also practiced—better practiced, some would argue—by more independent and diverse institutions that promote knowledge of the language and culture of a country, such as the Goethe Institut in Germany or Alliance française. Nevertheless, from 1951 to its closing in 1974, the NIS remained an instrument and voice of the Dutch state, also subject

to how a particular government wished to promote its agenda.

Culture-directed diplomacy, ipso facto, enjoyed a lower political—and budgetary—priority, and declining financial support cut into the NIS's cultural programming. Throughout the 1950s, 1960s, and early 1970s, the NIS continued, through thick and thin, to supply wide-ranging economic and cultural information to individuals, schools, social organizations, and companies, answer thousands of letters, arrange many exhibits and lectures, and expand its film library and its circulation. For nearly twenty-five more years, millions of Americans had their questions answered by the NIS both in person and by letter; used its materials sent to schools, libraries, and individuals; heard its radio programs; saw its films; read its accounts in daily newspapers based on its press releases; and attended its exhibits and talks.

The end of the NIB/NIS and what took its place

With the agency's declining budget and political support, the Dutch government closed the NIB/NIS in 1974 and transferred some of its functions to the diplomatic services.[12] Albeit with varying degrees of support, activities, and levels of output, for thirty-four years, there had been a continuous program of Dutch-government public diplomacy in the United States, covering all aspects of the country. What took its place, beginning in 1975 and continuing until today, were sporadic bursts of Dutch public, diplomatic attention at historical occasions important to both countries at both a national and a local scale (e.g., 1982, the bicentennial of

---

[11] Snyder, "The Problem of Power," 59–61.

[12] See endnote 2:11, p. 398.

ties between the two countries[13]); growth of private Dutch public diplomacy, a trend that had been present for some time already; and commercialization of Dutch visual media.

With the increase in income, resources, education, and leadership in Dutch American communities, Dutch American cultural investments—not financed by the Dutch government—were made in education, research, and Dutch festivals, each a form of private public diplomacy. Dutch-studies programs and academic chairs were launched at a number of American colleges and universities, and organizations to promote and share scholarship on Dutch Americans and Dutch topics were established and are still active. These programs and organizations have produced a substantial and growing body of journal literature and book-length accounts and have informed and shaped Dutch American and American perceptions of the Netherlands and its overseas territories.[14] Community-funded Dutch festivals have been held regularly in Dutch American centers and attract many non-Dutch American visitors. Dutch documentaries have largely remained missing after the closing of the NIS, but Dutch feature films with English subtitles have become more widely available to interested American viewers, and Dutch art is present in the permanent collections and special exhibits at many American museums and increasingly available online in high definition. In sum, Dutch public diplomacy in the United States changed from governmental, promotional outreach to private, differentiated, and multivocal programs.[15]

When the NIS shut its doors in 1974, the Dutch government allowed the Holland NIS branch office to keep all its materials and records, including its film library with its circulation records. In part, this arrangement was made because NIS-Holland shared space with the Netherlands Museum, founded in 1937, and the holdings of the NIB/NIS could potentially be augmented and expand the museum collections. Willard Wichers, director of the museum, was also director of the Holland NIB/NIS throughout its entire existence (1941–74). Wichers was a meticulous record keeper, a well-intentioned hoarder, and an assiduous collector of all things Dutch and Dutch American.[16] All this, in time, made possible the establishment at the Netherlands Museum of a very extensive and complete archive of NIB/NIS-Holland materials, as well as an equally extensive archive of Wichers' personal records, many also related to the information agency.

NIB/NIS public diplomacy: materials, media, and tactics

The NIB/NIS made use of all available media and varieties of Dutch and Dutch colonial materials: newspapers (clippings) and press releases, magazines and journals, photographs, material objects, films, filmstrips, slides, books, radio scripts, music recordings, art, cultural artifacts, lectures and speeches, telegrams, newsletters, and government publications and pamphlets.[17] Information and viewpoints about the Netherlands were disseminated through exhibits; libraries of films, books, magazines and other print materials in each

---

[13]   Snyder, "Dutch Cultural Policy," 979.

[14]   Ibid., 977–78.

[15]   See ch. 8 for discussion of the post-NIS Dutch visual media landscape in the United States.

[16]   Snyder, "The Netherlands Information Service Collection," 203.

[17]   See endnote 2:16, p. 398.

NIB/NIS office; lecture tours by prominent Dutch authorities or American surrogates; press releases; and regular radio programs throughout the United States.

In considering the voice and viewpoints of the NIB/NIS, it is important to note that, besides the production of its own materials, it mainly vetted and approved those produced by others and disseminated them as widely as possible. The New York head office sent a wide variety of materials down to the branch offices and gave the directors freedom to employ them as they saw fit.[18] Such modi operandi gave the NIB, unlike a propaganda agency that produced all its own material, a more diverse set of voices and interpretations, although all agreed with governmental policies and put the country and its colonies in a positive light.

To advance its objectives, the foreign-policy-directed public diplomacy of the NIB used its materials and media in more proactive, reactive, and tactical ways than the more consumer-driven, culture-directed, public diplomacy. In addition, the foreign-policy-directed activities made use of media and tactics not employed in the agency's role as an education and promotion agency. Materials for such initiatives were, in general, produced by the NIB itself since they could not be easily gleaned from already available sources.

The proactive and reactive foreign-policy-directed campaign waged by the NIB during the 1940s included covert oversight of the Dutch wire services to manage the news; speeches to prominent audiences by well-known Dutch figures, such as Queen Wilhelmina, the Dutch

ambassador, and American surrogates; the production of films; the commissioning and use of books and pamphlets making the Dutch case; the staging of moveable exhibits of photos of the Netherlands in wartime; and press releases and other quick responses to unfavorable newspaper accounts and editorials.[19] The campaign also sought to bring Dutch Americans to its side. For example, the NIB circulated Dutch news reports and enjoyed close cooperation in placing its materials with the editors of the *Knickerbocker Weekly*, an East Coast magazine for those of Dutch American ancestry and others with an interest in the history of Dutch America.[20]

The very detailed, monthly, point-by-point descriptions written by Willard Wichers to the New York head office about his planning of specific events and publications as head of NIB-Holland during the war years reveal the breadth (topical and geographic), complexity, and public-relations and meeting-driven nature of his work. The pressing issue of communicating with as many sectors of the American public as possible, the grave circumstances surrounding the Netherlands, and the war pervaded his work life. For every exhibit, lecture, interview, and publication, extraordinary attention was given to publicity and audience. There is the example of arranging a photo exhibit of the occupied Netherlands with and at the Chicago Museum of Science and Industry in 1943, which included a press release sent to 253 community newspapers, spot announce-

---

[18]   Snyder, "The Netherlands Information Service Collection," 202.

[19]   Snyder, "The Problem of Power," 64–73.

[20]   Charlotte Kok, "The Knickerbocker Weekly and the Netherlands Information Bureau: A Public Diplomacy Cooperation during the 1941–1947 Era" (MA thesis, American Studies Program, Utrecht University, 2011).

ments to radio stations throughout the region, invitations to principals of area day schools to send their classes to the exhibit, and signs for bulletin boards.[21] And there are the six general and wartime stories about the Netherlands supplied by the NIB to the Wisconsin Anti-Tuberculosis Association. Later, these were chosen (with lobbying, to be sure) for the November 1943 issue of *Junior Crusader,* a magazine also used in elementary schools and read by 1.7 million people—school children, teachers, nurses, and social workers.[22]

The monthly activity reports from Wichers made clear that, with the United States on a wartime footing, there was more public acceptance of and no lack of venues for foreign-policy-directed public diplomacy from Allied countries, such as the Netherlands. In addition to the standard outlets—museums, newspapers, magazines, and radio stations—Holland-NIB sent displays, films, and speakers to civil defense organizations, department stores such as Lazarus and Gimbels for window displays, and local and state chapters of the United Nations, War Chests, and War Funds. Traditional, culture-directed diplomacy, such as exhibits of Dutch paintings at art museums, took on additional significance for the American public because the country that had produced these treasures was torn apart by war and occupied and looted by the German oppressor.

Once the public lobbying for the war and postwar needs of the Netherlands and its colonies no longer drove the agenda, the work of the NIS became less diverse,

less assertive, and more consumer driven. The NIB arranged art exhibits and music performances to tour major cities and organized in-person lectures and radio appearances by prominent Dutch diplomats, writers, and academics. Much of its more routine business became sending out information, literature, and films in response to requests from thousands of telephone calls and letters from individuals, schools, and libraries; other queries required research by NIS staff to request and gather information and publications before responses could be sent out. The activity reports from the 1950s and 1960s reflect these changes; they became more standardized and statistical, with records of the number of phone calls, letters answered, and films sent out and lists of lectures, interviews, films, radio appearances and programs, and speaking engagements.

Films in public diplomacy and propaganda

The main title of this study—"Eyes on the Netherlands"—references Americans taking in Dutch visual media: paintings, sculptures, drawings, photographs, maps, films, and graphic designs. Readers of print media also use their eyes to decode words on the page to learn about the Netherlands; such knowledge may take the form of cognitive visual images. Reading a book without pictures, for example, about the genesis and organization of Dutch polders, will produce and also draw upon already existing learned visual imagery on the subject; one's mind will create a picture—a gestalt—of the information read. If a book includes photos of polders, learning is fast-tracked, enhanced, and more effectively retained (fig. 2.5). If a book or film contains only visuals of polders, without captions,

---

[21] "Report for the period of September 1 to 30, 1943," p. 2, in folder, "Monthly Reports to the Bureau, 1942–1943," box 3, NIS archive, HCASC.

[22] Ibid., "Report for the period of November 1 to 30, 1943," p. 8.

Fig. 2.5. Old and new land, part of and next to the Shermer Polder in Noord-Holland. At the bottom of the oblique aerial photo, linear farmsteads at the head of narrow, poorly drained (by gravity) fields—early medieval parcels—suitable only for livestock. At the top of the photo, former Lake Schermer (1635), drained by fifty-two windmills, centrally organized into large rectangular fields suitable for crops (*Edward Burkynski, courtesy of Nicholas Metivier Gallery, Toronto*).

explanations in the text, or voice-overs, learning is more limited and conjectural. Clearly, print and visual media together enrich and reinforce understanding; a picture may be worth a thousand words, but without explanatory text, much of what it might say will remain unknown.

Films, the subject of this book, began to find a place alongside familiar older media used in the programs of public diplomacy—newspapers, magazines, books, photographs, slides, posters, radio broadcasts, and exhibits. Films were first used in campaigns of propaganda and public diplomacy in WWI. Even though the

Netherlands was neutral in the First World War, its neighboring belligerents—Britain, France, and Germany—were given the opportunity to influence Dutch public opinion by screening their propaganda films in Dutch theaters.[23] With film becoming the most popular form of entertainment, its use for propaganda ramped up during WWII. Most of the Allied and Axis powers employed propaganda films to persuade

---

[23] Klaas de Zwaan, "Film/Cinema (the Netherlands)," in: *1914–1918-Online. International Encyclopedia of the First World War*, ed. Ute Daniel, et al., issued by Freie Universität Berlin, 29 May 2017. DOI: 10.15463/ie1418.11103.

domestic as well as foreign audiences of the rightness of their positions and actions and the wrongness of their enemies.[24] The NIB began using films in its public diplomacy in late 1943, well after the United States had entered the war immediately after the Japanese aerial bombing assault on Pearl Harbor on December 7, 1941.[25] What was relatively new at this time for film in public diplomacy was the use of lending libraries; both the NIB and the British Information Service used this method to distribute their films. They capitalized on the recent and growing availability of affordable 16 mm projectors for organizations other than movie houses. Rather than contracting only with movie theater chains to include NIB films as shorts, any organization or individual could borrow films for the cost of postage and insurance. This opened much larger markets—both numerically and geographically—no longer tied to movie houses and their showtimes.

The NIB got its start in the United States under wartime conditions; its primary purpose was to bring the United States into the war against the Axis powers and draw attention to the plight of the Netherlands. Without this dire emergency, it is most unlikely that something like the NIB would have been established at all. Beyond the foreign-policy-directed films related to wars—hot and cold—and international tensions, culture-directed films made it possible for a country to promote itself beyond its boundaries under more normal, reciprocal, friendly, and respectful diplomatic relations with other nations. Once the war and its immediate aftermath

were in the rear-view mirror, culture-directed films became the rule in the public diplomacy of the NIS.

The larger, changing consumption patterns of film also extended to how documentaries were deployed for public diplomacy. The period from 1941 to 1974 (the lifespan of the NIB/NIS) covers the continuing widespread popularity of movie theaters and the growing use of 16 mm film for the educational and home markets (schools, libraries, churches, workplaces, etc.), as well as the arrival and growth of television for home entertainment. Beginning in the early 1950s, 16 and 35 mm films were broadcast via television. Just like the many other distributors of nontheatrical films, the NIB/NIS chose direct lending to every kind of interested organization—educational, religious, civic, military, commercial, government—as its most effective marketing method from the beginning of and throughout its more-than-thirty-year existence. Especially during the 1940s, it also placed its films with American, nontheatrical film distributors. The practice of using—and paying—distributors to show promotional and propaganda films as shorts in theaters was enhanced by the widespread availability and use—not to mention the lower costs—of 16 mm projectors for all kinds of small-group screenings. Television stations were interested only in films with a large, broad-based appeal, and the NIS was successful in broadcasting only a small number of its more popular documentaries via this new mass medium.

Dutch documentary films in Dutch public diplomacy

What defines a "Dutch" documentary film, and what kind of Dutch nonfiction

---

[24]   See endnote 2:23, p. 398.

[25]   The earliest NIB-Holland circulation records are from December 1943, but it is possible that films circulated earlier without recordkeeping.

films were in the lending library? The vast majority of the two hundred-plus films in the NIS/NIB film library over the thirty-three-year life of the agency were *about* the Netherlands and its overseas territories; they were filmed in the Netherlands and its territories abroad, and they covered Dutch and Dutch-colonial topics. Dutch documentaries, of course, do not have to be made by Dutch filmmakers. The travelogues of the 1930s about the Netherlands—directed, produced, sold, and rented by American filmmakers and distributors—were an especially important part of the early NIB film library; they were regarded as Dutch documentary films by both the NIB and American viewers.

Even though, in general, documentaries about the Netherlands and its colonies/territories made by Dutch filmmakers comprise the largest subset of Dutch documentary films in the collection, Dutch nonfiction films do not need to be made by Dutch filmmakers or even be about the Netherlands or its overseas territories. One might rightfully expect Dutch filmmakers to be especially interested in their own country, but they have also increasingly addressed all manner of topics—European, international, and other, non-Dutch topics. This is how a variety of topics was made accessible to Dutch audiences in their own language. Among the nearly seven hundred, Dutch documentary films listed and described on FilmVandaag[film today].nl, there are as many about the Netherlands and its territories as there are not.[26] When such Dutch-made films about non-Dutch topics and places are distributed internationally, with voice-overs and/or subtitles in English or other world languages, viewers often do not regard them as Dutch films. Rather, they see them as general, topical documentaries, and the treatment of their topics is not necessarily driven by Dutch cultural sensitivities but sometimes by the vision of their filmmakers. In short, it is important to recognize that the NIB/NIS film library is a subset of Dutch documentaries—films about the Netherlands and its overseas territories not made exclusively by Dutch filmmakers. To this subset, other selection criteria were applied by the NIB/NIS, such as a film's promotional and propaganda value and its interest to Americans.

Learning about the Netherlands and its territories: public diplomacy, media, and tourism

Increased information and a variety of promotional media, including film, also combined to a greater degree with visitor travel during the lifetime of the NIB/NIS. International mass tourism was revived after WWII, albeit still with very modest numbers and directed almost exclusively to Europe and the Americas. More middle-class Americans were exploring Europe in larger numbers than ever before. The days of American international knowledge based solely on formal education and print and film materials were gone forever. For example, already in 1960, 50.4 million international tourists visited European countries, and with the somewhat usual Dutch share of about 2 percent, a million or so of these international visitors visited the Netherlands.[27] Neighbors of the Netherlands always made up a large share of those tourists, but Americans made up the

---

26 https://www.FilmVandaag.nl/nederlandsefilms?-genre=documentaire. See ch. 8 for a closer look at the "Dutch" documentaries listed on this site.

27 World Tourism Organization, "International Tourist Arrivals, 1950–2005," *Tourism Market Trends, 2006 Edition* (WTO, 2007), annex, 3.

largest group of those who had traveled a long distance. A visit to the Netherlands could now enhance the learning that came via education and through various forms of media, including film.

Seeing and experiencing a country in person and not only through the eyes of film directors, authors, and artists can add another modality of learning about places unknown. And reading about the country and its places to visit and learning from the commentary of tour guides will also help make sense of one's sights and experiences. Place encounters combine with commentary en route and relevant print and visual media to give depth, retention, understanding, and enjoyment to international travel and knowledge.

Films were one, but only one, important medium for both the foreign-policy and culture-directed public diplomacy of the NIB/NIS. As with other media, the foreign policy propaganda arm largely either produced its own films or modified existing ones, whereas the information services vetted films produced by others. Given the aims of the NIB/NIS, how did their films stack up against other media and programming? During the 1940s, foreign-policy-directed propaganda was the dominant form of public diplomacy prosecuted by the NIB; by nature, it has more definite, shorter-term goals than culture-directed public diplomacy. There were more foreign-policy-directed films screened, with a larger total viewership, during this decade than in the other decades. In the main, however, film distribution remained consumer- not NIB-driven; people, on behalf of organizations, ordered films from the NIB. The film screenings were not targeted to specific groups or organizations or included in selected events for a politically active pub-

lic. As such, and compared to other foreign policy diplomacy tactics, films were less nimble, less targeted, and less influential than timely responses to editorials, other unfavorable accounts in metropolitan dailies, or speeches to audiences by well-known and influential citizens.

Foreign-policy-directed films were chosen from a catalog for a particular audience; they were not chosen by diplomats or movie houses but by teachers, librarians, and church and army staff, among others. They were picked primarily for their general educational and pastime value, not typically for any particular foreign policy viewpoint they put forward. They were seen by regular, everyday people—mainly students—who, even if they were convinced by the message of the film, were not in a position to really change or bolster current public opinion. Unlike speeches, newspaper editorials, and staged events, the messages of these films worked their way slowly into the general population at a pace not very useful politically, considering the war-related urgency of these Dutch, foreign policy initiatives. Although they were foreign-policy-directed films, their actual impact was more like that of the culture-directed documentaries. Films, however, were probably more effective than some other kinds of print materials, such as books and magazines, because they were bought or borrowed by individuals, and they reached fewer people. Moreover, because of their entertainment value, films reached a greater cross section of people than print materials.

As Wichers' activity reports to the New York head office, however, make clear, a small number of foreign-policy-directed films did figure into NIB-initiated events and, in that context, were meant to be

Fig. 2.6. Evacuation of the flooded Island of Walcheren, Zeeland, by horse and wagon after the Allies bombed the dikes (*Broken Dykes, 1945*) (*NIS archive, HCASC*)

more immediately effective. For example, NIB-Holland partnered with the civilian defense authorities throughout the Midwest; at the beginning of the American involvement in WWII, the civilian defense was tasked with protecting citizens against military attacks by means of preparation and emergency operations, such as evacuation and recovery. At civilian defense meetings in more than thirty centers throughout the Midwest, NIB foreign-policy-directed films were regularly screened for a six-month period. Here, a direct connection could be made between American preparedness for war and the Dutch foreign

policy messaging of the film.[28] Another example of a more proactive use of films in foreign policy diplomacy was the more familiar practice of sending a speaker along with the film; in that way, the point of the film could be reinforced with an introduction, a Q and A session, or a separate talk.[29]

Because culture-directed films were not part of a campaign with more immediate political goals, the broad, longer-term aim of helping the American people come to know more about the Netherlands could

[28] "Report for the period of February 1 to 28, 1943," pp. 1–2, "Monthly Reports to the Bureau, 1942–1943," box 3, NIS archive, HCASC.

[29] Ibid., 2.

be much more realistic and successful. In this regard, it is important to remember that all films, including foreign-policy-directed films, do show viewers the people, places, and activities of a country and, as such, spread knowledge about that country. For example, a foreign-policy-directed film about the 1944 flooding and evacuation of the island of Walcheren in Zeeland as the result of the invasion by the Allies (*Broken Dykes*, 1945) to expel the German forces also conveyed general cultural information about the island, its people, its landscape, and its way of life (fig. 2.6).[30] The message that the NIB wanted Americans to take to heart from this film, which was not put into circulation until 1947, was the suffering of the Dutch people and their need for American aid, but along the way, viewers also came to see this place in particular and the Netherlands in general. This is true for all the foreign-policy-directed films.

The establishment of the Holland-NIB/NIS archive made it possible to study this program of film public diplomacy and examine how it continued to shape American perceptions of the Netherlands during WWII and the immediate postwar decades.

---

[30] See endnote 2:29, p. 398.

CHAPTER 3

The Influence of NIB/NIS Films in the United States: Sources, Data, and Methods

NIB/NIS-Holland 16 mm documentary film archive and circulation records

The services of the NIB/NIS film lending libraries were much in demand throughout the life of the agency; NIB-Holland began lending films in 1943. The demand for films was actively fostered by clever marketing and publicity as the activity reports from the Holland office during the 1940s make clear.[1] Film lists were sent out upon request but, more importantly, placed in publications and newsletters of educational/teacher, defense/military, church, and civic organizations in the states served by the Holland-NIB/NIS service region. State school directories were enlisted to send film lists out to individual schools. During the 1940s, the film lists were published as a booklet, with suggestions for teachers noted after the description of each film (fig. 3.1).[2] The films were listed under the auspices of both the Netherlands Museum and the NIB.

In general, and throughout the entire lifetime of the NIB/NIS, any organization or individual could borrow—for just postage, insurance, and a small service fee—a film either from the catalog or on the film list from the regional office. Films could be screened multiple times and even circulate locally. Copies of selected films were also placed with different colleges and universities and other film libraries throughout the region; these then circulated within their own systems. Throughout WWII, organi-

[1] "Monthly Reports to the Bureau" and "Activity Reports," box 3, NIS archive, HCASC.

[2] Film Records, box 2, NIS archive, HCASC.

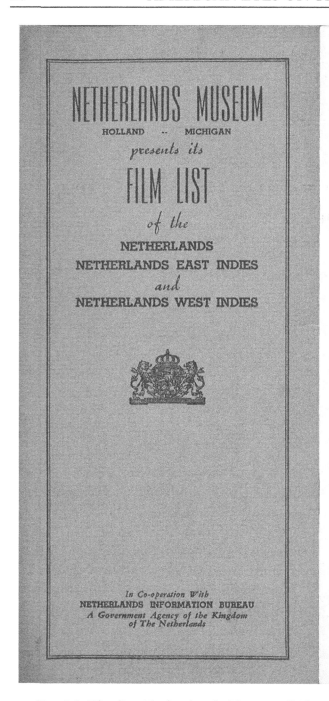

Fig. 3.1. Film list, Netherlands Museum/NIB, 1940s. The cover gives equal prominence to the Netherlands and the Dutch colonies; the Netherlands Museum is more prominent than the NIB as the source of the films (*NIS archive, HCASC*).

zations such as War Chests and other war information centers could keep and show films for their fundraising and education programs for a specified period. There were multiple copies of popular films; for example, there were forty-three copies of *Holland Today* (1962; 113,615) in 1973.[3]

---

[3]   Ibid.

When the NIB was founded during the early 1940s, the lower cost of the 16 mm compared to the 35 mm format brought the film-viewing experience out of the theater and into the classroom, boardroom, living room, library, and church. Although films at that time had, of course, already been around for quite some time (films with soundtracks were more recent), during the 1940s and early 1950s, documentary films were still something quite special and attractive to a very broad public, combining entertainment with learning, something that print media could not deliver as easily.

Later, in the 1941 to 1974 lifetime of the NIB/NIS, television, in general, increasingly competed with film screenings for the public's attention. This is reflected in the lower annual attendance figures for NIB/NIS films during the 1950s, 1960s, and 1970s (fig. 4.2). Film projection, however, remained the only way to show films to particular interest and user groups at set times and places. At the beginning of the 1950s, some NIS films began to be broadcast by metropolitan television stations (for example, in the Detroit and Houston areas), generating very large estimated household viewership, based on television ratings.

The digitized versions of the 16 mm films along with their circulation records, are the principal primary sources for this study.[4] NIB/NIS-Holland prepared monthly, and later, semiannual, film reports.[5] These were alphabetically organized by film title and listed the name, place, and state of the individual and/or organization borrowing and screening the film,

the number of viewers, and beginning in 1952 the number of showings. Borrowers or others in charge of the screening recorded the size of the audience and the number of showings. The film reports for the years from 1966 to 1972 have not been found. Fig. 3.2[6] shows the first page of the NIB-Holland Film Showing Report for September 1945. It lists as moviegoers: campers from the Walther League and YMCA camps, Sunday school groups, convalescent patients in a hospital, grade school pupils, workers at the American Seating Company, and members of women's clubs, among others. Occasionally, other details, such as school grade level, accompanying talk, and so forth, were added to the film-showing reports. Film circulation summaries, based on the film-showing reports, were also part of the monthly (later biannual) activity reports submitted by Wichers to the director of the NIB/NIS in New York (fig. 2.4). Other information about the films in the reports and the correspondence of the NIB/NIS archive was related, among other things, to acquisitions, special screenings, and placement of copies in university film libraries. Each of the 11,300 borrowing records from these film reports was entered into an Excel database, together with all the attributes enumerated above (figs. 3.3a and 3.3b). The films, together with their borrowing records, made an analysis of the cultural and geographic influence of these documentaries possible, something not possible with the films alone.

The attendance records are of two kinds. Nearly all are counts and estimates made by those who presided over the screenings; a very small number (36 of the

---

[4]   See endnote 3:3, p. 399.

[5]   Report on Films, 1940s, box 2, NIS archive, HCASC.

[6]   Ibid.

FILM SHOWING REPORT FOR SEPTEMBER, 1945

```
An East Indian Island
     Campers, Walther League, Arcadia, Michigan              230
     Junior Sunday school class, Medina, Ohio                 50

Celebes and Komodo
     YMCA Camp, Terre Haute, Indiana                          140

Ceremonies on Bali
     Junior Sunday school class, Medina, Ohio                 50

Dutch East Indies
     Church group, Christian Ref. Church, Worthington, Minnesota    200

Dutch Guiana
     YMCA Camp, Terre Haute, Indiana                          140

Glimpses of Picturesque Java
     Junior Sunday school class, Medina, Ohio                 50
     Sunday school teachers, Zeeland, Michigan                20
     Grade school pupils, Holland, Michigan                   24
          American Seating Company                            130
High Stakes in the East
     Convalescent patients, Station Hospital, Lake Charles, La.    21

Holland and the Dutch
     Church group, Christian Ref. church, Worthington, Minnesota    200

Landbuilders
     Grade school pupils, Holland, Michigan                   24
     Sunday school teachers, Zeeland, Michigan                20
     Women's Club, Orange City, Iowa                          275
     YMCA Camp, Terre Haute, Indiana                          140
     Church group, Christian Ref. church, Holland, Michigan   50

Little Dutch Tulip Girl
     Church group, Christian Ref. Church, Worthington, Minnesota    200

Netherlands America
     Church group, Trinity Ref. church, Holland, Michigan     50
     YMCA Camp, Terre Haute, Indiana                          140

Peoples of Java
     YMCA Camp, Terre Haute, Indian                           140
     Junior Sunday school class, Medina, Ohio                 50
     Opening of DEI show, Art Gallery, Grand Rapids, Michigan 302

Quaint old Holland
     Convalescent patients, Station Hospital, Lake Charles, La.    21
```

Fig. 3.2. NIB-Holland, first page of film-showing report for
September 1945 (*NIS archive, HCASC*)

11,000-plus borrowing records) are from television stations. Unfortunately, they (especially those from the 1950s) often omit the attendance figures based on Nielsen ratings for international documentaries. Television audiences are, of course, larger by several orders of magnitude than audiences at traditional film screenings. Even with these omissions and the tiny number of broadcasts, as compared to screenings, television viewership still made up some 13 percent of the total estimated viewership enumerated in the circulation records. That percentage would at least have been doubled had the size of television audiences been supplied more consistently.

The Netherlands Museum and the Holland NIB/NIS each maintained its own film lending library, but the lending management was a joint operation. The circulation records, whose summaries became part of the regular reports sent to the New York head office, were of the NIB/NIS, not the Netherlands Museum films. The Holland Museum film archive includes sixty-four films and newsreels not found in these circulation records. Presumably, these were part of the Netherlands Museum film collection. Because these titles were not part of the film service of the NIB/NIS, they are not included in this study. Although the Netherlands Museum films also helped form American perceptions of the Netherlands in the twenty-state, Holland, Michigan, service area, they were not part of the countrywide propaganda and promotional public diplomacy program directed by the Netherlands' national government. They were part of the holdings of the Netherlands Museum. The film lists that were sent out by the Netherlands Museum to attract the interest of various organizations combined the films of the NIB/NIS with those of the museum (fig. 3.1); there are no circulation statistics in the archive for the museum's films.

During the lifetime of the NIB/NIS (1941–74) and until 1992, the Holland Museum was called the Netherlands Museum. For much of this time, its collection was entirely devoted to Dutch and Dutch American materials, particularly those related to the Dutch settlement of West Michigan and Holland, its principal center. The Netherlands Museum and the NIB/NIS were both entirely focused on Dutch and Dutch American exhibits and materials, including films; they shared the same facilities, and Willard Wichers was the director of both organizations. It is not at all surprising, therefore, that the museum had its own Dutch film collection, in addition to the one belonging to the NIB/NIS. In 1992 the museum moved to its present location on Tenth Street and changed its name to the Holland Museum, underscoring that there was more to Holland's past and present than Dutch American history and culture.

My focus is on the films that were part of the Holland NIB/NIS lending library. As with any such library, however, over time, items are either lost or retired from or added to the collection. The archive of films that belonged to the lending library is considerably smaller than the actual lending library was during its thirty-one-year lifetime. There are sixty-eight films in the circulation records that are not present in the film archive. Over the entire period, from 1943 to 1974, the lending library, as shown by the circulation records, held 227 titles (see p. 401, n. 4:12). The NIB/NIS film archive contains by far the largest share of influential films. Fortunately, most of the films missing from the archive had a small viewership. Of the films not in the archive, only seven about the Netherlands and one about the Dutch colonies had more than ten thousand viewers each; many missing films had audiences of less than a thousand. Films with small total audiences over their lending lifetime were much more likely to be missing from the archive. Of the seventy-four film titles in the circulation records with fewer than one thousand viewers, forty-seven (63.5%) were not part of the film archive. That should not come as a surprise. Films that were rarely borrowed and consistently failed to attract many viewers would understandably be removed from the library, sent back to New York, or disposed of in some other way.

Information about some (not many) of the films missing from the archive was found in online film databases in the Netherlands, the United Kingdom, the United States, Australia, and Canada. It proved to be nearly impossible to locate

	A	B	C	D
1	ID	Film	Venue	Borrower Type
1325	7677	Peaceful Conquest	Evanston International Club	3
1326	8846	Holland Today		12
1327	8896	Speaking of Glass		12
1328	8909	Steamboat to Holland		12
1329	9028	Speaking of Glass		12
1330	6274	Bells of Holland	International Steel Company	2
1331	2952	Friesland	Group of Holland People	11
1332	2975	Holland and the Zuider Zee	Group of Holland People	11
1333	3017	Outside the Border	Group of Holland People	11
1334	3057	Celebes & Komodo	Evergreen Park Public School, Junior High School	1
1335	3062	Dutch East Indies, The	Evergreen Park Public School, Junior High School	1
1336	4011	Dutch Guiana	Evergreen Park Public School, Junior High School	1
1337	4276	Netherlands East Indies	Evergreen Park Public School	1
1338	4466	Holland Carries On	Evergreen Park Public School	1
1339	4636	Gateway to Germany	Evergreen Park Public School	1
1340	4760	Roaming the Netherlands	Evergreen Park Public School	1
1341	4154	An East Indian Island	Evergreen Park Public School	1
1342	4282	New Earth	St. Isidore School	1
1343	8317	New Guinea		12
1344	913	Dutch Guiana	Station Hospital patients	6
1345	7416	Medieval Dutch Sculptures		12
1346	659	Dutch Tradition, The	Freeport Commercial Geography class	1
1347	5223	Holland and the Dutch	Freeport Public Schools, Senior High School	1
1348	5408	New Earth	Freeport Public Schools	1
1349	79	Quaint Old Holland	Excelsior Christian School	1
1350	83	Roaming the Netherlands	Excelsior Christian School	1
1351	923	High Stakes in the East	Alumni Association	3
1352	936	Netherlands America	Alumni Association	3
1353	961	The Dutch Tradition	Alumni Association	3
1354	2387	An Empire In Exile	Second Reformed Church	4
1355	2708	High Stakes in the East	Second Reformed Church	4
1356	9221	Holland Today	Med. Arts Building	10
1357	11426	Holland Today	Medical Arts Building	10
1358	2420	Celebes & Komodo	YMCA	3
1359	2185	Ceremonies on Bali	YMCA	3
1360	8279	Land Below the Sea		12
1361	9826	The House	Lombard Junior High School	1
1362	10834	Amsterdam Concerto	High School	1
1363	5720	Holland Blooms Again	Gardner Elementary School	1
1364	5793	Landbuilders, The	Gardner Elementary School - Grade 3-6	1
1365	6308	Holland: A Meritime Nation	Elementary School	1
1366	6321	Holland: Its Land and Its People	Elementary School	1
1367	6060	Holland: A Modern Country #I Country and People		12

◄ ► | Films | Showings | Borrower Type | Missing Pages | +

Fig. 3.3a. Extract from the NIB/NIS-Holland film circulation database

copies of the missing films, let alone find a way to view them. Learning more about these films was important, especially the ones with sizable total audiences and, therefore, some cultural impact—films, such as *NATO Tattoo* (1958–65; 42,671), *Quaint Old Holland* (1935; 30,173), *Adventures in Perception* (1971; 17,040), *Celebes and Komodo* (n.d., 13,276), *Garden Granary* (n.d.,

12,828), *Introducing the Netherlands* (1955; 9,491), *Men against the Sea* (n.d., 10,712), and *The Language of the Flowers* (1960; 10,616).[7] For example, the British Film In-

7   Throughout this study, besides the release year, numbers cited parenthetically after a film title reference the total attendance for the entire 1943–74 period for the NIB/NIS Midwest region. This is one crude measure of the overall impact of a film. Commonly, the attendance for a film was con-

Borrower	City	State	Showings	Viewers	Month	Mont	Half Year	Year
	Evanston	IL	1	50			1	1959
Mr. Robert Girard	Evanston	IL	1	110			2	1964
Mr. Frank Kulasiewicz	Evanston	IL	2	22			2	1964
Mr. Robert Girard	Evanston	IL	1	110			2	1964
Mr. Frank Kulasiewicz	Evanston	IL	1				1	1965
	Evansville	IL					2	1953
Mr. Ralph De Groot	Evergreen Park	IL		64	November	11	2	1947
Mr. Ralph De Groot	Evergreen Park	IL		64	November	11	2	1947
Mr. Ralph De Groot	Evergreen Park	IL		64	November	11	2	1947
	Evergreen Park	IL		300	December	12	2	1947
	Evergreen Park	IL		300	December	12	2	1947
	Evergreen Park	IL			January	1	1	1948
	Evergreen Park	IL			February	2	1	1948
	Evergreen Park	IL		435	March	3	1	1948
	Evergreen Park	IL			April	4	1	1948
	Evergreen Park	IL			April	4	1	1948
	Evergreen Park (Chicago	IL			February	2	1	1948
	Famersville	IL		75	February	2	1	1948
Mr. Carl van Waning	Flossmoor	IL	1	80			1	1962
	Fort Sheridan	IL		115	June	6	1	1945
Mr. Francis G. Baptist	Fort Wayne	IL					1	1958
	Freeport	IL		60	November	11	2	1945
	Freeport	IL	3	80	May	5	1	1949
	Freeport	IL			May	5	1	1950
	Fulton	IL			October	10	2	1944
	Fulton	IL			October	10	2	1944
	Fulton	IL		90	June	6	1	1945
	Fulton	IL		90	June	6	1	1945
	Fulton	IL		90	June	6	1	1945
	Fulton	IL		160	February	2	1	1946
	Fulton	IL	3	160	February	2	1	1946
Dr. Brookstra	Fulton	IL	1	28			2	1973
Dr. Brookstra	Fulton	IL					1	1974
	Galesburg	IL	3	103	January	1	1	1947
	Galesburg	IL	3	103	January	1	1	1947
Mr. William Goodwin	Galesburg	IL	1				1	1962
S. Hinman	Galesburg	IL	2	60			1	1973
Mr. J. Griffith	Galesburg	IL	2	50			2	1973
	Gardner	IL	2	85			2	1952
	Gardner	IL	2	86			2	1952
	Gardner	IL	2	67			2	1953
	Gardner	IL	2	67			2	1953
Margaret Fisher	Gardner	IL					1	1953

Fig. 3.3b. Extract from the NIB/NIS-Holland film circulation database

stitute includes a useful, timed description of scenes of the British-made film, *Quaint Old Holland*.[8] The film about M. C. Escher, *Adventures in Perception*, is on YouTube, as is *Introducing the Netherlands*, a film introducing the country to other NATO members.

fined mainly to one decade: the 1940s, 1950s, or 1960s/70s. Films singled out for discussion in one of these three periods (chs. 5, 6, and 7, respectively) report the total attendance, not the attendance for just that period. Attendance for a specific period is supplied elsewhere in the narrative.

[8] British Film Institute, Film and TV Database, *Quaint Old Holland*. http://collectionssearch.bfi. org.uk/web/Details/ChoiceFilmWorks/150453761 (accessed 14 Mar. 2016). The film itself can be viewed only on site at the BFI in London by appointment.

Films in the archive with small total audiences were treated as having a very minor influence on the American public perception of the Netherlands and its colonies/territories and, therefore, were not included in the closer content analysis. One could argue that including *all* the films would be necessary to construct exactly what the NIB/NIS agency wanted the American public to know about the country and its dependencies. But discounting films with marginal attendance and focusing on the more influential ones—as measured by total viewership—helped to recreate the actual, rather than the intended, perception. The influence of individual films in helping to shape the American public perception of the Netherlands and its colonies/territories was assumed to be proportional to the number of people who, over time, saw them. This, of course, also got around the problem of not having any reasonable access to most of these missing minor films, many of which, after more than fifty years, have no surviving copies and are not present in the online film databases.

Secondary data and research design

Type, number, and ethnicity of borrowers

By querying the database, several secondary data were added to the primary data taken from each borrowing record, such as the type of borrower (fig. 3.3a, column D) and the Dutch ancestry of viewers. Borrowers were classified into one of twelve types—churches, schools, libraries, civic organizations, and so forth (fig. 4.11). In addition, the audience for each borrowing record was identified as of Dutch ancestry on the basis of screenings at Dutch

Reformed Churches (such as the Reformed Church in America and the Christian Reformed Church), Christian schools that were part of the then National Union of Christian Schools, and other Dutch American organizations.[9] All other audiences were categorized as non-Dutch viewers. This does undercount Dutch American viewers somewhat because at *any* screening of a Dutch film, those of Dutch ancestry would likely make up a disproportionate share of the audience.[10] Finally, the films were also classified on the basis of their title and content as about one of three geographic areas: the Netherlands, Dutch colonies/territories, and "other" (for example, populations of Dutch ancestry in other countries).

Total viewers for every film title for every year, decade, and the entire 1943–74 period were generated and rank-ordered to assess the strength of the film's influence. In addition, total viewers of all films for every year, from 1943 to 1974, were logged. Where the number of viewers at screenings was not provided in the records, the average number of viewers for that type of borrower (church, school, etc.) was inserted.[11] Because of their minor cultural impact, documentaries with relatively few viewers

[9] See endnote 3:8, p. 399.

[10] An alternative to using audiences at Dutch Reformed churches and schools as a measure of how many Dutch Americans attended screenings of NIB/NIS films in a county or state would be to apply the percentage of Dutch-born by county from the US census to the viewership. The measure I used and prefer is based on actual viewership rather than assumed attendance based on the percentage of people born in the Netherlands. Moreover, US censuses for these decades list the number of Dutch-born persons and not the more encompassing—and for this purpose, the more appropriate—number of all those with Dutch ancestry.

[11] See endnote 3:10, p. 399.

were left out of the close reading and analysis of individual films but not out of the statistical patterns and trends.

Periodization

In the next chapter, I will outline the general features of the Holland NIB/NIS film library and its patrons and then divide the study of these films—their circulation, viewership, and content—into three periods and chapters, roughly corresponding to three decades: the 1940s (1943–49), the 1950s, and the 1960s/70s (1960–74). These three chapters are bookended by the beginning of the NIB's circulation of films in 1943 and the shuttering of the NIS in 1974. These three decades are not just convenient time holders; they are, in fact, distinctive Dutch historical periods that, to some extent, are reflected and expressed in the documentary films. The 1940s period was that of the German occupation, the liberation by the Allies, the aftermath of the war, and the ending of the Dutch Empire. The 1950s saw a more nationally focused economic reconstruction and recovery; this period was the beginning of democratic socialism and required adaption to the loss of the colonies. The 1960s/70s were marked by first-time, broad-based affluence and major structural social changes.

The geography of film

Because I am a geographer, particularly important to me is the distribution of screening locations, the selection of Dutch and Dutch colonial/territorial places shown in the films, and the representation of the geographic and/or landscape identity of the Netherlands and its colonies/territories, including their regions and places. A subfield—the geography of film—arose already more than thirty years ago.[12] Today, it encompasses an extensive body of published journal and book literature, special sessions at conferences, vigorous theoretic debate, and scholars who survey the field, distill and sort out its theoretical direction, and suggest ways forward. The geography of film has applied itself more to the imagined places of fiction films, set in the story line and actions of the protagonists, than the bona fide, nondramatic places of nonfiction films, the subject of this study. Both fiction and nonfiction films, however, represent places, from streetscapes to continents and, as such, have to address the relationship between what Lukinbeal and Sharp call "the 'real' off-screen world and the 'reel' on-screen world."[13] The directors of documentary films represent places by selection, camera shots and angles, musical score, and voice-over; these, in turn stem from the film director's aesthetic vision, ethics, and worldview.

Geography (as well as other disciplines) studies films, on the one hand, as economic and cultural goods that are produced, distributed, and consumed and, on the other hand, as visual cultural texts whose contents and meanings are worthy of attention. I will use both approaches throughout this study. As economic and cultural goods, the two hundred-plus, 16 mm documentaries in the library of the NIB/NIS in Holland, Michigan, were mostly commissioned by Dutch government and nongovernmental agencies and industries for particular educational, jour-

---

[12] A substantial, theoretical, methodological, and bibliographic overview of this subfield is found in Christopher Lukinbeal and Laura Sharp, *Geography and Film* (Oxford University Press, 2014), oxfordbibliographies.com.

[13] Ibid., 2.

nalistic, and promotional purposes; others were made possible by awards from private and state film funds to directors, producers, and film companies for necessary and promising projects. Production companies making the films were commercial enterprises, but once they produced and delivered their films and received their contractual payments, their films, with some exceptions, earned only modest box office and nontheatrical rental revenue. Unlike feature films, which when released in multiple movie theaters to full houses for weeks on end could produce growing revenue and mounting profits, these documentaries, with just moderate commercial value, chiefly had educational and cultural value. Distributors either sold or rented these films to theaters, libraries, educational institutions, exhibitions, civic organizations, and film festivals.

The documentaries, acquired by the NIB/NIS in the United States, were lent out to any interested group or individual nearly free of charge. As a result, they circulated widely both demographically and geographically. They were seen by an estimated more than six million viewers in all parts of the country and in venues large and small. Although viewership numbers exist for nearly all of the screenings, there are no recorded comments or reviews from audiences on the tally sheets returned with the films.

In order to focus on the spatial organization of this public diplomacy by film, the geographic coordinates of each screening location and its related viewership numbers were added to the database and imported into GIS software, and attendance maps of the Holland-NIB/NIS service region were made for the entire lifespan of the NIB/NIS and for its three

historical periods. The resulting geographic patterns were analyzed.

Further, places in the Netherlands and its colonies/territories, either shown or mentioned in the films, were inventoried, and if the identity of a place was unclear, it was left out.[14] Places were classified into three groups by scale: small—villages, towns, cities, and historic polders (e.g., the city of Veere); intermediate—physical regions (e.g., the Wadden), economic regions (e.g., bulb growing), and larger islands (e.g., Walcheren); and large—physical regions and provinces (e.g., the Low Netherlands or the province of Groningen). The "small" places shown in the films were mapped for particular decades and for the entire 1943–74 period, along with how often they made an appearance and how many viewers saw them. In addition, all the places shown in the films—small, intermediate, and large—were combined to produce maps showing the percentage of Dutch places in the films from each province for particular decades and for the entire lifespan of the NIB/NIS.[15] In this way, the location and types of Dutch places presented to American viewers could be surveyed and analyzed.

The exposure of American audiences to Dutch places by way of these films also depended on attendance. A small, relatively unknown place, seen by a large number of moviegoers, would receive much more exposure than a larger and more prominent place seen by a small audience. I weighted the Dutch places shown in these films with their attendance to produce a

14 See endnote 3:13, p. 400.

15 Although the province of Flevoland was not established until 1986, film locations in the Noordoostpolder and the Flevopolder were associated with this future province rather than with the existing province or national government to which they were first legally bound.

Agriculture/rural countryside
Architecture/planning/building/housing
Church/religion
Cities
Demography
Education/science/museums
Fisheries
Folk life (dress/dance/games/etc.)
Health and health care
Industries
International relations (political/legal/cultural)
Military/war
Natural environments
Natural resources
Political life/government/public ceremony
Post WWII reconstruction
Recreation/sport/hobbies
Royal family
Services (retail/gov't/financial/community/etc.)
The arts
Towns and villages
Trade
Trades
Transportation
Water/water technology/polders

Fig. 3.4. Classification of the subjects of topical threads in NIB/NIS films

place-exposure index. The highest index scores belong to places shown in multiple films with a high aggregate attendance; the lowest exposure scores belong to places shown in just a single film that had low attendance.

The topical profiles of the films

Another approach to the geography of film is the study of the content—the cultural text—of films, particularly as it relates to such geographic fundamentals as landscape, spatiality, and geopolitics. While not ignoring these geographical approaches, I will tackle the contents of this film library and its groups of films—as well as individual films with significant viewership numbers—more broadly, first by classifying and tracking the subject matter of the films, then by a critical reading of individual films that are part of a particular

group, for example, the entire Netherlands, the Dutch colonies/territories, particular places (e.g., Amsterdam), and various broad topics (e.g., water).

Films were partitioned into content threads that were in turn cataloged into one of twenty-five subject categories (fig. 3.4). This gave a topical profile of the film collection for particular geographic divisions and periods and made it possible to track and assess leading and neglected subjects, as well as the changing attention paid to various topics over time. I define film threads as segments of film about a particular topic without regard to length. Most commonly, they constitute a single, continuous, defined segment, but sometimes, a thread is made up of several discontinuous segments. A film entirely devoted to a single topic, say, glass manufacturing, as in Bert Haanstra's, *Speaking of Glass* (1958), is made up of one segment, whereas a more encyclopedic film, like Gerard Raucamp's, *Holland Today* (1962), contains multiple topic segments. Arguably, a single-topic film could well be subdivided into further subtopics, much as places can be, but such a fine differentiation would not add insight into the comparative topical profiles of the films. Every thread was associated with one subject category only; in cases where a segment could fit into more than one category, the one with the clearest and strongest association was chosen. Admittedly, there was a subjective element contained inherently within this categorization system. The categories arose from viewing the films, not from a predetermined classification system.

Most individuals, of course, saw only a single film or a small selection thereof; the imprint on their knowledge and perception of the Netherlands would be quite different from that of seeing the entire collection—as I have—or some group of films. And depending on a variety of parameters, such as interest, age, gender, class, employment, and place, different viewers would take away very different impressions from each film. So, any kind of topical content analysis of some subset of the films would not correspond at all to what stimulated the mind and stayed in the memory of viewers, whether as individuals or as a group. But such an analysis does show which topical film threads and their audiovisual representations are found rarely in the films and which are featured more commonly. The topical profiles of the films are the raw material for the viewers' perception and knowledge, as filtered by the parameters identified above.

Critical reading of the films

Finally, given the propaganda and promotional ambitions of the NIB/NIS for the American public, the rhetorical claims and aims of various groups of films are analyzed and interpreted by means of a critical reading of individual films, including their audio/visual/narrative content and meaning, as well as related cinematographic approaches. Such analysis makes up the greater part of this study. The NIB/NIS film library was unique in that it made available to American borrowers and audiences mostly Dutch-made films—many originally meant for Dutch audiences—about the Netherlands and its overseas territories. English-language voice-overs were often added, either translated from the Dutch or newly written for non-Dutch—principally English-speaking—audiences. These cultural visual texts, many attuned to Dutch viewers and Dutch sensibilities, were now interpreted through American eyes.[16]

[16] As a Dutch American/Canadian geographer, born in the Netherlands, and with considerable research and field experience in my native country, I consider myself well placed to discuss both Dutch and American perceptions.

CHAPTER 4

Distinguishing Features of the NIB/NIS-Holland Film Library and Its Viewership, 1943–74

Factors affecting the makeup and character of the film collection

The most influential external conditions shaping the make-up and character of this film library were threefold: Dutch foreign policy objectives during the 1940s, the occupation of the Netherlands by Nazi Germany from 1940 to 1945, and from 1950 to the early 1960s, the widely known and internationally acclaimed school of Dutch documentary film. For the remainder of the lifespan of the NIS, the so-called VPRO film school (Vrijzinnig Protestantse Radio Omroep, lit. Liberal Protestant radio broadcaster), with origins in the Netherlands during the turbulent 1960s, had little-to-no impact on the NIS film library, even though the VPRO was transformative in the country itself.

WWII, its aftermath, and the colonial question

With NIB films, as with other media, the Dutch government in exile projected several recurring themes to the American public: the Netherlands was a reliable and useful partner in the Allies' war against Germany and Japan led by the United States; as a country occupied by Germany, it suffered from tyranny, destruction, and plunder; and, compared to others, it was a different colonial power committed to "civilizing" its territories and leading them to independence.

The films in this foreign policy category were produced very quickly, often from existing films and footage, and with an English-language voice-over that carried their message. The German occupation of the Netherlands shut the Dutch government out from the country's own existing films and film production. It could not easily produce films or use existing ones for its promotional and propaganda purposes; instead, it had to source many of its culture-directed films about the Netherlands and the Dutch colonies from American and British suppliers. This explains why many pre-WWII American travelogues about the Netherlands and some of the islands making up the Dutch colonies in the NIB film library were used as promotional films during the 1940s. In general, these were not at all suited for the NIB's foreign policy campaigns and, one would think, were ill-chosen for promotional purposes because of their dated and stereotyped imagery. But with or without the NIB's deliberate intent, these films segued right into America's favorable perception of the Netherlands, cultivated during its "Holland Mania" period from 1880 to 1920. With the NIB unable to change these films in any way, the American travelogues about several islands that happened to be part of the Dutch East Indies did not make any arguments in favor of continuing Dutch colonial rule.

The Dutch Documentary Film School

It is telling that the early lifespan (1943–65) of the NIB/NIS coincides with the early development, full flowering, and denouement of the distinctive and internationally much-admired and prize-winning Dutch Documentary Film School.[1] Its filmmakers saw documentaries as an art form of visual poetry, and its directors

and producers aimed to achieve a creative balance among image, form, editing, and sound. Imparting information and knowledge about the Netherlands and its people was secondary to composition and aesthetics. With such a paradigm, films' transmission of knowledge about the Dutch natural and human material world, let alone about real people and social issues, was more of an incidental byproduct. Among its better-known practitioners were John Fernhout, Ytzen Brusse, Bert Haanstra, Herman Van der Horst, Hattum Hoving, Max de Haas, Louis Van Gasteren, Jan Hulsker, and Charles Van der Linden.[2]

By the early 1950s, the Dutch film industry had recovered from the war, and documentaries made by Dutch filmmakers and producers could become the principal source for the NIS film collection. This is what one would expect from an agency of the Dutch government abroad making Dutch films available to the American public. Promotional documentaries commissioned by the Dutch government, its agencies and departments, or marketing associations and industries would have pride of place but so would highly acclaimed examples of the Dutch art of making documentary films. Not all Dutch filmmakers of the period were in the grip of or influenced by this Dutch documentary school, but many were. Aspects of the genre seeped into Dutch documentary making more generally, and it could also be put toward clearly promotional purposes. The best example of this is John Fernhout's *Sky over Holland*, 1967; it was commissioned for the Netherlands pavilion at Montreal's world's fair in 1967 (Expo '67) and represents the apogee of this docu-

---

[1] The definitive reference work for this film school is Bert Hogenkamp, *De Documentaire Film, 1945–1965. De Bloei van een Filmgenre in Nederland* (Uitgeverij 010, 2003).

[2] See endnote 4:2, p. 400.

mentary school at a time when it had already been bypassed. The 70 mm film was wildly popular at the world's fair that year, and I was among those impressed; it also won a Golden Palm at Cannes.

The NIB/NIS film collection includes ten of the Dutch documentary school's notable and prize-winning examples. Because films of this genre were principally studies in visual composition, pattern, and aesthetics, often of Dutch subject matter, they were ideal for the NIS in the United States, as well as for public diplomacy elsewhere. Content did not need to be explained or understood; its visual forms, dynamics, and interplays invited aesthetic appreciation and wonder. More difficult—and perhaps controversial—subjects were avoided. Dutch viewers likely reacted more emotionally than Americans to these films because the substance of the forms and patterns on view was their lifeworld.

There was a lag between the release of these and other documentaries in the Netherlands and their acquisition and distribution abroad. A national film-lending library abroad, such as the one of the NIS, faced delays, sometimes because of the need for international versions in different languages or with subtitles and at other times because of costs, copyright, and distribution issues. It took between five and ten years after the release of these films before the NIS could acquire and circulate them. Most were produced and released in the Netherlands during the 1950s but were not seen by American audiences until the midsixties to the early seventies. They were a decade behind Dutch audiences then already taking in the recent works of the VPRO school. For both the more routine films and these Dutch documentaries' cutting-edge content and cinematography,

American viewers were many years behind their Dutch counterparts.

One would expect that especially these ten noteworthy films in the collection would have translated into correspondingly high American attendance figures, but such was not the case. The attendance numbers in the United States for these notable Dutch films by title in order are:

Speaking of Glass	(1958; 68,236)
Amsterdam, City of Canals	(1957; 45,890)
Broken Dykes	(1945; 25,914)
The Building Game	(1963; 4,367)
Steady as She Goes	(1952; 3,643)
Mirror of Holland	(1950; 2,918)
Praise the Sea	(1959; 1,073)
New City, New Land	(1960; 752)
Sailing	(1962; 522)
Vincent van Gogh	(1953; 270)

Attendance depends on many factors, including how long a film remained in the lending pool, as well as its promotion, but I would suggest that American borrowers and viewers made their decisions based more on topics, information, and American associations than on film style or directors. Whereas Dutch moviegoers may have rushed out to see the latest Haanstra or Van der Horst film—two leaders of the movement—Americans, understandably not up on prominent Dutch filmmakers, made different choices. They came in much larger numbers to a film closely related to one that had garnered an Oscar, an American and international honor (*Speaking of Glass*). Likewise, they chose a film about Amsterdam, a city with high imageability for Americans (*Amsterdam, City of Canals*), and a film about the liberation of part of the Netherlands by Allied forces, in which Americans had played a leading role (*Broken Dykes*). Some other titles and topics from these prominent Dutch filmmakers, such as documentaries about the Dutch building industry (*The Building Game*), sailing (*Sailing*), and Dutch artists (*Vincent van Gogh*), drew low numbers because they lacked such associations and/or were acquired just several years before the NIS was shut down. All in all, even though American viewers of Dutch films about the Netherlands and its colonies did not gravitate to films just because they had been produced by prominent figures in the Dutch documentary school, they did encounter this film genre unselfconsciously, one that helped shape Dutch documentaries during the middle years of the lifetime of the NIB/NIS.

The VPRO Documentary School

By the early 1960s, this homegrown paradigm for cutting-edge, Dutch documentary filmmakers had run its course and was increasingly replaced by new international movements shaping documentary filmmaking, captured by a more artistic and experimental school, La Nouvelle Vague (New wave), originating in France, and Direct Cinema, a genre committed to realism that had its roots in North America. In the Netherlands, the VPRO Documentary School label was in time applied to these movements. Originally, VPRO was the broadcasting corporation associated with the liberal wing of Dutch Protestantism, and it gained independence from its religious leaders and context to make and broadcast on television outstanding representatives of these new directions in documentary filmmaking.[3] These cine-matographic changes developed coincident with and were also stimulated by the turbulent social criticism that brought profound social change to the Netherlands during the 1960s (ch. 7). The VPRO documentary school in the Netherlands, as part of a larger international movement, did not achieve the same level of widespread European acclaim accorded the earlier, more national, Dutch documentary school. Because of its very particular Dutch subject matter, there were few international or American releases. It was a respected Dutch film movement among other national documentary schools that had moved in the same cine-matographic directions.

Many of these innovator filmmakers were journalists, at home in the world of television broadcasting. Others made more abstract and experimental documentaries. Leaders included Jan Vrijman, Ed Van der Elsken, Louis Van Gasteren, Philo Bregstein, Johan Van der Keuken, Roelof Kiers, Hans Keller, Frans Bromet, and Pieter Verhoeff, among others.[4] Filmmakers of the VPRO school commonly used lightweight, versatile, shoulder-held cameras that synchronized video and sound and, as such,

---

[3] Bert Hogenkamp, *De Nederlandse Documentaire Film, 1965–1990. De Ontwikkeling van een Film-*

genre in het Televisietijdperk (Boom, 2015). In ch. 2, Hogenkamp discusses the decline of the Dutch documentary school and in chs. 1 and 3, the development, growth, and characteristics of the VPRO documentary school. My description of this school in the following paragraphs is based on these two chapters of Hogenkamp's book.

[4] *Hoogtepunten uit de Nederlandse Documentaire Film, 1945–1977.* The second boxed set in this series singles out the innovators that paved the way to the establishment of the VPRO school and contains seven films: pt. 2, *Vernieuwers*, 1962-70. The third box, pt. 3, focusses on the settled VPRO school itself and includes five of its noteworthy directors and films: *VPRO Documentaire School*, 1971–77. The list of exemplary directors chosen by Bert Hogenkamp included here is taken from the liner notes accompanying these two sets.

removed more of the barriers between who/what was filmed and the camera person with equipment. Lightweight, easily portable cameras led to smaller film crews and significantly lower filmmaking costs, and freelancers could enter the profession more easily. To show just what was there or just what was going on, these filmmakers preferred not to have any filters such as voice-overs or musical scores in their documentaries. As film directors, they regarded themselves as the true authors of their documentaries and did not take kindly to additional editing by producers or production companies.

Unlike the linear structure and serial order of the more conventional documentaries, these films employed unusual shots, novel editing (jump edits), and spontaneity to entertain, pique, and provoke audiences. The message and meaning of the films was often equivocal, ambiguous, and delivered with emotion and irony. As film journalists, the film makers were keenly interested in societal issues and what individuals, companies, and government authorities thought and did about them, not only in the Netherlands but also throughout Europe, the United States, and the developing world. This generation of Dutch filmmakers was far more international and socially engaged than their predecessors, and their work included a greater number of both journalistic and experimental artistic documentaries.

Ten of the eleven films featured in the boxed DVD set about the Dutch documentary school, 1945–63, were included in the NIS film library, a measure of the considerable exposure, recognition, and influence this film movement had in the United States. For the VPRO school of documentary film (1962–77), the opposite was the case. Not one of the notable films in the two boxed DVD sets devoted to this school was selected to be part of the NIS library. There were several reasons for this. As journalistic documentaries, they tackled—either as a topic or in passing—hot-button and often difficult Dutch social issues and historical events, such as police violence, prostitution, and the genocide of Dutch Jewry. Such subjects were naturally deemed not suitable for public diplomacy and promotion of the Netherlands. Other films of this school dove deep into the weeds of particular Dutch local issues which, without more context and explanation, could not be easily grasped and enjoyed by American viewers.

For other films in these boxed sets, given their dialogue, interviews, and lack of voice-over, it would have been very challenging, if not impossible, to prepare versions suitable for international audiences. That is why very few of them enjoyed international releases. The NIS, as an agency of the Dutch government in the United States, however, was not bound by whether a film had been licensed for international or American distribution. It could screen any Dutch-made film in the United States as part of its mandate. Nevertheless, the NIS also found such films at odds with its goals. For general non-Dutch audiences, such films were either overly particularistic or too controversial. The NIS needed its films to feature more positive, generally recognized, and neutral aspects of the country. A final, more practical reason is that it often took considerable time after their release for films to be acquired by the NIS; the film library was years behind in the distribution of films in the Netherlands. When the NIS ceased operation in 1974, some of the VPRO-type films that might have passed its selection standards would not have been acquired in time.

This underscores that film diplomacy carried out by one country in another does not necessarily reflect its most distinctive and best, highly recognized filmmaking. The films of the Dutch documentary film school of the 1950s and early 1960s suited the promotional requirements of the NIB/NIS films program, those of VPRO school did not.

Size of the film lending library

Most libraries grow in size over time as accessions outpace deaccessions. The NIB/NIS film library was no exception. There are no records in the archive of the dates of the acquisition or de-acquisition of the films, only the first and last borrowing dates recorded in the circulation data. During the 1940s, the collection grew to fifty-five films, ten of which are not in the archive. These numbers represent all the films that were circulating for all or part of that period. Some films may have been available but not borrowed for part of that period. During the 1950s, the library expanded to seventy films (49 new and 21 carried over from the 1940s); twenty-one of these films are not present in the archive. The size of the library more than doubled during the 1960s/70s to 161 films (114 new and 47 left from the 1940s and 1950s); sixty-one of these films are not in the archive. Many of the films not in the archive had very small viewership numbers. The growth in the number of films available was not matched at all by a proportional growth in total film attendance.

Film attendance

Fig. 4.1 presents the estimated total viewership for the three NIB/NIS ser-

vice regions for the 1940s, 1950s, and 1960s/70s.[5] The figure of 2.8 million people in the Midwest region who came out to see NIB/NIS films is derived from the actual borrowing records in the archive. This figure underreported the actual number for several reasons. For one, the circulation records from 1966 to 1972 were not recovered; applying the average annual viewership for the years 1960–65 and 1972–74 to those years with no data would add well over seven hundred thousand viewers.

For another reason, twenty-two television borrowing records did not report an estimated number of viewers, as based on their Nielsen ratings. By virtue of the nature of the medium, viewership for a film broadcast by a television station is several orders of magnitude (tens of thousands) higher than those of, for example, schools, libraries, and army bases (tens and hundreds). If those television stations that did not supply the viewership for broadcasting an NIS documentary film had contributed the average viewership for television showings recorded in the database, then more than six hundred thousand viewers would have been added to the numbers for the Midwest region.

Still another reason for a much higher total viewership of NIB/NIS films has to do with the practice (as reported in the semiannual reports submitted by Wichers to the New York head office) of placing copies of a number of films on permanent loan in several university and other film libraries. Their viewership numbers are not

5   Only the records for the 1950s are for the entire decade. Films circulated for seven years in the 1940s, beginning in 1943. The borrowing records from 1966 to 1972 have not been found in the archive, so the 1960 to 1974 period spans eight years.

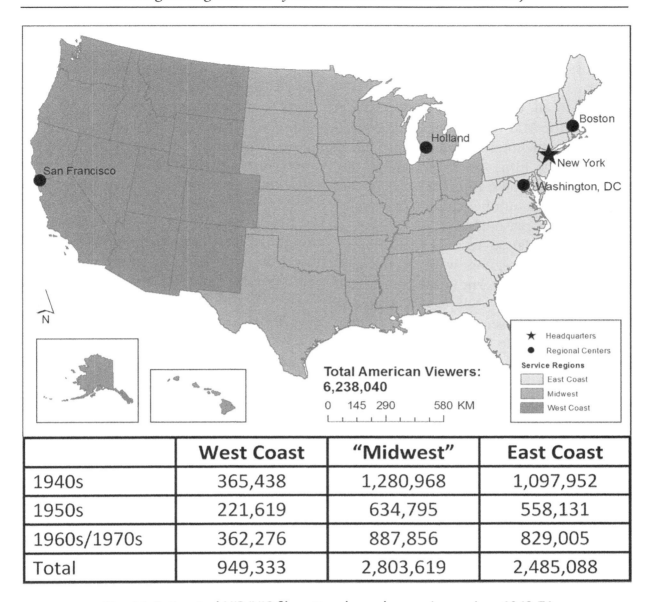

Fig. 4.1. Estimated NIB/NIS film attendance by service region, 1943-74

	West Coast	"Midwest"	East Coast
1940s	365,438	1,280,968	1,097,952
1950s	221,619	634,795	558,131
1960s/1970s	362,276	887,856	829,005
Total	949,333	2,803,619	2,485,088

part of the film circulation records of the NIB/NIS.[6]

Finally, beyond the borrowing records of the NIB/NIS itself, there is the circulation of some of these films in the United States via other suppliers. Especially during the German and Japanese occupation, with the Netherlands cut off from its own film collections, the NIB acquired a significant number of American-made travelogues and shorts about the Netherlands and some of its colonies. These films were also shown during the 1930s and 1940s as shorts in theaters and available from educational film distributors and lending libraries throughout the country. The attendance generated by the NIB/NIS from these films was, of course, only a fraction of the total number of those who

6   Activity Reports, 1940s, box 3, NIS archive, HCASC.

saw these films at other venues. Without any attendance data from such showings, it is impossible to put a number to this viewership.

All in all, the 2.8 million attendance figure for the Midwest region is a floor not a ceiling for the total attendance for Dutch documentary films borrowed from the NIB/NIS and shown in other ways in the United States; a number closer to four million is entirely reasonable.

The circulation records of the West and East Coast regions were, as far as I have been able to determine, not preserved or archived once the NIS closed its doors in 1974. To get a sense of the size of the national viewership for Dutch documentary films during this period, I applied the percentage of the census population of the states in the Midwestern region that came out to see these films during the 1940s, 1950s, and 1960s/70s to the census populations of the states making up the East and West Coast NIB/NIS regions (fig. 4.1).[7] That calculation yields a ballpark number of more than six million viewers nationwide. Although it is based on several limiting assumptions, such as equal borrowing rates and similar film lending libraries for the three regions, this attendance figure does underscore that the impact of these films on American perceptions of the Netherlands and its colonies had cultural weight. It was of a size to make a difference even in as large a country as the United States. Had this number been even one order of magnitude lower, let alone two, and/or had the viewership been confined to a small area of the country, these films, albeit interesting in and of themselves, could easily be dis-

missed as inconsequential for American perceptions of the Netherlands.

Because, in general, films were sent down from the head office in New York, there was a large overlap between the film libraries of the three NIB/NIS service regions. The total American attendance for most film titles was likely on the order of about 2.23 times the attendance of the film in the Midwest region. This needs to be kept in mind when the total attendance for individual films (in parentheses, after the title) and the total yearly viewership, based on the circulation records from the NIB/NIS Holland region, are given and discussed.

For the Midwest service region, fig. 4.1 shows total viewership reduced by half from the 1940s to the 1950s and then recovering slightly during the 1960s and 1970s. Fig. 4.2 provides more detail with total viewership by year from 1943 to 1974. It shows viewership ramping up rapidly from 1943 to 1946 as the NIB's film library became more established, larger, and better known.

The 1948 attendance peak is higher than any other year of the NIB/NIS. From the peaks of more than two hundred thousand annual viewers during the late 1940s, the general annual pattern during the 1950s and into the mid–1960s is much lower, often less than fifty thousand. There are, however, upsurges (1953/1954 and 1965/1973), occasioned by the acquisition of what would be a particularly popular film and by the broadcasting of such a film and others on television.

The consistently higher viewership during the 1940s and generally lower attendance figures during the 1950s and 1960s/70s reflect two conditions: the political—and follow-on fiscal—priority given

7   See endnote 4:7, p. 401.

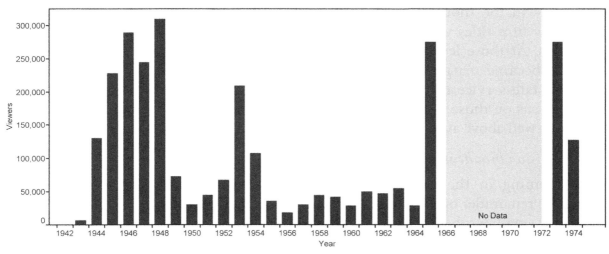

Fig. 4.2. Yearly attendance of Holland NIB/NIS films, 1943-74

the NIB during the 1940s and film projection as the dominant technology for showing movies. With the aim of influencing American public opinion in favor of Dutch foreign policy goals, comparatively large investments were made in staffing, promotion, materials, and programming for the NIB. But as these foreign policy objectives were overtaken by events and failures, the Dutch government began to scale back and change the operation. Already after the victory of the Allies in 1945 and again after Indonesian independence in 1949, budgets were reduced, resulting in staffing and programming cuts and the closing of some field offices. When foreign policy goals ceased to be the *raison d'être*, and the agency was repurposed into a more passive Dutch information service, it lost its place of political priority, and with that came reduced budgets, staffing, investments, and attention.[8] From these reductions came smaller audiences at NIS film screenings.

The other condition keeping attendance higher was that film and film projectors remained the dominant technology

for showing moving pictures during the 1940s. Television had not yet made many inroads into entertainment and education at home; to see a movie, one would have to leave home for the theater or other venue, such as a library, church, or school. That began to change during the early 1950s as television ownership became more widespread and added another mass medium, besides radio, for entertainment and edification at home. This new broadcast technology curbed going to movies for a variety of occasions and people borrowing NIS films and attending scheduled screenings.

Another measure of the declining cultural impact of these films on Americans is the change over time in the average and median total attendance of a film title. For the 1940s, the average attendance was 23,290 and the median 14,917; the same figures for the 1950s were 9,068/3,561, and for the 1960s/70s, they were 5,514/1,402. This again shows the sharp falling off after the 1940s as the number of films in the collection actually increased, spreading fewer viewers over more films as marketing weakened, and competition from television rose. If the average attendance for

8   Snyder, "The Problem of Power," 73–74.

a film was in the thousands, then there were many film titles with just hundreds of viewers. At those levels, their cultural influence became marginal, especially in a twenty-state service region. One would need to focus on those films whose attendance was well above average.

Television broadcasting of NIS films

Beginning in the early 1950s, and during the remainder of the NIS's lifetime, a relatively small number of NIS films were broadcast on television. Single showings reached unheard of viewership numbers in the tens of thousands. A film on TV could reach an audience equal to hundreds of film screenings. Twelve television stations in metropolitan markets in the NIS-Holland service area, including Southfield (Detroit), St. Louis, New Orleans, Houston, and Columbus, accepted one or more films from the NIS for broadcasting. Of the eleven thousand borrowing records, there are only thirty-six with television stations as borrowers and, of these, just fourteen provided attendance figures based on Nielsen ratings for the NIS film records. Fig. 4.3 ranks the top twenty-five borrowers by their total attendance during the lifetime of the NIB/NIS. Of the top five borrowers, four either included or were a television station: Southfield (Detroit), Houston, Columbus, and East Lansing, Michigan, as part of Michigan State University. Holland's annual Tulip Time, in third place, drew the largest attendance for conventional film screenings.[9]

_____
[9] Because the estimated size for a television showing was often not recorded, attendance and borrowing frequency for television broadcasts in fig. 4.3 are not linked. Michigan State College was an unusual borrower in that it showed films via its television station to a largely off-campus viewership and via conventional screenings by projector to the

With film projection, many different decision makers throughout the region selected films from the catalogs for their organizations—librarians, military officers, teachers, civic and community leaders, church staff, and business people. Their choices reflected the goals of their institutions and the reason for showing films. NIS staff made suggestions, but borrowers made the final decisions. Marketing NIS films for broadcasting engaged NIS staff more directly, reaching out to and working with station program managers to air particular films. Television stations looked for films with broad general appeal in their broadcasting region; traditional film projection could encompass the interests and purposes of many different small groups, making room for more specialized films. Deciding on films for projection involved many decision makers, but only a few were required for television broadcasts.

The geography of viewership of NIS films also changed with television broadcasting. For film titles that also included television broadcasts, the entire market area of television stations was saturated with viewers, whereas the rest of the NIS-Holland service region showed dispersed locations of film screenings with small audiences. Nor did the location of the television station that was broadcasting NIS films pinpoint where the audience was (unlike, for instance, an elementary school). Depending on signal strength, the Southfield, Michigan, television station, for example, could have been broadcasting to the entire Detroit urban region and beyond.

This new broadcast medium offered the NIS an opportunity to counter declin-

_____
on-campus educational community.

Borrower	Place	State	Borrowing Frequency	Estimated Attendance
Mrs. Sue Martin (TV Showing)	Southfield	MI	8	206128
KUHT, University of Houston (TV Showing)	Houston	TX	1	100000
Tulip Time	Holland	MI	10	86180
Mr. Frank Cozzolli (TV Showing)	Columbus	OH	6	36000
Michigan State College	East Lansing	MI	8	31053
Army Personnel	Camp Polk	LA	14	26595
Kane County Schools	Geneva	IL	3	19125
Catholic School Department	Buffalo	NY	4	18436
Mr. Frans	Holland	MI	1	17100
Board of Education	Akron	OH	3	12975
El Paso Public Schools, School Children	El Paso	TX	8	12581
El Paso Public Schools	El Paso	TX	19	12509
Circulated	Muncie	IN	3	11827
Federal Correctional Institute	Seagoville	TX	17	11632
Mary E. Bivins Memorial Library	Amarillo	TX	47	10965
Volunteer Film Association	St. Louis	MO	19	9931
Dutch Immigrant Society	Grand Rapids	MI	22	9888
Winter General hospital	Topeka	KS	13	9530
Christian School Rally	Grand Rapids	MI	3	9000
Circulated	Louisville	KY	11	8945
Major H. van Hoof	Fort Bliss	TX	11	8506
Civilian and Military Personnel	Camp Polk	LA	11	8205
Lincoln High School	Warren	MI	6	7954
Southern Michigan Prison	Jackson	MI	7	7539
American School Equipment Co.	Maplewood	MO	3	7342

Fig. 4.3. Top twenty-five borrowers by attendance and borrowing frequency, 1943-74

ing borrowing and viewership and reach and influence much larger segments of the population than before. Like radio earlier, television had the ability to grow audiences to levels unimagined with a conventional film lending library. Television was the new, up and coming medium for mass communication that brought entertainment and informal education into homes, and the NIS had to get onboard. Especially in settings other than schools, television vied with, provided alternatives to, and replaced going to and watching movies, such as those distributed by the NIS. The main incentive was the prospect of a meteoric rise in viewership—and impact—that television offered, over and above film projection.

Television was available to the NIS for more than twenty years, yet television stations broadcast its films just thirty-six times, compared to more than eleven thousand borrowings for film projection. But just one television broadcast could reach more viewers than hundreds of screenings with projectors in classrooms, libraries, churches, and civic organizations throughout the region. The relatively small number of broadcasts, however, brings into relief the limitations of television for a niche film library such as this Dutch documentary film collection with a focus on a wide variety of Dutch topics and places. Television broadcasting, with its advertising-driven income, was much more interested in programming that appealed to a large cross section of people in its reception area. A larger market for viewers bolstered Nielsen ratings, increasing advertising revenue. Marketing the films to profit- and advertising-driven television stations was something very different for NIS staff from the more passive sending out film lists, making suggestions, and filling requests for films from the general public. It was challenging to persuade television program managers and advertisers to include an NIS film in their line-up. In any television market, interest in the Netherlands and Dutch films would extend only to a small percentage of the population. But without many viewing choices, viewers during the 1950s and 1960s were more passive consumers of television programming, and as a result, such broadcasts would garner larger audiences than in today's highly segmented viewer markets. As part of a film series about other countries, for example, some NIS films would be quite suitable for television.

The nature and economics of television forced stations to focus on a smaller range of NIS films than the general public. Those films successfully marketed to television stations by the NIS automatically shot to the top of the viewership by virtue of the broadcast medium. Films thought to have more general appeal—those about the entire country, traditional Dutch culture, or an internationally recognized place such as Amsterdam—would more likely be shown on television. This is clearly borne out by the sixteen television broadcasts from eight stations during the 1950s. All were episodes from the four-part survey documentary series, *Holland: A Modern Country Full of Old-Time Charm*, pt. 1, *Country and People*, the introductory and most general and traditional episode of that series, was broadcast seven times.

This series was an overview of the entire country; each film was in the top twenty-five films shown during the 1950s.[10] By contrast, five different TV stations broadcast sixteen very different films during the 1960s/70s; nine of them made up the top ten films for that period. Again, most of these films were about the entire country and explored general themes. Eight of these borrowing records did not include attendance; if their estimated audiences had been recorded, these films would certainly have also climbed into the top tier of viewership.

Television broadcasting of all these films caused their attendance to spike. They derived their viewership totals and rankings mainly from TV broadcasts, and they markedly increased the annual total attendance numbers for all NIS films in the year they were shown. Coincidentally, 1953 and 1965 witnessed the most television broadcasts of NIS films—six and thirteen respectively—more than half the film broadcasts. These years clearly stand out in the total attendance by year from 1943 to 1974 (fig. 4.2). In those two years, several television stations opened their doors to the NIS, broadcasting quite a number of its films; once they showed the films, other stations, however, did not take their place in succeeding years. When that four-part series was added to the NIS collection in late 1952, both KUHT in Houston, the first public television station in the United States, and K-TAG in Lake Charles, Louisiana, broadcast the film in 1953. Even with most television broadcasts not providing viewership numbers, this quickly

---

[10] Thirteen of these sixteen television showings lack attendance figures; had these been included, the four episodes of this film series would have been the top four films in the 1950s.

added more than one hundred thousand recorded viewers to the 1953 NIS film attendance, causing total viewership to sky-rocket. Then, just as quickly in the years following, the film's numbers and the general attendance dropped to more expected levels. Similarly, in 1965, two television stations, one in Southfield, Michigan, and the other in Columbus, Ohio, broadcast a spate of NIS films. Between them, twelve films (more than in any other year) were shown, leading to an upsurge of recorded moviegoers from less than 50,000 for 1964 to more than 250,000 for 1965. There may well be another banner year or two brought on by television broadcasts hidden in the missing data for 1966–72.

Television showings of NIS films picked viewership winners and the strength of the films' influence. In general, they reinforced and accentuated the upper rankings of films from the traditional showings by projection because their higher viewership numbers were also from the more synoptic, traditional, and countrywide films. At the same time, there are several more specialized films in the collection, which, without a television showing, would have had such low attendance that their contributions to American perceptions and knowledge of the Netherlands would have been negligible and, therefore, not worth pursuing. *Vibration* (1951), a film about training deaf-mute children, for example, was screened by projection in only twelve locations, with just over two thousand total viewers; one single television showing in the Detroit area was estimated to have drawn forty-one thousand.

Would there be a difference between the impact on learning from a film at a traditional screening and the same film seen on television? I would suggest that film projection (larger screen, more color films, and group viewing with possible introduction and discussion) created conditions more conducive to learning and retention than television viewing (small screen, little color at the time, more individual viewing with little opportunity for reflection). On the continuum between education and pastime, television broadcasts of NIS films would trend toward the latter.

Film attendance by place

Had the nearly three million moviegoers been concentrated in, say, a three hundred-mile radius around the service area center of Holland, Michigan, as some might expect, the films' cultural impact would have been restricted to the Great Lakes states and only regional, not national, perceptions could be considered. The acquisition of international knowledge is measured not only by the number of people who are exposed to such knowledge but also by the geographic reach of visual media. Viewers of the NIS/NIB films, however, are found throughout the entire twenty-state service region. Fig. 4.4 shows the geography of viewership for the entire period, 1943–74. Films were screened in some 2,292 different places to audiences of varying sizes at different venues and at different times throughout the twenty-state service area.

On the map, screening locations are combined with the total number of viewers in these places and expressed as proportional circles to give an overall distribution of NIB/NIS film attendance. Some localities with a relatively large number of viewers/screenings have a single borrower, for example, Fort Polk, an army base in Louisiana. Others have many different borrowers, for example, Pella, Iowa. Fig. 4.5 zeroes in on the film attendance in the

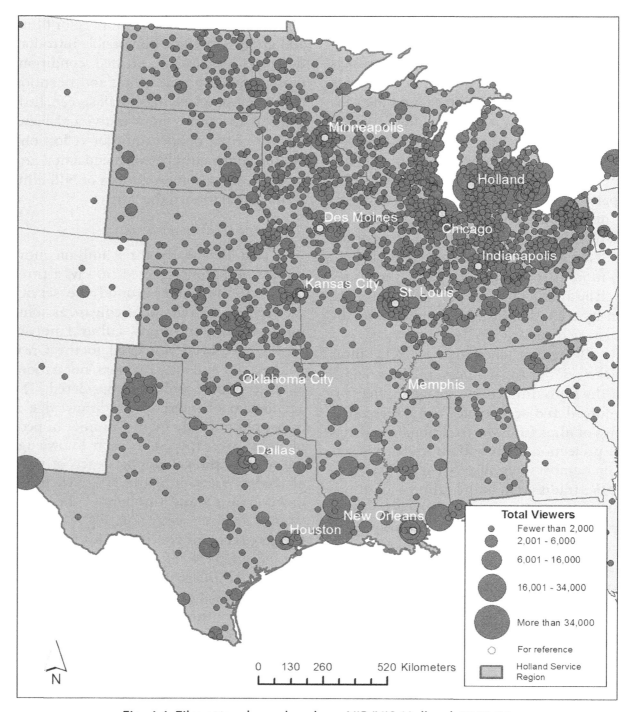

Fig. 4.4. Film attendance by place, NIB/NIS-Holland, 1943-74

Great Lakes states of Michigan, Ohio, In-diana, Illinois, and Wisconsin to present a clearer picture of this zone of the highest density of moviegoers. Fig. 4.6 presents the same data of the number of viewers and screening locations, but now by county, creating a more continuous density surface of viewers. This gives a more realistic picture of the distribution of viewers rather than of screening locations.

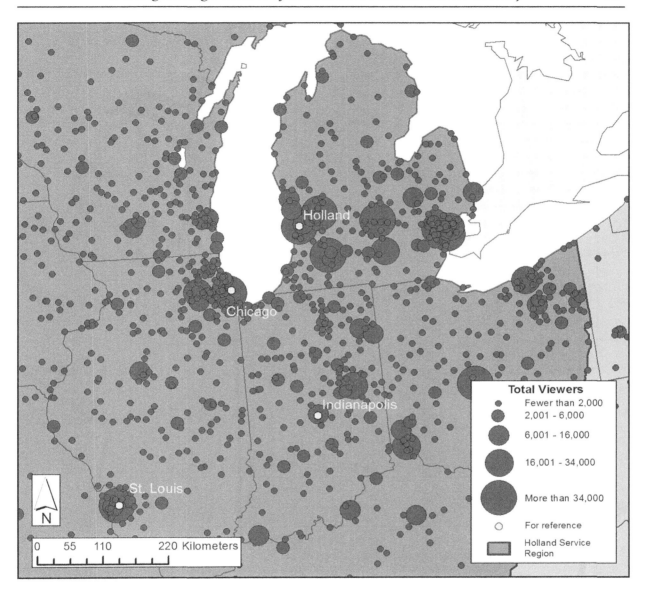

Fig. 4.5. Film attendance by place, Great Lakes states, NIB/NIS-Holland, 1943-74

In considering the total 2,292 different places where these films reached people (figs. 4.4, 4.5, 4.6), it is important to underscore that the maps of film attendance for the three different periods— the 1940s, 1950s, and 1960s/1970s—look much the same but are actually very different (compare figs. 5.2, 6.2, 7.2). Only some 112 places screened films in all three periods and 325 in two periods. For each period, more than 60 percent of the places showed films only in that period. In other words, the same users in the same places did not keep borrowing films; other users and places stepped in. This process accelerated the geographic dispersion of the films and their information and knowledge about the Netherlands and its colonies/dependencies throughout the entire Holland service region.

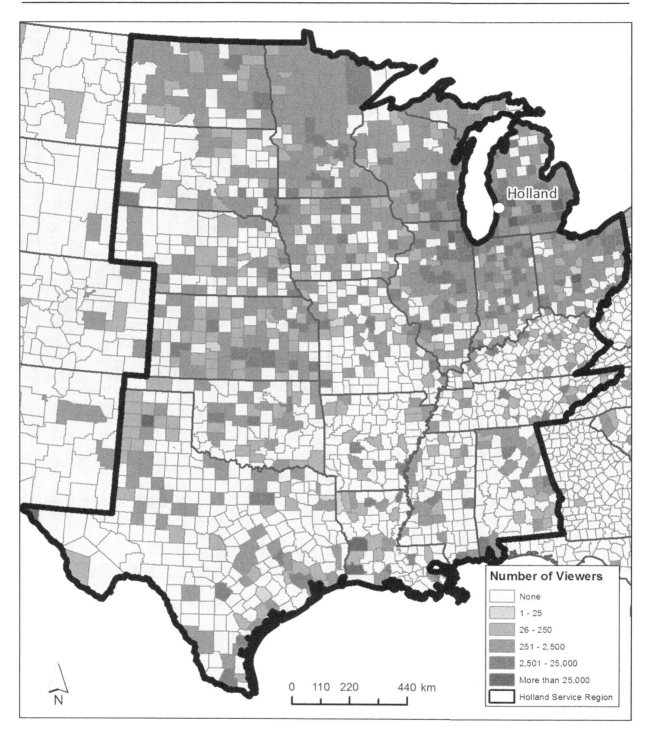

Fig. 4.6. Total viewership of NIB/NIS-Holland films by county, 1943-74

It is noteworthy that on figs. 4.4, 4.5, and 4.6, there are borrowers from NIB/NIS-Holland outside of its own service area; in fact, they are present not only in the border zone, as shown, but also throughout the other two areas, especially the East Coast region. This suggests that there were some titles held by only one film library and/or that the branches shipped titles outside their regions when they were unavailable for a screening date from the other service centers.

Overall, the distribution of viewers and screenings follows the general population distribution of the region: from a peak around the lower Great Lakes coasts and southern Michigan, most of Indiana and Ohio, population density falls off and then levels off to the south and west, interrupted, of course, by density peaks associated with urban areas. Because population density in the region does decline and then levels off south and west, the number of screenings and viewers declines with distance from Holland. But this is not because of the so-called distance decay concept in geography, which holds that an activity falls off with distance because of declining interaction with and knowledge about the services a center provides. Rather, in general, the number of screenings and viewers tracks the population density, which just happens to decline with distance from the Great Lakes region. There is also a significant statistical correlation throughout the region between the number of screenings by county and the county population; population is a good predictor of the number of screenings in a county. In general, the films were seen by a representative, geographic cross section of the population of the twenty-state, NIB/NIS-Holland service area.

That pattern, however, does not hold everywhere. In fig. 4.4, North Dakota and Missouri, for example, show higher film screening/viewer rates than their low-population densities would suggest. But it is especially along the Lake Michigan coast (the Milwaukee area, Chicago region, and West Michigan), as well the southern part of Lower Michigan, that the number of screenings/viewers is considerably greater than population alone would predict (figs. 4.4, 4.5). Two factors played a role in this heightened use of the film library in this region: proximity to Holland, Michigan, and the much higher concentration of Dutch Americans in these areas. Knowledge about the NIB/NIS and its services would be more widespread closer to Holland and in the state of Michigan, resulting in higher borrowing rates. Dutch American institutions, such as Dutch Reformed churches, Reformed Christian day schools, and other organizations, like the Dutch Immigrant Society, Holland Tulip Time, and Chicago's Knickerbocker Society, are much more prevalent throughout this zone. These institutions were borrowing NIB/NIS films at a higher rate than the general public, and there is a high density of such institutions in this area. When more prevalent Dutch American users are combined with non-Dutch American borrowers in this region, higher film-use rates than predicted by population alone resulted.

From the film circulation database, attendance maps by place may be produced for any area and film title. Examples are shown in figs. 4.7 (*Holland and the Zuider Zee*, 1939; 72,865) and 4.8 (*They Said It with Tulips*, 1946; 72,866). Above their lower margin, these maps also include a graph of the duration and totals for attendance by year. Both films attracted the same total number of viewers and were accessioned soon after the NIB's founding, but the distribution of their viewership through time and space is quite different. *Holland and the Zuyder Zee* circulated for only four years (1945–48), with substantial yearly attendance. *They Said It with Tulips* was borrowed for thirteen years (1946-58). The last

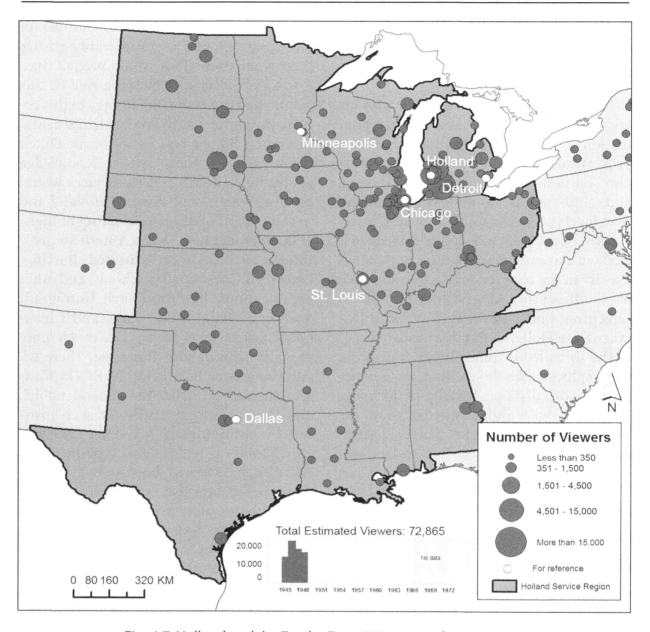

Fig. 4.7. *Holland and the Zuyder Zee*, 1939, viewership, 1945-48

three years do not show up on the graph because of very low attendance; numbers peaked quickly to over thirty thousand annual viewers in 1948 and then declined over the next ten years.

It is not possible to explain the distribution of the viewership of a particular film over time except that in general, one would expect to see some approximation of a log-normal distribution. As a new film first becomes available, viewership rises quickly, soon peaks, and then, as demand becomes saturated, declines much more slowly and over a longer period than when it rose. But the decisions of many borrowers and viewers do not always conform to such a pattern, as the records for *Holland and the Zuyder Zee* demonstrate. Other

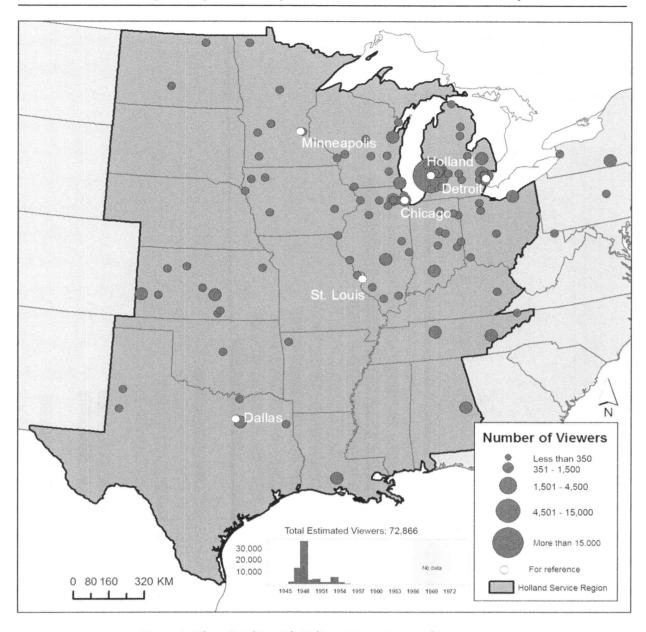

Fig. 4.8. *They Said It with Tulips*, 1945, viewership, 1945-55

factors, such as the number of copies, lost or damaged films, marketing, local borrowing networks, and mass showings at special occasions, may well change such an expected model.

The same may be said for the geography of attendance for individual films: one cannot explain why there were few viewers of a particular film in certain areas and many more moviegoers of another film in these same areas. Compare the maps for these same two films: few moviegoers from Iowa, and South and North Dakota for *They Said It with Tulips* and comparatively many for *Holland and the Zuyder Zee* from the same three states. It is possible that local and regional information networks (teacher, church, and civic organizations) reinforced borrowing and attendance. For individual film titles shown at the local

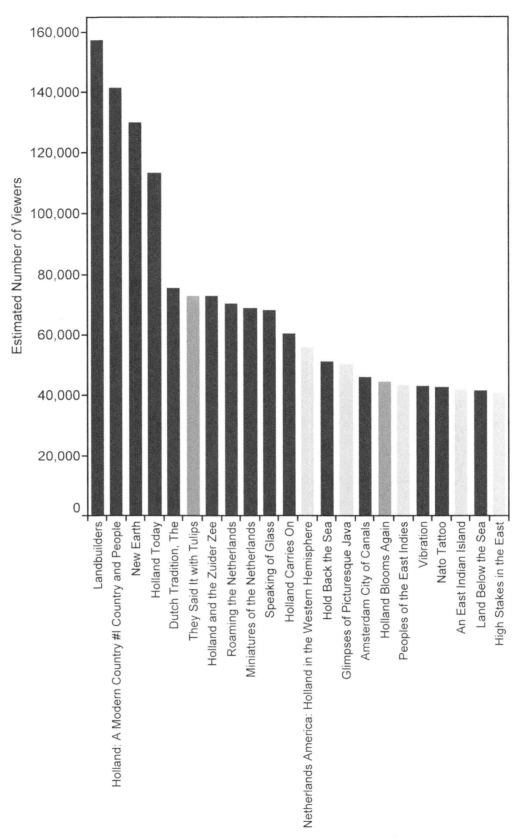

Fig. 4.9. Attendance for top fifty films, 1943-74

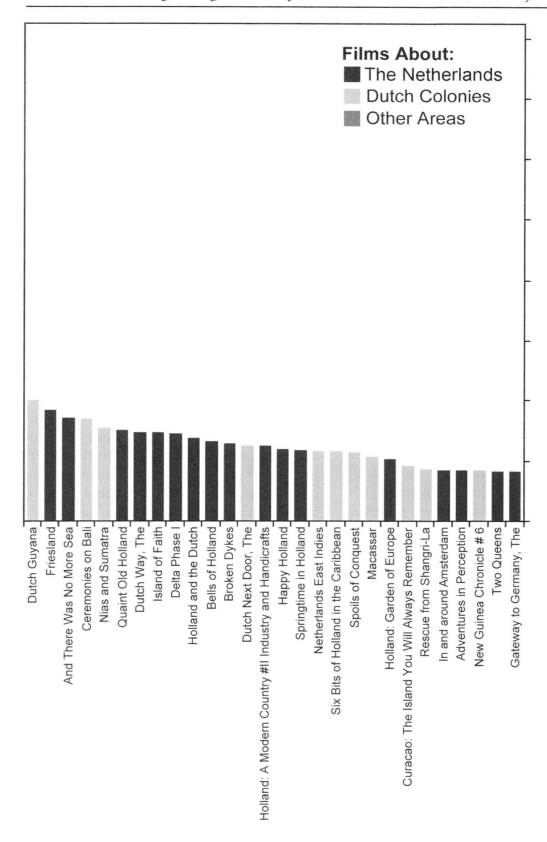

2,229,113 viewers, 79.5% of the total attendance (see endnote 4:11, p. 401)

level, there is more of a geographically random process at work since both borrowers and moviegoers make independent decisions. But even on the attendance maps for particular films, albeit not everywhere nor in all directions, one can still see the overall effects, discussed above, of the general regional population density gradient and of various concentrations of Dutch Americans and their institutions. At the macro level of decision making of both borrowers and viewers—the aggregate attendance of all films—these geographic patterns are more reliable and pervasive.

Attendance by film title

As with any lending library, there were films constantly in circulation, drawing large audiences, and films hardly ever borrowed, seen by very few. When the 227 titles for the entire 1943–74 period are ranked by the size of their total audiences, the list for all the films (app. 1) and the graph for the top fifty (fig. 4.9) shows a few toppers, with a steep decline from 160,000 to 80,000 viewers, followed by a relatively flat attendance plateau of some six films. From sixty thousand to less than one hundred viewers, the list reveals a shallow and relatively proportional decline in viewership of the films. At the sixty-fifth film in the ranking, viewership already drops below ten thousand, and at the 162nd film, it falls below a thousand. A graph and ranking that includes all the films over the entire period, however, has real limitations because many of these films were not in the lending library at the same time. They were not part of the same collection, competing with each other for viewers. The dynamics of borrowing some films more than others can better be observed at a smaller time scale, such as the decades

of the 1940s, 1950s, and 1960s/70s. In the chapters on each of these three periods, I will examine the ranking of the viewership by film title. It is, however, clear that films with staying power—that is, those that remained popular for more than one period—came out on top in total viewership. *New Earth* (1933/1943), for example, was the third most popular film, with nearly 130,000 viewers, as well as the only film screened in each period; it ranked second in the 1940s, third in the 1950s, and eleventh in the 1960s/70s.

Because NIB/NIS films did not benefit from advertising, newspaper reviews, and word-of-mouth marketing, it is hard to know how and why there are such large disparities in viewership. At a movie theater, box office hits and flops were driven by movie reviews and word-of-mouth publicity. For these films, a strong endorsement or a big yawn in one place may not have been readily communicated to people in another place. The title and brief catalog description must have had some impact, but the titles and descriptions for, for example, *Landbuilders* (1932/1940; 157,362), and *Holland: A Modern Country*, pt. 3, *Trade and Transport* (1950; 9,484), would not have produced enough divergence in appeal to explain such extreme differences in viewership. Films that either featured the entire country or focused on a topic or place of interest to Americans (Amsterdam, or water and the Dutch) would naturally generate more filmgoers. The NIB/NIS archive offers little help with the question of the differences in viewership for film titles. A plausible explanation combines marketing by the Holland office itself with local centers of film borrowers identified in fig. 4.4. On the one hand, the Holland office would have been asked by borrowers to recommend and send films for different occasions and interests; such preferences would help to build or dampen viewership for individual films. On the other hand, there are clusters of borrowers in some counties or centers but not in other adjacent ones. In such geographic borrowing clusters, school, church, and civic networks would informally circulate information about the films that would direct further borrowing decisions of individuals, families, and groups.

There is another reason to pay attention to the films with the largest attendance figures (fig. 4.9). Throughout this study, I focus my analysis particularly on those films with a large viewership on the straightforward assumption that such films likely made a larger difference in Americans' understanding of the Netherlands. The top fifty films took in 2,229,113 moviegoers, nearly 80 percent of the total attendance for the 227 NIB/NIS-Holland films for the entire 1943–74 period.[12]

Another meaningful statistic taken from this graph (fig. 4.9) is that films about the Dutch colonies are overrepresented in the overall top fifty: sixteen fit that category—seventeen, if one includes *The Dutch Tradition*, a film that pays attention to both the Netherlands and its colonies. The percentage of attendance from films about the colonies is 34.0 percent of the top fifty films compared to 19.8 percent for the entire film library. Related to this is the overrepresentation of attendance from the 1940s films among the all-time top fifty: 36.3 percent as compared to 23.2 percent for all the films, using as a measure, films shown entirely or primarily during the 1940s. The overrepresentation of 1940 films among

the all-time, top fifty and their follow-on greater cultural impact is due to the nearly two-times higher average attendance for the 1940s films than for all the films of the entire period (23,290 vs. 12,350 moviegoers per film title). Again, this is related to the smaller number of films in the library and film as the exclusive movie medium during the 1940s. A significant number of films about the Dutch colonies ended up in the more influential, overall top fifty because there were many more of these films in the 1940s library than in other decades.

Dutch American and non-Dutch American viewers

The NIB/NIS's purpose was to favorably shape American public opinion in relation to particular Dutch foreign policy objectives and to advance knowledge about and regard for the Netherlands in general. A broad American public, not just Dutch Americans, was the primary target. Press releases were sent mainly to regional dailies, not to Dutch American institutions, newspapers, and magazines; radio programs were not marketed to Dutch Americans but to a broader audience. The film circulation records bear this out as well: of the 2,803,619 estimated viewers of NIB/NIS films in the Holland-NIB service region, only about 12 percent (336,434) were Dutch Americans, and this number is based on screenings at Dutch American institutions. This percentage is a floor; the real number was certainly higher because at all other screenings, those of Dutch American ancestry would likely be disproportionately represented because of their special interest in all things Dutch.

The number of Dutch American viewers, of course, varied widely by state (fig. 4.10), from a high of more than 21 percent

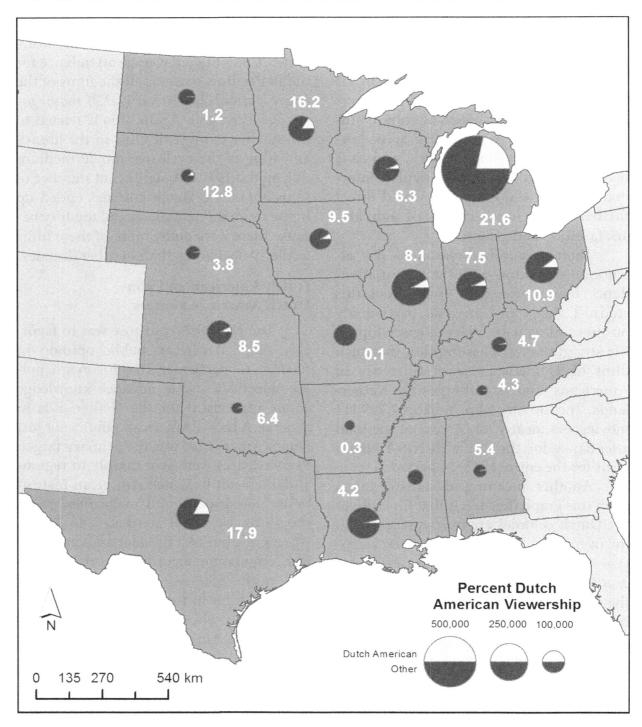

Fig. 4.10. Size and percentage by state of Dutch American viewership of NIB/NIS-Holland films, 1943-74

Screenings at Dutch Reformed churches, Reformed Christian day schools, and other Dutch American organizations

for Michigan to a low of only 0.1 percent for Missouri. Understandably, the upper Midwest Dutch immigration zone, in general, has the higher percentages and larger numbers of Dutch American viewers. Texas is an exception, partly because there was a field officer of NIB/NIS-Holland working in Nederland, Texas, for some time.[13] The upper Midwest, of course, was home to the largest populations of Dutch Americans in the country; much smaller total numbers resided in the states of the East and West Coast regions of the NIB/NIS. The percentages of Dutch Americans of the total viewership by state for the rest of the country, with some exceptions, would have been quite similar to the southern half of the Midwest NIS/NIB service region.

These modest percentages of Dutch American viewers (except for the upper Midwest) are related to the mission of the NIB/NIS: to influence American public opinion at large. It was an agency of the Dutch government led by diplomats from the Netherlands and not by Dutch Americans. Willard Wichers, director of NIB/NIS-Holland, was an important exception: a Dutch American leader whose life and career was entirely bound up in that ethnic subculture. More than others, Wichers did see Dutch Americans as important ambassadors in the NIB/NIS's public diplomacy and urged the New York head office to also send its materials to Dutch American institutions and print media.[14]

There is another reason why Dutch Americans made only modest use of NIB/NIS resources, including the documentary films. Beginning in the mid-nineteenth century, Seceders from the Dutch Reformed state church and their descendants, particularly in and around Holland, Michigan; Pella, Iowa; and Sheboygan, Wisconsin, as well as their secondary settlements, made up a significant proportion of the early immigrants and their leadership. They and those who had left for economic reasons were of two different mindsets and disagreed about their former motherland. David Zwart carefully examines these two perceptions with the help of the NIS archive as well as the Wichers archive.[15] One mindset was a rather dim view of the ancestral homeland: a country they or their forebears had left because of economic hardship and/or religious persecution, and compared to America, it was out-of-date economically, technologically, and politically. This perception was restated and re-enacted at public anniversaries. The other mindset was a more favorable appreciation of their Dutch heritage, albeit a very nostalgic view of the country as a quaint, nineteenth-century, preindustrial homeland with tulips, traditional costumes, windmills, wooden shoes, and cheese markets. This viewpoint conformed with the general American view of the Netherlands that arose during the second half of the nineteenth century. Yearly "Tulip Time" festivals around the country embodied and reprised these stock images and narratives.

From the circulation records and his own experience, Willard Wichers knew that many of the NIB/NIS films were not very popular among Dutch Americans.[16]

---

13   Activity Reports, 1940s, box 3, NIS archive, HCASC.

14   David Zwart, "Constructing the Homeland: Dutch Americans and the Netherlands Information Bureau during the 1940s," *Michigan Historical Review* 33, no. 2 (Fall 2007): 99.

15   Ibid., 81–100.

16   Ibid., 99.

It is this deeply anchored negative view of the Netherlands as a country that lacked essential freedoms—of religion and from want—that, in addition to the NIB/NIS goals, also helps explain the more limited interest Dutch Americans had in these films.[17] At the same time, it must be remembered that the percentage of Dutch American NIB/NIS filmgoers was considerably higher than their share of the population: less than 2 percent compared to 12 percent. Dutch American viewers still stood out in the general viewership.

Americans also helped steer the American public to NIB/NIS films. With a special interest in the Netherlands, Dutch American teachers, academics, librarians, and military officers all borrowed the films for their classes, programs, and troops. For example, Major H. van Hoof, stationed at Fort Bliss, Texas, borrowed films on eleven occasions and arranged screenings for more than eighty-five hundred army personnel (fig. 4.3). The best example of such facilitation, one with a great impact on viewership, was the city of Holland's Tulip Time festival. This annual festival organized by the Dutch American community brought tens of thousands of non-Dutch Americans into the city's downtown. Tulip Time regularly screened NIB/NIS films and, except for several television stations,

generated the third-largest viewership of more than eighty-six thousand (fig. 4.3).

Types of borrowers

The monthly and semiannual film reports were compiled by the NIB/NIS staff from the film borrowing records. The film borrowing report for September 1945 (fig. 3.2) lists a wide variety of different users along with the attendance: Sunday schools and other church groups, camps, grade schools, a commercial firm, civic organizations, an art gallery, and a military hospital. When all borrowers are classified into one of twelve types, the viewership of these different kinds of borrowers may be compared (fig. 4.11).[18] Educational users, especially schools and universities, tower above all the others; civic organizations, the military, libraries, and church schools count among minor types of borrowers. The school/education category alone has more than six times the number of viewers than civic organizations, the next lower ranked category. Film catalogs of the 1940s included notes to teachers (fig. 3.1). The remaining types of users steadily ramp downward from about one hundred thousand to only several thousand viewers.

The preponderance of educational users clearly strengthened the films' cultural impact. On a continuum between education and pastime, schools, universities, church education, civic organizations, and

---

17 Ibid., 93–94, 100. Zwart also attributes the lack of interest of Dutch Americans in the Netherlands to the more modern and up-to-date image of the country that the NIB/NIS was promoting, also in the films. Many Dutch Americans clung to traditional nostalgic images of their homeland. I, however, argue that the films about the Netherlands shown during the 1940s, with very few exceptions, somewhat surprisingly, almost all reiterate and reinforce this traditional imagery. Because the films very much conform to Dutch Americans' image expectations, at least, during those years, they should have liked and frequented them much more.

18 Most borrower types are self-explanatory. Users classified as "circulated" were organizations that in turn also further distributed the films to other local users. "Religious" users were all organizations administered by churches. "Care Facilities" include hospitals and institutions for the elderly. As shown, a large number of borrowers did not report their institutional affiliation in the circulation records. If these would be distributed over all types of borrowers in the same fashion, the predominance of educational users would even be more pronounced.

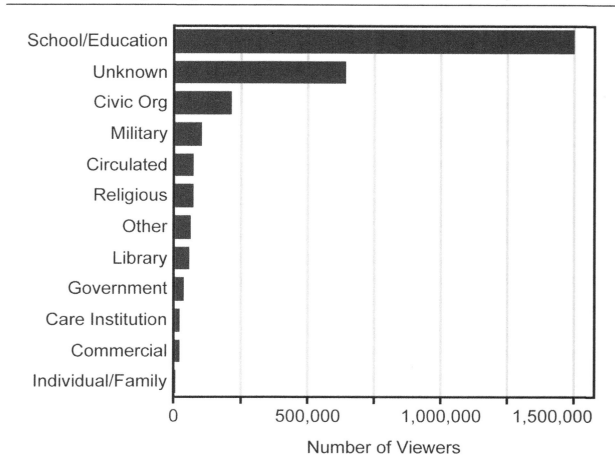

Fig. 4.11. NIB/NIS-Holland film attendance by type of borrower, 1943-74

libraries point more to the former, and the military, care facilities, and commercial entities, more toward the latter. Educational institutions and their teachers would most likely show these films as part of a curriculum unit with possible previewing commentary by the teacher, class questions with discussion before and after a film, written reports by the students, and tests on the contents. Such teaching and learning strategies would enhance the impact and retention of the material, message, and meaning of the film. At the same time, students would more likely be taught to be somewhat more discerning and critical about the information and points of view of a film than those gathered at a military

base for an evening's diversion. Politically, however, student consumers of these films would have less impact on operational, short-term, American public opinion than adult viewers at a care or military facility. All in all, the large majority of educational users blunted the more desired and immediate foreign policy goals of the NIB during the 1940s but bolstered the longer-term cultural impact of the films on American viewers.

Subject matter of the films

No agency for political and cultural diplomacy can cover its entire information waterfront, but it does need to build out its resources with the goal of representativeness. Moreover, it has to be nimble enough to know where and how to find information that is not among its own materials. This agility is clear from the activity reports submitted by the directors of the branch offices to the headquarters in New York. An example of the NIS both supplying and obtaining information is the report for the six-month period of July to December 1952. During that period, as reported, Holland-NIS received 869 telephone calls; 366 people came into the office, and 2,810 letters were written, many of them accompanying the 1,235 packages of literature sent out to schools, libraries, and individuals. Under the heading of public relations, another 287 of these outgoing letters were inquiries for information related to further research, special attention, and development.[19]

There is both topical and geographical representativeness. Do materials about, for example, mining in the Netherlands cover the different types of this activity? Does a film that aims to provide a general introduction to the country include much or very little of its regional diversity? For a national information agency, comprehensiveness—both topical and geographical—was an important benchmark. It would fall short of that standard if there were no materials about, say, the railway system or the province of Limburg.

Topical diversity would certainly also serve as a guiding principle for the acquisitions of a film library such as this one, and this makes sense, considering the materials a film library about the Netherlands and its territories ought to include, given the different consumer-driven information needs and interests. In this chapter, I will measure and discuss the subject makeup based on the topical threads in the films in the entire collection for the lifetime of the NIB/NIS, and, in subsequent chapters, for each decade. These are meta profiles of the topic mix in the film library, an aggregate image of the Netherlands and its colonies provided by the films but certainly not one communicated to Americans in general.

Not one person or group, of course, saw all the films available at any one time. Individuals probably saw no more than several films, which helped construct *their* perception of some aspect(s) of the country. This made their knowledge far different from and less representative of the aggregate image. For the perception of the Netherlands conveyed by the films to individuals or groups of viewers, it is necessary to analyze the topics and rhetoric of specific films on the assumption that most people viewed only one or two. This, I will do in the following chapters. Just as the topical profile for the entire collection, or divisions of it, may be measured and appraised for its representativeness, any individual film under scrutiny on a particular topic (*New Earth*, 1933/1943) or places (*Six Bits of Holland in the Caribbean*, 1950) also needs to be assessed as more or less representative in relation to its title, topic, and aims.

The scrutiny of films with large viewership numbers is particularly imperative because they cemented widespread specific perceptions: if *Landbuilders* (1932/1940; 157,362), with more viewers than any other film, was one of the few films seen by an individual, its perceptions would be more widely shared. Rather than any kind of meta image that Americans who viewed

19   Willard C. Wichers to Jerome Heldring, Activity Report for July to December 1952, 1, "Monthly Reports to the Bureau" and "Activity Reports," 1951–59, box 3, NIS archive, HCASC.

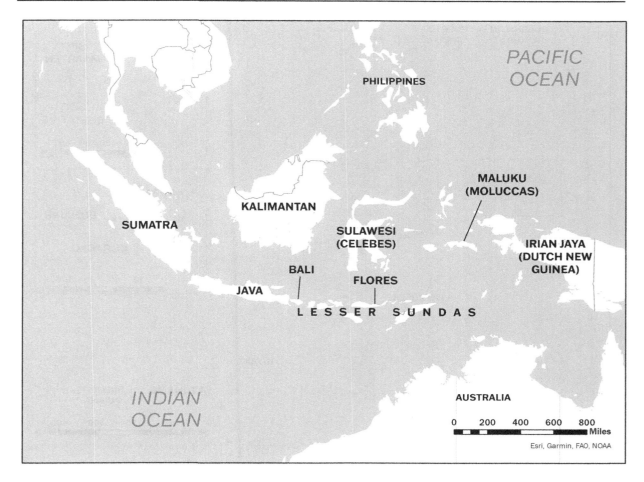

Fig. 4.12. The Dutch East Indies in geographic context

films from the NIB/NIS shared, it is better to think of a kaleidoscope of different, albeit related, images conveyed by the well-attended films that Americans saw in different decades.

Films about the Netherlands and films about the Dutch colonies/dependencies

Geographic coverage was a first consideration for organizing the content of the films. For the entire film library, the breakdown between films about the Netherlands itself and those about its colonies/territories was about 80:20. In addition, there were a few films (e.g., *They Said It with Tulips*, 1946; 72,866) about the Netherlands in North America. In the 1940s,

the Dutch colonies around the world included all of what today is Indonesia and East Timor (then together known as the Dutch East Indies) in Southeast Asia (fig. 4.12); the Dutch West Indies included the islands of Aruba, Bonaire, Curaçao, Saba, Sint Maarten, and Sint Eustatius in the Caribbean; and Suriname (Dutch Guiana) in South America (fig. 4.13). Fig. 4.9 organizes the top fifty films for the entire 1943–74 period into these three geographic classes. In this group of especially influential films, sixteen (32%) are about the Dutch colonies, a higher figure than the overall percentage about the colonies from all the films. During the 1940s, when the NIB pushed hard to convince the American public of

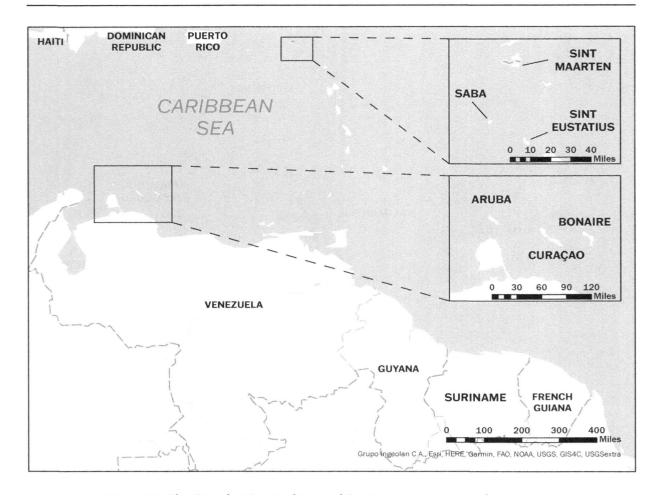

Fig. 4.13. The Dutch West Indies and Suriname in geographic context

the rightness and strategic necessity of its colonies, nearly half of the film library's fifty-five films (and 12 of the top 25 in attendance) in the collection were about the colonies.

More than seven hundred thousand Americans viewed these sixteen films about the Dutch colonies/territories among the top fifty films from 1943 to 1974, some 25 percent of all viewers in the Holland-NIB/NIS region. Of these viewers, more than six hundred thousand attended screenings for these films during the 1940s (nearly 50% of all moviegoers for that decade), again, a reflection of the urgency of the colonial question for the Netherlands in the United

States at that time. After WWII, and the political independence of Indonesia, the number of films in the collection about the colonies/territories and their viewers shrank dramatically. During the 1950s, only eight of the top fifty films dealt with the colonies/territories, with four in the top twenty-five and during the 1960s, five of the top fifty films, with only one in the top twenty-five (figs. 6.1, 7.1).

Similarly, the viewership of films about the Dutch colonies/territories declined from over six hundred thousand during the 1940s to less than one hundred thousand for the period from 1950 to 1974. Moreover, the geographic focus

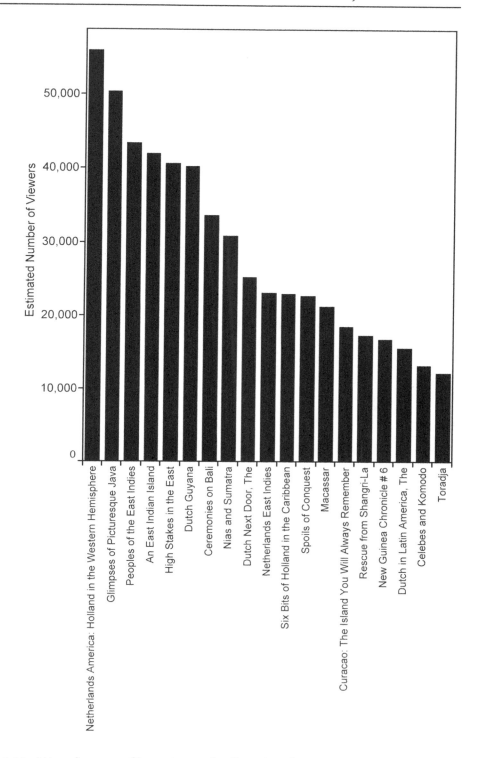

Fig. 4.14. Attendance at films about the Dutch colonies/territories, 1943-74

of this much smaller number of films and viewership shifted from the East Indies to the West Indies and the topical focus from geostrategic locations and resources to economic development and tourism. Fig. 4.14 ranks the attendance of each of

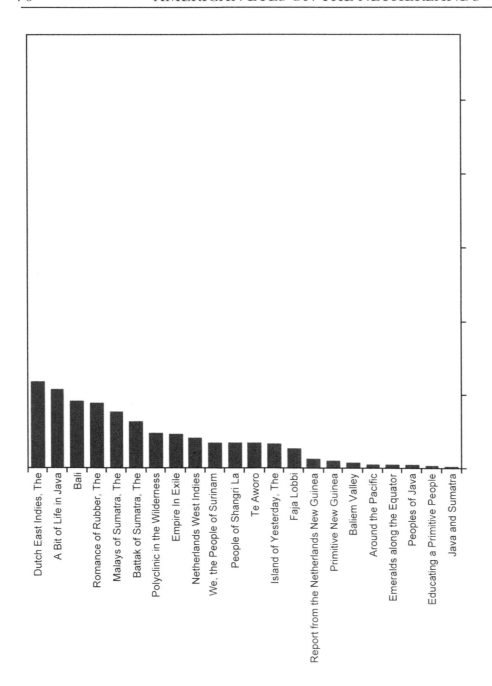

the forty-one films about the Dutch colonies/territories. Those screened during the 1940s entirely dominate the region of larger audiences on the graph. With the exception of the four national blockbuster films about the Netherlands that each attracted more than one hundred thousand viewers, films about the Dutch colonies/ territories were found at every attendance level (fig. 4.9). The average attendance at films about the colonies/territories was not significantly lower than that of films about the Netherlands, suggesting—for the entire lifespan of the NIB/NIS—equal interest among Americans in the Netherlands overseas and in the country proper. This is somewhat counterintuitive: one would think that an agency called the Netherlands Information Bureau/Service would garner the greatest interest among those who want to know more about the country by that name, one already well known to the general public. The strong attendance at film screenings about the colonies/territories was due to the propaganda campaign of the NIB in the 1940s that was designed to put the colonies in a favorable light in American public opinion. This reflected the considerable financing of the NIB by the Dutch East Indies, as well as the leadership of Slotemaker de Bruine, director of the NIB and—significantly—former head of the Dutch East Indies news wire service. Another more general factor was the attraction of exoticism associated with these Dutch tropical possessions.

Content inventory: films about the Netherlands, 1943–74

For each of these two principal groups of films—those about the Netherlands and those about the Dutch colonies/territories—a content inventory was carried out, one based on the twenty-five subject categories previously introduced (fig. 3.4). This helped to identify the principal content categories for all of 1943–74 for a large number of the top films and for the lion's share of viewers. This inventory also documents how the subject matter of the films changed throughout the lifespan of the NIB/NIS and, therefore, what was on offer for Americans about the Netherlands and its possessions at different times.

Fig. 4.15 singles out eight subject categories—those each making up more than 5 percent of the subject threads—standing out above the rest. The palette of knowledge available to Americans about the Nether-

lands throughout the life of the NIB/NIS, as shown, was especially made up of information about eight broad subject categories, each further expanded in fig. 4.15; in descending order of prominence, they are: water, cities, architecture, the arts, recreation, agriculture, military, and transportation. With this many films, subject categories, and actual subject threads, any single subject could not attain a high score and dominate the portrayal of the country. Those subject categories listed in fig. 4.15 provide the principal colors of the knowledge palette for Americans. That issues broadly related to water constitute nearly 15 percent of the subject threads (5.5% more than cities), the second-ranking category, does cement this feature as an inescapable, albeit a stock, stand-out image of the Netherlands for Americans.

Scores lower than 5 percent are equally telling. That subjects such as demography, natural resources, international relations, and health care failed to even reach the 1 percent threshold of threads, shows that these colors are largely indistinguishable on the palette. The films are even largely silent about Christian worship and the church in the Netherlands, still very much a pervasive dimension of Dutch life during the 1940s and 1950s; that topic commands only 1.6 percent of the nearly nine hundred subject threads.

As the NIB/NIS changed from an agency whose principal objective was influencing American foreign policy to a much less proactive information service making materials about the country available to the American public and organizing cultural events and exhibits, the knowledge palette placed on offer to Americans about the Netherlands saw perceptible changes.

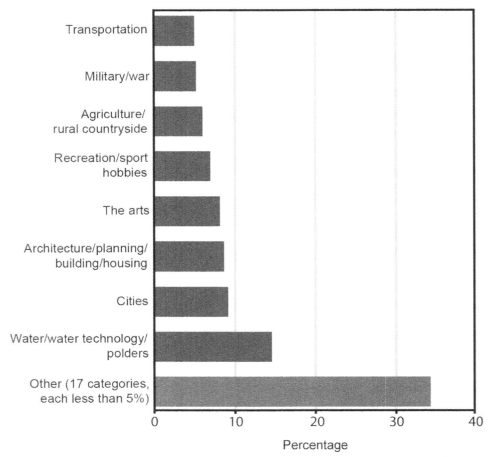

Fig. 4.15. Films about the Netherlands, 1943-74: percentage of
film threads by subject

899 film threads, top 71 films about the Netherlands, 1,821,248 viewers (92.1%)

Similarly, as the agency worked to remain up-to-date and represent leading trends at work in the country, the mix of subject matter changed from decade to decade. Fig. 4.16 tracks leading content categories in the film collection that show significant decline from the 1940s to the 1960s/70s. It is hardly surprising that film threads related to war and the military declined from more than 18 percent of content in the 1940s to less than 2 percent during the 1960s/70s. The peace in Europe kept by international mutual defense pacts and the strong national aversion to war in the

decades following WWII precipitated the steep decline of this once very prominent and, at that time, fitting subject category. Less easily associated with modernization, the category of traditional towns and villages, fostered by long-standing American preferences, as well as the American-made travelogues shown during the 1940s, slipped into obscurity. Attention paid to Dutch cities also waned, but a focus on new, rebuilt, and modern parts of cities, especially during the 1960s/70s, rescued this category and kept it before American eyes. Even water/water technology, the trade-

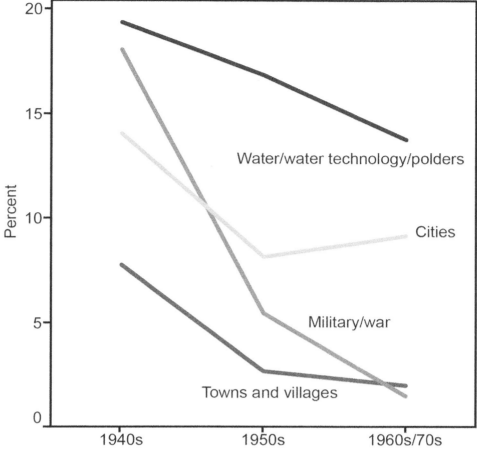

Fig. 4.16. Films about the Netherlands, 1943-74: percentage decline
in topical film threads by subject

1216 film threads, top 92 films (71 titles) about
the Netherlands 1,821,248 viewers (92.1%)[20]

mark brand, while continuing as the most prominent category throughout the entire period, slipped from more than 19 percent to just shy of 14 percent of the threads. It too had become part of the overly traditional image of the country.

With this high-flying category as a benchmark, fig. 4.17 charts the subjects that rose from insignificance to a prominent place during the lifespan of the NIB/NIS—the arts from 0 percent to 13.7 percent, recreation from 1.0 percent to 10.9 percent, and architecture from 3.4 percent to 9.0 percent. Individually and together, these film subject lines, albeit with a pro-

motional and uncritical statistic, exhibited the postwar economic and societal conditions of the country—reconstruction, economic recovery, modernization, and growing affluence.

The colors of the knowledge palette offered to the American public by viewing

20 A significant number of films were viewed during more than one decade. To measure the growth and decline by decade of these subject categories, the content profile of these films had to be entered for each decade in which they were viewed. This accounts for the many more threads and films in figs. 4.16 and 4.17 compared to fig. 4.15; the number of unique film titles remained the same, but some titles were surveyed twice or even three times. Their total viewership, however, remained the same.

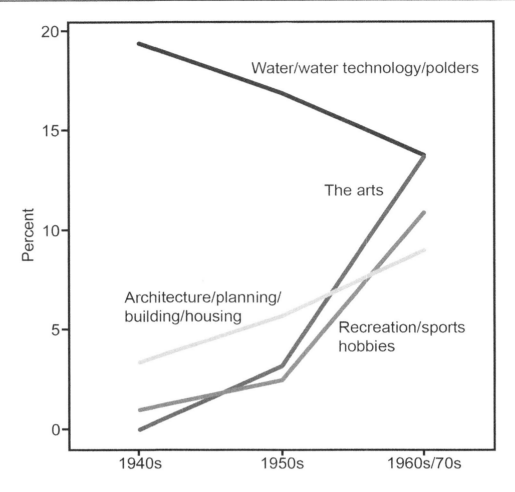

Fig. 4.17. Films about the Netherlands, 1943-74: percentage growth in film threads by subject

1216 film threads, top 92 films (71 titles) about the Netherlands 1,821,248 viewers (92.1%)

NIB/NIS films about the Netherlands itself were gradually reconfigured during the lifetime of the agency. The more traditional American perceptions related to Dutch identity already in place during the late nineteenth century were given additional impetus and reinforcement by the NIB films of the 1940s. Beginning in the 1950s, however, a more modern, up-to-date, and progressive Dutch identity was on offer to the American public, as the changing topical mix in the films surveyed above attests. In the next three chapters, I will endeavor to match the choices for and viewership of individual films and groups of films to this changing knowledge palette. It will become clear that the traditional perceptions had a lot of staying power that affected the choices of films and the size of viewership.

Content inventory: films about the Dutch colonies, 1943–74

The information and imagery palette on offer to Americans via films about the Dutch colonies/territories showed similarities but also differed in noteworthy ways from the one about the Netherlands itself (compare fig. 4.15 with fig. 4.18). The

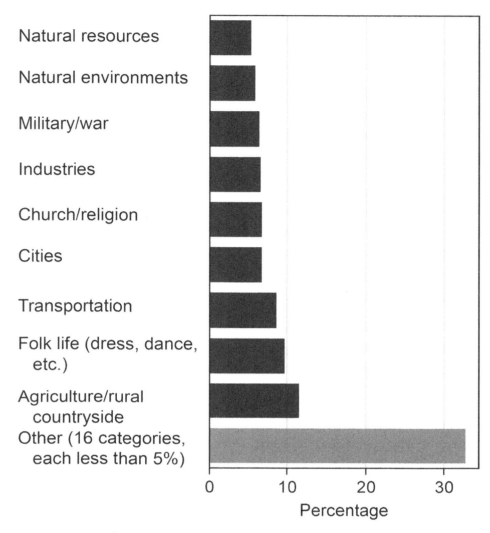

Fig. 4.18. Films about the Dutch colonies, 1943-74: percentage
of film threads by subject

445 film threads, top 26 films about the Dutch colonies, 651,190 viewers (92.6%)

subjects of transportation, agriculture/ rural countryside, military/war, and cities exceed 5 percent of the threads on both graphs, although the films about the colonies track higher percentages for the first three, especially for the rural countryside. The largest numerical difference was related to the water/water technology/polders category: nearly 16 percent of the threads for the films about the Netherlands and not even 1 percent for those about the colonies. For the Netherlands, that subject was and part of its very unique DNA, reiterat-

ed and elaborated over and over again in the films. The colonies, of course, enjoyed a much greater variety of natural settings than the Dutch delta lowlands, and even though quite sophisticated surface water management systems (e.g., wetland rice) existed, they did not define the Dutch colonies as did the hydraulic society of the low Netherlands. Filmmakers took little note of them.

A number of subjects that failed to reach the 5 percent threshold for topic threads for the Netherlands exceeded them for the colonies, notably, natural resources (cf. 5.8% to 0.2%), natural environments (cf. 5.4% to 2.4%), industries (cf. 6.5% to 3.3%), church/religion (cf. 6.7% to 1.6%), and folk life (cf. 9.7% to 4.4%). The place of the colonies in the Dutch economy, as well as their environmental and anthropological otherness, helps explain these differences. In the eyes of the Dutch authorities, these dependencies were, of course, especially valued for their natural resources and related industrial processing (bauxite, tin, rubber, sisal, oil, etc.) and the revenue they created for the Dutch economy. Moreover, Dutch and American filmmakers and their audiences were drawn to differences from their own setting and culture—exotic and unspoiled tropical and subtropical environments, a way of life with unique religious practices, and strange but fascinating customs.

Moviegoers in different decades saw different facets of the colonies take up smaller and larger parts of the collective imagery. If audiences during the forties saw especially rural and farming scenes, folklife, and religious practices (36.0% of threads), audiences during the 1960s/70s saw many more scenes of natural environments, industries, tourism, and the provision of, especially, retail services (these together, made up 39.8% of threads). These same subjects, respectively, accounted for only 11.8 percent during the 1940s and 8.2 percent of the threads during the 1950s.

Figs. 4.19 and 4.20 chart the rapid and significant rise and fall of these subject categories. Through the eyes of the filmmakers, there certainly was a basic shift in the perception of the Dutch colonies. In the 1940s, the composite image had an ethnographic focus with attention to religion, folkways, and indigenous live-

lihood (fig. 4.19). These dependencies were presented as presided over by a beneficent Netherlands bent on economic and societal development for the general betterment of the colonies. But by the time of the 1960s and 1970s, the geographic focus of the Dutch territories had shifted entirely to the Caribbean islands and Suriname in South America; the ethnographic and civilizing focus was largely gone, replaced by a tourist and an industrial image, with attention in the films to scenic natural environments, recreational pastimes, vacation shopping, and modern factories (fig. 4.20). Other more modest rises and falls of attention to subjects also fit into this same shift in perception—increases in the percentage of topical threads for health and health care, the arts, education/science/museums, and transportation, but declines for towns/villages and trades.

In the next chapters, when I line up the changing palette of knowledge about the Dutch colonies/territories presented to American audiences in these films with their choice of films and size of their audiences, it will become clear that Dutchness had little influence on their viewing decisions. Rather, there was a *National Geographic* magazine factor at work: places very different from their own were of interest, either because of their exoticism or their potential as vacation destinations.

Dutch places in the films

Geographical representativeness and comprehensiveness serve as important benchmarks for any national information agency. Such standards also apply to a national film library abroad. For the NIB/NIS film library as a whole, the questions are: which places of the country and its territories are shown repeatedly? which

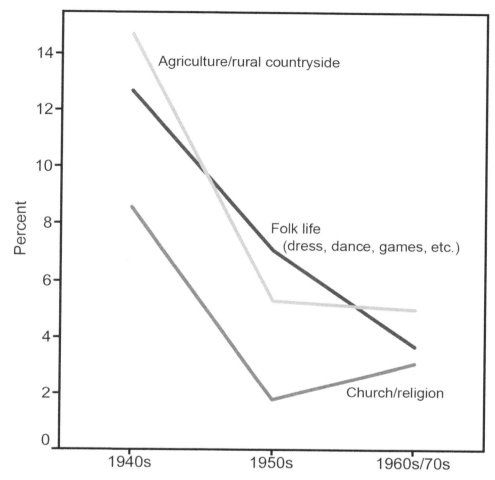

Fig. 4.19. Films about the Dutch colonies: decline
in selected films threads by subject, 1943-74

521 film threads, 33 films (26 titles), 651,190 viewers (92.6%)

receive just a passing interest? and which are entirely ignored? Of course, an entire film may be about either a particular place (Amsterdam), a region (Friesland), or the country as a whole. At each scale, geographic representativeness is one issue for a filmmaker and one yardstick for reviewing a particular film and the entire film library. Is Amsterdam represented only by noteworthy buildings and sites in the historic core of the city? Why leave out the Frisian Wadden Islands in a film about that province? Does the island of Java, as is often the case, stand for all of the Dutch

East Indies? Is the eastern Netherlands ignored in broad surveys of the country?

Geographical representativeness is particularly important in film surveys of either the entire country, a region, or a place. In topical films, it is replaced by geographic particularity and identity. Clearly, the main purpose of such films is to pass knowledge on to an audience about a particular topic in the Netherlands or its territories. That purpose may be achieved with varying degrees of success, even when the names and geographic context of villages, cities, rivers, polders, and regions are left

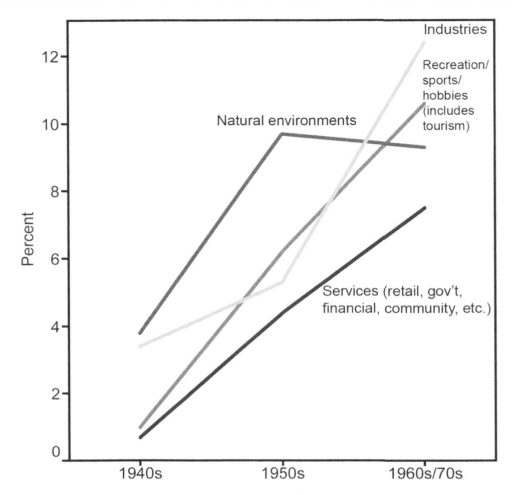

Fig. 4.20. Films about the Dutch colonies: growth
in selected topical threads by subject, 1943-74

521 film threads, 33 films (26 titles), 651,190 viewers (92.6%)

out. But whatever the topical focus/foci of a film—farming, industry, the military, religious worship, transportation—they are invariably place based, and these places have names, identities, and relative locations. A filmmaker always shoots scenes set in time and space for a topic, whether a particular factory assembly line, a specific open-air shopping street, a certain nature reserve, or an aerial view of an actual port. The identification of places and spatial information in the voice-over, dialogue, or visual track promotes further learning about the Netherlands in reference to a par-

ticular topic. Regrettably, the actual places in such films are sometimes not identified, limiting geographic learning, as when a fishing village stands for all such villages, or a polder represents all such landscapes. Alternatively, the geographic settings of a film are generic backgrounds for particular subjects, but they do not enter into the subject matter itself and are left unidentified in the voice-over or the visual content. Many films produced by the Dutch documentary school featured such unnamed generic and nonoperational places; there was no need to identify places and geographic context because the content related to all places. Similarly, there were Dutch documentaries (albeit not many in the NIB/NIB collection) that were about particular products (Heineken Bier, *Het Meest Getapt*, 1952) and trades (plasterers, *De Stukadoor en zijn Werk*, 1950) and public health (radioactive fallout, *De Onzichtbare Vijand*, 1958).[21] Such films often also lacked any geographic particularity.

Because people did not see the entire collection but just a few films, geographic representativeness and identity can best be discussed as part of the scrutiny (undertaken in the succeeding chapters) of particular films screened during each decade. Nevertheless, the overall distribution of places in the Netherlands shown in the films of the NIB/NIS library does track the conscious and inadvertent geographic selectivity of all the actors together—filmmakers, film production companies, and the directors and staff of the national and regional NIB/NIS offices. An average viewer was much more likely to see Amsterdam and Volendam in a film than Nijmegen or Stellendam.

In the sixty-six most-viewed films about the Netherlands (88.9% of viewers), I counted eighty-five "small" places (principally cities and towns) that were shown and/or mentioned—thirty-eight (44.7%) of them multiple times (fig. 4.21), and forty-seven (55.3%) of them only once (fig. 4.22). Not surprisingly, Amsterdam is shown twenty-seven times, more than two times more often than the second most-filmed place, Rotterdam, at thirteen times. Of the places with five or more film appearances, 60 percent are in the province

of Noord-Holland. Among places shown three times or more, small traditional touristic towns (fishing, cheese, flower bulbs) do stand out: Volendam, Scheveningen, Urk, Edam, Spakenburg, Lisse, and Marken. One looks in vain on this table for other nationally dominant urban places such as Maastricht, Groningen, Zwolle, and Enschede.

When these eighty-five filmed places are mapped, along with the number of times each appears (fig. 4.23), clear patterns emerge. Whether measured by the number of different places shown or total showings of places in all sixty-six films, there is a distinct west-to-east gradient for filmed Dutch places in the NIB/NIS-Holland collection. In fig. 4.23, there are many more different places in the western part of the country. What strengthens the representation of the western Netherlands even more is the preponderance of much larger multiple showings of the same place in that region compared to the rest of the country. When single and multiple showings of all places at all scales (from village to region to province) are assembled by province (fig. 4.24), a distinct geography emerges. The western coastal provinces of Noord-Holland, Zuid-Holland, and Zeeland dominate the representation with 75 percent of the filmed places. The midsection of provinces—Friesland, Flevoland, Utrecht, and Noord-Brabant—makes up a second north-south tier, with some 20 percent of the places, and the provinces along the eastern border—Groningen, Drenthe, Overijssel, and Limburg—a third tier, with less than 5 percent of the places. As distance from the west North Sea coast increased, the films presented less and less of the country, with the eastern provinc-

Place	Times Shown	Place	Times Shown
Amsterdam	27	Schiedam	2
Rotterdam	13	Beemster	2
Alkmaar	13	Schermer	2
Volendam	12	Haarlemmermeer	2
Schiphol	11	Monnickendam	2
Afsluitdijk	10	Haringvlietdam	2
The Hague	8	Giethoorn	2
Middelburg	6	Gouda	2
Scheveningen	5	Bunschoten	2
Urk	4	Westkapelle	2
Eindhoven	4	IJmuiden	2
Edam	3	Keukenhof	2
Spakenburg	3	Oostkapelle	2
Delft	3	Arnhem	2
Lisse	3	Leiden	2
Marken	3	Scheveningen Haven	2
Veere	3	Kampen	2
Utrecht	3	Hindelopen	2
Velzen	2	Aalsmeer	2

Fig. 4.21. Dutch places shown more than once in NIB/NIS-Holland films about the Netherlands, screened in the United States, 1943-74

Sixty-six top films about the Netherlands (88.9% of viewers)

es a *terra incognita* for American viewers. In addition, fig. 4.24 makes clear that the visually dominant west coast has its own north-south gradient: Noord-Holland with well over 35 percent, Zuid-Holland with nearly 25 percent, and Zeeland with about 15 percent of the total filmed places.

The provinces of Noord- and Zuid-Holland are a suitable approximation of the demographic, political, economic, urban, and cultural center or core of the country, with the other ten provinces designated as more of a periphery. For Dutch places in the films viewed by Americans, the center/periphery contrast ratio for the entire 1943–74 lifespan of the NIB/NIS is 61/39: 61 percent of the places are from the two provinces making up the center, and 39 percent are from the other ten provinces. That geographic contrast becomes somewhat stronger during the lifetime of the NIB/NIS: from 58/42 during the 1940s, 61/39 during the 1950s, and 66/34 during the 1960s/70s. In the following chapters on each of the three periods of the NIB/NIS, I will compare its map of filmed places with the 1943–74 overall pattern, as well as with those of the other decades.

The strength of place exposure was measured in figs. 4.21 and 4.22 by the num-

Places Shown Once	
Baarn	Madurodam
Biggekerke	Meliskerke
Bolsward	Middelharnis
Breukelen	Nijmegen
Den Oever	Noordzeekanaal
Drimmelen	Noordoostpolder
Elburg	Oosterland
Enkhuizen	Oude-Tonge
Geertruidenberg	Purmer
Haaksbergen	's-Hertogenbosch
Haarlem	Serooskerke [Walcheren]
Harlingen	Souburg
Heerhugowaard	St. Michielsgestel
Hilversum	Stellendam
Holwerd	Tilburg
Hoorn	Veerse Gat
Kaatsheuvel	Vlissingen
Katwijk	Wieringermeer
Kimswerd	Workum
Kortehemmen	Wormer
Krimpen aan de IJssel	Zaandam
Leerdam	Zandvoort
Leeuwarden	Zierikzee
Lelystad	

Fig. 4.22. Dutch places shown once in NIB/NIS-Holland films about the Netherlands, screened in the United States, 1943-74

Sixty-six top films about the Netherlands (88.9% of viewers)

ber of times a place was shown in the films; for example, Amsterdam was shown twenty-seven times, Gouda twice, and Workum once. That measure of place exposure may be enhanced and made more accurate by taking into account the actual number of people who viewed a particular place shown in the films. For example, the city of Delft, between The Hague and Rotterdam, was shown in three films: *Girls of Holland* (1966; 3,273), *Quaint Old Holland* (1935; 30,173), and *Happy Holland* (1954; 24,062),

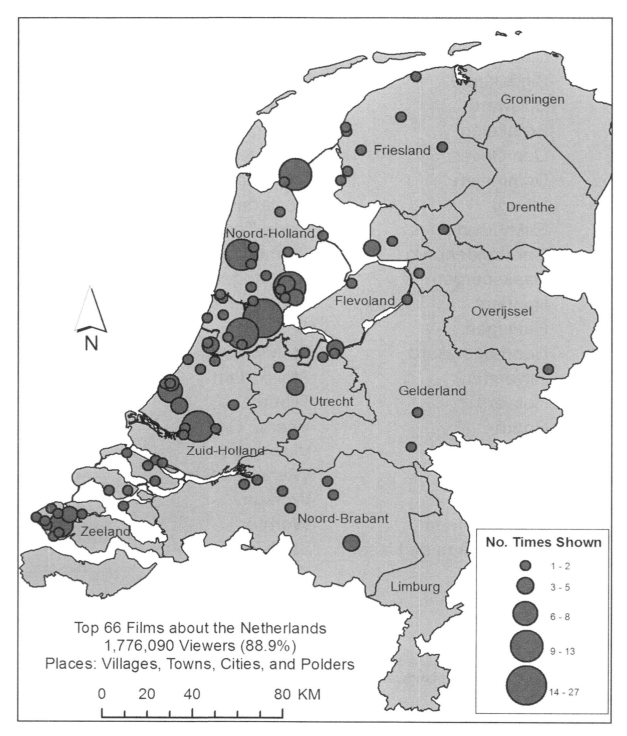

Fig. 4.23. Dutch places shown in films screened in the United States, borrowed from the Holland-NIB/NIS 1943-74

Top 66 films about the Netherlands
1,776,090 viewers (88.9%)
Villages, Towns, Cities, Polders, Regions, and
Provinces

Percent of Places Shown

	2% or less		15.01% - 25%
	2.01 - 5%		More than 25%
	5.01% - 15%		

0　15　30　60 KM

N

Fig. 4.24. Percentage of Dutch places by province in films shown
in the United States, borrowed from the Holland-NIB/NIS, 1943-74

Place	Viewership (000s)	Place	Viewership (000s)
Amsterdam	1012.1	Leiden	44.4
Rotterdam	537.9	St. Michielsgestel	43.1
Afsluitdijk	512.6	Kampen	41.9
Middelburg	479.8	IJmuiden	38.2
Alkmaar	478.3	Hindelopen	37.9
Schiphol	424.5	Lisse	37.9
Volendam	291.5	Holwerd	36.7
Eindhoven	215.5	Kortehemmen	36.7
Scheveningen	209.8	Leeuwarden	36.7
Westkapelle	199.6	Aalsmeer	35.4
Velsen	182.4	Elburg	34.2
Veere	170.9	Enkhuizen	34.2
Urk	162.8	Hoorn	34.2
Biggekerke	157.3	Veerse Gat	29.3
Souburg	157.3	Meliskerke	25.9
Spakenburg	151	Serooskerke	25.9
Gouda	146	Madurodam	24.1
Giethoorn	134.2	Scheveningen-Haven	24.1
Hilversum	134.2	Haarlem	23.7
s'Hertogenbosch	134.2	Nijmegen	16.4
Den Oever	129.8	Tilburg	16.4
Keukenhof	116.8	Vlissingen	16.4
Pernis	113.6	Haringvliet	16.1
Rijpwetering	113.6	Monnickendam	16.1
Rotterdam	113.6	Purmer	16.1
Marken	112.8	Wormer	16.1
Utrecht	100.7	Zaandam	16.1
Schiedam	84.3	Oude - Tonge	13.5
The Hague	82	Stavenisse	13.5
Haaksbergen	70.3	Stellendam	13.5
Leerdam	68.2	Zierikzee	13.5
Beemster	67.3	Baarn	10.6
Haarlemmermeer	67.3	Breukelen	9.5
Schermer	67.3	Noord Zee Kanaal	9.5
Edam	62.1	Zandvoort	7.4
Arnhem	59.3	Haringvlietdam	7.3
Delft	58.2	Katwijk	3.8
Oostkapelle	55.2	Harlingen	3.7
Bunschoten	51.3	Kimswerd	3.7
Bunschoten	51.3	Workum	3.7
Heerhugowaard	51.2	Bolsward	3.7
Krimpen aan den Ijssel	51.2	Kaatsheuvel	3.2
Lelystad	51.2	Drimmelen	1.9
Noordoostpolder	51.2	Geertruidenberg	1.9
Wieringermeer	51.2		

Fig. 4.25. American viewership of Dutch places in NIB/NIS-Holland films shown in the United States, 1943-74

Top 66 films about the Netherlands, 1,776,090 viewers (88.9%), places: villages, towns, cities, and polders

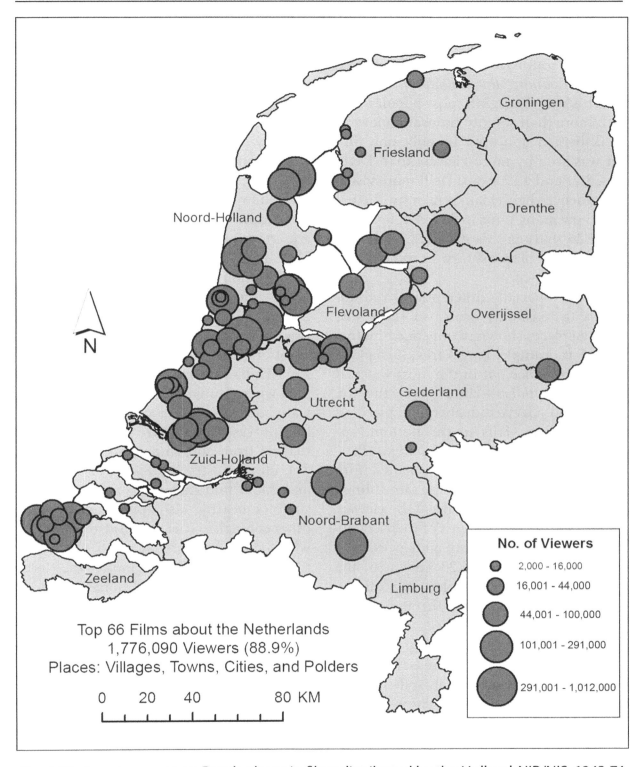

Top 66 Films about the Netherlands
1,776,090 Viewers (88.9%)
Places: Villages, Towns, Cities, and Polders

0   20   40   80 KM

No. of Viewers

2,000 - 16,000

16,001 - 44,000

44,001 - 100,000

101,001 - 291,000

291,001 - 1,012,000

Fig. 4.26. American eyes on Dutch places in films distributed by the Holland-NIB/NIS, 1943-74

together with around fifty-eight thousand moviegoers. Haaksbergen, on the German border in southern Overijssel, was shown only in *Roaming the Netherlands* (1934). Yet, this was the eighth most popular film with more than seventy thousand viewers. Haaksbergen appeared in only one film but was seen by more viewers than Delft. Figs. 4.21 and 4.22 award Delft more visual prominence than Haaksbergen on the basis of how many films included it; figs. 4.25 and 4.26 sharpen this measure further by weighing the places shown in the films by their attendance.

This especially differentiates and upgrades the visibility scores of those forty-seven places shown in only one film (fig. 4.22). For example, Biggekerke, Zeeland—shown only once but in the most-watched film, *Landbuilders*—climbs into the top ranks, and Geertruidenberg, a place in Noord-Brabant, falls to the bottom, appearing only once in *The Amphibian Postman* (1954; 1,886), a little-watched film (fig. 4.25). Fig. 4.26 maps these same filmed places, but now the total size of the viewership measures the strength of their collective exposure to American audiences.

Comparing figs. 4.23 and 4.26, the west-to-east gradient in place exposure is retained but recalibrated. Throughout the map, places with one or just a few showings but with high viewership numbers wax in visual exposure, whereas those with low viewership numbers—in spite of multiple showings—wane. This can especially be seen on the former island of Walcheren, situated in the southwest of the province of Zeeland. Three films with relatively large total audiences—*Landbuilders* (157,362), *Island of Faith* (29,336) and *Broken Dykes* (25,914)—brought a great deal of American visual attention to places on Walcheren. As

fig. 4.26 makes clear, even relatively small Zeeland towns, such as Oostkapelle and Souburg, balloon in visual significance. At the same time, the persistently and unrealistically low scores of places throughout the middle and eastern sections of the country, shown on fig. 4.23, are replaced by values comparable to the western provinces. The rest of the country may have had many fewer filmed places but those that were captured on film were often seen by American audiences in numbers comparable to many in the west.

It should be no surprise that films about the Netherlands and particular Dutch subjects and places also follow this long-standing geographical arrangement of center and periphery. Noord- and Zuid-Holland comprised (and still do) the area where things were happening—politically, economically, socially, and culturally. This was largely where visitors and filmmakers from abroad entered the country. The film industry itself was centered here and could find material for filming most subjects nearby, also for directors from other countries. This region also embodied what many directors regarded as the distinguishing qualities and look of the Netherlands, whether traditional—polders, fishing villages, and towns traversed with canals—or more modern—apartment blocks, electric trains, factory assembly lines, and abstract art.

The north-south decline in American visual exposure to Dutch places along the coastal provinces in NIB/NIS films (fig. 4.24) had less to do with the economic and population geography of the region and more to do with tourist destinations, current events, and particular films. Places in the province of Noord-Holland, more so than in Zuid-Holland, became the iconic filmed tourist destinations—Amsterdam, Volendam, Edam, Marken, and Alkmaar. The capital city Amsterdam, with twenty-seven showings and more than a million American viewers (figs. 4.21 and 4.25, respectively), attracted a great deal of visual attention, and together with Schiphol Airport, formed the principal entry and starting point into the Netherlands from abroad.

At the southern end of the coastal region, the province of Zeeland is part of this western core region, in terms of visual attention from the films, although, as shown (figs. 4.23, 4.24, 4.26), somewhat less so than its northern neighbors, but it has not been part of the Dutch core region for centuries. During the Dutch Golden Age (17th century), Zeeland benefited from its coastal location and island geography and participated in and prospered from the Dutch-led international seaborne trade. But it stagnated economically and became a part of the Dutch periphery, losing out to the larger and better-connected industrial ports to the north. The surplus visual attention conferred on Zeeland in the NIB/NIS films was therefore not because it was part of the core region of the country but because its twentieth-century warfare, flood calamity, and reconstruction were captured on film and included in the NIB/NIS film library. This surfeit of visual consideration for Americans came from a number of transformative events depicted in the films: the German assault on Zeeland during May of 1940 (*Landbuilders*, 1932/1940; 157,362); the British-led attack on Walcheren and the evacuation and restoration of the island as part of the liberation of Europe by the Allies (*Broken Dykes* 1945; 25,914, and *Island of Faith*, 1950; 29,336); the restoration of

the country with the help of, among other things, the Marshall Plan (*Island of Faith*); the devastating North Sea flood of January 31–February 1, 1953 (*Stormramp*, 1953; 13,931, and *Life in Holland*, 1953; 1,307); and the floodproofing of the province by means of the Delta Works plan (*Delta Phase One*, 1962; 29,278, and *Dam the Delta*, 1969; 16,041). More than for any other Dutch region, current events related to war and flood hazards shaped the filmography and visual rhetoric of Zeeland for Americans in the NIB/NIS film library.

The center/periphery relations of the country are articulated not only in the distribution of places featured in the NIB/NIS films, but the entire corpus of films produced in the home country during the same period also displays the same pattern. When one surveys the filmography in Bert Hogenkamp's *De Documentaire Film, 1945–1965*—the authoritative work on Dutch documentary films for this period—the same dominance in place showings, especially in the provinces of Noord- and Zuid-Holland, is evident.[22] And that is completely understandable because the place showings in all Dutch documentary films, of which the NIB/NIS films were a subset, were geographically structured by the same center/periphery relations.

From this discussion of the more general features that distinguished the Holland-NIB/NIS film library in the United States during its entire lifespan, I will now turn to an examination of the film library and groups of individual films in three different periods in three chapters: World War II, the colonies, and reconstruction during the 1940s; economic redevelopment, modernization, and cultural nation-

[22] Hogenkamp, *De Documentaire Film*, 283–305.

alism during the 1950s; and internationalism, affluence, and nonconformity during
the 1960s and early 1970s. This will allow
me to place films into their cultural and
societal context and make room for a close
reading of the visual content and rhetoric
of the more influential films for Americans
in each period.

CHAPTER 5

The 1940s: Propaganda, Exoticism, and Nostalgia

Introduction[1]

As the NIB began to ramp up its foreign-policy-directed public diplomacy—at this point, still without films—the United States had still not entered the war. The destructive effects (e.g., the bombing of Rotterdam) of the German invasion of the largely helpless Netherlands and the hardships of the German occupation were used to gain sympathy for the Dutch and importune America to join the Allied powers. When the United States did enter WWII

after the Japanese attack on Pearl Harbor on December 7, 1941, the NIB's outreach to the American public continued this theme of a suffering and innocent little country and added some other themes, in particular, the Netherlands as a useful ally of the United States in the war effort. American-trained Dutch airmen, as well as the Dutch navy and merchant marine, had escaped from the Netherlands and made themselves available for the war effort. Strategically located Dutch colonial bases and Dutch colonial natural resources were offered as valuable resources in prosecuting the war. These assets, the NIB asserted, made the country a desirable and deserving Allied partner.

With the end of the war, the foreign-policy-directed diplomacy of the NIB as related to the Netherlands itself turned

---

[1] An earlier, much shorter version of this chapter, with a focus on the foreign-policy-directed propaganda films, was published as Henk Aay, "Dutch Propaganda Films in America: Documentaries from the Netherlands Information Bureau in the 1940s," in *Dutch Americans and War: United States and Abroad*, ed. Robert P. Swierenga, Nella Kennedy, and Lisa Zylstra (Van Raalte Press, 2013), 220–49.

more toward the physical and human destruction of the country and assistance for improving public health and rebuilding infrastructure. The NIB budget and personnel were substantially reduced, internal departments merged, and the Boston and Washington offices closed.[2] The NIB would no longer be the agency that channeled and managed the bulk of Netherlands-United States cultural diplomacy. Instead, the plan was to convert it more fully into a culture-directed marketing and educational agency. But then came the Indonesian crisis and with that a renewed need for propaganda and policy-directed diplomacy.

No other immediate postwar issue received more attention from the NIB than restoring and maintaining Dutch sovereignty over the East Indies in the face of a growing Indonesian independence movement and the American public and political sympathy for decolonization.[3] To counter the strong anticolonial sentiments among the American public and political leaders, the NIB waged an information campaign that rested especially on the claim that the Dutch were different colonizers than other nations. Included in this claim were assertions and demonstrations of genuine improvement in the lives and conditions of the Indonesian people as a result of Dutch-led development, integration of Dutch and Indonesian society and institutions in the East Indies, and significant political participation by indigenous communities at all levels.

The other principal claim in this propaganda campaign was unrelated to the Netherlands as a colonial power but was leveled against the leadership of the Indonesian independence movement and the kind of country it would fashion. The NIB reminded the American public that these nationalist leaders had not only earlier collaborated with the Japanese occupiers—the enemy of the United and the Allied powers—but also sympathized with communism, an ideology the United States and other Western nations regarded as a threat to democracy and world stability. In Dutch hands, Indonesia would be safe from both fascism and communism.

Although this propaganda campaign did reach its targets, its strength was not tied into any hard economic, military, or international bargaining power to keep American foreign policy under President Truman from forcing the Netherlands' hand and grant independence to Indonesia, which it did in December of 1949.[4] This marked the end of the NIB's activist foreign policy diplomacy programs; henceforth, the NIB as a passive information provider and cultural programmer took over completely. Alongside the foreign policy films, the NIB distributed American-made travelogues about the Netherlands and parts of

---

[2] David J. Snyder, "The Problem of Power in Modern Diplomacy: The Netherlands Information Bureau in World War II and the Early Cold War," in *The United States and Public Diplomacy. New Directions in Cultural and International History* (Martinus Nijhoff Publishers, 2010), 73.

[3] David Snyder documents the various information strategies the NIB employed to try to win the American public over to the side of supporting continuing Dutch colonial rule in Indonesia. Films played a role in this propaganda; about half of the films distributed during the 1940s were related to the Dutch colonies. David Snyder, "Representing Indonesian Democracy in the US: Dutch Public Diplomacy and the Exception to Self Determination," in *Democracy and Culture in the Transatlantic World*, ed. Charlotte Wallin and Daniel Silander (Växjö University, 2004).

[4] Cees Wiebes and Bert Zeeman, "United States 'Big Stick' Diplomacy: The Netherlands between Decolonization and Alignment, 1945–1949," *The International History Review* 14, no. 1 (Feb. 1992): 45–70.

the Dutch East Indies during this period. Those about the Netherlands played into the nostalgic American perceptions engendered during Holland Mania (1880–1920); those about the Dutch East Indies were not about the Dutch footprint in these colonies but about the exoticism of their environments and native peoples.

Film attendance

Circulation records for the 1940s include fifty-five film titles; forty-five of which are present in the film collection archive. Those records show that an estimated 1,280,968 people throughout the twenty-state, Holland-NIB service area saw these films. When one applies the percentage (1.82) of the total 1950 census population of this region that viewed the films to the 1950 populations of the other two NIB service regions, a rough, but still useful approximation of the national total comes to more than 2.8 million viewers (fig. 4.1).[5] Such a figure assumes identical viewer participation rates and overall similar film libraries in each region—something not likely. Still, it provides something of a national ballpark figure and one measure of the collective societal impact of the films in the United States during the 1940s.

Film attendance from year to year in the 1940s is included in fig. 4.2. It was not until late in 1943—more than a year after Holland-NIB was organized—that the first films were borrowed and screened. It took time to produce and acquire films, arrange for and add English-language narration to Dutch-language films, and prepare and distribute a film catalog. With the German occupation of the Netherlands and the Japanese occupation of the Dutch East Indies,

the NIB was largely cut off from the stock of Dutch films about the Netherlands and its colonies. This lack of access to Dutch-made films also contributed to the decision by the NIB to acquire a substantial number of earlier, mainly American-produced, documentaries about the Netherlands and its colonies. Later in this chapter, I will discuss what kind of American films these were and the consequences thereof for the American perception of the Netherlands and its colonies.

The average film attendance per year for Holland-NIB/NIS was much higher (182,995) in the 1940s than in the 1950s (63,479) and 1960s/70s (110,982). The total attendance for a specialized film library such as that of the NIB was driven by a wide variety of general factors, including marketing, the size and diversity of the film library, the rate of acquisition of new films, and the accession of particularly popular films that skyrocket viewership. The especially high viewership numbers during the 1940s, and the equally low numbers during the 1950s, however, may be explained by two additional unique and potent factors. First, the Dutch government, in exile until 1945, gave high priority to foreign policy and follow-on resources to the NIB due to the country's WWII national emergency and the postwar Dutch East Indies crisis. Beginning in the 1950s, these priorities were no longer in force, and the newly named Netherlands Information Service (NIS) became solely an information agency.

Second, the shift from projection to broadcast technology for moving pictures began to change viewing behavior. The 1940s was still a decade of 16 mm film projection for viewers other than movie theater patrons. But once television at home

5   "Historical Population Change Data (1910–2020)" at census.gov.

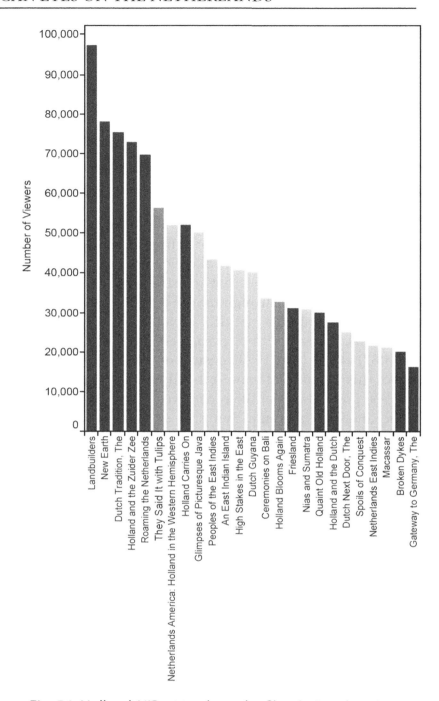

Fig. 5.1. Holland-NIB, attendance by film during the 1940s

became commonplace in the 1950s, going out to see 16 mm documentary films began to decline as television programs became popular, and films were broadcast. The NIS was able to have only a small number of its films broadcast via television.

Fig. 4.2 shows viewership ramping up from 1943 to 1948 as the NIB's film library became more established and better known. The 1948 attendance peak was higher than any other year during the life of the NIB/NIS; from that peak, the gen-

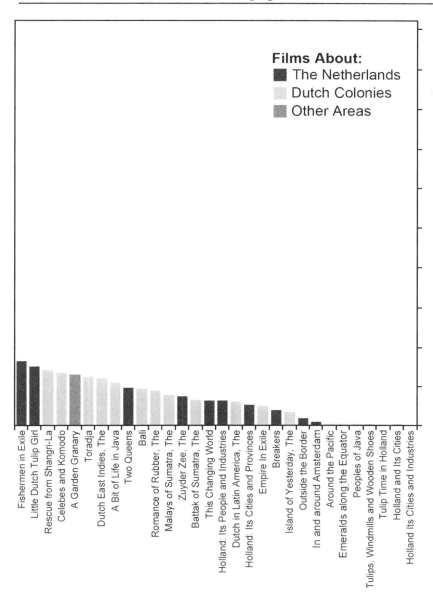

eral annual pattern was one of declining viewership that continued into the 1950s, punctuated by an irregular upsurge occasioned by a particularly popular film and the television broadcasting of films.

The total attendance in the 1940s of nearly 1.3 million viewers was, of course, also distributed unevenly over the fifty-five films. Fig. 5.1 shows the 1940s attendance for each film, arranged in descending order, from *Landbuilders* (1932/1940), with more than ninety-seven thousand viewers

(7.6% of total), to *Holland, Its Cities and Industries,*[6] with just sixty viewers (0.0%). This decline in viewership is fairly steep for the first six films and then continues downward at a relatively constant rate. The first thirty-three films capture more than 93 percent of the total 1940s viewership.

---

6 This film is in the circulation records but not the NIB/NIS archive. It is not cataloged in the national film collections and archives of the United Kingdom (the British Film Institute), the Netherlands (Institute for Sound and Vision), or the United States (Internet Movie Database [IMDb]).

Because films with relatively small numbers of viewers have an equally small, collective cultural impact, the more detailed analysis was reserved for these films (each with over 10,000 viewers).[7]

In part, the attendance figures for particular films for any decade may have little to do with the popularity and impact of the film. The year the film was added to the library also helped determine the buildup of its circulation. The film *In and around Amsterdam* (1949; 17,096), for example, was not acquired by the NIB until 1949 and drew only nine hundred viewers during the 1940s. For the entire 1943–74 period, however, more than seventeen thousand people saw the film; it ranks forty-sixth in overall attendance among the two hundred-plus films. If the impact of the film during the 1940s is measured by its attendance figures then, indeed, its influence was marginal; that is why, when the attendance is reported in parentheses after the title of a film, it is always the total 1943–74 viewership and why the close reading of a film is assigned to the decade (chapter) when it garnered the largest attendance.

Again, it is difficult to really understand why some films had a much larger total audience than others. Size of viewership and topic, along with up-to-date cinematography, appear not to be strongly related. That an excellent, four-part compilation film with Dutch narration, *Buiten de Grenzen* (Outside the borders, 1939–44; 1661), is way down on the list, with some sixteen hundred viewers, is entirely understandable but not *Roaming the Netherlands* (1934; 70,335), a silent film from the 1920s,

yet the fifth-most-attended film, with nearly seventy thousand viewers during the 1940s.

Films about the Netherlands were not seen by more people than films about the Dutch colonies. And it is not at all apparent why films of roughly the same subject class, for example, *People of the Indies* (1942; 43,519) and *The Malays of Sumatra* (1928; 7,774), should be separated in attendance by more than thirty-five thousand viewers. Nor do the films with higher numbers of viewers appear to be dominated by the venues with large audiences, such as military bases or the Tulip Time festival in Holland, Michigan. Marketing by the NIB, as well as local and regional referrals, must have played a significant role in differentiating the size of any film's viewership. Nevertheless, as fig. 5.1 shows, such large differences in viewership among individual films did exist and did influence the perceptions of the Netherlands and its colonies by Americans, even if the reasons for the differences are not all apparent.

Geography of viewership

The million-plus viewers for the 1940s were found throughout the twenty-state, Holland-NIB service region. Fig. 5.2 shows the geography of viewership during the 1940s. In that decade, Holland-NIB films were screened in 1,182 different locations to audiences of varying sizes not only in that service area but also in a substantial number of other locations, especially throughout the East Coast states. Around 70 percent of these screening locations are unique to this decade. Overall, the 1940 attendance map conforms to the general viewership geography on the composite map for the entire 1943–74 period (fig. 4.4).

---

[7] This was also to economize on the research required.

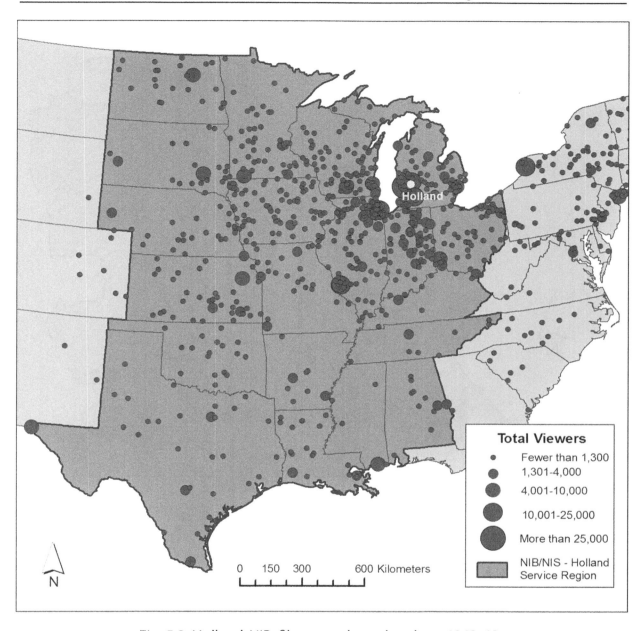

Fig. 5.2. Holland-NIB, film attendance by place, 1943-49

Dutch places shown in the NIB films screened during the 1940s

The most important feature of figs. 5.3 and 5.4, and one shared by many other national Dutch statistics and measures, as noted for the entire period from 1943 to 1974 of the Holland-NIB/NIS, is the importance of the western, coastal region as compared to the eastern and southern parts of the country. For the 1940s, there are no places shown in the films from the provinces of Groningen, Drenthe, and Limburg and, with the exception of Friesland, just a smattering from the other southern and eastern provinces. If the number of different (unique) and geographically small places, such as villages, towns, cities, and historical polders, is the measure (fig. 5.3), then 69.7 percent of them are in the three western provinces (Noord-Hol-

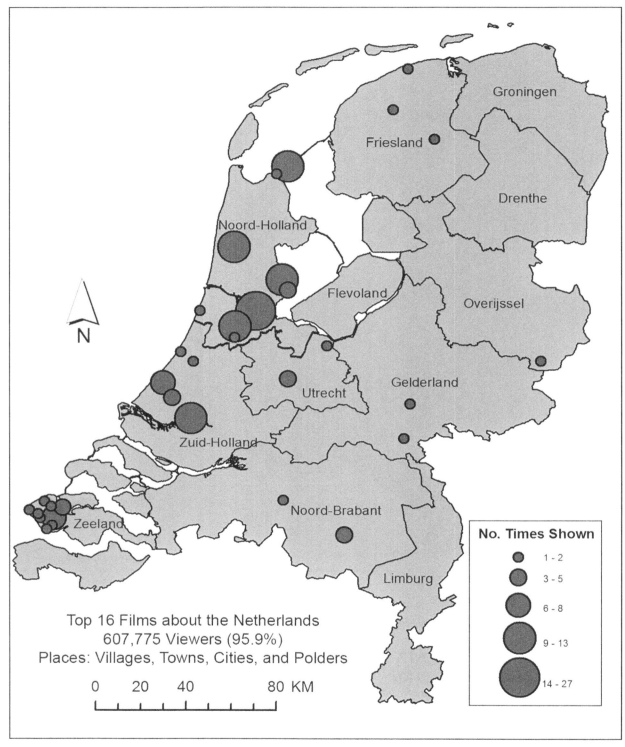

Fig. 5.3. Dutch places in films screened in the United States,
borrowed from the Holland-NIB, 1940s

Top 16 Films about the Netherlands
607,775 Viewers (95.9%)
Places: Villages, Towns, Cities, Polders,
Regions and Provinces

Percent of Places Shown

2% or less	15.01% - 25%
2.01% - 5%	More than 25%
5.01% - 15%	

0   15   30   60 KM

N

Fig. 5.4. Dutch places by province in films screened in the United States,
borrowed from the Holland-NIB, 1940s

land, Zuid-Holland, and Zeeland), 21.2 percent in the middle tier (Friesland, Flevoland, Utrecht, and Noord-Brabant), and 9.1 percent in the provinces along the eastern border. If the measure is all places, including multiple showings, and also taking into account regions, national polders, and provinces (fig. 5.4), then sixty of the seventy-four places shown—an even greater concentration (81.1%)—were in the three western provinces, with even smaller showings in the middle tier (14.9%) and eastern provinces (4.1%). As fig. 5.3 makes clear, places in the western provinces were much more likely to be shown in multiple films, reinforcing the preeminence of the western Netherlands in American eyes. In the middle tier of provinces shown on the maps, places in the future province of Flevoland made hardly any appearance during the 1940s—only the Noordoostpolder was settled—but that would quickly change as the remaining Zuiderzee—now the IJssel Lake (IJsselmeer) polders—were laid dry and occupied. This was a project with large international bragging rights for the Dutch government and Dutch filmmakers. It quickly grew in visual attention during the following decades as a comparison of these maps with those of the 1950s (figs. 6.4, 6.5) and 1960s/70s (figs. 7.4, 7.5) makes clear.

From the beginning of the Dutch Republic, the western Netherlands has been the economic, demographic, urban, economic, political, and cultural heartland of the country. Historically, the periphery received much less attention, especially from foreign writers. During the Dutch Golden Age, the province of Zeeland was also part of this heartland, but it became a part of the periphery in the ensuing centuries. The strong focus on this province in

the films shown during the 1940s (figs. 5.3, 5.4) came from mainly two films: *Landbuilders* (1932/1940) and *Broken Dykes* (1945)—war-related, foreign-policy-directed films—and the spotlight was not on the province as a whole but on only one island: Walcheren. A film about that island just so happened to be chosen by the Dutch National Information Service (Rijksvoorlichtingsdienst), in London, very early in the war, as one that could well be used for its war propaganda objectives; stills showing the bombardment of the late-Gothic, city hall of Middelburg by (supposedly) German forces could easily be added to the end of the film, along with an entirely new propagandist, English-language voice-over and musical score.[8] The film had been a 1930s folklorist film about the cultural landscape of the island. In *Broken Dykes*, however, Walcheren is strategically important in and of itself, protecting the entrance to the Western Scheldt and, with that, the port of Antwerp. John Fernhout filmed the intentional flooding of the island and its settlements by British forces in 1944 to remove the German defenders and the subsequent necessary evacuation of many of its people and much of its livestock. This military campaign opened the estuary to shipping and provisioning into Antwerp, already liberated by the Allies.

The war-related, foreign-policy-directed films of the 1940s did not feature many places from the core of the country—Noord- and Zuid-Holland. Although Rotterdam is shown in connection to the bombing it suffered during the German invasion (*The Dutch Tradition: Three*

---

[8] Today, historians agree that the retreating French forces actually shelled the center of Middelburg. http://www.waroverholland.nl/index.php?page=Middelburg.

Years of the Netherlands' Fight against the Axis, 1940–43, 1944; 75,419), the liberation drives were in the southern and eastern sections of the country. These bring the places of Walcheren onto the map, as well as other liberated cities, such as Tilburg and Eindhoven (Noord-Brabant) in the south and, as part of the drive across the major rivers, Nijmegen and Arnhem (Gelderland) (fig. 5.3).

That the large majority of (unique) places shown during the 1940s were located in the core of the country, with nearly 50 percent from the province of Noord-Holland (fig. 5.3), stems from the culture-directed, not the foreign-policy-directed, films. The former were American-made travelogues, seen not only by NIB film viewers but also by very many American moviegoers. American filmmakers had decided which Dutch localities American moviegoers would view. They especially favored the tourist places north of Amsterdam and helped make some of them into international destinations; places such as Marken and Volendam stand out on the map. For other larger places, such as Alkmaar, Amsterdam, and The Hague, this is not as clear, but the sites in the cities profiled by the films were almost all tourist destinations. These filmmakers' preferences also resulted in the showing of many fewer places (just over 10%) from the province of Zuid-Holland, also very much part of the Netherlands' core. During the 1940s, this province had its weakest place representation during the entire lifespan of the film library. As films from Dutch filmmakers took up more of the film library during the fifties, sixties, and seventies, Zuid-Holland place representation for American viewers steadily increased to fall more in line with its place as part

of the core of the country. This becomes clear when one compares these maps for the 1940s with those of the 1950s (figs. 6.4, 6.5) and 1960s/70s (figs. 7.4, 7.5).

Descriptive content analysis: topical threads in the 1940s Holland-NIB films

Before I discuss individual films screened during the 1940s (to present, document, and group their distinguishing features, rhetoric, and meaning) a more general overview of their subject matter will serve as an introduction. Classifying film threads by topic headings (fig. 3.4) and measuring their relative frequency—as was done for the films for the entire 1943–74 period—provides a content inventory and snapshot of the collective imagery of the films. Again, combining into a single chart the five hundred subject-classified threads of films about both the Netherlands and its colonies shown during the 1940s is not very helpful. The topic of military/war comes out on top with more than 12 percent of all the film threads, but that is about the only subject the films about the Netherlands have in common with those about its colonies. Many other topics—cities, water, farming, religion, and industry—are at opposite ends of the frequency distributions for these two groups. Given their very different societies and economies, each group has distinctive topical foci; splitting the films into these two groups and linking the data to each group made meaningful distinctions and comparisons possible.

Fig. 5.5 summarizes the distribution of subjects for sixteen films about the Netherlands shown during the 1940s. If these subjects all received equal consideration, each would make up about 4 percent of the total number of threads. But, as can be seen, the subjects vary widely in their

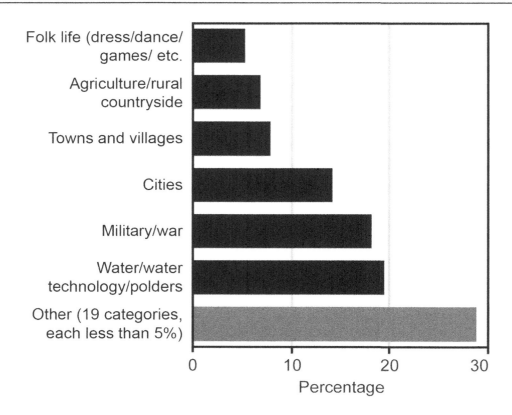

Fig. 5.5. Films about the Netherlands, 1940s: percentage of
film threads by subject

208 film threads, top 16 films about the Netherlands, 607,775 viewers (95.9%)

distribution. Nineteen of the twenty-five subjects have very low frequencies. There are no threads at all related to demography, natural resources, services, political life, or the arts, and the remainder of these nineteen subjects are each less than 5 percent of the total number of threads. Just three subject categories—water management, cities, and issues related to the war and the military—dominate the rhetorical attention of these films with together over 50 percent of the threads. The first two are perennial favorites of movie directors and producers filming the Netherlands for foreign viewers; the importance of the third subject is unique to the war and postwar conditions

of the 1940s and particularly important to the foreign policy objectives of the NIB in the United States.

When films about the Dutch colonies screened during the 1940s are singled out for attention (fig. 5.6), the mix of their focus shifts away from those about the Netherlands.

Understandably missing is the preponderant attention to water management; in the colonies, this category slips from nearly 20 percent to only 1 percent of the film threads. Both groups, of course, include plenty of footage about WWII and its aftermath (Netherlands, 18.1%, and colonies 8.6% of film threads), although the

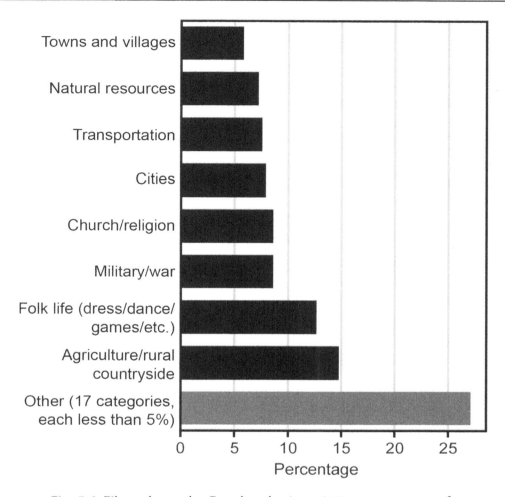

Fig. 5.6. Films about the Dutch colonies, 1940s: percentage of topical film threads by subject

292 film threads, top 20 films about the colonies, 564,456 viewers (91.3%)

perspectives are quite distinct. The colonies are shown as having geostrategic clout and necessary resources for the entire Allied war effort, whereas the home country chafes under German occupation and is liberated with great sacrifice.

Footage about the countryside, farming, folk culture, and religion tops the content list in films about the colonies (36%) compared to just 14 percent in those about the Netherlands itself. Such differences may be explained by divergences in modernization and attention to cultural differences. Premodern rural economies and

ways of life predominated in the colonies. Traditional, native farming methods (e.g., paddy field rice in *An East Indian Island*, 1930) and commercial export crops (e.g. rubber plantations in *The Dutch East Indies*, 1931) receive particular attention. Filmmakers in the colonies were also fascinated with folkways (Balinese dances in *People of the Indies*, 1942) and religious ritual (head towers with fruit and other offerings brought to the temple gods in *Bali, Paradise Isle*, 1946; 9,749).

Even though the percentage of film threads having to do with trade, trades, natural environments, industries, demography, and political life all track at less than 5 percent, these topics receive much more serious attention (68 threads compared to 8) in the films about the colonies compared to those about the Netherlands: natural resources (21–0), trades (13–2), natural environments (11–3), industries (10–1), demography (7–0), trade (6–2), and political life (6–0).

These disparities again reflect the place of the colonies in the Kingdom of the Netherlands at large and in the Allied war effort—stores and industrial processing of natural resources and trade—as well as a natural tendency to highlight what is different in the colonies and the home country (natural environments, traditional crafts, and indigenous populations). Americans, like other Western viewers, were intrigued, fascinated, and charmed by the unfamiliar and the rare; in the twentieth century, documentary film could now contribute to the trend that had been the purview of art and literature.

Films about the Netherlands and films about the Dutch colonies

Fig. 5.1 divides the 1940s films into those mainly about the Netherlands and those about the Dutch colonies. More than half the films are about the Dutch colonies, a reflection of how important the Dutch government regarded the issue of American support of the Netherlands as a colonial power. It also references the enduring perception of itself as a world power. With the loss of the East Indies and a prevailing anticolonialism, the percentage of films about the colonies understandably declined sharply in the ensuing decades.

The top thirty-three (those above ten

thousand viewers) of the fifty-five films shown during the 1940s received closer scrutiny; they drew 93.1 percent of the 1940s attendance (1,191,310 viewers). I divided the films into those that were about the Netherlands and the Dutch colonies; those that were foreign-policy-directed, that is, WWII, postwar reconstruction, colonial policy; and those that were culture directed—improving the general understanding and appreciation of the Netherlands and its colonies. Two of the top thirty-three films could not be placed into these groups.[9] During the 1940s, the NIB was first and foremost working to advance Dutch foreign policy aims among the American public; a measure of its success in meeting this objective is a total audience of 689,868 for sixteen, foreign-policy-directed films, compared to 474,690 moviegoers for fifteen, culture-directed films. That pattern flipped in the ensuing decades, with the number of foreign-policy-directed films steadily dwindling.

Almost all culture-directed films were American made, not Dutch. Conversely, most foreign-policy-directed films were produced by Dutch government agencies, principally the NIB, but also by the RVD (the Rijksvoorlichtingsdienst, the government information service) and the Netherlands Indies Government Information Service. A few films about the liberation of the Netherlands by Allied forces (*Broken Dykes*; *Gateway to Germany*, 1945) were acquired by the NIB from the British Information Service.

Foreign-policy-directed films were frequently compilation films, composed entirely, or almost entirely, of footage from

---

[9]   See endnote 5:9, p. 401.

other films, usually with new narration and music, and the same footage may have been used to produce several different films. The most extreme form of borrowing footage to produce a "new" film would be to use all or most of an existing film, give it a new ending and a new voice-over. The two films with the highest attendance during the 1940s, *Landbuilders* (1932/1940) and *New Earth* (1933, ca. 1943), are examples of this filmmaking technique. Compilation films could of course be produced more quickly and cheaply. Here, the narration drives the rhetoric and meaning more so than the motion picture; in some cases, the same footage with different narration takes on an entirely different message. When filming locations are inaccessible, or filming on location is prohibitively expensive and time-consuming, a documentary film can still be produced. Such circumstances certainly applied to the film production units of the NIB and RVD, but although the principal messaging of these films was related to foreign policy goals, the video footage still communicated cultural information to some extent.

One, however, should not assume that compilation films could just be slapped together and that, as such, were therefore inferior productions. Suitable footage had to be located, permissions secured, new voice-over narrations written, voice actors hired, and recordings made. Reputable filmmakers and motion picture companies were involved in their production. For example, John Fernhout, a well-known Dutch cameraman and filmmaker who worked for the NIB film unit in New York and for the National Film Board of Canada (NFB) during the war years, made, among others, the compilation film, *The Dutch Tradition*, an overview of the Netherlands

and its colonies in relation to the war effort.[10] The NFB is listed as the producer of the film.

Culture-directed films include travelogues, ethnographic films, newsreels, and shorts about the Netherlands and its colonial lands; during the 1940s, these were mainly filmed, directed, and produced by American filmmakers and purchased and distributed by the NIB. They were distributed not only by the NIB but also by the American commercial film industry and by public and education film libraries throughout the country, which had total audiences many times those of the NIB.

Films about the Dutch colonies

I will begin, not with the documentaries about the Netherlands—as one would expect from a Dutch information service—but with those about the Dutch colonies among the top thirty-three films. During the 1940s, there were seventeen of these, with 548,489 viewers, compared to fifteen about the Netherlands, with 691,488 viewers.[11] This is a measure of the remarkable and somewhat surprising success the NIB enjoyed bringing to the attention of the American public the existence of and the Dutch sovereignty over these territories. It is also a barometer of American curiosity about these places at a level matching that of the mother country. One would have thought that the Dutch colonies would have been a lagging interest compared to what drew people to borrow films from the NIB in the first place. Not so.

---

[10]   For an account (in Dutch) of Fernhout's filmmaking career go to: http://www.historici.nl/Onderzoek/Projecten/BWN/lemmata/bwn4/fernhjh.

[11]   One film, *The Dutch Tradition*, fits both categories (the Netherlands and the Dutch colonies), and its title and viewership was counted for each.

Fig. 5.7. NIB-Holland letterhead during the 1940s

Films about the colonies produced or commissioned by the NIB employed a trope that David Snyder calls "large Holland."[12] The size, global presence, population, geostrategic locations, and essential natural resources and the democratic, economic, and social development found throughout the Kingdom of the Netherlands all project the country as a global player in peacetime and a world power needed for success in WWII and the Cold War. "Large Holland" is given cartographic expression (fig. 5.7) on the letterhead of the NIB. Shown—each at a different scale—are the Dutch colonies in the Eastern and Western Hemispheres, as well as the home country itself; the Netherlands East Indies dominates the center of the map and overwhelms the mother country in area and population. The NIB letterhead declares that the Kingdom of the Netherlands is not a small but a large country with a presence throughout the world.

Propaganda in films and other NIB media about the Netherlands itself sometimes used the opposite and contradictory image of a small and vulnerable country destroyed by war to engender sympathy and merit aid from the United States. The NIB tried to have it both ways.

Foreign-policy-directed films about the Dutch colonies

Most of these films make twin rhetorical claims. First, both the West and East Dutch Indies have military, geostrategic, and economic assets of importance for the successful outcome of the war and for a postwar, free trade, global economic system. Second, the Netherlands is an enlightened colonial power: honoring the cultural traditions of its indigenous peoples; helping them achieve the benefits of modernization/innovation; and including them as fully participating citizens of the country.

The compilation film, *The Dutch Tradition* (1944; 75,419), the third most-viewed 1940s NIB documentary, in its second half,

[12]   David J. Snyder, "The Problem of Power in Modern Diplomacy: The Netherlands Information Bureau in World War II and the Early Cold War," in *The United States and Public Diplomacy. New Directions in Cultural and International History* (Martinus Nijhoff Publishers, 2010), 65.

Fig. 5.8. Dutch army in American-made tanks, plowing through rice paddies in the Dutch East Indies before the Japanese occupation (The Dutch Tradition: Three Years of the Netherlands' Fight against the Axis, 1940-43; *1944*) (*NIS archive, HCASC*)

(See endnote 2:29, p. 398, regarding the resolution of these stills.)

hits all these notes. It is a synoptic look at the Netherlands and its empire (both East and West Indies) as related to its assets and efforts to defeat the Axis powers and its commitments and contributions to extend the sphere of "civilizing" Western values and liberal democracies in the post-WWII world. The film extends the tradition of progressive accomplishments of the country itself in housing, transportation, water management, science, and health care (shown in the first part) to that of a progressive, enlightened leader of a world empire and a reliable, strategic, and useful global ally. The subtitle—*Three Years of the Netherlands' Fight against the Axis,*

1940–43—is instructive. The Netherlands capitulated to the German invasion forces on May 14, 1940, after just five days of fighting, and had been occupied ever since. Nevertheless, from outside the country, the film shows that it had carried on the fight against the Axis powers already for three years (fig. 5.8). The film makes the record of such endurance and fight for freedom also part and parcel of the Dutch tradition and national character.

The Dutch West Indies

Sheer size, population, and economic investments and returns made the Dutch East Indies by far the most important col-

Fig. 5.9. Festively dressed Maroon (freed slave) women gathered in Paramaribo for Queen's Day celebrations (Dutch Guiana, *1942*) (*NIS archive, HCASC*).

ony for the Netherlands. Yet, because of their proximity to the United States, the Dutch West Indies received more attention in these films than one would expect. Besides *The Dutch Tradition*, which included the East Indies as well as the Netherlands itself, three of the thirty-three top films cover the Dutch West Indies exclusively: *Netherlands America: Holland in the Western Hemisphere* (1942; 56,063), *Dutch Guiana* (1942; 40,268), and *The Dutch Next Door* (1942; 25,225). If *The Dutch Tradition*, which also included a section on the Dutch West Indies, is added, then 196,975 Americans in the NIB-Holland service region

saw these films during the 1940s, a viewership similar to that of the East Indies. Few Americans knew that these nearby parts of the Netherlands even existed, and seeing these places for the first time must have been an eye-opener. All these titles, especially *The Dutch Next Door*, brought the Netherlands geographically closer to the United States and therefore, as a neighbor, more deserving of American interest and consideration.

Although every film also includes details about the history and culture of the various islands of the Dutch Antilles and Suriname (Dutch Guiana) in South

Fig. 5.10. Bauxite awaiting processing into alumina in Dutch Guiana
(The Dutch Next Door, *1942*) (*NIS archive, HCASC*)

America, it is quite clear that they are all foreign-policy-directed films. Except for parts of *Dutch Guiana*, an American 20th Century Fox, short-subject film—also shown in movie theaters—there are no exclusively culture-directed films about the Dutch West Indies among the NIB films of the 1940s. The second half of *Dutch Guiana* portrays the daily life of the Maroon people living in the interior of the country; they are expert boatmen on the wild rivers of the region. For the annual Queen's Day—then, Queen Wilhelmina—people would come to Paramaribo, the capital, from all over the country for celebrations (fig. 5.9).

The Dutch West Indies were not occupied by an Axis power; they were the only parts of the country that retained Dutch sovereignty during the war. They were placed under American protection because the Netherlands government in exile was not in a position to safeguard the Dutch Antilles and their strategic resources. This meant that they were open to film crews and readily accessible from the United States. The Dutch West Indies was the only region where the NIB and American filmmakers could work on location and produce the films in the United States.

Visually and narratively, often with identical footage, the same points were

Fig. 5.11. Oil storage tanks and refineries on Curaçao (Netherlands America: Holland in the Western Hemisphere, *1942*) (*NIS archive, HCASC*)

covered in these films. Much is made of the fact that the first WWII German attack in the Western Hemisphere was the February 16, 1942, shelling by a submarine of the oil refineries on the Dutch island of Aruba. The Dutch West Indies and Suriname (Dutch Guiana) provided resources critical for the war effort, especially bauxite and refined oil products, as well as potash.

Film viewers saw bauxite mining in the interior of Dutch Guiana and the shipment of the ore by river barge (under the protection of Dutch and American troops) to the coastal capital of Paramaribo for enrichment and shipment to the United States. Moviegoers learned that 60 per-

cent of American-made aluminum came from Dutch Guiana, that it was required to make warplanes, and that, without Dutch bauxite, air warfare would be crippled (fig. 5.10). American audiences saw the oil refineries (guarded by troops) on Curaçao and Aruba that turned Venezuelan crude into fuels and lubricants (fig. 5.11). From *Netherlands America: Holland in the Western Hemisphere* and its voice-over, they learned that "Dutch West Indian oil is fueling the warships and the convoys, the tanks, and the combat cars of the United Nations. In fighting planes and in bombers, it is helping knock the Fascist menace out of the skies of the world."

Fig. 5.12. Javanese dancer welcoming Princess Juliana as one of the many cultures of Dutch New Guiana/Suriname (The Dutch Next Door, *1942; NIS archive, HCASC*)

Another common point made by this group of films is related to the geostrategic position of the Dutch West Indies. With maps of the Caribbean, filmgoers saw that especially the southern Dutch Antilles— Curaçao, Aruba, and Bonaire (fig. 4.13)— garrisoned and with a naval base, provided valuable military protection for the Panama Canal, an extremely vital asset in a two-ocean war. Moreover, these islands were nodes on shipping lanes and air routes; port facilities for the supply chain, trans-

shipment, and repair; and a gateway to the Venezuelan oil fields, fifty miles away. Audiences saw American war materiel being used in joint military training exercises, to guard oil refineries, and to build roads on the islands. Such scenes promoted the strategic value of these places for American viewers. Another film, *The Dutch in Latin America* (1947; 15,610), not among the top thirty-three films, with 6,004 viewers during the 1940s, was produced after the war; it stripped all the war-related footage from the earlier NIB films but kept the rest to press the economic and multicultural assets of the Dutch West Indies.

The other foreign policy issue tackled in these films was the legitimacy and morality of Dutch colonial rule in the West Indies itself. This was not tackled as overtly as wartime questions were, but it was there in every film. It is the racial and cultural diversity of these colonies, especially Dutch Guiana, the films assert, that points to an egalitarian, multiethnic, and global Kingdom of the Netherlands. In *The Dutch Next Door*, the different groups within the population are each profiled in turn: Carib Indians, Africans (freed slaves, called Maroons), Javanese from the Dutch East Indies, people from the Indian subcontinent, and the ethnically Dutch (fig. 5.12). The film's voice-over concludes: "These many cultures exist side by side in harmony. The entire Netherlands Kingdom may be a commonwealth of nations tomorrow [after WWII], but the Dutch West Indies is a community of nations today." *The Dutch Next Door*, however, is silent about the more than two hundred years of harsh slavery and the skewed economic power relations among these constituent groups at the time the film was produced.

The NIB liked to employ American surrogates to make its claims; they would be more credible and trustworthy for the American public than Dutch spokespersons and productions.[13] Surrogates could be American-produced news programs or well-known American personalities making similar pro-Dutch claims. Among the NIB-distributed films about the Dutch West Indies, was an American newsreel, *Dutch Guiana*, a 20th Century Fox short

subject, screened in many American movie theaters in addition to its distribution by the NIB. *Netherlands America: Holland in the Western Hemisphere* was filmed by Philip Hanson Hiss, a well-known American writer, photographer, and traveler who worked for the government of the Netherlands and became an expert on both West and East Dutch Indies.[14] This production was also filmed in color, something still fairly rare and expensive in 1942, enhancing its appeal and boosting its attendance.

The Dutch East Indies

There are eight foreign-policy-directed films about the Dutch East Indies among the fifty-five films, with five in the top thirty-three. Unlike the films about the Dutch West Indies that did not include any culture-directed films, however, there are sixteen (9 in the top 33) in that category about the Dutch East Indies in the 1940s film library, twice as many as the foreign-policy-directed films about this region. This increased attention is understandable given the region's size, economic importance, and cultural diversity. Several of the films open with an overlay of an outline map of the coterminous United States on a map of the Dutch East Indies; without Alaska, the two have the same North-South and East-West extent (fig. 5.13). Of the top thirty-three films that received closer study, five were foreign-policy-di-

---

13   Snyder, "The Problem of Power," 72.

14   Philip Hanson Hiss, *Netherlands America: The Dutch Territories in the West* (Duell, Sloan, and Pearce, 1943); Philip Hanson Hiss, *Holland Carries On; The Netherlands West Indies* (NIB, 1945); Philip Hanson Hiss, *A Selective Guide to the English Literature on the Netherlands West Indies, with a Supplement on British Guiana* (NIB, 1943); Philip Hanson Hiss, *Bali* (Duell, Sloan, and Pearce, 1941).

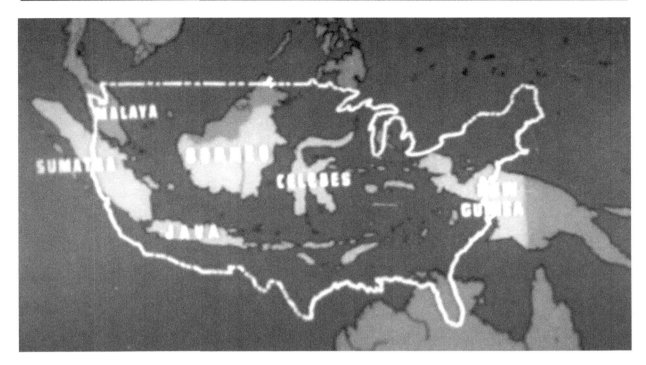

Fig. 5.13. Maps of the United States and the Dutch East Indies superimposed
(People of the Indies, *1942*) (*NIS archive, HCASC*)

rected films about the Dutch East Indies: *The Dutch Tradition* (1944; 75,419), *Peoples of the Indies* (1942; 43,519), *High Stakes in the East* (1942; 40,734), *Spoils of Conquest* (1940; 22,811), and *The Netherlands East Indies* (n.d., 23,205). In all, the circulation records show that 204,214 Americans saw these films in Holland's NIB region during the 1940s.

Like Philip Hanson Hiss's *Netherlands America: Holland in the Western Hemisphere*, the film *Spoils of Conquest* was an ideal American-made surrogate film for the foreign policies the Dutch government was promoting as part of its relations with the United States. *Spoils of Conquest* was the August 1940 episode of *The March of Time*, the controversial and influential American newsreel series of Time Inc., screened in American and foreign movie houses to millions of viewers from 1935 to

1951.[15] The NIB-acquired copy of *Spoils of Conquest* was not screened until late 1943, two years after its theater run, and well after the relatively easy Japanese invasion, in spite of all the efforts by the Dutch to put the colony on a wartime footing, as shown in the last section of the film. Even though the episode predicted that Dutch defenders would be no match for the Imperial Japanese Army when it invaded the colony and that all its assets would become "spoils of conquest," the film put Dutch colonial rule in quite a positive light and emphasized its strategic importance to the United States of particular natural resources produced for export in the Dutch East Indies.

[15] Raymond Fielding, *The March of Time, 1935–1951* (Oxford University Press, 1978); "The March of Time as Documentary and Propaganda"; http://xroads.virginia.edu/~ma04/wood/mot/html/home_flash.htm.

Fig. 5.14. Molding rubber made from tree sap (*Hevea brasiliensis*)
(Spoils of Conquest. The March of Time, *1940*) (*NIS archive, HCASC*)

Authorities in the Dutch East Indies must have cooperated closely with *The March of Time* production unit, making film locations and much stock footage available, helping to shape the voice of the film. The governor-general of the colonies is described in the voice-over as a "liberal autocrat" and the Dutch as "the most efficient colonizers" who treat "the natives not as subjects but as citizens of the empire." "Of all European colonists in the Orient, the Dutch are the most democratic" is perhaps the most congratulatory line. Little wonder the NIB kept this outdated film in its film lending library. Notwithstanding the praise for the Dutch brand of colonialism in the narrative, when the film showed scenes of the everyday life of the colonists (home, family meal, men's club, swimming pool), viewers saw a life of privilege. And while the narrator's focus was elsewhere, the Javanese served meals at a colonist's home and drinks at the club, and the pool had only white swimmers.

Besides the focus on the Dutch style of colonial rule, the film also underscored that the Japanese "spoils of conquest" would threaten American reliance on tin and rubber supplies (fig. 5.14) from the region, as well as divert other essential resources and products, such as crude oil and quinine, to Japan. A film can make such a point more real. In rapid review, viewers take in Dutch East Indies' scenes of harvesting tobacco as well as tea, cutting and processing of sisal into rope and cinchona bark into quinine, surface mining and processing of tin, tapping and mold-

Fig. 5.15. Model modern and integrated Javanese village
(Peoples of the Indies, *1942*) (*NIS archive, HCASC*)

ing of rubber, and extracting and refining of oil. Overlaying this panorama, the narration gives the intended meaning to these scenes: all these assets will most likely fall into the hands of the Japanese and produce shortages and hardships for the United States and the Allies. The film may be seen as urging the United States to consider coming to the aid of the Netherlands in defending the Dutch East Indies against Japanese aggression. This was precisely the foreign policy goal of the Dutch government at the time. It was not until January of 1942, however, that a joint command of American, British, Dutch, and Australian (ABDA) forces was formed, but it was too little, too late; they were no match for the Japanese.

The other three films—*Peoples of the Indies, High Stakes in the East,* and *The Netherlands East Indies*—are compilation films that share much of the same older footage and many of the same claims. The voice-over carries the message and the meaning in these films; the visuals are stock and illustrative, not closely woven into the narration. *Peoples of the Indies* was produced prior to the Japanese occupation, *High Stakes in the East* during the occupation, and *The Netherlands East Indies* after the defeat of the Japanese; the selection of footage reflects that staging.

Fig. 5.16. Hydraulic mining of tin deposits in the Dutch East Indies
(High Stakes in the East, *1942*) (*NIS archive, HCASC*)

In *Peoples of the Indies* (43,519) the Dutch-advertised ideal of colonial development takes center stage, guiding the highly civilized cultures of Indonesia into modern standards of living and global economic development. In the defense of the East Indies against the Japanese invaders, the Dutch are fighting for the "idea that freedom can be a real thing today in the 20th century and for people whose skins are brown."[16] The first part of the film shows American filmgoers aspects of traditional Javanese and Balinese civilization, including Buddhist temples, Balinese dancers, wetland rice cultivation, and religious flower processions. The second part shows how "the Netherlands has guided Indonesians to their place in the modern world." Shown are plantations, factories, modern roads and conveyances, and model villages (fig. 5.15). The Japanese will enslave the Indonesians to produce war-related materials, but the Dutch will preserve their

[16]   Voice-over from *Peoples of the Indies*.

Fig. 5.17. Traditional mows of harvested rice in the Dutch East Indies
(The Netherlands East Indies, *n.d.*) (*NIS archive, HCASC*)

freedom in order to bring their traditional cultures into the modern world.

High Stakes in the East (40,734), an early, color film, nominated for an Oscar as best documentary in 1943, makes the strategic and global importance of the Dutch East Indies economy its centerpiece. Tin (fig. 5.16), rubber, crude and refined oil, quinine, rice, sisal, and rope—all essential to the prosecution of the war and all developed by Dutch skill and knowledge—are now flowing into Japan to maintain and expand its conquests, whereas before the Japanese occupation, large percentages of these essential resources were imported into the American market. The Dutch

East Indies settings for the excavation, cultivation, processing, and manufacturing of these resources and commodities are again shown in this film. These economic losses, the film asserts, must and will be reversed by defeating Japan; in the post-WWII world, there must be equal access for all nations of the world to the trade in raw materials and the products made from them.

The postwar version of all these claims—using the same prewar footage—is the compilation film, *The Netherlands East Indies* (23,205). With the Indonesian independence movement gaining ground, and with postwar American global hegemony an established reality, there was a need to restate for the American public why the Netherlands should be permitted to continue to maintain its more than three hundred-year-old colonial empire. The film voice-over contrasts the plunder and oppression strategy of the Japanese occupiers, now departed, with that promoted by the Netherlands, that is, the transfer of technical knowledge and global marketing acumen to bring these traditional societies and their livelihoods into the modern era. For example, before the Japanese occupation, the Dutch East Indies exported large quantities of rice both within and outside the region; modernization would expand those exports worldwide (fig. 5.17). It is noteworthy that, in spite of opportunities to film new material for the first time in many years, there is no new footage in the film of postwar conditions, documenting Japanese economic destruction and plunder (closing of mines, cutting down of plantations, and disruption of transportation). The ramping up of the Indonesian struggle for independence likely made the region too unstable, and the Dutch suffered from a critical lack of all kinds of resources after the war. The narration drives the meaning of the film's recycled visuals. The same footage, for example, of a model Javanese village in the *The Netherlands East Indies* represents integrated (Indonesian and Dutch) education, but in *Peoples of the Indies*, it represents the desirable blend of Indonesian traditions and twentieth-century innovation (fig: 5.15).

Culture-directed films about the Dutch colonies

There are nine films about the Dutch colonies in the top thirty-three that are culture-directed with nearly a quarter mil-

lion viewers by way of Holland-NIB; these aimed to provide information, improve understanding, and generate appreciation for these "Dutch" places and regions. In contrast to foreign-policy-directed films, no explicit Dutch foreign policy goals steer culture-directed films, although one can argue that any film by a mother country about its colonies is, by definition, a justification of its foreign affairs. All these films are about various parts of the Dutch East—not West—Indies. What is most significant about this group of films is that, with one exception, they are all American-made travelogue and ethnographic shorts (from 10 to 12 minutes long), both silent with intertitles, and sound with voice-over, produced for Hollywood movie studios during the late 1920 and 1930s. They were shown mainly in movie theaters before the main feature and to a lesser extent in classrooms. Five are films of Andre de la Varre from his Film Traveler and Screen Traveler Series; two are Eastman Classroom Films, produced for the Eastman Kodak Company.[17]

These films were acquired by the NIB or, independently, by Holland-NIB. Why these—largely, American-made films—were acquired and not Dutch films about their own colonies is an interesting question, but without a definite answer. A sizable body of films about the Dutch East Indies and Dutch New Guinea made by Dutch filmmakers certainly existed. In

---

17   Andre de la Varre was a successful American pioneer filmmaker who traveled the world making documentary shorts. He was an associate of Burton Holmes, one of the originators of the travelogue-film genre. Consult the Travel Film Archive, http://www.travelfilmarchive.com, and the Burton Holmes Archive, http://www.burtonholmesarchive.com. For a brief biography of Andre de la Varre by his son Renee de la Varre, consult: http://www.burtonholmes.org/associates/andredelavarre.html.

Fig. 5.18. Western-led expedition on Nias, Dutch East Indies
(Nias and Sumatra, Islands of Netherlands India, *1936*) (*NIS archive, HCASC*)

Bert Hogenkamp's *De Nederlandse Docu-mentaire Film, 1920–1940*, the filmography lists more than thirty films, particularly those by the *Haghe Film* and the *Nederlandsch-Indische* [Dutch Indies] Film companies.[18] The Dutch national audiovisual archives, the Netherlands Institute for Sound and Vision, lists hundreds of films and film footage about the Dutch East Indies and Dutch New Guinea.[19]

There were certainly Dutch-made films that would have been candidates for an English-language narrative track, for example, those that were commissioned and supported by the Dutch government ministries of colonies and education.[20] And there was an abundant supply of footage to make compilation films. Several factors together most likely led the NIB to not turn to these Dutch-made films. Most importantly, if the NIB was going to spend its scarce resources on commissioning and producing films, its foreign policy objec-

[18]   Bert Hogenkamp, *De Nederlandse Documentaire Film, 1920–1940* (Van Gennep, 1988), 131–49.

[19]   The search engine for the Netherlands Institute for Sound and Vision is https://www.beeldengeluid.nl/collective.

[20]   Hogenkamp, *De Nederlandse Documentaire Film*, 136.

Fig. 5.19. Funeral pylon with bodies on a bamboo rack carried across a river for cremation ceremony (Ceremonies on Bali, *1936; NIS archive, HCASC*)

tives would be the driving force; it would produce foreign-policy- not culture-directed films. Additionally, after the occupation of the Netherlands by Germany in May of 1940 and the Dutch East Indies by Japan in February of 1942, access to these film materials most likely became very difficult, if not impossible. Finally, unlike John Fernhout and Philip Hanson Hiss in the Dutch West Indies, the NIB could not send filmmakers into the region to film on location.

The NIB in general and NIB-Holland in particular, however, did pay a price for having its culture-directed films about the Dutch colonies—and also even more, as I will argue, about the Netherlands itself—consist largely of American-produced films. In general, these films have more of an ethnographic focus and are not really about the "Dutch" East Indies but about the indigenous and immigrant Asian cultures of this archipelago region. A smaller number of these travelogues do also show the workings of the resource-based, export-oriented industries as well as the monetized handicraft systems that formed the basis of the colonial economies; in some of these scenes, American audiences see local workers and their Western supervisors. Where more Western-style development is shown—steam tram, rail transport of sugarcane—it is

Fig. 5.20. Clustered village on Sumatra (Nias and Sumatra, Islands of Netherlands India, *1936; NIS archive, HCASC*)

often not explicitly associated with the colonial power. In some of the films, such as *Nias and Sumatra, Islands of Netherlands India* (1936; 30,932) and *The Dutch East Indies* (1931; 11,860), occasional, white-suited supervisors bring out the colonial power's presence, although few moviegoers would have noticed (fig. 5.18).

These culture-directed documentaries can hardly be called promotional films for the Dutch East Indies or for the Kingdom of the Netherlands for that matter. On the plus side, as with the foreign-policy-directed films about the colonies, American viewers may have realized for the first time that little Holland was not so little. On the

minus side, the films' locations may be islands making up the Dutch colonial empire in Southeast Asia, but there was little or nothing in these shorts, however, referencing the more than three hundred-year-old Dutch economic and societal footprint, nor did they show the indigenous world and Dutch life, side by side, separate but also interrelating. Few of the films have the words "Dutch" or "Netherlands" in their titles, and there are only passing references to the Dutch as the colonial power.

In travelogue style, the films internally sequence rapidly from one "different" cultural custom or artifact to another without much integration. The travelogue

Fig. 5.21. Traditional weaving and threshing rice among Toradjan women of Celebes (Sulawesi) in the Dutch East Indies (Toradja, *n.d.*) (*NIS archive, HCASC*)

filmmakers were recorders but not qualified to be interpreters. The films—often the first-ever movies of a place or area—are fueled by exoticism—the attraction of the different—aimed at Western consumers: cremation rituals in *Ceremonies on Bali* (1936; 33,763, fig. 5.19); a Sumatran clustered village with its raised houses/grain storage barns and steep, curved thatch roofs in *Nias and Sumatra, Islands of Netherlands India* (1936; 30,932, fig. 5.20); cradle coffin rock graves; traditional weaving and rice threshing in *Toradja* (n.d., 12,1288, fig. 5.21); plowing flooded rice paddies with water buffalo in *An East Indian Island*

(1930; 41,984, fig. 5.22);[21] planting rice in flooded fields (*sawah*); and washing clothes in the river in *A Bit of Life in Java* (1928; 10,768, fig. 5.23).

In addition to the remarkable customs recorded in these documentaries in different places of the Dutch East Indies, American viewers also became acquainted with indigenous handicrafts and the making of spices, which had become global export industries with Western colonialism. Wood carving on Bali in *An East Indian*

[21] There are two films in the NIB/NIS library with this title (see index of films). The circulation records do not show which film was screened, so the viewership for these two films was combined.

Fig. 5.22. Plowing flooded rice paddies with water buffalo
(An East Indian Island, *1930*) (*NIS archive, HCASC*)

Island (41,984, fig. 5.24) and batik on Java in *Glimpses of Picturesque Java* (50,380, fig. 5.25) are examples. Then, there are the export-oriented, resource-based industries, not part of the indigenous economies, developed in this region by Dutch commercial interests and dependent upon indigenous labor. These required plantations, mines, rail lines, and ports. There are segments in these films about sugar, rubber, bamboo, sisal, rattan, cinchona, and kapok. *The Dutch East Indies* (1931; 11,860) portrays sugarcane production and its transport on Java (fig. 5.26). *Macassar* (n.d., 21,368) paints a picture of the principal trading port of the Island of Celebes by that name; it shows that the loading,

off-loading, and transportation of goods moving through this port, whether from land or sea, is all by means of human muscle power (fig. 5.27).

One cannot be sure, of course, how Dutch films about their own colonies would have differed from these American ones. I do, however, think that they would have had a more distinctive Dutch-colonial signature. They would likely have blurred the distinction between culture- and foreign-policy-directed films. They would have featured a lot more scenes of Dutch economic and social development of this very diverse region and the mix of indigenous and more modern ways of life (health care, education and technical training, and

Fig. 5.23. Men washing clothes by pounding them on wooden platforms in the river (A Bit of Life in Java, *1928*) (*NIS archive, HCASC*)

agricultural innovations, among others). Such is certainly the case with the later, Dutch-government-sponsored films about Dutch New Guinea released during the 1950s and 1960s.

If there were nearly a quarter million Americans who saw these nine films by way of the Holland-NIB, one can only imagine the viewership from other distributors by way of shorts in movie houses and classrooms throughout the region. The public likely did not associate these movie shorts with the Netherlands but with faraway, fascinating lands and people. But when these films were borrowed from the NIB, there must have been a stronger association with the Netherlands; they would have been regarded as "Dutch" films or films with a Dutch imprimatur. Yet, in many important ways, they were not Dutch films at all.

Films about the Netherlands

Nearly seven hundred thousand American moviegoers in the Holland-NIB region during the 1940s took in fifteen films about the Netherlands among the top thirty-three. It is important to underscore again the overriding importance of foreign policy for the NIB during the 1940s: nine foreign-policy-directed films compared to six culture-directed films, with a split in attendance of 443,417 to 248,071.

Fig. 5.24. Woodcarving on Bali, Dutch East Indies
(An East Indian Island, *1938*) (*NIS archive, HCASC*)

Foreign-policy-directed films about the Netherlands

Nine of the top thirty-three films examined more carefully belong to the group of foreign-policy-directed films about the Netherlands itself. This category of NIB films had the highest attendance in NIB-Holland during the 1940s—443,417. Like those about the colonies in this category, almost all these films were commissioned and produced by the NIB and other Dutch and British government agencies and, unlike the culture-directed films, they were largely distributed and circulated only by these same organizations. In terms of production methods, it is a diverse group: older, existing, complete films with new endings and narration (*Landbuilders*, 1932/1940; *New Earth*, 1933/1943), compilation films (*The Dutch Tradition*, 1944; *Holland Carries On*, 1944), and completely new films shot on location (*Fishermen in Exile*, 1944; *Friesland*, 1946; *Broken Dykes*, 1945; *Gateway to Germany*, 1945; *They Said It with Tulips*, 1946).

One would expect that more films would have had Dutch postwar conditions, challenges, reconstruction, and related appeals for aid as their subject. Filmmakers had complete access to the country once

Fig. 5.25. Women making batik cloth on Java (Glimpses of
Picturesque Java, *1933*) (*NIS archive, HCASC*)

again and the physical devastation, plunder, and economic hardships were appalling. *Friesland* and, to a lesser extent, *Holland Carries On* tackled that subject. United States Marshall plan films and newsreel footage about the American role in rebuilding the country did not reach Dutch movie theaters and other venues, including the NIB film library, until the early fifties.[22]

[22] Anne-Lijke Struijk, "Negotiating the Marshall Plan: Dutch Marshall Plan Films, 1948–1954" (master's thesis, American Studies, Utrecht University, 2010), 88–92. See also, Ralph Dingemans and Rian Romme, *Nederland en het Marshall Plan. Een Bronnenoverzicht en Filmografie* (Rijksarchief Den Haag, 1997). The second half of the book (109–98) is a filmography of Marshall Plan films.

The foreign policy objectives of these films are quite ideological. Several portray Germany as a ruthless expansionist aggressor with no regard for civilian populations, their way of life and accomplishments (*Landbuilders*, 157,362; *New Earth*, 129,872). In addition, these films assert that the Dutch have always been committed to an internal and peaceful expansion of their population and economy. The NIB's goal was to build up aversion among the American public to Germany's destructive expansionism, evoke sympathy for the Dutch, and secure a commitment to vigorously pursue the fight to liberate their country and provide aid. Another ob-

Fig. 5.26. Loading sugarcane onto a railcar on Java for transport to the mill (The Dutch East Indies, *1931*) (*NIS archive, HCASC*)

jective was to show that, in spite of all the hardships of the German occupation and postwar life, the Dutch had carried on, doing what they had always done, also within their own country—fighting for their freedom, this time against the German occupiers (the resistance movement), providing valuable services to the Allies, and rolling up their sleeves to begin reconstruction immediately after the liberation (*The Dutch Tradition*, 75,419; *Holland Carries On*, 60,335; *Friesland*, 36,733; *Fishermen in Exile*, 16,110).

Several of these films also make the claim that the Netherlands is a country like the United States, with the same pro-gressive political philosophy based on individual achievement, science, technology, economic development, and social organization. These are qualities the United States was prepared to defend at home and in the Netherlands (*The Dutch Tradition*; *Holland Carries On*). The films about the Netherlands also needed to show the American public the actual fight for and success in liberating the Netherlands; alongside the other Allies, American involvement in the war, although difficult and costly, was leading to success and to the end of tyranny for the country (*Broken Dykes*, 25,914; *Gateway to Germany*, 16,408).

Fig. 5.27. Moving bulk goods from warehouses to the port
in Macassar (Macassar, *n.d.*) (*NIS archive, HCASC*)

Landbuilders and *New Earth* occupy a special place in the NIB-Holland film collection; these were the two most popular films in the 1940s and took first and third place for the lifetime of Holland-NIB/NIS.[23] Unlike most others, these two films had staying power. *Landbuilders* (157,362) is a repackaged 1932 film, *Walcheren*, about the former island at the mouth of the Scheldt estuary of the same name, part of the province of Zeeland. One filmmaker (Adrian van der Horst) was responsible for the overall direction, as well as the filming and the script for the narrator; the music track of *Walcheren* is a composition based on old Dutch folk songs.[24] *Landbuilders* retains most, if not all, of the original footage and music track of *Walcheren*; it adds English-language narration with a British accent and phrasing, and most importantly, it splices a new, minute-long piece onto the very end of the film.

Although *Landbuilders* is a foreign-policy-directed film in intent, it functions equally as a culture-directed film.

[23] The film borrowing records from 1966 to 1972 were not recovered. *Holland Today* attracted nearly 50,000 viewers in 1965, just after it had been acquired, and in 1973, it still drew more than 40,000 viewers. Any extrapolation of its viewership makes *Holland Today* the most-viewed film in the NIB film collection.

[24] See endnote 5:24, p. 402.

Fig. 5.28. The age-old Dutch skill of building and repairing dikes to create and safeguard land (Landbuilders, *1932/1940*) (*NIS archive, HCASC*)

This helps account for its popularity and staying power well into the 1950s. Anyone viewing the first seventeen minutes or so of the film would be enjoying traditional scenes and commentary about Walcheren—dunes and handmade dikes as sea walls protecting the land (fig. 5.28); drainage to make fertile farmland; prosperous farming landscapes with fields, pastures, villages, roads, and canals; rural crafts and pastimes; people leaving church in traditional costumes; and the bustle on the market square in Middelburg, the capital. Together with its lyrical and moving music, the film is an ode to the way of life created and followed on the island—one that would fill any viewer with admiration. Then comes the last minute. Scenes of the beautiful, late-Gothic city hall situated on Middelburg's market square dissolve into stills with discordant music of the ruins of the building (fig. 5.29) caused by the "German" bombardment of the city (but see note 8 above). Then, against a background of the bombarded and burned-out city hall and of waves running up against a dike, the narrator makes a summary stern

Fig. 5.29. Destroyed city hall of Middelburg, Zeeland, May 1940
(Landbuilders, *1932/1940*) (*NIS archive, HCASC*)

declaration that adds other layers of meaning—those of concern and sympathy—to the earlier feelings of admiration and respect. It is worth quoting this declaration because several other films in this category make much the same claim:

> A new order reigns in Holland. Zeeland was the last province to resist the German hordes and had to pay the price. This man [the film shows a dike worker] has enemies a million times as powerful as any human foe and more relentless. With bare hands, they have torn the soil inch by inch from the clutches of the waves, and bare-handed, they stood guard over the land they so rightly own. They did not come with guns and tanks and bombs like bandits to steal their fields and homes. They also needed Lebensraum [living space] and found an answer. It was not mass murder. They built their islands and owned them with just pride. With your help, they will again be masters of their hard-earned soil, reconstruct their damaged homes and reclaim their barren fields.[25]

---

[25]   Voice-over from *Landbuilders.*

Fig. 5.30. Constructing willow mats for protecting the base of the dike on the floor of IJssel Lake (New Earth,*1933, 1943*) (*NIS archive, HCASC*)

The film closes with a picture of the coat of arms of the province of Zeeland: *Luctor et Emergo* (I wrestle and emerge).

If *Landbuilders* celebrated the millenniums-old practice of making and protecting land from sea and, from this precondition, fashioning a rich and enduring cultural landscape, then the film *New Earth* (129,872) brought this defining Dutch practice into the scale and technology of the modern era. The national project to drain large parts of the Zuiderzee that began in 1927 now attracted Dutch film-makers, including Joris Ivens, pioneer and internationally renowned filmmaker of political and social documentaries.[26] His 1933 film, *Nieuwe Gronden* (*New Earth*), looked at this monumental undertaking (over 600 square miles of new land when finished), especially the then modern technology of dike building (fig. 5.30), land drainage, and preparation and cultivation of the new soil. He aimed his camera particularly at

[26]   For a biography of Ivens, consult: Hans Schoots, *Living Dangerously: A Biography of Joris Ivens* (Amsterdam University Press, 2000).

Fig. 5.31. Plowing the former Zuiderzee bottom (now, the Wieringenmeerpolder) for the first time (New Earth, *1933, 1943*) (*NIS archive, HCASC*)

the workers and skilled machine operators whose hard, physical labor produced this progress (figs. 5.30, 5.31). In the last part of the 1933 film, Ivens indicts the world economic system of the Great Depression that would rather destroy food than feed it to the poor and hungry.

Nieuwe Gronden is the source for the documentary, *New Earth*, produced by the RVD in 1943. Even though Ivens was strongly antifascist, and his home country was occupied by the Nazis, it is still quite remarkable— given, what was left out in the 1943 version—that he gave the Dutch government the rights to use and alter his film. That the Dutch government used his film in its public diplomacy in the United States is also remarkable because Ivens was a well-known socialist filmmaker who had recently directed *The Spanish Earth*, a propaganda film in support of the political left in the Spanish Civil War. Moreover, the film's score was composed by Hanns Eisler, a leftist composer, deported in 1948 from the United States by the House Committee on Un-American Activities. Given the foreign policy objectives of the RVD, it is not surprising that the third part of the film, a denunciation of the global capitalist economic system, was not part of the government film. Eisler's modernist musical score, however, was left intact, even though it did not fit the propaganda goals; for that, a much more stirring triumphant score would have been more effective.

There are two versions of *New Earth* in the Holland-NIB film archive with only very slight differences. Both use short excerpts at the beginning from the film *Walcheren/Landbuilders* to set the historical context for the longstanding United States-Netherlands friendship and American knowledge of the country. Then the footage from *Nieuwe Gronden* is inserted. The close-up look at the Zuiderzee polder project in *Nieuwe Gronden* is given a new meaning in *New Earth* for American moviegoers. More than tulips, wooden shoes, and traditional costumes, the key to the identity of the country is to be found in the ubiquitous dikes, pumps, sluices, drainage canals, and other water works. These have created the country and its dispositions from the beginning and continue to do so today: "We were conquering a new portion of the Earth's surface, and these [the workers on the Zuiderzee project] were our armies; this was our answer to a need for *lebensraum*. This is how a peaceful nation fights for its homeland. Holland is bounded by frontiers that Dutchmen have made."[27]

One version ends with a brief scene representing the dike breach of the Wieringermeerpolder—the first Zuiderzee project polder—by the retreating Germans in 1945. The narrator tells his American viewers that this land that feeds the country and helps feed the world is now under water again: "Our crops are submerged once more under a treacherous tide of invasion as they were once under the ocean

tide. But we Dutch once pushed back the Atlantic Ocean. This time, we will have your [American] help."[28] The film asks Americans for aid to redrain this polder and, more generally, to help reconstruct the entire country. The other version leaves out this and other particular visual and narrative references to the war, signifying that this was probably the postwar version of the film.

The fact that there are two slightly different versions of *New Earth* also underscores the flexibility of compilation films; a slight tweaking of the footage and narration to keep things up to date preserves the usefulness of a film. *New Earth* had the longest run of any film in the Holland NIB/NIS collection; attendance peaked in the immediate postwar years but continued until 1965 (and most likely into the data gap). This, I suspect, had less to do with the film's message and more to do with Ivens as a celebrated Dutch filmmaker with an international following, as well as the worldwide fascination with the Zuiderzee project. That an NIB film with Ivens' footage but a different foreign-policy-directed message taking the place of the original Ivens film, *Nieuwe Gronden*, shows how readily a different public understanding of this film could be shaped for the American public.

The dominant rhetorical theme asserted by these two influential films (and others) is that the Netherlands' need for new land, more agricultural production, and greater economic welfare in the face of an expanding population had always been achieved, not by military aggression against its neighbors but rather by wresting more land from the water. Although this is

---

27   Voice-over from *New Earth*.   28   Ibid.

more or less the case for the coterminous Netherlands, it glosses over the Dutch naval military campaigns during the seventeenth century against especially the British, Spanish, and Portuguese to carve out and maintain colonial commercial spheres of influence around the globe. Apparently, expansion over sea is different than expansion over land.

Moreover, this rhetorical claim creates the impression that taking land from the sea and other flood-prone areas was a planned national goal, when in fact, for much of Dutch history, it was prompted by local and regional community and business interests, needs, and hazards. And when this did become a national goal, as with the Haarlemmermeer Polder (19th century) and the Zuiderzee project (20th century), it was public safety from flooding and the loss of surrounding land from flooding that provided the immediate impetus for these projects. Additional land was an important collateral benefit but not the driving force behind these public works.[29] There was never a political calculus, that is, winning land from water or war against our neighbors; the Netherlands was militarily far too weak as a land power for such undertakings. These films attempt to give a moral meaning to a general Dutch local and regional practical matter: winning land from water and marshland to expand livelihood and protecting such lands and other areas from flooding in order to safeguard agriculture and the community.

The compilation films, *The Dutch Tradition* (75,419) and *Holland Carries On* (60,335), advance another rhetorical claim. These two share a lot of imagery, although the latter includes footage from the liberation, as well as the bleak immediate postwar period. By pointing out parallels between the United States and the Netherlands—they are like us—the filmmakers bring the two countries closer together, give them a common identity, and as a result, aim to evoke more understanding and sympathy from the American public. Against a background of iconic scenes from the Netherlands and from Holland, Michigan, *The Dutch Tradition* asserts:

> For centuries, the people of the Netherlands have been creating the tradition that today inspires their fight for freedom. We all know the outward appearance of that tradition—tulips, windmills, and wooden shoes. But what lies behind these surfaces? What is the spirit that moves every Dutchman in the world today? . . . The spiritual [mental] legacy is the most important: a structure made up of layers of individual achievements and social progress. It was one aspect of the Dutch tradition; it has become the American way as well.[30]

Then follows a visual survey of noteworthy modern Dutch achievements. In *The Dutch Tradition* and *Holland Carries On* these national accomplishments are shown in scenes of Schiphol Airport, modern highways, diesel-electric trains, modern housing (fig. 5.32), and most

---

[29]   There is extensive literature on the history of empoldering and protection against flooding in the Netherlands. For English-language overviews, consult: G. P. van de Ven, ed., *Man-made Lowlands. History of Water Management and Land Reclamation in the Netherlands*, 2nd rev. ed. (Stichting Matrijs, 1994); Robert Hoeksema, *Designed for Dry Feet* (ASCE Press, 2006).

[30]   Voice-over, *The Dutch Tradition: Three Years of the Netherlands' Fight against the Axis, 1940–43.*

Fig. 5.32. Modern pre-WWII Dutch housing (The Dutch Tradition: Three Years of the Netherlands' Fight against the Axis, 1940-43, *1944*) (*NIS archive, HCASC*)

prominently, the Zuiderzee project—both the construction and the settling of the new land.

Footage from Ivens' *New Earth* gets even more use. It is clear that compilation films such as *Holland Carries On* were put together quickly, without careful editing and even with known inaccuracies, since American viewers would not spot them anyway. One conspicuous example of such sloppiness is found in the account of the new IJssel Lake polders in that film. As the narrator describes the dikes, fields, set-tlements, and churches of these modern, twentieth-century, new polders, the film footage shows these features—hundreds of years old—on Walcheren, Zeeland, taken from *Landbuilders*. The narrator describes people coming out of a church in one of the new towns in the IJssel Lake polders, but the film shows worshippers leaving a church on Walcheren, in traditional cos-tumes from Zeeland. But, then again, perhaps even this is intentional, given the American taste for traditional Dutch ico-nography.

Fig. 5.33. Destruction from flooding and fighting on Walcheren, Zeeland (*Holland Carries On, 1944*) (*NIS archive, HCASC*)

These two films argue that the Dutch have long fought and continue to fight for their political, social, economic, and religious freedoms, which were precious in American life as well, and the United States would be inclined militarily and economically to help the Dutch recover them. Like the United States, the Dutch championed individual achievement and social progress (in housing, education, transportation), but the German occupation had trampled on them. As an ideological ally, the United States would want to help the Netherlands restore the same freedoms

and accomplishments to which it was also strongly committed.

For American audiences, this rhetorical claim that the Netherlands was like the United States was probably not all that convincing. Not that Americans were indifferent to the Nazis' abrogation of Dutch freedoms, rights, and accomplishments, of course, but the comparison needs to be nuanced. The contributions of the seventeenth-century, New Netherland colony in America to the founding and making of the United States have recently received

Fig. 5.34. Dutch fishermen on board sorting their catch destined for the British market (*Fishermen in Exile, 1944*) (*NIS archive, HCASC*)

a lot of convincing attention.[31] But the Netherlands of the nineteenth and twentieth centuries was quite different from that of the Dutch Golden Age and from the New Netherland produced by it. In the collective memory of European, immigration-derived communities such as the Dutch, throughout the Midwest, the *differences* between America and Europe stood out. These communities remembered that, unlike the United States, Europe lacked religious freedom as well as economic liberty and opportunities; it suffered under rigid class distinctions, economic hardships and poverty, and more state control.

Despite all the hardships of German occupation and a devastated postwar country, the NIB films strove to portray the country as carrying on as a loyal member of the Allied powers and a sovereign nation in exile (fig. 5.33). This theme of "Holland carries on"[32] resonates in the films *The Dutch Tradition, Holland Carries On, Friesland,* and *Fishermen in Exile.* The establishment of the NIB itself may of course be seen as an expression of this idea. It was

---

[31] See, for example, Russell Shorto, *Island at the Center of the World* (Doubleday, 2004).

[32] David Snyder coined this useful phrase; Snyder, "Problem of Power," 69.

much easier to provide filmic examples of this for the Dutch colonies—the East Indies before March 1942, and the West Indies during the entire duration of the war.

But actions undertaken within the Netherlands itself also had to be shown as carrying on the fight and doing the hard work of reconstruction. The Dutch underground is shown coordinating airstrikes on military targets in their own country, distributing underground newspapers, sabotaging German trains, fighting alongside the Allied forces liberating the country, and rounding up Dutch collaborators after the liberation (*Holland Carries On*). The film *Fishermen in Exile* (16,110) provides another angle on the "Holland carries on" theme. Dutch fishermen escaped to British ports with their vessels when Germany invaded the country. They put their vessels at the disposal of the British navy and engaged in sweeping for mines and detonating them at sea while continuing with their traditional fishing operations in the North Sea. Their catches helped feed their British ally (fig. 5.34).

The NIB got out of the business of producing and commissioning its own films soon after the war's end, which is one reason why there are so few films in the NIB collection of the 1940s about the physical devastation and the necessary reconstruction of the country. One would think that independent and commercial filmmakers would have wanted to document the war's ravages, but the economic conditions were so dire, film supplies so scarce, and mobility so limited that it took several years for the Dutch filmmaking sector to come to life once again. *Friesland, Holland's Northernmost Province* (36,733), however, is an exception. It takes a rather

surprisingly lighthearted look at the province of Friesland coming back to life after five years of occupation—a period that had become increasingly repressive as the years passed. The narration is not the customary authoritative voice-over but a relaxed, even joking, conversational style. After very graphic scenes of the human toll of the war in Friesland, accompanied by a minister in a church service reading from the book of Lamentations, the film shows people (and cattle) coming out of hiding to pick up living somewhat normal lives once more, albeit against a lot of odds.[33] The entire film underscores the "Holland-carries-on" and "can-do" themes: trucks for cattle transport become busses; cars are ferried across canals because bridges have been destroyed (fig. 5.35); bricks from destroyed buildings are cleaned and repurposed; and traffic moves very deliberately across temporary bridges built by Canadian forces during the fight for liberation. Much of this restart also immediately served a larger purpose: to send farm resources, such as cattle and foodstuffs, to the west of the country, which had experienced so much human suffering, shortages, and plunder during the Hunger Winter.[34]

This restart of Frisian life after the liberation is related not only to these more tangible and practical matters but also to

---

[33] Another level of humor in this film for English-speaking viewers, and especially for those who also know Dutch, is the use of the Dutchism "underdiver" (*onderduiker*) for those who spent time hiding from the German authorities. It would probably have been better to either keep the Dutch word or to simply use "hider."

[34] The Dutch Hunger Winter (Hongerwinter) was a severe famine, especially in the western provinces of Noord- and Zuid-Holland, in 1944–45, during WWII. By the time of the liberation, in May 1945, around 20,000 Dutch people had died from it.

Fig. 5.35. Cars and bicycles ferried across a canal with bridges destroyed
(Friesland, Holland's Northernmost Province, *1946*) (*NIS archive, HCASC*)

the gamut of Frisian culture—the film shows scenes of recreational sailing and sailing races on the Frisian lakes and a parade of Frisian carriages pulled by Frisian horses with riders wearing Frisian traditional costumes. The scenes of suffering—executions of resistance fighters, the religious mourning for all the physical and human destruction the province had endured during the occupation, the long-awaited liberation by Canadian forces and the exuberant celebrations that followed, and the "get back up, dust yourself off, and get going" posture shown in this film—as well as the other life-changing scenes must have been very moving for

audiences and further cemented goodwill and sympathy for the Dutch people among the American public.

The American public saw plenty of newsreels and shorts about the progress of the Allies in the war, but the NIB also wanted to show those who borrowed its films that the Netherlands was a theater of war for the liberation of the country. *Gateway to Germany* and *Broken Dykes* fall into this category. Both films were produced by the British Information Services, and both were filmed and directed by John Fernhout, the Dutch filmmaker who was appointed war correspondent with the Allied forces invading German-occupied western Eu-

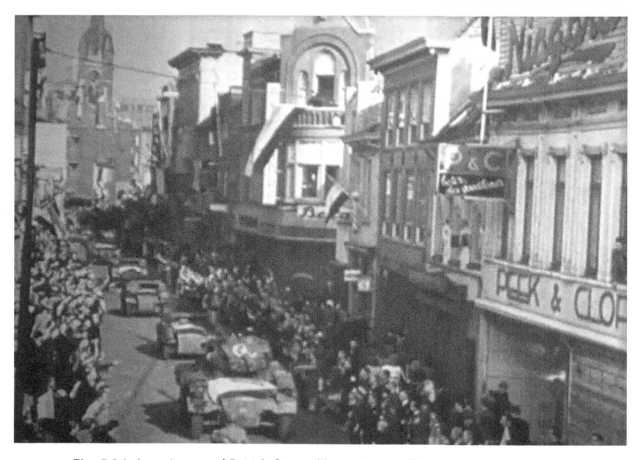

Fig. 5.36. American and British forces liberating Eindhoven, Noord-Brabant, driving through its city center (*Gateway to Germany, 1944*) (*NIS archive, HCASC*)

rope. Fernhout filmed the liberation of the Netherlands. *Gateway to Germany* (16,408) is a military film focused on the campaign to secure the approaches to the port of Antwerp, which was to serve as the principal supply depot for the Allied drive into Germany. Included in that campaign were the partially successful encircling drive into the southern Netherlands to secure bridges across the major rivers (fig. 5.36) and the invasion and flooding of Walcheren, Zeeland, by British forces to remove the Germans from the estuary leading to the port of Antwerp.

Broken Dykes (25,914) commemorates the heartbreak and courage of the fifty thousand residents of Walcheren who had to be evacuated—along with their livestock—from their flooded island home when the British Air Force breached the dikes to drive out the German defenders (fig. 2.6). Moviegoers watched horses being lifted in slings and set into the holds of ships and people being evacuated to the mainland in amphibious vehicles called "Ducks" (fig. 5.37).

The liberation from German occupation would require a second liberation from the floodwaters; the narrator concludes: "The time will come, and not so distantly, when they will ask us for the pumps, the pile drivers, the bulldozers, and the ma-

Fig. 5.37. Six-wheeled amphibious vehicles ("Ducks") used to evacuate the population of Walcheren, Zeeland, in 1944 (Broken Dykes, *1945*) (*NIS archive, HCASC*)

chinery to liberate their land again, this time from the sea."[35]

The films, of course, also show the destructive effects of war—the Rotterdam and Middelburg bombings and bombardment, the breaching of the dikes by the retreating Germans in the Wieringermeerpolder in Noord-Holland and by the British on Walcheren in Zeeland, and the general destruction of the Dutch infrastructure toward the end of the war. Such scenes were intended to instill repugnance and sympathy among American viewers and were sometimes accompanied by "We need your help to recover" in the audio script.

Normally, the films themselves were instruments of public diplomacy. The last film in this class, *They Said It with Tulips* (1946; 72,866), is a film that reports on a Dutch public diplomatic undertaking and, in so doing, makes it more widely known among the American public. The film tells the story of tulip bulbs as an instrument of public diplomacy after WWII, a Dutch international gesture that has continued to the present-day. In gratitude for liberation and other support, gifts from the people of the Netherlands in the form of tens of thousands of tulip bulbs—of many different varieties—were made to Allied countries such as the United States and Canada.

---

35   Voice-over, *Broken Dykes.*

Fig. 5.38. Workers planting Dutch bulbs in New York City parks
(They Said It with Tulips, *1946*) (*NIS archive, HCASC*)

They were planted in parks (fig. 5.38) and other public spaces of the capitals and other major cities. The film was made by Maurice T. Groen, resident American director/producer of many Dutch films in the United States; it was sponsored by the Associated Bulb Growers of New York. *They Said It with Tulips* breaks still more ground. Nearly all the other films in the collection are set in the Netherlands and its colonies; this one is about a Dutch diplomatic event set entirely in the United States and Canada, albeit still very much a "Dutch" film.

Culture-directed films about the Netherlands

Very surprising is that the culture-directed films about the Netherlands among the top thirty-three films of the 1940s are American-made films, nearly all from the 1920s and 1930s: *Holland and the Zuider Zee* (1939; 72,865), *Roaming the Netherlands* (1934; 70,335), *Holland Blooms Again* (1945; 44,390), *Quaint Old Holland* (1935; 30,173), *Holland and the Dutch* (1932; 27,569), and *The Little Dutch Tulip Girl* (1928; 14,917). With a total attendance of 248,071 during the 1940s, they made up

Fig. 5.39. Poster from the Dutch Tourist Information Office
(*Albert Hemelman, ca. 1919*)

about 20 percent of total attendance of the top thirty-three films and fell in line with the total attendance of the culture-directed colonial films. They belong to the American travelogue genre of the 1920s and 1930s, directed to curiosity and interest in the unique features of other countries. Like all travelogues, including those about the Dutch colonies, they were a form of virtual tourism—what it would be like to travel through a sequence of sites of interest, often with camera angles that provide the sensation of travel and of being in specific places. The text boxes in silent films and the voice-over in talkies both tell and explain what the filmgoers are seeing.[36] Although most people at that time could not afford to visit these filmed sites in person, wealthier viewers were motivated by travelogues—especially those about European countries and destinations—in planning their trips. The travelogues helped to create common tourist itineraries abroad, and the tourist industry sent travelers along those routes to these destinations.

At the same time, destination countries were beginning to launch their own tourist associations to advertise their attractions in promising outside markets. Fig. 5.39 is a poster from the Dutch Tourist Information Office in The Hague, distributed around 1919.[37] It shows an assemblage of Dutch lowland features, both premodern—the dike or other embankment, parallel seepage ditch, polder, and polder windmill—and modern—steam train, automobile, and telegraph lines—all set against the background of a typical expansive Dutch sky filled with towering cloud formations.[38] The visual weight of this color poster is on the left with two larger representations, one, the destination—the polder windmill,[39] the other, the agency of tourism—the chauffeured, open-air touring car with a visiting couple in the backseat. Countries eager for profitable tourism required not only attractions but also infrastructure for the mobility of people and information, here shown by the car, chauffeur, road, railroad, steam train, and telegraph lines. Group tourism was also beginning to add visitor numbers at this time, especially on the domestic side, but international tourism, as shown in this poster (a couple, privately chauffeured), often targeted a wealthier demographic.[40]

The Little Dutch Tulip Girl, a silent film—the earliest of these American, culture-directed documentaries—breaks with the customary travelogue style of description with learning about the Netherlands from a story. It is a film version of Madeline Brandeis' 1929 children's book of the same title, directed and produced by the author. In the story, an American boy named Tom, in unpacking a box of flower bulbs, finds

36   Jeffrey Ruoff, ed. *Virtual Voyages: Cinema and Travel* (Duke University Press, 2006).

37   Marcel Franciscono, *The Modern Dutch Poster: The First Fifty Years, 1890–1940*, ed. Stephen S. Prokopoff (MIT Press, 1987), 79.

38   See endnote 5:38, p. 402.

39   Not until the second half of the nineteenth century did the windmill become an iconic component of the Netherlands in the eyes of those living outside the country. Only at the beginning of the twentieth century, when the nascent Dutch tourism industry recognized its value to attract international visitors, did the windmill become a stock image in promotional materials. Jos Bazelmans, "De Windmolen; De Oorsprong van een Icoon van Nederland," *Tijdschrift voor Historische Geografie* 5, no. 1 (2020): 17–32.

40   For a history of Americans traveling to the Netherlands, see Herbert H. Rowen, "American Travelers in Holland through Two Centuries," in *A Bilateral Bicentennial, A History of Dutch-American Relations, 1783–1982*, ed. J. W. Schulte Nordholt and Robert P. Swierenga (Meulenhoff, 1982), 227–50.

Fig. 5.40. Looking more like a Dutch boy than an American, Tom meets Katrina (Trijntje) in Volendam, carrying the book *Wonder Tales from Windmill Lands* (Little Dutch Tulip Girl, *1928*) (*NIS archive, HCASC*).

a note from Katrina Schulder, a girl from Volendam, asking him to write to her. In reading *Wonder Tales from Windmill Lands*,[41] Tom travels to Volendam in his imagination and meets Katrina (fig. 5.40), who then shows him most of the same sites as in the travelogue films.[42]

The first striking thing about these five films, and several others with smaller viewership numbers, is how alike they are; they can all stand in for each other. Each film briefly recounts the environmental conditions of Holland's lowlands—the protection of dikes against incursions by the sea and the making and maintenance of polder drylands by continuous drainage with windmills. Steam-driven pumps had already replaced windmills for some time, but these films show only windmills. In

[41] Frances Jenkins Olcott, *Wonder Tales from Windmill Lands* (Longmans, 1926).

[42] Madeline Brandeis, *The Little Dutch Tulip Girl* (Grosset and Dunlap, 1929); Olcott, *Wonder Tales from Windmill Lands*. Both children's books also mirror the traditional stock imagery of the country found throughout these travelogue films. Sometimes, major geographical gaffes show up: in *The Little Dutch Tulip Girl*, it is very unlikely that a letter from a girl in Volendam, a Zuiderzee fishing village, would show up in a box of bulbs, likely from

Haarlem, Hillegom, or Lisse, then centers of the Dutch bulb-growing industry behind the North Sea dunes. Geographically, "Little Dutch herring girl" would be a more fitting title, with Tom finding the letter in a case of smoked herring.

Fig. 5.41. Pedestrian and bicycle ferry across a canal in Amsterdam; the operator pulls
the ferry along a cable (shown) and is paid by each passenger
(Holland and the Dutch, *1932*) (*NIS archive, HCASC*).

Holland and the Zuyder Zee, the narrator refers to the current, state-of-the-art Zuiderzee drainage project, but at the same time, the film shows only traditional dikes and windmills.

It is as if each filmmaker starts in Amsterdam, pivots to Volendam and Marken, and then moves over to Alkmaar, with possible side trips to Delft and The Hague. The films follow and perhaps even create a tourist itinerary. In Amsterdam, the scenic focus is always on the historic inner core: canals (fig. 5.41); canal houses; bicycle traffic; iconic streets, such as the Damrak and the Kalverstraat, and individual attrac-

tions, such as the Rembrandt House, the Rijksmuseum, and Palace on the Dam; and the Central Railway Station. *Holland and the Zuyder Zee* erroneously asserts that most of the city's commerce is conducted via its canals. Then, it is on to the Zuiderzee's old fishing villages of Volendam and Marken. Repeated stock scenes include all villagers dressed in the traditional local attire, the fishing fleet leaving the harbor (fig. 5.42), herring readied for smoking, streets scrubbed, windows washed, and laundry hung out to dry over the street.

Noteworthy is that, in several of the films, Volendam and Marken are shown

Fig. 5.42. Herring boats leaving a Zuiderzee harbor for the fisheries
(Roaming the Netherlands, *1934*) (*NIS archive, HCASC*)

to be on the itinerary for what was then group tourism. In *Holland and the Dutch*, a tourist boat is seen coming into the harbor of the island of Marken; the passengers disembark *en masse*, and retailers in traditional attire, wearing vendor trays and postcard strips, meet the tourists to sell souvenirs (fig. 5.43). The sloped roof of one of the stores has the words "Art Store" in English worked into the roof tiles; another, in *Holland and the Zuyder Zee*, has the word "Kodak" signed with roof tiles.

Alkmaar is the next tourist destination, and most of these films devote detailed attention (for twenty-minute films) to its cheese market. Tourists are seen watching from the perimeter and looking down on the market from the tower of the weigh house in *Holland and the Dutch*. They take in the theater of bargaining between sellers and buyers, the guild cheese porters carrying the round cheeses on barrows to and from the canal barges and the weigh house (fig. 5.44), and the official weighing of the cheeses.

Some of the films give their audiences a glimpse of other touristic places: the Queen's palace, as well as the Peace Palace, housing the International Court of Justice in The Hague; the diamond district of Amsterdam; and Delft's Nieuwe Kerk on the market square. Geography does not

Fig. 5.43. Hawking souvenirs from vendor trays to tourists in Volendam
(Holland and the Dutch, *1932*) (*NIS archive, HCASC*)

seem to matter: Middelburg's (Zeeland) market—shown with many of its buyers and sellers in traditional local costumes—is the last scenic unit in *Holland and the Zuyder Zee*. In fact, this film does not really deal with the Zuiderzee at all. Again, in this film, the touristic intent is very clear: visitors pose with and pay for pictures of women in their folk costumes (fig. 5.45), and signs in English point tourists to the wooden shoe souvenir stand.

An altogether different, nontravelogue, and last film in this class is *Holland Blooms Again* (1945; 44,390). It is a commercial and advertising film from the Associated Bulb Growers of Holland about the Netherlands' most iconic export—flower bulbs. Advertising and political propaganda films have a lot in common. The Netherlands was not facing any competition in the bulb export industry, but *Holland Blooms Again* was announcing to the United States that the Netherlands was ready to resume bulb exports to its largest market that had been cut off during the war.

The film begins with brief, black-and-white, stock scenes of bombs dropping from German aircraft, buildings ablaze, bridges in ruins, and crowds cheering as Allied tank units liberated their city. Next are stock scenes of the country rebuilding

Fig. 5.44. Porters at the Alkmaar Cheese Market (Holland
and the Zuyder Zee, *1939*) (*NIS archive, HCASC*)

and getting back to business, including the flower bulb industry (fig. 5.46). The film enlisted the horticultural editor of the magazine *American Home* as the surrogate expert and narrator for the newly filmed portions. He assures his viewers that the bulb varieties had been hidden from the Germans during the war and are now all available again, along with new varieties. At this point, *Holland Blooms Again* becomes an educational film, narrated by the same expert, but now about the metabolism of bulb and flower and how deep, where, and when to plant different bulbs in American residential gardens; this part is set in the United States. *Holland Blooms*

Again had strong staying power and added another 11,547 viewers in the 1950s.

The aggregate attendance number of 248,071 from NIB-Holland of these six NIB culture-directed films about the Netherlands among the top thirty-three films is not at all a meaningful measure of their influence because, as with this class of films about the Dutch colonies, they were also shown as shorts before feature films in American movie theaters and made available for rent and sale by distributors to schools, libraries, and other organizations. The Holland-NIB viewers joined this much larger audience of theatergoers and others, especially students, who came away with

Fig. 5.45. Tourist at the Middelburg market paying Zeeland women in traditional attire and shoulder yoke to take their photo (Holland and the Zuyder Zee, *1939*) (*NIS archive, HCASC*)

very consistently clichéd and dated traditional views of the country and its people—views that also cemented American public perceptions formed earlier.

In movie theaters, these films did not pretend to be something they were not; they were travel and tourist films, shown as much for entertainment as education. Borrowing these films from the NIB, however, came with somewhat different expectations. An agency of the Dutch government was furnishing official information about its country; the films therefore came with an imprimatur and had a more serious intent. The NIB films were shown mainly to students. To have these films collective-

ly serve as an official representation of the Netherlands and borrowers accept them as such were significant failures of Dutch public diplomacy. The NIB did not offer, as one would have expected, given its mission, an alternative to these American touristic perceptions of the Netherlands. These films may be seen as representing and reinforcing existing American public perceptions of the Netherlands and, for that matter, extending already long-held views. They fed right into and perpetuated the earlier affectionate and nostalgic American perceptions focused on the early Dutch Republic (1649–1784) and its nineteenth- and early twentieth-century legacies. They contain many enduring icon-

Fig. 5.46. Hand cutting flowers to produce larger and more productive bulbs for sale (Holland Blooms Again,*1945*) (*NIS archive, HCASC*)

ic components that continue to be worked and reworked even today by Dutch tourist industry advertising aimed at international travelers. This iconography also structures the Holland festivals held yearly in Dutch American regions throughout the United States.

Except for *Roaming the Netherlands*, the travelogues do not appear in the borrowing records after the 1940s, and even this remaining film dropped from fifth to fifty-ninth place during the 1950s, with only 631 viewers from 1950 to 1952. Their absence indicates that they were quickly deaccessioned with the recognition that they promoted an extremely stereotypic, touristic, and overall dated image of the country. Beginning in the 1950s, the NIS committed itself to portraying a more modern, diverse, and international country; such subjects had not received their due in the press of wartime and colonial foreign policies.

The question remains: Why did the NIB acquire these American-made tourist films and travelogues that set back the general and up-to-date understanding of the country by the American public? Although at a slower pace than some other Western countries, the Netherlands had been going through a scientifically based modernization since the middle of the nineteenth century with, among other things, rail-ways between cities, telegraph capabilities, modification of rivers and the building of canals, a roadway system between major cities, national postal services, technologi-cally advanced ports, and modern housing for the working and middle classes.[43] These films show nothing at all about these de-velopments.

The factors at work in the acquisition of American- (rather than Dutch-) made, culture-directed films about the Dutch colonies also apply to these films. One ex-ception—although it was the greater part of a compilation, foreign-policy-directed film—was *New Earth*. More than twen-ty minutes of this film is taken from Joris Ivens' film footage of the construction of the Zuiderzee reclamation project. Here was part of a film that featured a modern Dutch development project.

There certainly were fitting, Dutch-made documentary films for the NIB, some about the entire country, and oth-ers—with broad relevance—about specific industries, places, and activities.[44] Several films representing the entire country were produced in the 1920s and 1930s. Willie Mullins of *Haghe Film*, a pioneer of Dutch cinema, directed a film titled *Nederland* (1921, 1937), a compilation of films he had shot over the years; it premiered in 1921 and went through several versions with different lengths. It was distributed out-side the country by the Association of the Netherlands Abroad (Vereeniging Neder-land in den Vreemde).[45] Yet this film was not part of the Holland-NIB collection. Unlike the American-made travelogues, *Nederland* had a much broader geographi-cal orbit—every province is included—and presented the country as it was in the first part of the twentieth century and not as a nostalgic, premodern vacationland with stock imagery of windmills, tulips, cheese, and traditional costumes. One section is about the Dutch and water; it shows mod-ern shipping, canals, polders, sea dikes, and the harbors of Amsterdam and Rot-terdam. Another section surveys Dutch agriculture, including oyster culture, horse breeding, and dairying. Additional sec-tions survey industries and watersport, es-pecially ice skating.

In the early 1930s, the Dutch Associ-ation for Tourism (Algemene Nederlandse Vereniging van Vreemdelingenverkeer) commissioned Visie Film to produce a new film about the Netherlands. Max de Haas, another pioneer of the Dutch film indus-try, directed the film, released in 1934 with the title *Nederland Spreekt*, 1934 (*The Netherlands Speaks*). What especially sets this film apart is the use of aerial shots.[46] The film is organized by seasons and plac-es, and like the earlier film, *Nederland*, it is geographically much more representative of the country than the American-made films. It often juxtaposes traditional and modern subjects—a diesel-electric train rushes past a windmill, and folklore and orthodox Calvinist villages like Staphorst are placed side by side with Scheveningen's beach with men and women in swimsuits. *Nederland Spreekt* was an early twenti-eth-century survey of the look and activ-ities of Dutch landscapes, cities, and vil-lages, blending old and new. It was pro-

---

43 Ouke van der Woud, *Een Nieuwe Wereld. Het Ont-staan van het Moderne Nederland* (Bert Bakker, 2007).

44 See endnote 5:44, p. 402.

45 Hogenkamp, *De Nederlandse Documentaire Film*, 17–18.

46 Ibid., 85–86.

duced especially for foreign viewers, but again, it was not part of the Holland-NIB film collection. There were certainly other films commissioned and kept by the government information services and tourist organizations that would have been a good fit for the mission of the NIB: for example, films about Schiphol Airport; the Rhine River, from where it entered the country to where it emptied into the North Sea; and the North Sea fisheries.[47]

Again, the most ready explanation for films such as these to not have been included in the NIB film library is that, with the German occupation of the Netherlands, the Dutch government in exile in London was shut out from the country's films. In need of 16 mm films about the country in general, each with English intertitles or voice-overs, the NIB turned to American-made ones. But even after the liberation of the country in May of 1945, the NIB did not decide to acquire and make ready Dutch-made films for American viewing.

It appears that, aside from the high-priority, foreign-policy-directed compilation films produced or commissioned by the NIB that addressed the country's war, reconstruction, and colonial policy, more general, Dutch-made, culture-directed films were not chosen for the film library. This was not where the NIB spent its scarce resources. Films that provided more general information about the Netherlands proper and its various colonial possessions were acquired from American filmmakers. This was far less expensive than reproducing Dutch-made, 35 mm films into 16 mm format and adding English subtitles and voice-overs for Americans who would come to see these documentaries, not in movie theaters, but in schools, libraries, and churches. This choice, however, came with a price of significant misrepresentation and outdatedness.

There may be an additional, but less likely, explanation, one related more particularly to Holland-NIB. Albeit employed by the Dutch government, Holland-NIB director Willard Wichers was a Dutch American leader and not, as other NIB directors, an expatriate or a professional diplomat. Many Dutch Americans had a love/hate relationship with their motherland. The love side of this equation squared well with the kinds of imagery found in the American-made travelogue films. Dutch Americans were much less interested in the modern, up-to-date Netherlands than in the premodern, rural, and folkloric country.[48] Wichers, living in a predominantly Dutch American enclave, understood that and was able to move back and forth between the interests of Dutch American communities and those of the larger American public the NIB was trying to reach and influence. NIB directors had considerable freedom in selecting films. Wichers could well have been adding American-made films about the Netherlands on his own to cater to both American and Dutch American tastes and preferences. But for this explanation to be credible, the other two NIB branches would not have had any of the Dutch-made, culture-directed films in their libraries either; if any of these films were generally available to the NIB branches, they would have been part of the NIB-Holland collection as well.

47   Ibid., 131–49 (filmography).

48   David Zwart, "Constructing the Homeland: Dutch Americans and the Netherlands Information Bureau during the 1940s," *Michigan Historical Review* 33, no. 2 (Fall 2007): 81–100.

Without the film records of the other NIB branches, there can be no definitive answer to this question. I consider the priority placed on foreign-policy-directed films; the war-time inaccessibility of Dutch-made, culture-directed films; the cost of converting these films from 35 mm to 16 mm format and the addition of English-language subtitles and voice-overs; and the immediate need for such culture-directed films to be much more compelling explanations. These factors also apply to the culture-directed colonial films.

Conclusion and transition

With its kit of diplomatic tools and media, including films, the NIB was successful in drawing the attention of the American public more to Dutch foreign policy goals (17 films, 765,287 viewers from the top 33 films) than to general introductions to the country and its colonies (15 films, 474,690 viewers). This reflected the agency's priorities during the 1940s. Films did not become part of the Dutch public diplomacy in the United States until late 1943; messaging urging the United States to enter the war, therefore, was not part of the content of its foreign-policy-directed films. With the exception of helping to bring much sympathy and aid to a war-torn country, the NIB instruments of public diplomacy employed for achieving the Dutch foreign policy goals did not bring the United States into WWII (the Japanese attack on Pearl Harbor did that), nor did they vouchsafe the Dutch colonies. The foreign-policy-directed films were part of this failure of public diplomacy. The culture-directed films continued and gave new impetus to the preferred American, nostalgic perception of the Netherlands as a romanticized, premodern republic of traditional communities organized around livelihood, principally farming, fishing, and trade. The culture-directed films about the Netherlands' colonies, particularly those about the Dutch East Indies, helped extend American perceptions of Southeast Asia as an exotic realm, environmentally and culturally; they did not attach an image of Dutchness to these places among American viewers.

At the end of the 1940s, the most pressing need for the NIB, as constituted, disappeared, with no new vital foreign policy differences between the United States and the Netherlands in sight. But the consumer-driven distribution of all kinds of information about the Netherlands, via different media, including film, unrelated to foreign policy aims, had also proved to be quite successful and broad-based; an agency, an infrastructure, and a market for continuing the dissemination of such knowledge was already in place. These, together with cultural programming, were enough for the NIB to continue to carry on its public diplomacy mission in the United States—albeit with diminished priority and budgets—for another twenty-four years.

CHAPTER 6

The 1950s: From Political Propaganda to Cultural Nationalism

Introduction

With the victory of the Allies, the Marshall Plan, NATO, and the independence of Indonesia, the Dutch foreign policy objectives related to the war, reconstruction, and the colonies had run their course. Dutch and American foreign policy had become quite congruent, and the need for concerted foreign policy activism to shape American public opinion disappeared. The NIB was rechristened the Netherlands Information Service (NIS) and shaped into more of a cultural institute, although still an agency of the national government. Gone, of course, were the activist campaigns to bring the war and postwar plight and destruction of the Netherlands before the American public. Gone were the programs to manage and correct the news related to the war and the colonies. Dutch academics and American surrogates were no longer needed to make the case for the Dutch point of view on these urgent foreign policy issues. The information and cultural service by letter, printed materials, phone, radio, lectures, and film continued—both consumer- and NIS-driven—but no longer prioritized by war and the colonies. This change reshaped the content of the materials that the NIS collected and distributed, including its documentary films. Foreign-policy-directed films were no longer made or accessioned, although several about the Netherlands—those with enduring cultural value—were carried over from the 1940s. Cultural programming was freed from foreign policy imperatives and priorities.

The semiannual reports submitted by Willard Wichers to the NIS director in New York City during the 1950s—and into the 1960s—were divided into a number of different tasks, including lectures and tours, radio, press, films, public service, and service projects. Tens of thousands of letters were written and sent out yearly by the staff of Holland-NIS to administer these different responsibilities. NIS staff replied to requests for information from libraries, schools, and individuals; other letters required research and follow-up before answers and other information could be provided. Radio stations throughout the twenty-state area were solicited to carry Dutch programs. The January to June 1954 activity report, for example, reported that the program *Dutch Light Music* was placed at 371 stations.[1] Speaking tours and engagements were arranged for attachés and other diplomatic staff at the Dutch embassy, Dutch scholars, and Dutch business leaders. Among the detailed reports about the NIS's differentiated responsibilities, the film library's screening summaries by title always had a prominent place in Wichers' reports. They were headed by a statistical overview, listing—for the six-month period—the total number of incoming telephone calls, in-person visits to Holland-NIS, letters written, and packages sent out, followed by five summary statistics related to the film lending library—number of films booked, showings (booked and reported), attendance, and average attendance (fig. 2.4). This statistical breakdown for the films is another measure of their importance among the

other instruments of public diplomacy. All such twice-yearly summaries about the film library's work were derived from the detailed film borrowing records that, together with the films themselves, are the primary sources for this study.

During the 1950s, the Netherlands continued to rebuild a country devastated by war. It had been plundered of everything useful to Germany's war effort and destroyed as part of a scorched-earth policy during the enemy's retreat. Nearly one hundred thousand homes had been destroyed and six times as many seriously damaged. Housing shortages persisted well into the decade. The food-supply chain had been seriously disrupted, and rationing was needed to provide country-wide food security during the years immediately after the war. More than half of the transportation system lay in ruins. The ports—backbones of the export-oriented economy—although kept in operation by the German authorities for their own wartime requirements, needed much investment to become engines of growth once more. Much farmland had deteriorated and needed rehabilitation to return it to prewar productivity. The American Marshall Plan substantially aided reconstruction efforts in all these areas; it made money available to many different Dutch companies without working capital, cash flow, or access to credit because of the war and its aftermath. With these funds, companies could purchase the materials and other inputs required for their operations and manufacturing—all necessary for the reconstruction of the country.[2]

[1]   Activity Report, Jan. to June 1954, 3, Activity Reports, box 3, NIS archive, HCASC.

[2]   Anita Blom, Simone Vermaat, and Ben de Vries, eds., *Post-War Reconstruction in the Netherlands, 1945–1965: The Future of a Bright and Brutal Heritage* (NAi Publishers, 2017).

Government-sponsored films distributed abroad during this period had a nationalist cast. With the necessary preoccupation with reconstruction, human welfare, and economic recovery, it is very understandable that the country, including its films (especially those exported outside its borders) further exposed and reinforced this orientation. Films focused on and highlighted the accomplishments of a country rising from the ruins of war and the occupation by a ruthless enemy. The Netherlands needed to be made whole again. International security arrangements, such as NATO in 1949 and the beginnings of pan-European alliances with the European Coal and Steel Community (ECSC) in 1951, were essential for the future, but the Netherlands was more focused on its own reconstruction, social programs, and economic progress, not that which it held in common with other developed nations.

Many 1940s NIB films were taken out of circulation but fortunately kept in the collection. Some seventy films circulated during the 1950s, an increase of more than 20 percent over the 1940s.[3] Sixteen titles (22.9%) were carried over from the 1940s. Twenty-one (30%) of the films borrowed during the 1950s are not present in the archive; only one, *Men against the Sea* (1953), had over ten thousand viewers; this compares to 18 percent for the 1940s. Every film library needs to remain up-to-date, and the 1950s saw a predominately new collection.

---

[3] The precise number is tricky because, occasionally, separate titles appeared as stems or abbreviations of full titles in the circulation records. When there were no records of these as their own titles, I combined them—together with their circulation data—with the larger encompassing title. I may have missed an independent title or incorrectly combined films.

1940s and 1950s films compared

Topical films

An important trend in relation to the films' subject matter became noticeable in the 1950s. Most films shown during the 1940s were place-based and general, synthetic overviews with multiple threads about the Netherlands, particular colonial islands and possessions, and regions and their cities, towns, and villages. During the 1950s, more specialized, topic- and event-based films with fewer subject threads made their entry into the library—films such as *Bells of Holland* (1951), *It's Just a Postage Stamp* (1952), *Mediaeval Dutch Sculpture* (1951), and *The Amphibian Postman* (1954), to name just a few. This trend became even more pronounced during the 1960s/70s. To be sure, such films also highlight a topic in one or more places, but they do not paint a more holistic picture of such places. For example, the 1950 documentary, *Island of Faith* (1950), is set on the island of Walcheren in the province of Zeeland; its topic is the agricultural restoration of the island following the war-related flooding in 1944. It is more of a topical film than one about a place, and although such a distinction is sometimes blurred and sometimes clear, it does mark an important difference. Films about places assemble their personality, landscape, culture, history, and identity for the viewer. They provide either a regional or place synopsis. They create imagery that often gives entry to lasting impressions. Landscapes, whether natural or human made, are important ingredients of such films; they engage viewers' aesthetic, emotional, and cognitive sensibilities.

The travelogue is one of the oldest types of films about places: the filmmaker surveys the attractions for interested outsiders, virtual travelers, and those (with the means) who, after viewing such a film, might even consider traveling to the area to experience it firsthand. When films about places are not travelogues but more carefully developed, balanced, and holistic portraits of a place (e.g., Amsterdam, the Veluwe), they present particular challenges for a filmmaker, including representativeness and synthesizing multiple subject threads and diverse layers into a coherent portrayal. Topic-based films often evoke a more cognitive response. Films about the history of the Dutch post office (*It's Just a Postage Stamp*) or bell casting and carillon building (*Bells of Holland*) do tell and teach viewers about Dutch crafts and institutions, but they produce a different kind of knowledge about the country than films about places, large and small.

Thirty-one (62%) of the top fifty films—twenty-eight about the Netherlands and three about the Dutch territories—distributed by the NIS during the 1950s were topical films. This was a dramatic change from the 1940s, when only fifteen of the fifty-five films (27.3%)—ten about the Netherlands and five about its overseas territories—were topical films; all the others were place-based surveys.

In general, topical films about the Netherlands and its territories that were circulated by the NIS would either zero in on an already internationally known Dutch contribution (printing), export (bulbs), or skill (water management) or focus on a quality or practice regarded as distinctively Dutch that set the country apart (flower pageants). This provides a clue about the film-selection standards of the NIS. Other topical films in the NIS collection that did not conform to such markers would draw fewer viewers. Some were produced for the Dutch market, but later, a producer/distributor or government agency might take a chance and add an English, French, or Spanish voice-over. But even if a subject generated strong interest among Dutch viewers, it did not mean it would appeal to people in other countries. The film might be too specialized, arcane, complex, or without adequate context. Or its content might not relate to what those outside the Netherlands already knew or interest them in either the country or its overseas territories.

Emerging technical and cinematographic qualities of NIS documentary films

The most obvious cinematographic difference between the 1940s Holland-NIB documentaries and those of the 1950s was the transition to color film. For the 1940s, only four films were in color; among the top fifty films screened during the 1950s, there were more than twenty in color, including most top-tier films as measured by attendance. Color was fast becoming the standard for new productions.

The NIS library required films with English voice-overs. Except for *Hans Brinker's Return* (1954), all the NIB/NIS documentaries of the 1940s and 1950s were films with English voice-over only, without spoken parts or dialogue. After 1950, the NIS could no longer rely either on American films or propaganda films produced by the Dutch government. The RVD (first, in exile in London and then back in The Hague) had looked after the production of the foreign-policy-directed compilation films with English-language narration during the 1940s. The culture-directed films about the Netherlands and the Dutch colonies acquired from American film companies came with English voice-overs.

English subtitles at that time were not an option. Creating subtitles—mechanically or chemically stamped on every frame—for a documentary film that had a continuous, Dutch voice-over made a film more difficult to follow; viewers might miss the subtitles while focusing on the visuals or miss the visuals while reading text. All the while, the Dutch voice-over would still be audible and intrusive. To add English-language voice-overs and revoice (dub) the spoken parts was considered to be more effective. English voice-overs were commonly translated from the Dutch ones, although additional information could be added.

The decision to add voice-overs in other languages after 1950 was made not by the NIS but by the producers, government agencies, sponsors, and distributors of the documentaries who assessed their films' potential beyond Dutch borders. Films that presented either a snapshot of the country as a whole or its internationally valued places, regions, customs, and activities were at the front of the line for voice-overs in other languages. Films commissioned by the ministries of foreign affairs and economic development of the national government would also be more likely released in several other languages, thereby serving the aim of international diplomacy and promotion and not profitability and returns on money invested. Whether or not the more specialized topical films about the Netherlands and/or Dutch territories were suitable for voice-overs in other languages was much more difficult to ascertain: some film production companies would make certain films for the domestic market only; others would judge that a par-

ticular film project might well generate interest abroad and decide to produce at least an English-language version. In any event, the NIS had little to no say about such decisions; they could consider only films that came with English-language narration and were shut out of what were otherwise suitable films for their diplomatic purposes but lacked an English version.

Musical scores, soundscape, and dialogue were incorporated into feature (fiction) films already in the 1930s, and during that time, documentaries also became sound films with voice-over narration and some music but not soundscape or dialogue. Soundscape is the acoustic environment of what is filmed: waves crashing, doors closing, sheep bleating, and the background buzz of conversation. Voice-over was considered suitable and sufficient for description and explanation in documentary films. Whereas character dialogue was essential to realistically portray and tell a story in fictional film, the same was not true for documentaries; they usually lacked a story line or dramatis personae. Moreover, during the early decades, adding soundscape and dialogue was expensive, and the profit margins of documentary films were always much smaller than those of fictional films.

The late arrival of soundscape and dialogue in documentary film clearly shows up in the NIS lending library of the 1950s. In the 1940s, the NIB-Holland films included some eleven silent films produced during the 1920s and 1930s; the rest had sound as voice-over and music. In some films, background music was continuous, in others, episodic. The silent films disappeared from the film library in the 1950s, but as in the previous decade, nearly all the documentaries continued to be sound films, if only by virtue of their film score and voice-over narration.

Documentaries with either sound-scape or dialogue, or both, were few and far between. Of the top fifty films of the 1950s (99% of viewership), eight films are in neither the archive nor the relevant Dutch- or English-language film databases, such as the Netherlands Institute for Sound and Vision, IMDb Pro, and the British Film Institute. Of the remaining forty-two films, thirty-five (83%) have neither soundscape nor dialogue. Some do have prerecorded music for specific scenes (barrel organ and street musician scenes in *In and around Amsterdam*), but sound and video are not synced. Seven films do have a soundscape but not typically throughout the entire film, primarily just for selected stationary scenes (pile driver in *In and around Amsterdam*, playing the bells of a carillon in *Bells of Holland*). Only two films with soundscape also have dialogue that advances the subject of the film: *Hans Brinker's Return* (1954) and *Shoot the Nets* (1951). In both films, but especially in *Hans Brinker's Return*, dialogue replaces voice-over narration. Although viewers do not actually see them speak, a question-and-answer conversation between father and son traveling through Amsterdam and surroundings provides the knowledge about the city and the country in *Hans Brinker's Return*. Strictly speaking, it is not filmed dialogue but a voice-over in the form of a conversation. In *Shoot the Nets*, the conversational camaraderie and the lilting commands by the fishing supervisor while his crew is shooting and, later, pulling in the nets, create an intimate picture of life onboard a herring boat at sea. Dialogue brings viewers closer to the subject at hand; it softens

and diversifies the authoritative knowledge of the narrator.

All in all, the NIS film library of the 1950s was keeping pace with the cinematographic developments of the documentary film industry.

Attendance

Compared to the 1940s, viewership of Holland-NIS films dropped off markedly during the 1950s (fig. 4.2), even though the 1950s enjoyed a full decade of attendance, compared to just seven years for the 1940s. Total 1950s attendance for Holland-NIS was more than halved from the 1940s, from 1,280,968 to 634,795 (fig. 4.1); total estimated attendance for the entire country stood at more than 1.4 million viewers, down by more than a million from the 1940s. Reasons for this steep drop had nothing to do with the number of films on offer because that number had increased from fifty-five to some seventy. Rather, the NIS—now more of a cultural institute—did not have the same high-Dutch, foreign-policy priority as the NIB had enjoyed. This reconfiguration brought on smaller operating budgets and reduced staffing and marketing, also for films. For most years, annual attendance for Holland-NIB did not top fifty thousand (fig. 4.2). Only when the four-part series, *Holland: A Modern Country Full of Old-Time Charm*, was acquired, soon after its release in 1952, did attendance spike to above two hundred thousand for 1953 and above one hundred thousand for 1954. Another reason for this significant overall drop in attendance was related to a shift away from films about the Dutch colonies/territories in the collection. This led to a steep decline in the total viewership for this group of documentaries. And last—apart from the film library itself—television ownership and home viewing cut into attendance at group showings organized by a wide variety of private, public, and governmental institutions.

When the 1950s films are ranked by attendance (fig. 6.1) and compared to the same pattern for the 1940s (fig. 5.1), additional differences for the 1950s stand out. The drop from first- to second- to third-ranked film is much steeper (130,000–60,000–33,000) than the 1940s pattern, indicating a greater reliance on a few "chartbusters," rather than a more proportional decline in attendance from all offerings. The ten thousand attendance floor is reached already by the eighteenth film (compared to the 34th for the 1940s) and more than a third (24) of the films contribute less than a thousand viewers each to the total attendance for the 1950s. It is instructive that two stalwarts from the 1940s, *Landbuilders* (1932/1940) and *New Earth* (1933/1943)—both foreign-policy-directed films but with much arresting cultural content—take second and third place in the 1950s viewership before a more even rate of decline takes over.

The geography of viewership

The significant decline in attendance from the 1940s to the 1950s was, as might be expected, matched by a decline in screening locations, from 1182 to 834, nearly 62 percent of which were new locations, active only during the 1950s (fig. 6.2). Compare the 1940s (fig. 5.2) with that of the 1950s. To a large extent, the 1950s saw a new distribution of screening locations and related total audience sizes, some in new areas of the region, for example, throughout Ohio. Examples on the map

of very sharp increases in attendance include Houston, a television broadcasting location, and Amarillo, Texas, at the Mary E. Bivins Memorial Library. The decline in viewership, of course, was much steeper than that of the screening locations so that the average attendance per location for the decade also saw a sharp drop. Screening locations dropped across Southern states, as well as around the east and west coastlines of the Great Lakes; the crowding and superimposition of these locations on the map in the latter region makes the decline less apparent there (cf. fig. 5.2).

Change and carryover in the film collection

Although half of the films shown in the 1940s were about the Dutch colonies, only ten of seventy films and just 72,143 viewers (11.5%) of the total 1950s attendance were related to these territories during the 1950s, a reflection of the "loss" of the Dutch East Indies and the depoliticization of the issue. The few colonial films that carried over from the 1940s to the 1950s were about either the Dutch West Indies, with footage related to the war deleted (*The Dutch in Latin America*, 1947), or Netherlands New Guinea, then not (yet) part of Indonesia (*Rescue from Shangri-La*, 1947; 17,445).

In the interest of more balanced and modern and less touristic films about the Netherlands itself, all of the American travelogues from the 1930s—except *Roaming the Netherlands*, which dominated American viewing of films about the Netherlands in the 1940s—were retired from circulation. And even *Roaming the Netherlands* was seen by very few, just until 1951. In their place came a group of Dutch- and American-made films that sought to

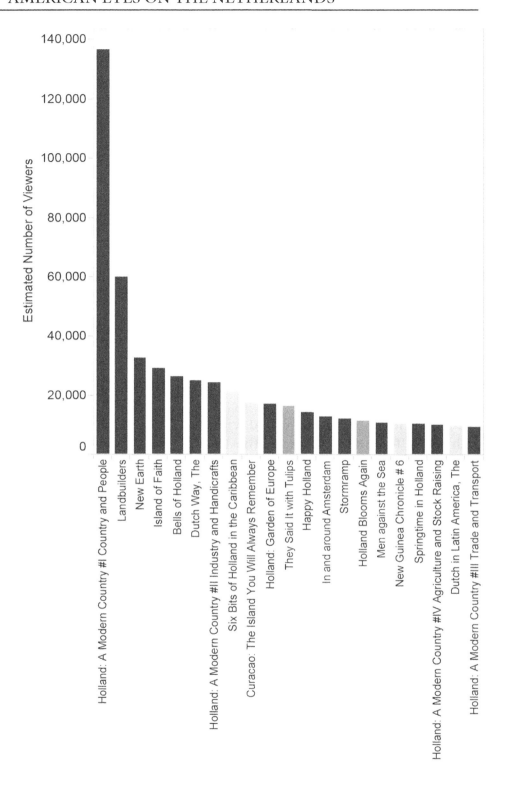

Fig. 6.1. Holland-NIS: Attendance by film during the 1950s (top 50 films)

99.3% of total 1950s attendance

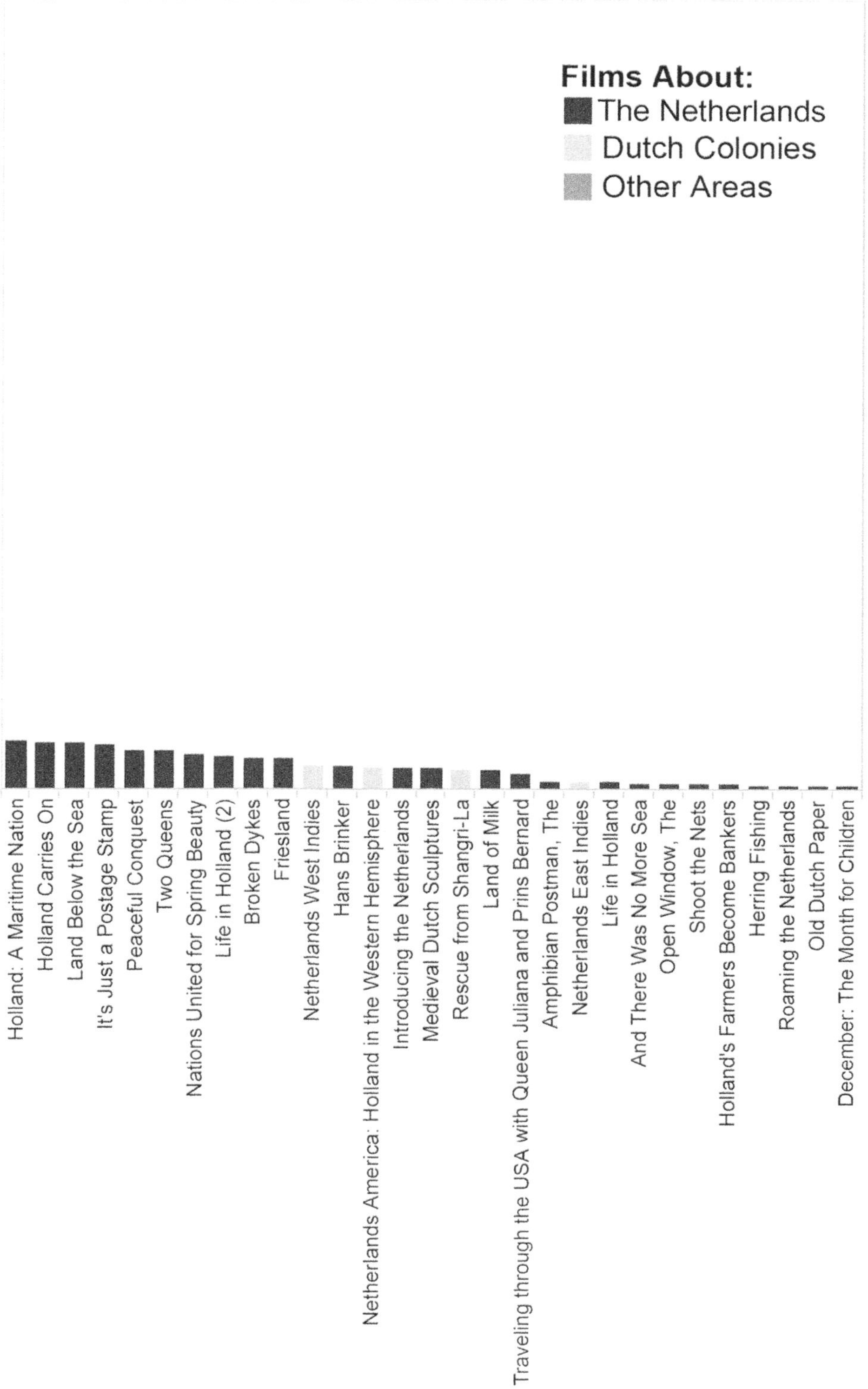

Films About:
■ The Netherlands
▢ Dutch Colonies
▣ Other Areas

Holland: A Maritime Nation
Holland Carries On
Land Below the Sea
It's Just a Postage Stamp
Peaceful Conquest
Two Queens
Nations United for Spring Beauty
Life in Holland (2)
Broken Dykes
Friesland
Netherlands West Indies
Hans Brinker
Netherlands America: Holland in the Western Hemisphere
Introducing the Netherlands
Medieval Dutch Sculptures
Rescue from Shangri-La
Land of Milk
Traveling through the USA with Queen Juliana and Prins Bernard
Amphibian Postman, The
Netherlands East Indies
Life in Holland
And There Was No More Sea
Open Window, The
Shoot the Nets
Holland's Farmers Become Bankers
Herring Fishing
Roaming the Netherlands
Old Dutch Paper
December: The Month for Children

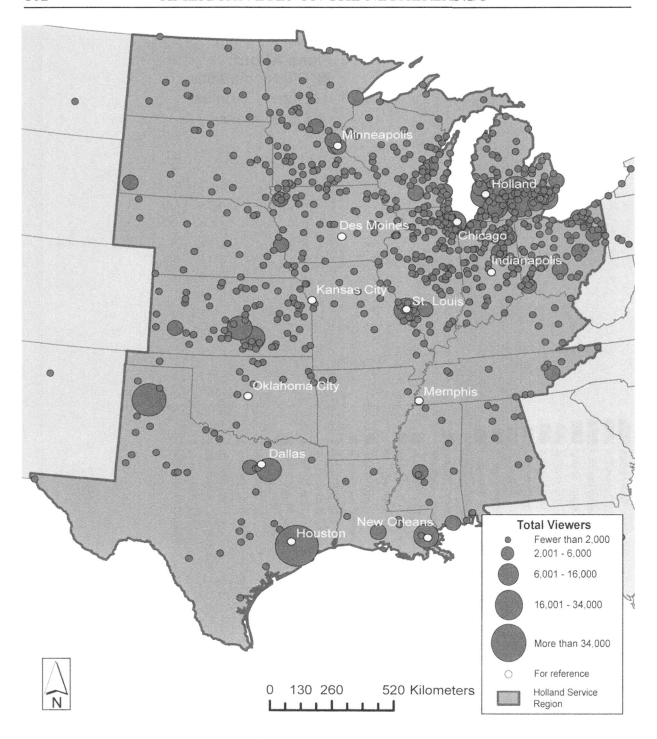

Fig. 6.2. NIS-Holland: Film Attendance by Place, 1950s

strike a balance between what one film se-ries called Holland's "old-time charm" and more across-the-board modern develop-ments.

One subcategory of films from the 1940s that did carry over into the 1950s, especially in terms of strong viewership, was the foreign-policy-directed films about the Netherlands, in particular, those related to the war and its aftermath. The significance of this becomes clear from the attendance records from the 1950s (fig. 6.1): *Landbuilders*, the number-one film from the 1940s moved down just one spot for the 1950s, with 59,879 viewers, and *New Earth*, the number-two film from the 1940s, also moved down just one spot, with 32,646 viewers for the 1950s. Several other films from the 1940s about the war and reconstruction—*Holland Carries On* (1944), *Friesland* (1946), and *Broken Dykes* (1945)—are also in the top-forty films for the 1950s. Why did these films remain in the library and continue to be quite popular with American audiences? There are several possibilities. First, *Landbuilders* and *New Earth* both have a moral tacked on at the end: the enduring Dutch commitment to the peaceable addition of new land. Second, the bulk of each film presents material compelling in its own right and not related to the war: *Landbuilders*, the traditional life on the island of Walcheren, and *New Earth*, the construction of the barrier dam across the mouth of the Zuiderzee, the lynchpin of the future IJssel Lake polders, as well as the ring dike and drainage of the first of the Zuiderzee polders, the Wieringermeerpolder. Last, the NIS wanted to continue to show viewers that the Dutch had suffered much during the war (*Holland Carries On, Friesland, Broken Dykes*) and engender American sympathy and support.

Films about the Netherlands shown during the 1950s

Topical threads

Again, because of their very different content and purpose, it is helpful to divide

the films into those about the Netherlands itself and those about the Dutch territories overseas.[4] Films about the Netherlands make up the largest group by far (60/70). Only one of the twenty-five categories—international relations—received no consideration in these 1950s films.[5] Compared to the 1940s, the same number of subject categories had less than 5 percent—these actually each had less than 4 percent—of all the topical threads for the 1950s and the same number of categories surpassed that threshold (fig. 6.3). There was, however, some shift in the distribution of the leading categories from the 1940s to the 1950s—those with the greatest percentages of the total. Understandably, film threads related to war fell sharply, from 18.1 percent to 5.5 percent. With the Zuiderzee project in high gear and the devastating 1953 flood garnering much international attention, issues related to water still retained the largest percentage of the film threads (from 19.4% to 16.8%). Curiously, attention both to cities, and towns and villages dropped quite sharply: cities from 14.1 percent to 8.2 percent, and towns and villages from 7.8 percent to 2.7 percent. In part, these particular changes had to do with taking out of circulation the American-made travelogue films that were very much focused on tourist cities and towns. The reason for the near doubling of film threads (from 6.8% to 12.1%) related to agriculture and the rural countryside is not clear.

4 After WWII, the loaded name "colonies" was increasingly replaced with the more politically neutral "(overseas) territories."

5 For the list of these categories, see fig. 3.4.

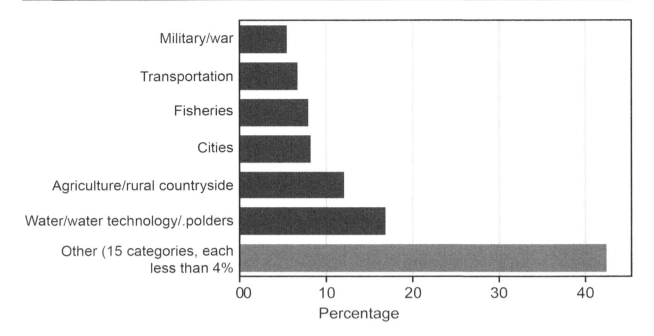

Fig. 6.3. Films about the Netherlands, 1950s: percentage of film threads by subject

404 film threads, top 27 films about the Netherlands, 464,525 viewers (91.8%)

Dutch places on view in 1950s films

Naturally, as the film collection grew in size from the 1940s to the 1950s, the number of Dutch places on view for American filmgoers also increased. And the number of films with sufficiently high viewership numbers to be influential and, therefore, part of the analysis in this study, also increased; this resulted in twenty-one more different villages, towns, cities, and small polders entering the analysis for the 1950s (fig. 6.4). When one compares the maps of Dutch places shown in the films during the 1940s (figs. 5.3, 5.4) to those of the 1950s (figs. 6.4, 6.5), the overall patterns look much the same: a steep west-to-east gradient in the number and frequency of places shown and a north-to-south gradient in place representation among the coastal provinces, the region with the greatest number of filmed places.

At the same time, there are some revealing similarities and differences in the numbers informing these two sets of maps. First, the similarities. The three western provinces remained very much in control of which Dutch places American viewers saw. During the 1940s, these three (of the then 11) provinces contributed 69.7 percent of the different (unique) places shown, and when multiple showings are included, the number rises to 82.6 percent; the comparable statistics for the 1950s are 70.4 percent and 81.7 percent, nearly identical figures. When the category of places is broadened to include showings of larger geographic units, such as economic regions, islands, water bodies, and even the provinces themselves (fig. 6.5), 74.7 percent (81.0% for the 1940s) of the places fell into the three western provinces, a slightly lower but comparable level of dominance. The eastern border provinces of Gronin-

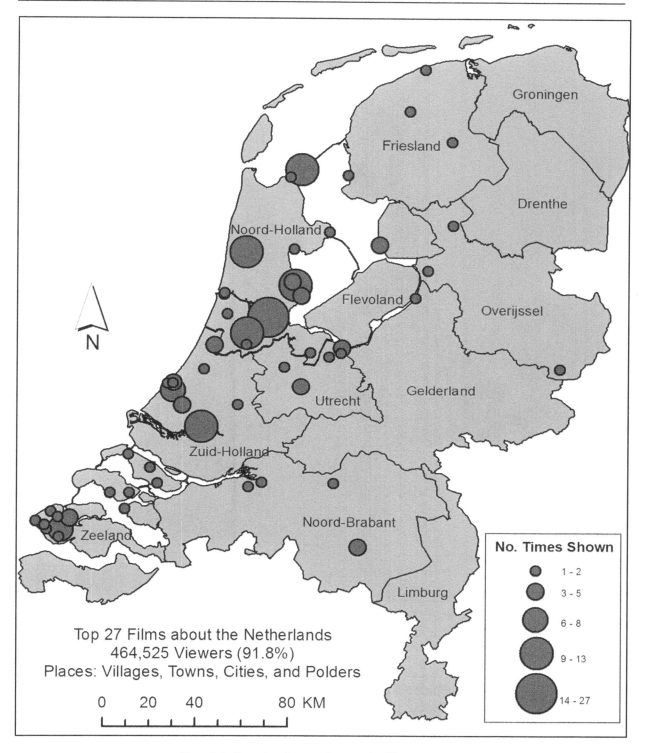

Fig. 6.4. Dutch places shown in films, 1950s

gen, Drenthe, and Limburg again had no place representation whatsoever in the films, and even Gelderland lost what lit-tle recognition it had during the 1940s. These center-periphery contrasts in place representation in films shown in America

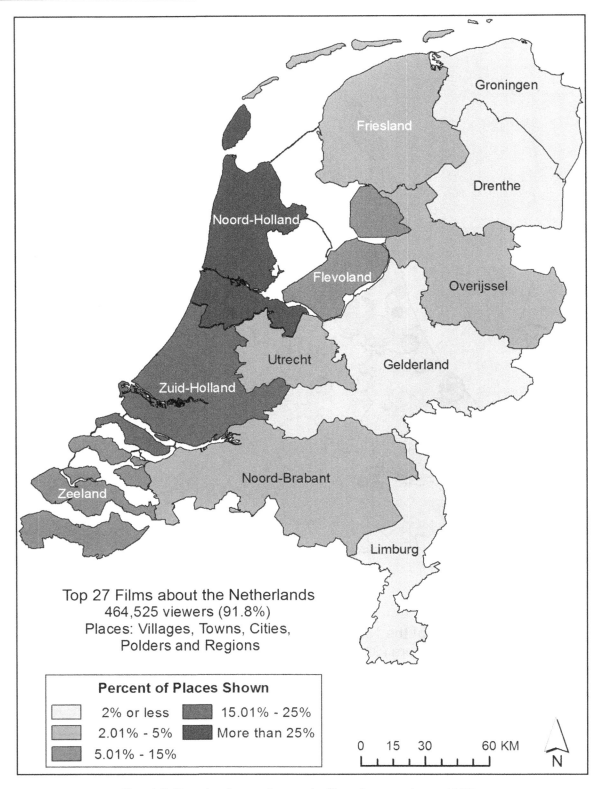

Fig. 6.5. Dutch places shown in films by province, 1950s

were even stronger than those related to the demographic and economic contrasts between the western coastal provinces and the rest of the country at this time.

Some differences between the 1940 and 1950 place representations do come out when the maps depicting the percentage of all the places shown by province are compared (figs. 5.4, 6.5). For one, Zeeland's contribution began a significant decline in the 1950s that continued into the 1960s and 1970s, one that was more in keeping with its actual place in the Dutch periphery. By contrast, Zuid-Holland, a province very much part of the core but much underrepresented during the 1940s, for reasons already outlined, began an upward climb, nearly doubling its percentage contribution, a trend that continued into the next decade. As a result, Noord-Holland, the perennial geographical champion, gave up some of its primacy. Among the middle-tier provinces, future Flevoland jumped two map categories to achieve the highest representation of any of the provinces in that grouping, approaching that of coastal Zeeland. The Zuiderzee "land reclamation" project—making new land from water and settling it with farms, drainage, transportation, villages, and towns—garnered a lot of attention from filmmakers commissioned by the Dutch government; these films were ideal for international promotion and much used for that purpose. Audiences abroad were impressed by them because they gave a new and modern version of the age-old and internationally known Dutch narrative of taking and keeping land from the sea.

Inspecting the distribution of the actual locations of "small" places (villages, towns, cities, and polders) shown on the islands of the southwest on the 1940s and 1950s maps (figs 5.3 and 6.4) reveals that

the monopoly the island of Walcheren had over the American perception of this area had begun to break. The 1940s map shows only places on Walcheren; the 1950s map also registered places shown in the films about the 1953 flood disaster that affected the entire island chain and beyond (including the island of Goeree-Overflakkee in Zuid-Holland) but left Walcheren largely unscathed.

A close reading of the 1950s films about the Netherlands

Introduction

Nine films about the Netherlands from the 1940s, with a total viewership of 153,226, carried over into the borrowing records of the 1950s. Some of these, for example, *New Earth*, *In and around Amsterdam*, *Broken Dykes*, and *Friesland*, even reached into the 1960s. Most are foreign-policy-directed films related to the war and its aftermath. These became historical documentaries, reminding American viewers of what the Netherlands had gone through during the war and the years following, much like the grip the war had and continues to have on the Netherlands itself, including its film industry. These films have already been analyzed and assessed, but it is important to note that they make up one strand of content during the 1950s, albeit without the more immediate propaganda goals of the 1940s. They helped create cultural memory about WWII and its results in the Netherlands among the American public, somewhat like the fiction films *Theirs Is the Glory* (1946) and *A Bridge Too Far* (1977), both about Operation Market Garden, which aimed to outflank the German military forces by seizing and securing the bridges across the major Dutch rivers. In several of the NIS films that were circulated mainly

Fig. 6.6. Laying underground drainage pipes by hand in machine-dug ditches on the newly made Noordoostpolder (Peaceful Conquest, *1950*) (*NIS archive, HCASC*).

(See endnote 2:29, p. 398, regarding the resolution of these stills.)

during the 1950s (e.g. *Peaceful Conquest*, 1950), one again sees and hears echoes of this war-related theme: the Netherlands does not take land belonging to others but makes its own land. *Peaceful Conquest*, with its oxymoronic title, carefully documents the making of the Noordoostpolder, the next drainage project in Lake IJssel—building the ring dike, pumping out and preparing the land for farming (fig. 6.6), and constructing the farmsteads and rural infrastructure.

National films

An always important group of films are surveys of (supposedly) the entire country or society, or those documentaries that speak to what they regard as the Netherlands' keystone qualities. Such national fields of vision attract larger audiences and make a substantial impact on the public perception of the country by those living outside its borders. They leave enduring impressions about the identity of the country as a whole or about its defining features. Recall that, these surveys and primers in the 1940s were largely American-made travelogues produced in the 1930s. These films fostered very outdated, folkloristic impressions of the country. During the 1950s, however, some Dutch-made national surveys made their way into the collection, although the NIS continued to acquire more of such films from non-Dutch producers.[6] Altogether, there are eleven documentaries that may be classified as national films, making up 38.8 percent (246,203) of the 1950s viewership.

The most important and influential film of this or any other genre in the NIS collection during the 1950s was the four-part series *Holland: A Modern Country Full of Old-Time Charm* (1952); the title was translated from the 1950 Dutch title.[7] This series was commissioned by the Dutch Economic Information Service and directed and produced by veteran Dutch filmmaker Max de Haas.[8] It was the first film of its kind released after the war. The film was screened in 1950, first for the Dutch public; soon thereafter, the film was released for distribution by the Dutch diplomatic corps in no fewer than seven other languages, including English. The film dramatically improved the overall attendance of NIS films, especially because there were sixteen television showings. In the Netherlands, its goal was to engender national unity and pride among a Dutch population divided, downtrodden, and demoralized by war and the German occupation. By featuring both the country's distinguished past *and* its modern achievements, the Dutch could begin to feel optimistic and energetic about their future once more.

Overall, *Holland: A Modern Country Full of Old-Time Charm* is cast in an economic mold, which is understandable, given its sponsor and the enormous un-

dertaking required to rebuild the country. Each of the four parts is about fifteen minutes long (suitable for a movie theater short) and covers several broad swaths of Dutch economic life, with the following four secondary titles for the English-language version: *Country and People*; *Industry and Handicrafts*; *Trade and Transport*; and *Agriculture and Stock-Farming*. In the region served by the Holland NIS, the series drew more than 180,000 viewers, but the viewership of the individual parts varied wildly. The first part, *Country and People* (140,451), saw more than 130,000 of those moviegoers and was the most popular film by far in the 1950s, outperforming by two-to-one the second most-viewed film, *Landbuilders*, a film from the 1930s. The other sections drew only a small fraction of the opening part: *Industry and Handicrafts* (25,179), *Agriculture and Stock-Farming* (10,551), and *Trade and Transport* (9,484).[9]

This series is perhaps the most transparent example of a dominant theme in the films about the Netherlands viewed during the 1950s, a theme captured perfectly by its title, *Holland: A Modern Country Full of Old-Time Charm*. Publics in other countries, such as the United States, needed to hold on to the iconic traditional imagery and, at the same time, move beyond it; the Netherlands would benefit from Americans adding a stock of knowledge that portrayed it as an up-to-date country with widely adopted, state-of-the-art technology, design, and modern conveniences throughout its economy and society.

Each of the four parts of this series presents its own balance of old and new. But it is revealing that the first part, *Country and People*, heavily favors the tradition

[6] See endnote 6:6, p. 403.

[7] See endnote 6:7, p. 403.

[8] For the career of the prolific Dutch filmmaker Max de Haas, see Bert Hogenkamp, *De Documentaire Film, 1945–1965. De Bloei van een Filmgenre in Nederland* (Uitgeverij 010, 2003), 105–8.

[9] See endnote 6:9, p. 404.

Fig. 6.7. Greengrocer punting his store through the water roads of Giethoorn (Holland: A Modern Country Full of Old-Time Charm, pt. 1, Country and People, *1952*) (*NIS archive, HCASC*)

and charm side of this balance (nearly 70% of the footage). All the venerable standbys make their appearance once again: windmills; regional costumes; bulb fields and flower tourism; traditional rural pastimes, such as tilting the ring in Zeeland and the Alkmaar cheese market; a parade of monumental historical buildings; towns, such as Volendam, Giethoorn (fig. 6.7), and historic Veere; and the art masterpieces of the golden age.

The other three parts of the series solidly lead with the modern side (from 85% to nearly 100% of the footage) and feature very little of the old. They show modern developments throughout the country, in manufacturing (blast furnaces, oil refineries, and factories for electrical appliances, foodstuffs, and textiles [fig. 6.8]), trade (modern shipbuilding, ports, cargo handling, and logistics), transportation (planes, trains, and automobiles and their infrastructure [fig. 6.9]), agriculture (plant and animal breeding, farm mechanization and high-yield commercial dairying, poultry [fig. 6.10]), and greenhouse production.

What is equally revealing and related to the old/new (charm/modern) balance is that the first and introductory part, *Country and People*—heavily invested in

Fig. 6.8. Modern carpet mill, part of the textile industry in Twente, Overijssel (Holland: A Modern Country Full of Old-Time Charm, pt. 2, Industry and Handicrafts, *1952*) (*NIS archive, HCASC*)

showing the "old-time charm"—drew 75 percent of the viewership for the entire series. Although it is true that this was the introduction to the series and, as such, would attract more viewers, it does underscore, as noted earlier for the 1940s, that American and Dutch American viewers were far less interested in the then current developments in the country than in its nostalgic and glorious past. The television broadcasts of this film series bring out the same imbalance: the first part was shown seven times and the other three parts, just three times each. Still another measure of this preference is that the two most-viewed films in the 1950s—*Country and People*, part 1 of *Holland: A Modern Country Full of Old-Time Charm*, and *Landbuilders*—

together garnered 196,678 viewers in the 1950s—31 percent of the total viewership of some seventy films. Both films are suffused with stock traditional imagery. Apparently, American viewers were not ready to see or much interested in the Netherlands as a country that enjoyed many of the same modern technical advancements as they did.

With the exception of *Roaming the Netherlands*—a silent travelogue devoted exclusively to familiar, old-time charm, with attendance almost entirely during the 1940s—other national compilation film surveys circulating during the 1950s also aimed to combine old and new. These enjoyed a combined 1950s viewership of 62,550: *The Dutch Way* (1950; 29,523),

Fig. 6.9. First divided highways (Holland: A Modern Country Full of Old-Time Charm, pt. 3, Trade and Transport, *1952*) (*NIS archive, HCASC*)

Happy Holland (1954; 24,062), *Holland Carries On* (1944; 60,335), *Land below the Sea* (late 1950s; 41,713), *Life in Holland: A Short Story about the Country on the North Sea* (1950; 6,690), and *Introducing the Netherlands* (1955; 9,491). Most were American-made films and so, again, because they were marketed by other film-distribution companies, they had far higher viewership numbers and impact than NIS circulation alone would have allowed. Differences between them rest on what ratios between old and new the directors and producers

had settled on and what old-time charm and modern developments they highlighted. These films do cover many of the same subject threads.

The Dutch Way and *Land below the Sea* were produced about a decade apart, the former during the late 1940s, and the latter during the late 1950s. Most of the total attendance of *Land below the Sea* took place during the 1960s/70s. Both films open with sea waves rushing toward the coast and show the environmental conditions and human environmental controls relat-

Fig. 6.10. Mechanized egg sorting (Holland: A Modern Country Full of Old-Time Charm, pt. 4, Agriculture and Stock-Farming, *1952*) (*NIS archive, HCASC*)

ed to water at work in creating the country. *Land below the Sea* presents a brief environmental history—which was a first—but one full of errors: sea dunes formed by deposition at river mouths, dune mounds connected by causeways to form a continuous barrier, and windmills invented by the Dutch to evacuate river floodwaters from the polders. *The Dutch Way* does a little better but wrongly asserts that the sea dunes would have "crumbled away" had it not been for the planting of Marram grass, a conservation measure not practiced until the early nineteenth century.

With an emphasis on the economic and technical sides, both films give a quick-paced overview of the country. The social, political, and religious aspects, however, are largely missing. Many modern technological, infrastructure, economic, and recreational scenes are juxtaposed with their premodern equivalents. The Alkmaar cheese market, warehouses and guildhalls from the Golden Age, a traditional Frisian wedding complete with an open carriage, and costumed farmers as well traditional fishing villages all make an appearance. But more recent developments and postwar reconstruction also have an equal place in these films: modern locks and current versions of boat portages (fig. 6.11), the IJssel Lake polders, Bauhaus architecture and residential housing (fig. 6.12), Formula 1 racing, enormous ship-

Fig. 6.11. Boat portage (*overtoom*) from canal to canal without water connection and at different levels, now with winch and rail (Land below the Sea, *late 1950s*)
(*NIS archive, HCASC*)

yards and busy ports with their dry-docks, bicycles (fig. 6.13) and their infrastructure, modern factories, export-oriented horticulture, and science-based plant and animal breeding. Somewhat surprisingly, not all the up-to-date developments are from the post-WWII era; many predate the war. The much admired, Dudok-designed city hall of Hilversum (fig. 6.14), for example, was completed in 1931.

Life in Holland: A Short Story about the Country on the North Sea (1950; 6,690), is a condensation of *Holland Carries On*, a compilation film carried over from the 1940s. To extend its circulation, along with its new title, footage related to the war was deleted to give this film a more "updated" look. It is ironic that the war-related material was actually the newer footage in this film. Most of it was from the 1930s and came, via *Holland Carries On*, from the film *Landbuilders* (*Walcheren*), and from Joris Ivens' *New Earth*. But because the greater half of this eight-minute-long film is about the massive national Zuiderzee polder project, it has a modern, forward-looking air, compared to the traditional imagery. And, when to this section

Fig. 6.12. Post WWII Dutch terrace housing (Land below the Sea, *late 1950s*)
(*NIS archive, HCASC*)

are added scenes, elsewhere in this film, of new modern housing, cars speeding by on highways, electrified trains, and Schiphol aviation (fig. 6.15), *Life in Holland* creates a somewhat more up-to-date canvas of the country. Of course, the geographic errors of *Holland Carries On* are also given extended life. For instance, footage of the island of Walcheren, Zeeland, is shown as newly settled land in the then completed IJssel Lake polders.

Introducing the Netherlands (1955; 9,491), another national survey, was part of the NATO film series, *The Atlantic Community*; it introduced each member state of this military alliance (in 1953) and sur-

veyed what they held in common.[10] The series may be seen as both acquainting the NATO states with each other and taking part in the Cold War propaganda efforts against countries belonging to the Warsaw Pact. The Netherlands and the United States were allies in the Cold War, and *Introducing the Netherlands* was the only film of its kind and tame compared to the intense ideological rhetoric of most Cold War cinema.[11] The NIS did not enter the Cold War propaganda war in earnest by

[10] This film is not in the archive but is available on YouTube.

[11] Consult, for example, Cyril Buffet, ed., *Cinema in the Cold War* (Routledge, 2016).

Fig. 6.13. Carrier bicycle outfitted for a window washer (Land below the Sea, *late 1950s*)
(*NIS archive, HCASC*)

assuring the American public and messaging the Warsaw Pact that it shared the ideology, geopolitics, and foreign policy goals of the United States and its allies. *Introducing the Netherlands* was made by Ytzen Brusse, a well-known Dutch director, part of the group of young Dutch moviemakers associated with the Dutch documentary school. Although beautifully filmed, with many different camera angles and distances, it was an entirely conventional film, with an encyclopedic format and an authoritative voice-over, without any of the more distinguishing hallmarks of this Dutch film style. The film was released in 1955, accessioned by NIS Holland

in 1958, and screened to more than twelve thousand viewers in nearly sixty places for more than a decade. It is important to underscore again that the NIS was not the sole distributor of this documentary in the United States.

Like other films in this group, *Introducing the Netherlands* also focused on modern developments especially in the economy and—given the interests of NATO—security. It opens and closes with a view along the Afsluitdijk, the barrier dam that closed a North Sea arm reaching deep into the country. Echoing the earlier NIB wartime hit, *Landbuilders*, the voice-over ends with the assertion that, even though

Fig. 6.14. The city hall of Hilversum (*The Dutch Way*, late 1940s) (*NIS archive, HCASC*)

a rapidly growing Dutch population needs more land, "only from the sea can it be taken," a reference to the historical territorial ambitions of war and the Dutch's peaceable taking of land from time immemorial. The film's closing shots show men and machines making more new land. For a film produced by a Dutch director to introduce the Netherlands to other countries, it contains some jarring inaccuracies: among others, that Dutch cities were built on timber piles to be safe from sea flooding.

Introducing the Netherlands devoted no footage or words to the destructive effects on the country of WWII and its aftermath. Rather, the remarkable economic progress and modernization of ports (fig. 6.16), agriculture, textiles, petrochemicals,

and electronics—all shown in the film— were made possible by postwar peacetime and NATO's commitment to defend that peace. The Dutch contributions to this military alliance are also featured—navy ships, amphibian forces, and readiness training exercises. Together with the other NATO members' films, *Introducing the Netherlands* showcased some of the common features worthy of protection in the Western societies making up NATO, such as parliamentary democracies, highly developed social services, trade and travel free from national restrictions, and economic planning and cooperation among employers, labor, and government. Historically, the Netherlands and the United States had been close allies, and NATO was

Fig. 6.15. Schiphol Airport in the 1930s, with seating for travelers and visitors outside
(Life in Holland: A Short Story about the Country on the North Sea, *1950*)
(*NIS archive, HCASC*)

now further proof of this continuing bond. Americans were interested in learning more about their fellow NATO members, including the Netherlands.

But not all these films tipped the scales in the direction of a modern country. *Happy Holland* (1954; 24,062),[12] for instance, took a much different approach to portraying Dutch identity for American audiences. In place of the economic

and technical sides—well suited to display modernity—this film highlights more of the cultural and recreational sides, naturally more given to tradition. As a result, the proportion between new and old slides toward the latter. The narration opens with "the Netherlands, where history steps out of the pages of a little Dutch story book." The settings were more contemporary, but the film capitalized on old American favorites: costumed dancers in wooden shoes, flowerbeds in Keukenhof, Amsterdam's canals, life and work in old fishing villages, and Frisian handball (*kaatsen*). There *are* modern scenes—bathers at Scheveningen's beach, children enjoying street puppet theater, and tourists at Madurodam (fig. 6.17),

---

12　The copy of *Happy Holland* in the NIB/NIS archive is missing the footage for the opening and closing credits. The film is not included in the Netherlands Institute for Sound and Vision, the Dutch national audiovisual archive, or any of the other relevant national archives. It is most likely an American-produced compilation film made up of segments from other Dutch films.

Fig. 6.16. Rejuvenation of the port of Rotterdam, where inland and ocean-going shipping come together (Introducing the Netherlands, *1955*. YouTube)

the park near Scheveningen, with 1:25 scale miniatures of famous Dutch buildings that had opened in 1952. But these scenes were familiar and not as easily associated with modernity as the advances in transportation, scientific research, factory technology, and farm machinery were. The film closes with a shot of four windmills along a waterway. *Happy Holland* is really a more up-to-date American travelogue.

Films about Dutch places and regions

Among the top fifty films that make up 98.8 percent of the 1950s viewership, there are only four that really focus on a Dutch region or place below the nation-al economic level: *Landbuilders, In and around Amsterdam, Friesland*, and *Hans Brinker's Return*. Together, these four films attracted 80,948 NIS-Holland filmgoers in the 1950s. Of these, only *Hans Brinker's Return* was acquired in the 1950s; *In and around Amsterdam* was added in 1949 and circulated predominantly during the 1950s.

Together with *Island of Faith* and *Broken Dykes*—both more topic and event oriented—*Landbuilders* continued the extraordinary attention these films lavished on the island of Walcheren and the province of Zeeland. *Landbuilders* alone added sixty thousand viewers to the nearly one hundred thousand from the 1940s. Like *Landbuilders, Friesland* had its greatest

Fig. 6.17. Madurodam (Happy Holland, *1954*.) (*NIS archive, HCASC*)

impact during the 1940s with more than thirty thousand viewers (see ch. 5). Nevertheless, the impact of their particular treatment of Walcheren and Friesland was extended into the 1950s and beyond. That leaves only two films, *In and around Amsterdam* (1949; 17,096) and *Hans Brinker's Return* (1954; 5,674), both principally about the city of Amsterdam and its wider region.

In different ways, both films carry forward the travelogue genre so prevalent in the made-in-America, culture-directed films about the Netherlands that were produced during the 1930s and shown by the NIB during the 1940s. Both also have an American flavor: *In and around Am-* *sterdam* is an American production,[13] and *Hans Brinker's Return*, commissioned by the RVD and made by a Dutch director, nevertheless, gives still more life to the American fiction of the Dutch boy who saved the community by putting his finger in a leaking dike.[14] Both films were

[13] *In and around Amsterdam* was produced by Maurice T. Groen, an American maker of travelogue films for DPM Productions and Films of the Nations distributors, based in NYC. Groen was also the producer of a number of other NIB/NIS-acquired films. The NIB/NIS archive has both a b&w and a color version of this film. There are errors in this film that would not have crept into a Dutch production. For example, the Kalverstraat, one of the principal shopping streets that starts at Dam Square is described as coming off the Muntplein. And the fishmonger is selling plaice or flounder (flatfish) not herring from his pushcart.

[14] See endnote 6:14, p. 404.

Fig. 6.18. Holding hands amid bicycle congestion on the streets of Amsterdam
(*In and around Amsterdam, ca. 1949*) (*NIS archive, HCASC*)

produced with English-language voice-over and dialogue; there is no record of a Dutch-language version of either film. They were intended for a non-Dutch, English-language viewership.

The American-made travelogue films of the 1930s, with titles like *Holland and the Dutch*, which referred to the entire country, were really formulaic films about Amsterdam, with a pivot to a nearby Zuiderzee fishing village, usually Volendam, and then on to the Alkmaar cheese market. The titles of these two films have more modest geographical aims. Both give a predominant visual focus to Amsterdam, but the old quaint ways of life not far from the capital city—the fishing/farming villages of Volendam and Bunschoten and the Alkmaar cheese market—are just too irresistible.

Amsterdam itself, with some exceptions, is shown still mainly as a collection of pre-eighteenth-century historical sites, both individual buildings, such as the Palace on the Dam, the Schreierstoren, the Oude Kerk, the Weigh House, and the Rembrandt House, and the larger scale attractions, such as the canal system with its associated residences and warehouses. More twentieth century are scenes of widespread use of the bicycle for personal mobility in congested streets (fig. 6.18). A

Fig. 6.19. Fishmonger preparing and selling flatfish from a pushcart (In and around Amsterdam, *ca. 1949*) (*NIS archive, HCASC*)

street barrel organ and a fishmonger selling from a pushcart (fig. 6.19) close out the section on Amsterdam in *In and around Amsterdam.*

Just like other films of the 1950s feature modern and postwar new Netherlands, these films also very briefly capture more areas of Amsterdam beyond those of the historic urban core. By 1950 the city had more than tripled in area, especially in a southerly direction but also to the north, across the IJ. In both of these documentaries, viewers are treated to scenes of preparing new land for development (fig. 6.20) and the thoroughly planned residential

quarters mandated by twentieth-century national housing laws (fig. 6.21) that put an end to laissez-faire, unit-by-unit construction. The film, however, ignores the large areas of crowded and poorly built nineteenth-century tenements, the result of the then unregulated construction industry. Of course, this is what one would expect from a promotional film.

The content of these two films is much the same, but their film style and technique could not be more different. *In and around Amsterdam* resembles the standard genre of nearly all the films examined thus far. Edited film scenes are independent units

Fig. 6.20. Driving concrete piles for new construction around Amsterdam
(Hans Brinker's Return, *1954*) (*NIS archive, HCASC*)

sequenced by geography or topic, and an authoritative voice-over describes, explains, and connects these scenes. *Hans Brinker's Return* has a much different cinematography, one that shows innovation, a trademark of the Dutch documentary film tradition at this time. The film begins with a Dutch American father and his young son deplaning from a DC-6 at Schiphol. The father is going to introduce his home country and Amsterdam—the city of his birth—to his son. The two characters are in every scene of the film, and the customary voice-over is a question-and-answer dialogue between them. Their presence and conversation at every place along the itinerary unifies the film. Viewers see what this father and son

see and experience and learn about various places via their dialogue. This brings the experience of visiting these places and appreciating and understanding them closer to the viewer than a more detached voice-over narration ever could. Unlike the single voice and interpretation of the narrator, dialogue also brings with it the possibility of introducing different points of view related to what the people in the film see and experience. Father and son may visit the same sites, but their perceptions are colored by, among other things, their age, roles, education, and previous experiences. In the film, the father is the teacher, and the son asks him questions and absorbs and processes his answers.

Fig. 6.21. Planned residential quarter in Amsterdam Zuid
(In and around Amsterdam, *ca. 1949*) (*NIS archive, HCASC*)

Hans Brinker's Return is pioneering in another respect as well. Documentaries, up until that time, were commonly quite serious treatments of a country, place, or topic; the goal was to inform and entertain viewers with interesting and instructive scenes with accompanying narration. Only rarely did filmmakers, by way of the narrator or of actual scenes, inject some lightheartedness into their documentaries. *Hans Brinker's Return* breaks new ground by sustaining a minor comedic thread throughout the film related to the Hans Brinker folklore. Here is an American boy who, like many American children, has read or heard about the Hans Brinker story. When, at the beginning of the film, he and his father visit the Afsluitdijk, between the North Sea and its former sea arm, IJssel Lake, he expresses his amazement to his dad that little Hans Brinker could put his finger into such an enormous dike and save the community. On two occasions, on their walk throughout Amsterdam, they come upon groups of boys and girls, thumbs in the air, flexing and readying them and the rest of their fingers for plugging holes in dikes (fig. 6.22).[15] These are genuinely funny (staged) scenes.

[15] It is curious that the future (female) Hans Brinkers in this film seem to be readying their thumbs (fig. 6.22) rather than their forefingers to stop dike leaks. Most visuals, including the statues, show the index finger as the stopper; using thumbs for this purpose would be rather improbable from an anatomical point of view. Perhaps they are exercising all their fingers.

Fig. 6.22. Dutch girls exercising their fingers for leaking-dike emergencies
(Hans Brinker's Return, *1954*) (*NIS archive, HCASC*)

The father dismisses these encounters, but his son becomes more convinced that an army of Dutch children is available as a first line of defense against flooding by plugging leaking dikes with their fingers. Toward the end of the film, as they walk together along the dike of IJssel Lake in the vicinity of Volendam, the son can no longer resist: he puts his finger to the test by plunging it into the dike and discovers it hurts to do so. In his father's mind, that settles the issue: Hans Brinker could never have prevented a dike leak—much less, a break—with his fingers. But, at the end of the film, even the father still remains ambivalent after they visit the statue of Hans Brinker in Spaarndam, close to Haarlem. The sculpture shows Hans with his finger in a dike. Why would the Dutch put up a statue to Hans Brinker if this act of heroism had never happened? This entire comedic thread is playful and imaginative, a continuation of the literary narrative of Mary Mapes Dodge and a welcome contrast to and break from the more serious purpose of imparting knowledge about the country and its capital.[16]

In conclusion, the earlier films about Dutch places that continued to be shown during the 1950s (*Landbuilders* and

---

[16] See endnote 6:16, p. 404.

Friesland) had traditional ways of Dutch life and the war's aftermath as their primary focus. The few new films about places—*In and around Amsterdam* and *Hans Brinker's Return*, both about Amsterdam—added to the NIS collection during the 1950s—continued the travelogue and tourist genre of the 1940s but in more up-to-date cinematic garb. Except for the national scale, few synoptic films about regions and places, large and small, were produced, and this trend has continued to the present day. Travelogues still dominate the genre, even though films about places could use many different scenarios and scripts and serve other purposes. Lists of Dutch-produced documentaries include few films about places; most are topical films with historical, biographical, scientific, and societal themes.[17]

Topical films

Twenty-eight (56%) of the top fifty films distributed by the NIS during the 1950s were topical films about the Netherlands; 234,790 filmgoers (37.4% of the top 50 viewership) went to see them. Except for the encompassing issue of water, these films covered different topics. Most were crossover films viewed in both the United States and the Netherlands.

Water: friend and foe

Landbuilders and *New Earth*—blockbusters in the 1940s and 1950s—had as their premise the struggle against and victory over water as a defining quality of Dutch identity. *New Earth* celebrated this triumph as a feat of engineering and human labor. This is also one important introductory theme in each of the national films of

the 1950s that have already been discussed. *Broken Dykes*, also carried forward from the 1940s, focused on the flip side—water as foe, in this case, as a scorched-earth strategy. Another seven films about this cornerstone relationship were added to the NIS-Holland film library during the 1950s: *Island of Faith* (1950; 29,336), *Stormramp* (Storm disaster) (1953; 13,931), *Peaceful Conquest* (1950; 7,728), *Life in Holland* (newsreel) (1953; 1,307), *And There Was No More Sea* (1955; 34,224), and *Men against the Sea* (1953; 10,712).[18] These may be seen as topical films elaborating on this one distinguishing feature of the country. More than one hundred thousand viewers saw these new films and those continuing from the 1940s in the NIS-Holland region during the 1950s. For these films, circulation outside of the NIS circuit was much more limited. Most were made by leading Dutch documentary filmmakers and directors, including John Ferno, Herman van der Horst, and Bert Haanstra.

If they knew anything about the country, Americans and others around the world had learned that the Netherlands was a small country, below the sea; it had won much land from the sea and its flood-prone coastal marshes, and it protected and maintained this land with dikes and windmills. This is certainly an ur-perception of the country, a preface to all the American-made travelogues shown in the 1930s and 1940s and of virtually every other film survey of the country as a whole that was shown to outsiders. As a group,

---

[17]   See endnote 6:17, p. 405.

[18]   *Men against the Sea* is not in the archive; it is listed in the British Film Institute collection but not by IMDb or the Dutch Institute for Sound and Vision. It is a film about the 1953 flood in the Netherlands. Because I was unable to view it, it is not included in the discussion here of the films about the Dutch and water.

Fig. 6.23. The assembly of prefab barns in the Noordoostpolder
(Peaceful Conquest, *1950*) (*NIS archive, HCASC*)

the films that focused on this theme of the Netherlands' relationship to water more exclusively during the 1950s delivered less triumphant and more nuanced and variegated knowledge about this subject. *Peaceful Conquest*, an American Films of the Nations release, filmed by Herman van der Horst and issued by the NIS and others, however, is an exception. This film does carry on the congratulatory, accomplishment-driven rhetoric, buttressed by the earlier antiwar message in the title, but most others in this group present the hazardous and more difficult sides of the country's relationships with water. *Peaceful Conquest* shows how new land is made

and furnished; the land drainage and regional planning for the Noordoostpolder is seen as applied science. Decisions about soil preparation, tile drainage, and the location and building of roads, farmsteads (fig. 6.23) and villages are based on carefully researched knowledge and standards.

The other six new films about the Dutch and water, however, have flood disasters and other cultural costs of land winning as subject matter. Throughout Dutch environmental history, regular damaging floods provided an important impetus for impoldering.[19] Some silent film foot-

---

[19]　In 2013, NTR, a Dutch public-service broadcaster that supplies educational and cultural programming for Dutch radio and television, released a

age was taken during the 1916 Zuiderzee flood—the disaster that led to the building of the barrier dam across the mouth of the Zuiderzee and to the IJssel Lake polders—but the craft of filmmaking had advanced, spread, and been institutionalized by the press, such that, major floods of the 1940s and 1950s could be documented much more fully with film.[20] These films make very clear that land taken from the sea is not a *fait accompli* as some earlier films had suggested; they make the relationship between people and water much more dynamic, with episodic winners and losers. Seawater, as well as lake and river water, can and does (re)flood occupied land, whether by storm on weakened dikes, breaching dikes in acts of war, or high-river flows that cause river dike failures. Moreover, when land takes the place of water, cultural ways of life based on water are displaced or extinguished.

The *national* films shown during the 1950s did headline water as friend *and* foe but included little to no footage of the destructive side. But John Ferno's films *Broken Dykes* and *Island of Faith* and the newsreels *Stormramp* and *Life in Holland* focused on water as a foe with all of its very unpleasant consequences. Together, they left a message about the Dutch and water

that was not nearly as triumphant as before. *Broken Dykes*, from the British Ministry of Information, and *Island of Faith*, from the Marshall Plan, both filmed by John Ferno, document the flood disaster and reconstruction that followed the bombardment in 1944 by the Allies of the dikes on Walcheren to dislodge German forces protecting the sea lane to the Belgian port of Antwerp. In *Broken Dykes*, a lead into *Island of Faith*, viewers see houses and barns on Walcheren collapsed, ruined by North Sea saltwater moving in with the tides; they are told that the saltwater was killing pastures and fruit trees and poisoning soil. Ferno uses footage from the 1930s film *Walcheren* (later, *Landbuilders*, 1940) to contrast this devastation with the prosperous rural landscape behind the dikes, built up over the centuries by hardworking Zeelanders. The people are depicted as courageous and accommodating during this flood and evacuation.

Island of Faith, a Marshall Plan film project, begins with the same, rather dated, human-powered pile drivers in action, shown at the conclusion of *Broken Dykes*; here they were used for constructing and repairing the dikes.[21] Again, this film shows thriving agricultural land secured by dikes for centuries until the bombardment of these sea walls in December 1944. The film is really part 2 of *Broken Dykes*, and its footage sets the stage with the destruction of buildings and the evacuation of the population and cattle. The new foot-

---

seven-part film series, *Nederland in Zeven Overstromingen*. It provides an overview of the history of floods in the Netherlands and how they helped shape Dutch identity and culture. *Nederland in Zeven Overstromingen*, Just Bridge Entertainment, 2014. The standard scholarly work on the history of floods in the Low Countries is M. K. E Gottschalk, *Stormvloeden en Rivieroverstromingen in Nederland*, 3 vols. (Van Gorcum, 1971–77).

[20] For film footage of the 1916 flood, consult the Eye Filmmuseum Nederland, http://www.filminnederland.nl/film/storm-en-noodweer-nederland; see also, YouTube, *Watersnood in Noord-Holland*, 1916.

[21] *Island of Trust* or *Confidence* would have been a better translation of *Eiland van Vertrouwen* than *Island of Faith*. The word "faith" is too readily associated with religious faith. It is not that Zeelanders lacked religious faith—on the contrary—but this film underscored that they inspire confidence and have faith in the future.

Fig. 6.24. The Visser farmstead moves from Walcheren, Zeeland, to the Noordoostpolder (*Island of Faith, 1950*) (*NIS archive, HCASC*).

age shows the environmental restoration with the help of government experts: repairing the dikes, pumping the land dry, removing flood-deposited sand from the upper soil layer, planting trees, and cultivating the land in such a way that the flood-borne salt leaches down farther into the soil, beyond the roots of the crops. Cultural restoration is next: barns and houses are rebuilt, farmers and cattle return, and pastures and cropland begin the road back to productivity.

But the goal is not just the restoration of the prewar agricultural way of life. More than half of *Island of Faith*—like other

films of the 1950s—shows further modernization and commercialization of the rural landscape with help of counterpart funds from the United States Marshall Plan and assistance from Dutch government agricultural experts. Documented in the film are the consolidation of scattered holdings, the leveling of land to even out soil moisture, the moving of field drainage underground to facilitate larger-scale mechanical cultivation and harvesting, and the building of new roads to bring products to market more easily.

The implementation of these economies of scale also makes clear that there are too many farmers on the land. The film follows the Visser family as they and their livestock move—with government help—to the new land and farms of the Noordoostpolder (fig. 6.24). John Ferno employs a film technique then little used in documentary films. He follows two families as they rally from the flood disaster—one stays on the island, and the other leaves. This draws viewers into their personal stories. But leaving Walcheren is not a defeat brought on by the flood.

Agricultural productivity is enhanced by government-sponsored out-migration, and the farming expertise is transferred to new land gained from the sea in the Noordoostpolder. Although the film is all about government assistance and intervention, the camera is trained on the people themselves. They apply these changes to their farming, and the film voice-over concludes: "The old values which brought them through will still endure in them: courage, hard work, and faith." Like other Marshall Plan films, *Island of Faith* gave American audiences an opportunity to see the very real results of American aid in the lives of ordinary Dutch farmers.

Less than a decade later, a much more calamitous flood struck the entire province of Zeeland and parts of Zuid-Holland and Noord-Brabant, although, interestingly, very little of Walcheren, the island featured in John Ferno's films, was affected. The breaching of the dikes of Walcheren in 1944 was planned and controlled, not caused by storms and high tides; it caused much environmental and property damage but little or no loss of life, and the evacuation was quite orderly. This flood, on January 31–February 1, 1953, was caused by a heavy storm and high tides and cost more than eighteen hundred people throughout

the southwest of the country their lives. Its aftermath was filmed more than any other previous national flood, and for Americans who viewed films about the 1953 flood, the reality of this hazard as part of Dutch identity became very real and tempered the triumphant perceptions of the Dutch and water.

Stormramp (Storm disaster) (13,931), *Life in Holland* (likely mistitled) (1,307), and *Watersnood 1953* (376) were produced by Polygoon-Profilti and Multifilm, commercial makers of popular newsreels for theaters in the Netherlands. All three have Dutch narration and so were seen by mainly Dutch American audiences, still able to understand the language, and others drawn to the imagery and visual narrative of the disaster. The other film about the disaster, *Men against the Sea* (10,712)—not in the archive—has an English voice-over. It is puzzling why these Dutch-language films about the 1953 flood were part of the collection, given the purpose of the NIS, the small potential audience, and the sympathy and understanding the films would have generated among the larger American public. An English-subtitled film, based on *Watersnood 1953*, was available but not acquired by NIS-Holland.[22] In the Netherlands, these were newsreels, available to moviegoers for only a short time after the disaster. From Holland-NIS, they were available for more than a decade, although attendance peaked in the first few years. Long after the 1953 flood, moviegoers in the United States could see and learn about this consequential disaster.

The first part of *Stormramp* is an aerial survey of villages and towns on the delta

---

22 Parts of *Watersnood 1953* were put into *Flood 1953*, with English-language subtitles inserted into the film.

Fig. 6.25. With help from the armed forces, flood evacuees get into amphibious vehicles, and others wait their turn (Stormramp, *1953*) (*NIS archive, HCASC*).

islands that were struck and destroyed by the flood and their death tolls. In succeeding sections, viewers see bodies removed in caskets, people fleeing *en masse* along dike roads, and others rescued from their homes by an international flotilla of helicopters and amphibious vehicles, many provided by American forces stationed in West Germany (fig. 6.25). The scenes in *Stormramp* are far more grim and dramatic than those in *Broken Dykes*. The presence in the disaster zone and evacuation centers of members of the Dutch royal family, especially Prince Bernhard, but also Queen Juliana, receives much attention in the film.

Whereas *Stormramp* is an aerial survey of the more familiar, hard-hit center of the disaster—the islands of the delta, also the focus of the international media—*Life in Holland* focuses on the perimeter, the zone more accessible from nonflooded lands to film crews on the ground. Together, these two newsreels provide comprehensive regional coverage of the 1953 flood. *Life in Holland* shows damage in locations not commonly shown to have been impacted by the February 1 storm and flood: coastal resorts, harbors, and industrial centers in the provinces of Noord- and Zuid-Holland, such as IJmuiden, Noordwijk, Katwijk, Hoek van Holland, Maassluis, and Vlaardingen. Viewers are informed about ruined beach boulevards, wrecked ships, and breached dunes in these places.

Fig. 6.26. Cattle transport assembled in Papendrecht, north of Dordrecht, to evacuate livestock herded by farmers from surrounding flooded polders out of the region (Life in Holland, *1953*) (*NIS archive, HCASC*)

They see people coping with flooded urban neighborhoods in Rotterdam, Dordrecht, and Papendrecht, cities not at the disaster's center of public attention. They learn about extensive flooded polders and the evacuation of people and cattle in the Alblasserwaard (fig. 6.26), a rural region well east of Rotterdam and Dordrecht.

Life in Holland films the situation on the ground in a broad semicircle around the core of disaster, the islands of the delta. This core suffered the greatest loss of life and destruction of property and infrastructure, but this film showed American moviegoers that the storm had also im-pacted a much larger region of the western Netherlands.

Besides the continuing vulnerability to flooding from storms and high water, there are other variables that make drainage of waterbodies to make new land something less than an unmitigated success. Throughout Dutch environmental history, there has been opposition to drainage projects from fishing, shipping, and trading interests, all facing the loss of these activities and their way of life. Examples include draining the many lakes in the western part of the country from the seventeenth century to the nineteenth century, as well

Fig. 6.27. Hanging out the wash with temporary posts and lines over the quay of a fishing village along IJssel Lake—no clothespins are used; corners of the laundry are wedged between strands of the clotheslines (And There Was No More Sea, *1955*) (*NIS archive, HCASC*).

as the Zuiderzee drainage project and the Delta Plan for the southwest Netherlands during the twentieth century.

Today, the opposition is largely from environmental organizations and their constituencies. The long era of "Dredge, drain, and reclaim" has largely ended in the Netherlands as the country makes *more* room for coastal and inland (river) waters when floods occur and appreciates the ecological services and recreational value of intact fresh and saltwater environments. Gone is the national need for more farmland to feed a rapidly growing popula-

tion; today the Netherlands is edging closer to zero population growth and is the world's second largest food exporter.[23] It is, however, important to underscore that, during the entire lifespan of the NIB/NIS, "Dredge, drain, and reclaim" remained the ruling national paradigm.[24]

[23] "The Netherlands is the second-largest exporter of agricultural products. See the cutting-edge technology that makes it possible," *The Washington Post*, 26 Nov. 2022. Online edition. Documentary film, "Food for Thought," Kadir van Lohuizen, VPRO, 2022.

[24] The classic text for the long Dutch national drive to make land from water is Johan Van Veen, *Dredge,*

The film, *And There Was No More Sea* (1956; 34,224) addresses one such drawback of changing water into land in relation to the impoldering of the Zuiderzee and makes this monumental project—also for American viewers—less of a resounding, once-and-for-all triumph. It visually documents the impending loss of the age-old fishing communities and cultures around the shore of the Zuiderzee—towns and cities such as Hoorn, Elburg, Urk, Hindeloopen, Kampen, Spakenburg, and Volendam. The film is by Bert Haanstra, a master among Dutch documentary filmmakers, known for his visual poetry.[25] Rather romantically, Haanstra focuses his camera precisely on the traditional features of these fishing places admired by Americans in general and Dutch Americans in particular: period costumes with elaborate lace caps, a wedding with folkloristic dancing, Dutch gables, clothes drying from lines on sticks strung across the street and quay (fig. 6.27), fishing boats hoisting their sails and setting out to sea, and fish catches hauled in and stored on board. Throughout, he uses close-up shots of individuals and groups from these local cultures. Although the filming is far more imaginative and accomplished and serves a much larger thematic purpose than the American-made travelogues shown by the NIB during the 1940s, the subject matter is remarkably similar; twenty minutes of this twenty-two-minute documentary showcase the centuries-old culture of these fishing villages. The footage was irresistible to American and Dutch American viewers.

Not until the last part of the film—when dike-building activities and reclaimed land with farms and their villages come into view—does it become apparent that these much admired and distinctive *genres de vie* are coming to an end. With resignation, fishermen stare at cranes building a new dike, and at a traditional graveside ceremony—representing a farewell to their culture—mourners are distracted by a steam shovel noisily discharging earth into water. At the end, the film's focus changes to the land newly won from the sea, furnished with the stuff of modernity: mechanized farming, churchgoers in modern attire (but with one couple in traditional costume) (fig. 6.28), cars, and a contemporary built environment.

NIS-Holland did not add *And There Was No More Sea* to its film library until 1958. Only 1,187 people saw the film in the 1950s, and the viewership continued to be very modest until 1965. But then, the film really took off with from five- to ten thousand viewers a year, taking nineteenth place among all the films about the Netherlands (1943–74). The growing international renown of Haanstra was certainly in play in the belated popularity of the film. It joined a group of popular films that met the American taste for the more traditional iconic and place-based ways of life in the country and added an extra level of nostalgia by dramatically showing their imminent loss.

All in all, the films shown during the 1950s (and later) that looked at the Dutch and water parsed this association in more

---

Drain and Reclaim: The Art of a Nation (Nyhoff, 1948). On the evolving and present-day paradigm shift in the relationships between water and the Dutch, see Tracy Metz and Maartje van Den Heuvel, *Sweet and Salt: Water and the Dutch* (NAi, 2012).

25   For Haanstra's career as filmmaker, see Hans Schoots, *Bert Haanstra. Filmer van Nederland* (Mets en Schilt, 2009).

Fig. 6.28. Church attendance in a new town in the Zuiderzee polders at the end of the film (And There Was No More Sea, *1955*) (*NIS archive, HCASC*)

detail, noting costs as well as benefits—the continuing water hazards in drained lowlands, the loss of ecological value, and the actual reclamation techniques and practices for occupying and furnishing the new lands.

Other topical films

There were twenty-one additional topical films among the top fifty documentaries (99% of the attendance) screened during the 1950s and seen by 137,790 filmgoers. Six are not in the archive and three—*They Said It with Tulips* (1946), *Holland Blooms Again* (1945), and *Two Queens* (1948)—carried over from the 1940s. Thir-

teen of these 1950s films remained in the library for all or part of the period from 1960 to 1974, extending their influence on American perceptions of the Netherlands.

Many different interlocking factors influenced viewership. With important exceptions, those documentaries with higher overall attendance often highlighted some internationally recognized contribution of the Netherlands, such as bulb and flower horticulture (*Holland: Garden of Europe*, ca. 1950; 20,542, and *Springtime in Holland*, 1954; 23,705), carillons (*Bells of Holland*, 1951; 26,575), the Royal Family (*Two Queens*, 1948; 16,459), and the dairy sector (*Land of Milk*, 1953; 11,841).

But other Dutch brands, such as herring (*Herring Fishing*, ca.1956; 3,485, and *Shoot the Nets*, 1951; 2,059) and the country as a water land (*The Amphibian Postman*, 1954; 1,866), fared surprisingly less well. Some less familiar Dutch subjects to outsiders, such as the postal service (*It's Just a Postage Stamp*, 1952; 8,081), did draw a respectable number of viewers, but others, for example, sculpture (*Mediaeval Dutch Sculpture*, 1951; 5,832) and banking (*Holland's Farmers Became Bankers*, ca. 1954; 942), drew smaller audiences overall.

Crossover films with perceived Dutchness

I will first examine those topical films that tie into an aspect of the Netherlands about which there was already some international acquaintanceship. As with other films from the 1950s, a subject could sometimes be given a more traditional treatment and interpretation and at other times, more modern. Of course, other films, beyond those that featured drainage, polders, dikes, and floods more narrowly, also tied into the Netherlands a special relationship with water. Whether the subject was fisheries, water sports, transportation, national defense, or landscape painting, the country's geographic fundamentals—maritime location, elevation in relation to sea level, and delta environment rich in water features of every kind—affected and colored every topic. *The Amphibian Postman: A Postal Delivery between Reeds and Rush* (1951; 1,886), commissioned by the Dutch Postal and Telecommunication Service, is clearly one such film.

American viewers should not have been surprised that the Dutch have an amphibian postal service; it is a fitting Dutch touch. Mail delivery by boat is shown for the Biesbosch (Dutch for "rushwoods"), a large region of freshwater tidal wetlands with rivers and islands of willow forests, wet grasslands and reeds, set between Dordrecht and Geertruidenberg, mainly in the province of Noord-Brabant. People of the area, however, had not always depended on water to get around. Before the St. Elizabeth Day flood of 1421, it was an agricultural polder with villages. Then it became a tidal wetland again for the next four centuries, but beginning in the nineteenth century, much of the area was again slowly being reclaimed and recolonized, and it is in this time frame that *The Amphibian Postman* was filmed.

At the end of the twentieth century and continuing today, the Dutch government began to buy out many farmers to allow water to inundate much of the polder landscape (Dutch—*ontpolderen*) and return the area to its natural state for reasons of ecology, flood control, and recreation. There was little or no need for water-based access to services anymore.

The film shows an orange postal cabin motorboat towing a rowboat with two letter carriers leaving Drimmelen, a small town on the southern border of the Biesbosch. Once they enter the area, the two go their separate ways: the motorboat stays on the major rivers with sufficient depth and the rowboat negotiates the shallow creeks. The timing of mail delivery depends on the tides. Both boats help deliver (and pick up) mail to farms, vacation spots, and pleasure craft locations (fig. 6.29) along and inland from the rivers and creeks. And it is not just mail delivery at the water's edge; walking is as important for these letter carriers as rowing and piloting because farms may be more than an hour of walking away

Fig. 6.29. Amphibian postman delivering mail to a vacation boat in the Biesbosch (The Amphibian Postman, A Postal Delivery between Reeds and Rush, *ca. 1954*) (*NIS archive, HCASC*)

from where the mail boat is moored.

In the film, the Biesbosch is shown under ideal conditions; viewers see these amphibian mailmen on very calm waters, under generally sunny skies and—judging from the farming scenes and leisure activities—in warmish temperatures. The film ends by noting that, even with icy winds, frozen water, driving rain, slippery roads, and limited visibility, these mail carriers will be on the job. The US Postal Service creed, "Neither snow nor rain nor heat nor gloom of night stays these couriers from the swift completion of their appointed rounds" apparently applied to these Dutch letter carriers as well.

Carillons are not as readily associated with the Netherlands as water drainage and dikes, but those knowledgeable about music and musical instruments are aware that carillons have their roots in the Low Countries. *Bells of Holland* (1951; 26,575) is a very instructive, nine-minute film about the craft of designing the shape and pitch of the carillon bells, the construction of the molds, and the casting of the bells. The middle two-thirds of the film details the technical aspects and craftsmanship of building such an instrument.

Carillons originated in the Low Countries in the sixteenth century. Here, the skill of playing them is well preserved

Fig. 6.30. Hoisting carillon bells aboard for export (Bells of Holland, *ca. 1951*)
(*NIS archive, HCASC*)

and carried on; here they are still manufactured and exported all over the world. They are present throughout this area in large numbers in houses of worship and public buildings and are played and enjoyed more than in other parts of the world. The association of this musical instrument with the Low Countries made a carillon and bell tower a logical and very appropriate public diplomacy gift in 1954 to the American people from the Dutch government in gratitude for all the help the Netherlands received from the United States during and after WWII; it stands at Arlington National Cemetery.

In the bookends of the film, the moviegoer hears carillons playing from different ancient church towers and civic buildings in the heart of old Dutch cities, one complete with a hand-operated drawbridge. They see men and women in traditional costume listening to a carillonneur testing a new instrument in public before it is shipped overseas (fig. 6.30). The framing of the film is entirely in iconic traditional imagery.

The same can be said of the films *Springtime in Holland* (1954; 23,705) and *Holland: Garden of Europe* (ca. 1950; 20,452), which, after *Bells of Holland*, were the most frequented films in this group. All three are in the top fifty in attendance among the more than two hundred films shown during the entire 1943–74 period.

Fig. 6.31. Guiding a flower-filled boat with poles through narrow canals to market
from Aalsmeer to Amsterdam (Holland: Garden of Europe, *ca. 1950*)
(*NIS archive, HCASC*)

These two films are about the Dutch flower industry. *Garden of Europe*, produced for the NIS, films the growing and marketing of cut flowers and potted plants in Aalsmeer, a world center of commercial flower growing southwest of Amsterdam. *Springtime in Holland*, an industry film, produced by the Associated Bulb Growers of Holland, is set mainly in the bulb-growing region between Haarlem and Leiden. The Dutch love for flowers—a national passion—their skills in plant cultivation and breeding, and their international export of flowers are well known to many outsiders. Flower gardens have helped fuel Dutch tourism since WWII, and Keukenhof, near

Lisse, Zuid-Holland, one of the largest in the world, has been a top destination in the Netherlands since 1950, with Americans one of the largest groups of its visitors. Floriade, an international flower and garden festival, has been held every ten years at different locations in the Netherlands since 1960; it also draws large numbers of international tourists. These skills, exports, and visitor attractions have made flower growing and tourism a very important domestic and international part of the Dutch economy.

With scene after scene of close-ups of flowers, flowerbeds, flower gardens and outdoor retail stalls, as well as commercial bulb and flower fields, the overall impact of these two films is largely aesthetic, and this, I think, does help account for their popularity. Viewers see only the results—the seas of flowers—and not the entire cultivation cycle. *Garden of Europe* captures the abundance of flowers in the everyday Dutch environment of parks, roads, and homes. It documents the harvesting of different varieties of commercial cut flowers and potted plants in the fields and greenhouses of Aalsmeer, south of Amsterdam, and the last part of the film pays significant visual attention to the transport of the flowers to outdoor retail outlets and markets in that city.

For American viewers, *Garden of Europe* privileges favored traditional settings. The film begins and ends in old Amsterdam as the Venice of the north, with its historic and distinctive canal network, towers, bridges, homes and warehouses. It talks about a modern city but shows the environment of the much-admired old historic core. The film's voice-over explains that any and all means of transport, including refrigerated trucks, are used to move flowers from Aalsmeer to Amsterdam, but the camera lingers nostalgically over the flat-bottomed barges, guided by men with poles walking alongside the canals all the way to the capital, the century-old way of delivering flowers to market (fig. 6.31).

Springtime in Holland might as well be publicity for bulb-flower sightseeing, a national and international destination already well established in the 1950s. The more immediate goal of this industry film becomes clear toward the end: to encourage American park managers and homeowners to buy Dutch bulbs for their flower beds and gardens by pointing to their availability at local dealers, reasonable prices, flo-

ral variety, and ease of cultivation. Visual instructions for planting, care, and garden design are included. The larger context of the film is the recovery of the Dutch bulb industry from the economically devastating war years.

The greater part of the film places flowering bulb fields squarely into the tourist iconography. Before they arrive at the subject of the film, viewers, in the introduction, are led past windmills, grazing Frisian Holsteins in a polder landscape, the Alkmaar cheese market, Volendammers in costume, and a boat guided from the bank with a pole through an urban canal.

From there on in, different and brightly colored flowering bulb fields take center stage as elongated carpets of crocuses, daffodils, hyacinths and, especially, tulips, in their many varieties of shapes and colors. The working, bulb-growing landscape also receives attention: mows of straw for protecting the bulbs in winter, drainage and transportation canals for the cut flowers and other farm materials, and the laborious manual labor of cutting the flowers to benefit the bulbs. And part of that working landscape is tourism; moviegoers see boats filled with tourists making their way through the waterways to give ready visual access to the flowering bulb fields.

Other cultural spin-offs and attractions of bulb growing are also shown, in particular, the decorative arts and celebrations made possible by the enormous surplus of cut flowers. Floral arrangements on the ground in parks and gardens make a statement and create an impression. Throughout the country—but especially in the bulb-growing regions—the immensely popular flower parades and pageants (Dutch-*bloemencorso's*), with their themed floats, completely covered in intricate pat-

Fig. 6.32. Float in a flower pageant thanking the Marshall Plan
(Springtime in Holland, *ca. 1954*) (*NIS archive, HCASC*)

terns of flowers of all colors, take such flower arranging to an entirely higher level. *Springtime in Holland* shows a cut-flower arrangement in a park with an American and a Dutch flag, telling its viewers—in flowers—that the Marshall Plan helps the Netherlands. One of the floats in the parade has "Thank You Marshall" (fig. 6.32) written in flowers on a flower heart and another has "U.S.A" written on its side with several women waving from it, backed by a Dutch flag. Such Dutch ties to the United States strengthened the attractiveness of the film for American audiences.

Although the Netherlands may be less well known abroad as the land of milk, it is very well known for a milk prod-

uct—cheese. *Land of Milk* (1953; 11,841), commissioned by the Dutch Dairy Bureau—and, therefore, another promotional industry film—has an entirely modern look from beginning to end. That may have something to do with the fact that the film was first produced in 1953, not for English—but for Dutch-speaking viewers (Dutch title, *Land van Melk*). A year later, an English-language version was released. In Holland-NIS, it had remarkable staying power, and in the 1960s and 1970s, it added another 8,572 viewers from eleven additional locations, six thousand alone from a television broadcast in Columbus, Ohio. *Land of Milk* is an example of a reasonably successful NIS film that did not pander to

Fig. 6.33. Vats for automated cheese curdling in a modern Dutch dairy factory (Land of Milk, *1953*) (*NIS archive, HCASC*)

the preferred American tastes for Dutchness.

The film does not neglect the historic crafts, looks, and rituals of the cheese trade in such places as Gouda, Edam, and Alkmaar but covers them only as the seventeenth-century beginnings of what is today the most important Dutch farm industry. Throughout the film, one sees the Netherlands of the 1950s with modern clothing, housing and domestic scenes, schools, sports, transportation, and factories. The focus falls not so much on dairy farming but more squarely on the modern Dutch dairy industry with its factory production of pasteurized milk, condensed milk, milk powder, butter, and cheese. The

film visually underlines the Netherlands' general economic importance, productivity, efficiency, mechanization, use of science, competitiveness, and public-health measures. Viewers see the manufacture of powdered milk using the process of spray drying in heated towers and heated steel rollers. They see Dutch school children drinking milk in the classroom and on the playing field. They witness the steps in the factory production of cheese (fig. 6.33). They observe the evaporation vats for making evaporated milk. They see the efforts and technology to safeguard the quality of dairy products in the factory laboratories. Overall, *Land of Milk* provides an up-to-date look at the Dutch dairy industry and

Fig. 6.34. Packing gutted and salted herring into barrels onboard for harborside delivery (Herring Fishing, *ca. 1956*) (*NIS archive, HCASC*)

broadens international knowledge about this industry in the Netherlands beyond its most recognized export, Edam and Gouda cheeses.

Inland, coastal, and high-seas fishing are part of the diverse relations of the Netherlands with water as a maritime nation and lake-rich land. But unlike the Dutch water technologies of polders, enclosing dikes, sluices, and drainage mills, fishing cultures did develop in most other maritime countries. Fishing villages, with their distinctive local folk attire, housing, and customs, were part of the Dutch iconography in the United States as the NIB

travelogue films shown during the 1940s confirm. Dutch fishing villages—like those of other European maritime countries—go back to the Middle Ages and in time developed characteristic localisms. *And There Was No More Sea* is a lament for the Zuiderzee fishing villages cut off from their traditional livelihood and facing extinction of their cultures. Fishing villages and towns with direct access to the North Sea, such as IJmuiden, Katwijk, Scheveningen, and Vlaardingen, faced no such threats to their livelihood. The focus of the earlier films was very much on the village around the harbor, and except for the boats setting out for the fishing grounds and the mending of nets, there was little visual attention on the fishery itself. Two somewhat similar films, *Shoot the Nets* (1951; 2,059) and *Herring Fishing* (ca. 1956; 3,485), set in Scheveningen and IJmuiden, on the North Sea, enhance the knowledge of Americans about these fishing cultures by following the fishing boats out to sea and documenting the catch and the onboard processing of the fish. They also move beyond a premodern rendering (common to films screened in the 1940s) to a more modern image, one that still shows traces of the traditions but is not defined by them.

Both films are about herring, the largest and best known of the Dutch fisheries and the one with the most cultural embellishment. *Herring Fishing* has the look and feel of an industry film. It covers the complete activity cycle: preparation, departure, and voyage to the fishing grounds, putting out and taking in the nets, onboard processing of the catch (gutting, salting, storage in barrels) (fig. 6.34), and the return, processing, and marketing. It pays lots of attention to the certification of quality and diverse herring products for consumption. *Shoot the Nets*, directed by Herman van der Horst, a Marshall Plan film—winner of the best documentary of 1952 in Cannes—has more of an artistic quality provided by carefully planned filming and creative editing. This film restricts itself to the preparations for setting out to sea and to the fishing activities themselves; the lens follows the choreography of the fishermen's work. The Dutch version, *'T Schot is te Boord*, is available in two parts on YouTube.

In *Shoot the Nets*, moviegoers see boats inspected and repaired, women mending nets, wagons piled high with nets making their way to the boats, nets rolled into the hold, barrels for storing herring repaired, and foodstuffs brought on board. Both films show the celebration of "flag day" before the fleet's departure: the boats are decorated with flags and, when they later put out to sea, they are seen off by the entire town (the way flag day was originally celebrated in the Netherlands). *Herring Fishing* also includes footage of what had become an important national tradition in the herring fishery: the race to bring the first new herring (Dutch: *Hollandse Nieuwe*) of the season into port for auction. For the winning boat, crew, and fishing port, this was a reason for celebration, including savoring the new raw herring.

The film documents the use of both the traditional drift net as well as the newer trawl net, a technology that increasingly took over. *Shoot the Nets* sticks with the drift net. It masterfully shows the strenuous labor required to pull miles-long drift nets out of the hold and into the water late in the day and then, in the middle of the night, the even greater effort required to haul them back in, all the while shaking out the herring trapped in the mesh of the net (fig. 6.35).

A number of different processing techniques are documented in these films, both on board and on land. Herring caught with drift nets are shown gutted onboard (gibbing) with a single knife stroke in the same manner these catches had been processed for centuries; this preserved the quality of the meat. Once gutted, they are then salted and sealed in wooden barrels, brought into the harbor at the end of the expedition, and marketed as well as enjoyed on site as fresh herring. In *Herring Fishing*, the harvest from the trawl net is shown sorted, gutted, iced, salted, and stored in barrels in the hold of the ves-

Fig. 6.35. The miles-long drift net, laden with herring trapped in the mesh by their gills, is hauled in and shaken by the fishermen for hours on end
(Shoot the Nets, *1951*) (*NIS archive, HCASC*)

sel (fig. 6.34). Once on land, the catch is off-loaded, transported in cold storage wagons, and further processed into fresh, brined, smoked, and pickled herring products for home consumption and export.

More than other topical documentaries, these two films about the herring fishery leave the earlier nostalgic stock imagery of Dutch fishing cultures behind and present a more practical labor- and business-oriented account of the industry. The

films occupy a point in the centuries-old Dutch history of the herring fishery when ever-larger vessels, factory ships, international competition, labor-saving technology, advanced nets, modern sonar tracking of fish, and ship-to-ship and ship-to-shore communication all began to change the industry forever. Once the pride of the Netherlands, today very few Dutch vessels are engaged in the herring fishery; the industry has internationalized to the point where one can buy plenty of herring in the country's shops and markets, but the Dutch herring fishery is almost completely gone.[26]

Yet, the imagery of the earlier Dutch fishing villages bulks large in the cultural memory of both the Dutch public and other people abroad. Villages such as Marken and others have become Disneyesque, open-air tourist places, where visitors can make their perceptions come to life. Dutch filmmakers have also produced materials that match and further develop these tourist tastes, making it possible to enjoy and learn about these fishing places without visiting them; alternatively, such movies may well act as a spur to actual visits. Such films are really more highly developed, well-crafted, homegrown versions of the travelogues about such places seen by Americans and others around the world in the 1930s.[27]

Just as with cheese and fishing villages, the Dutch royal family, in spite of American antimonarchical and pro-republican sentiments, was and is also relatively well known and admired in the United States, albeit not to the same degree as the British

monarchy. Both Queen Wilhelmina and Crown Princess/Queen Juliana visited the United States a number of times during the lifetime of the NIB/NIS. The film *Two Queens* (1948; 16,459) comes with an English-language narration and repackages the Dutch newsreel footage of the abdication by Queen Wilhelmina and the ascension to the throne by her daughter Queen Juliana, during the first week of September in 1948. The film was a DPM production in New York City, a company and production team headed again by Maurice T. Groen who worked with NIB/NIS to produce and cooperate on a number of other films. *Two Queens* belongs as much to the 1940s as to the 1950s. In a relatively short period of time, from 1949 to 1954, it was seen by more than sixteen thousand viewers in twenty-five places, including seven thousand viewers at Holland's Tulip Time in 1949. Nearly ten thousand people saw *Two Queens* in 1949, the year the film was accessioned; in the years following, attendance quickly dropped off, a not unexpected pattern for a current event.

Two Queens shows that week's pageantry—the events most likely to interest an international public, including American viewers. Moviegoers took in the last visit to the Dutch parliament in The Hague by the queen and crown princess, complete with a parade of women in regional costumes; the abdication by Queen Wilhelmina on the balcony of the Palace on the Dam; the introduction of the future Queen Juliana and her family to the crowd assembled on Dam Square and on the parade route through Amsterdam; the procession into the *Nieuwe Kerk* by dignitaries and royal guests, followed by the royal family itself (fig. 6.36); and the inauguration of Queen Juliana and her oath of office. Another

---

[26] The 2013 documentary *Hollandse Nieuwe* (*Raw Herring*) about a herring fishing expedition aboard the ships *Wiron 5* and *Wiron 6* out of Scheveningen makes the point that these are the only two ships in the country after herring still flying the Dutch flag. The *Wiron* ships are state-of-the-art, factory ships with the latest communication, remote sensing, conveying, lifting, automation, and refrigeration technology. Herring are sucked out of purse nets, pumped directly into the holds, processed, and packed into tubs or flash frozen.

[27] A good example is the Holland Heritage series, by Dutch filmmaker Menno Mennes. In Dutch and English, the series covers, among others, fishing villages, windmills, flower parades, river ferries, and winter scenery. The film in this series about fishing villages is of Marken, *Old Fishing Villages-Marken*, 2012.

Fig. 6.36. Queen Wilhelmina and her granddaughters, Princesses Beatrix and Irene, waiting in the Nieuwe Kerk in Amsterdam for the arrival and coronation of her daughter and their mother, Princess Juliana (Two Queens, *1948*) (*NIS archive, HCASC*)

version of this ten-minute film might well have been shown as a newsreel in American movie theaters during the weeks following the September 1948 event, thereby greatly increasing its public exposure.

Crossover films with no perceived Dutchness

It's Just a Postage Stamp (1952; 8,081) is one such film; it was shown in fifty-one different places, almost entirely in just two years, 1957 and 1958. Commissioned by the Dutch Postal and Telecommunication Services on the occasion of the one hundred-year anniversary of the Dutch post-

age stamp, the film documents the history of message and letter sorting (fig. 6.37) and delivery in the country, the establishment of the post office, and later, the postage stamp (1852). The greater part of the nearly twenty-minute film shows in detail all the steps in the design, engraving, photography, printing, and inspection of stamps. There is nothing distinctively Dutch about this technology; every country employed it. The same may be said about the balance between the mechanization and hand labor required for sorting mail in post offices and distribution centers in the 1950s. All economically advanced countries adopted

Fig. 6.37. Hand sorting mail into destination bags in a Dutch post office, 1950s
(It's Just a Postage Stamp, *1952*) (*NIS archive, HCASC*)

such mechanization for their postal services and adopted further enhancements as these came along.

Aside from several, wonderful Amsterdam street scenes of a busy outdoor stamp market and a frustrated customer trying—without success—to buy a stamp at various locations in the city, Dutchness does not enter the topic of the film itself; the Dutch postal system is like all others in advanced economies. The film was educational for the Dutch population; its purpose abroad was to show that the Netherlands postal service is right up there with other countries. It is an early example of

what I will designate in the next chapter as an international Dutch documentary.

Many of the same points may be made about *Holland's Farmers Became Bankers* (ca. 1954; 942), a film that documents and reenacts the rise of agricultural cooperatives and agricultural cooperative loan banks in the Netherlands. It is saying to the Dutch public and—by means of this English-language version—to other like-minded countries: we have also made progress in the development of cooperatives. The film was directed by Rudi Honecker, a leading Dutch documentary filmmaker best known for his images of

Fig. 6.38. Agricultural cooperative loan banks began in rooms of farmsteads. This farmer client has taken off his wooden shoes before entering the "office" (Holland's Farmers Became Bankers, *ca. 1954*) (*NIS archive, HCASC*).

the hunger winter in the Netherlands at the end of WWII. The film was acquired by Maurice Groen of DPM Productions in New York, given an English voice-over, and made part of their Films of the Nations series. Groen had also produced other Dutch films for American distribution. Again, here was a Dutch film, meant for a Dutch audience, but acquired by the NIS, as well as other American distributors.

Agricultural cooperative loan banks were part of a larger social movement that began in the latter part of the nineteenth century throughout Western Europe and then spread to North America. The historical context of this movement varies from country to country, but it produced very comparable institutions, for example, credit unions and marketing and production cooperatives. Farmers were the shareholders and, therefore, owners of these institutions; by pooling their money, individual farmers could receive low-interest loans to invest in, expand, and modernize their operations (fig. 6.38). By pooling their output of crops, livestock, and livestock products, farmers were able to market them more cheaply and widely, as well as process their output into consumer goods like butter, milk, and meat. The cooperatives also set up laboratories to test and improve the quality of their farm products and help

Fig. 6.39. Early Gothic Madonna and Child (Mediaeval Dutch Sculpture, *1951*)
(*NIS archive, HCASC*)

farmers improve their agricultural techniques. This social movement, in general, improved the economic position of farmers and helped them to modernize and become more productive.

Holland's Farmers Became Bankers includes all these developments but, again, its purpose was not to carve out a Dutch particularity but, rather, an economic and social innovation the Netherlands shared with other Western democracies. The look of the landscape, the farm exteriors and interiors, and the farm families themselves are certainly Dutch but the subject of the film lacks Dutchness. Remarkable, but understandable, given the aim of the film, is that the stock footage prior to the break-

through to cooperatives all has a premodern look (grain mill, box bed, farm interior, outdoor hand milking) but thereafter, a modern appearance (bank interior and vault, scientific animal husbandry, trains, trucks, and tractors, modern urban architecture, and factories).

Mediaeval Dutch Sculpture (1951; 5,832) is even less of a crossover candidate, and one can only be amazed that an English-language version of this highly specialized and cinematographically boring documentary was produced at all and, further, that Holland-NIS brought it into its film library. One can only imagine the reaction of the nearly six thousand viewers who turned out to see it in the United States. The film is really only for those who are interested in sculpture and, what is worse for any audience—non-Dutch, or Dutch—there is no commentary as the camera, in turn, pans and zooms in on specific pieces of medieval sculpture with accompanying medieval music (fig. 6.39). The character of these sculptures as representing the Low Countries receives no attention; only the modern technical age is contrasted, in general terms, with the Christian Middle Ages. I suspect that *Mediaeval Dutch Sculpture* is part of this film collection because Bert Haanstra, one of the most celebrated Dutch documentary filmmakers of the period, codirected the film. When this thirteen-minute film was released on DVD in 2007, one Dutch film critic opined that it belonged to those films Haanstra had wished would not be in circulation anymore.[28]

The Dutch colonies in the 1950s films

The Holland NIB Film library of the 1940s included no fewer than seventeen of the top thirty-three films (93.1% of the total 1940s viewership) about the Dutch colonies, two more than the number of films about the Netherlands itself, and 548,489 American viewers came out to view them. That is quite remarkable and underscores how vital propaganda about the justification of colonial rule was to the Dutch government. During the 1950s, only some 72,143 Americans—more than sevenfold fewer—attended just ten films about the colonies or territories—then a more acceptable name for these possessions. That is a drop from nearly 50 percent to around

11 percent of all viewers for this decade, a monumental shift in the geographic visual focus for Americans on all things Dutch.

Topical threads in films about the Dutch territories

Fig. 6.40 graphs the blend of topics in the films about the Dutch territories shown during the 1950s. With the Dutch colonial center of gravity in the 1950s shifted from Southeast Asia to the Caribbean, and with the economic recovery from WWII, the topical mix in the colonial films witnessed some informative changes (fig. 5.6, fig. 6.40). With agriculture less important in the Dutch Antilles, the percentage of film threads associated with that topic declined significantly, from some 15 percent in the 1940s to 5 percent in the 1950s. Similarly, the films about the Dutch East Indies shown during the 1940s contained a strong ethnographic element (folk culture and religion). In the Caribbean, this was a less conspicuous feature for filmmakers, and such threads became less dominant during the 1950s (from 21% to 9%). At the same time, other subjects related to tourism, the natural environment, and services saw noticeable growth: recreation from 1 percent to 6 percent of threads, natural environments from 4 percent to 10 percent, services from 1 percent to 4 percent, and transportation from 8 percent to 13 percent. The films about the Dutch overseas territories shown during the 1950s reflected the worldwide geographic and economic shifts taking place.

A look at the films about the Dutch territories shown during the 1950s

The Netherlands' civilizing mission

Taken together, films about the Dutch territories shown during the 1950s present

---

[28] http://cinemagazine.nl/nederlandse-beeldhouwkunst-tijdens-de-late-middeleeuwen-1951-recensie/. The review was written by Bart Rietvink and published on this Dutch film website 21 Oct. 2007.

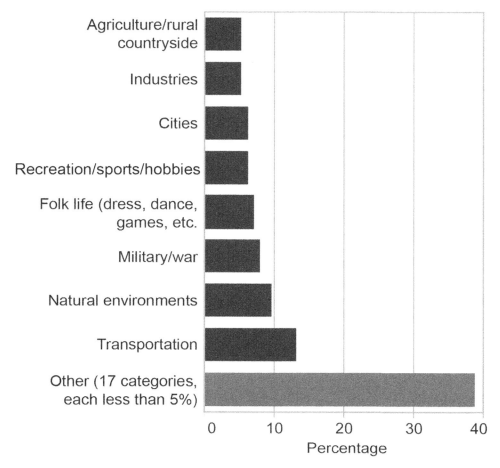

Fig. 6.40. Films about the Dutch territories, 1950s:
percentage of film threads by subject

Top seven films about the colonies/territories, 113 film threads, 70,391 (97.5%)[29]

a rather complicated picture. Gone from circulation were the older, American-made travelogue films shown during the 1940s about various islands that just happened to be Dutch colonies; they had a descriptive anthropological focus but revealed very little about the Dutch overseas enterprises. The new and remaining films of the 1950s focused more on the place and role of these areas as Dutch territories.

Five of the ten films about the colonies were carried over from the 1940s and include out-of-date information about the former Dutch East Indies and the supportive role the Dutch Antilles and Dutch Guiana provided for the Allied war effort (*Netherlands America: Holland in the Western Hemisphere*, 1942; 56,063). The attendance figures for these carryovers, however, are on the low side, and they disappear entirely from circulation by the midfifties. One new film, *Java and Sumatra*—not in the archive—was acquired and

29   The film, *The Dutch Way*, with 25,119 viewers, was not in the 1950s included in the content survey; it covered both the Netherlands and its territories.

deaccessioned all in the same year (1950) because of the loss of the East Indies in December 1949; it garnered just 228 viewers. Together with another new acquisition, these films continued to make the case for the Netherlands as a progressive, inclusive, and civilizing colonial power. The independence of Indonesia in 1949 did not take away this foreign policy issue once and for all, although the post-WWII decolonization drive caused it to be reformulated.

Although independence for the islands of the Netherlands Antilles in the Caribbean, either individually or as a group, was much less likely because of their small size, population, and economic base, the same was not true for Suriname (Dutch Guiana) in South America (fig. 4.13) and Dutch New Guinea (West Papua) in Southeast Asia (fig. 4.12). Helping these areas to grow toward independence by developing their political democracy, educational systems, health care, and more modern, market-oriented economies, among other things, was the stated goal. At the same time, retaining close economic ties with the Netherlands took the place of the older colonial ideology of more undisguised Dutch economic, military, administrative, and political control. Dutch filmmakers of the 1940s in the employ of their government had always made this case for eventual independence to American moviegoers, although it then was a far-off goal. This case could continue to be made with the older films, such as *The Dutch in Latin America* (ca. 1947), which garnered more than half of its viewership (9,606) during the 1950s. The film pronounced that Dutch Latin America already constituted a multinational part of the Kingdom of the Netherlands, where different ethnic cultures

were treated as equals and cooperated together.

The same case was made by new films, for example, those from the 35 mm, twenty-three-part series, *Nieuw-Guinea Kroniek* (New-Guinea Chronicle), commissioned by the RVD, released from 1954 to 1962, in black and white and in color, and shown as shorts (most around 20 min. long) in Dutch movie theaters. Each of these films focused on the civilizing mission and economic development of West Papua by the Dutch administration. They did show the indigenous Papuan ways of living but always side by side with what the Dutch territorial administration regarded as modern enhancements: police training schools, Christian missions, vocational training and education, disease eradication programs, international marketing of processed resources, and self-rule by Papuan-elected representatives. A number of these New Guinea chronicle shorts were released with English narration by the RVD to show the international community the Dutch version of enlightened colonialism and eventual decolonization, for example, no. 8, *Educating the Native Population*, and no. 21, *The Way to Self-Determination*. Neither of these films, however, was acquired for the NIS film library in the 1950s.

From many possible candidates, the Holland-NIS added just one film during the 1950s that promoted and defended more current Dutch policy and practice related to its remaining overseas territories— no. 6, *The Medical Care of the Native Population* (1956; 16,807), from the New Guinea Chronicle series.[30] It is not clear why this film was chosen and not others from either this series or the extensive corpus of Dutch

---

[30] See endnote 6:29, p. 405.

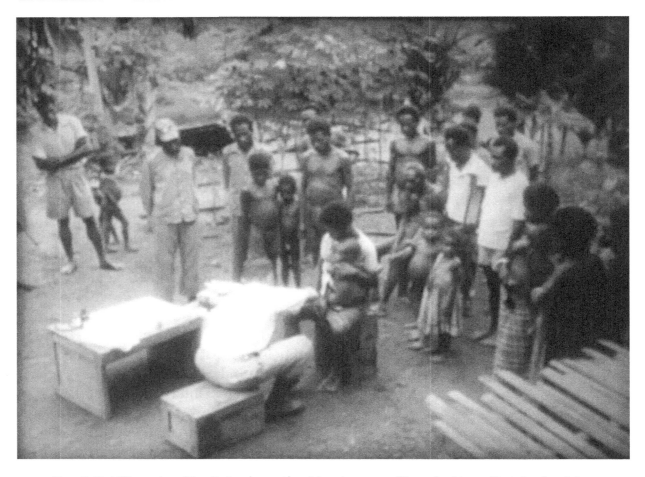

Fig. 6.41. Village health clinic along the Mamberamo River, led by a Dutch physician
(*New Guinea Chronicle, no. 6,* The Medical Care of the Native Population, *1954-1962*)
(*NIS archive, HCASC*)

documentary films about New Guinea. The availability of an English-language version was clearly the most important consideration. Six films from this series with English narration were added to the NIS library at the very beginning of the 1960s; their original Dutch versions were all produced during the 1950s, suggesting a possible delay in their availability abroad. Dutch moviegoers had plenty of opportunities to see a new spate of films about Suriname, the Dutch Antilles, and West Papua, but American viewers during the 1950s were largely kept in the dark about new developments in these areas from a Dutch point of view.

The Medical Care of the Native Population lacks the necessary larger Dutch political-colonial context for American viewers. The film shows the voyage of the Dutch government vessel, the *Kolff,* moving inland along the Mamberamo River, anchoring at different villages to run clinics, including vaccinations, blood tests, diagnostic services, pediatrics, and treatment of specific diseases (fig. 6.41). In addition to the medical team on the vessel, the commissioner of the government as well as the police chief from the district capital of Hollandia are also onboard, assessing the provision of other services, such as education and policing, at each village. Villagers are shown welcoming the vessel and expressing a high level of trust in the medical staff and the administrators as well as appreciation for their work. At Pionierbinak, a kampong along the river, the chieftain removes the dust from the clothes of the Dutch civil servant from Hollandia, a ritual and a sign of confidence in their mutual relationship. All in all, the film renders a thoroughly positive image of skilled and caring Dutch and indigenous medical staff who bring continuing and effective health services to highly scattered native populations never before able to benefit from such knowledge and care.

The Dutch Caribbean: from virtual to actual tourism

The new and best-attended films about the Dutch overseas possessions re-introduced the theme of travel and tourism but with a difference. The American-made travelogue films from the 1930s that were distributed by the NIB during the 1940s about a number of Dutch overseas territories were a form of virtual tourism or travel documentary; they were not really meant to promote travel to these destinations. The technology, facilities, and affluence necessary for tourist visits, let alone mass tourism, to areas such as these were not yet in place. Moreover, the Dutch-made films about the colonies shown during the 1940s were preoccupied with foreign policy issues.

Three new films, *Six Bits of Holland in the Caribbean* (1950; 23,107), *Curaçao: The Island You Will Always Remember* (1950; 18,575), and *Netherlands West Indies* (n.d., 4,190), ranked eighth, ninth, and thirty-sixth, respectively, among the films

shown during the 1950s, aimed to bring the Netherlands Antilles into the—especially American—tourist orbit. Suriname (Dutch Guiana) was not one of these six "bits," nor is there a separate film about that colony, partly because it is often not included in the Caribbean region and partly because it did not have the beaches of the Antilles or the infrastructure for tourism. The film *Netherlands West Indies* is in neither the Holland NIB/NIS archive nor any of the other relevant national film databases. The other two films had a Dutch cameraman/director but were produced largely for an American audience in 1949 and 1950 by the New York-based company Films of the Nations. Like the earlier American-produced travelogues, these two films were circulated not only by the NIS but also other American film distribution companies and institutions. They were also likely shown as shorts in movie theaters. So, again, the total number of American viewers, along with the impact of these films, far exceeded the NIS attendance.

Curaçao, The Island You Will Always Remember, is filmed from the point of view of tourists visiting the island. It opens with street scenes of snow-bound Manhattan with a voice-over asking viewers if they would like to leave for a nearby warm and sunny destination. The film shows Caribbean cruise ships calling on the island and DC-4 KLM airliners arriving. With the tagline, "A Little Bit of Holland in the Caribbean," the film advertises that the Netherlands provides the culture, and the Caribbean the sun, water, beaches, and everything else that comes with those attractions. With this, all the island's attributes can become tourist assets: the capital, Wil-

Fig. 6.42. Passengers disembarking from the ship, *New Amsterdam*, in Willemstad, Curaçao
(*Curaçao, The Island You Will Always Remember, ca. 1950*) (*NIS archive, HCASC*)

lemstad; heritage sites, such as the oldest Jewish synagogue in the Western Hemisphere; the oil refineries; the dry landscape; and the coasts with their beaches.[31]

Passengers disembarking at the airport are shown driving to Willemstad in a roadster and taking in the different natural, urban, and industrial landscapes. Cruise-ship tourists coming ashore (fig. 6.42) head for the historic old city, with its brightly colored, Dutch-style buildings, floating market, and duty-free shopping for luxury goods. Other visitors are shown taking in the beaches, sunbathing, swimming, fishing, and boating. All such activities have become staples (greatly scaled-up today) of the Caribbean tourist experience; in this film, one sees their early stages. The perception of Curaçao in the films has pivoted from a strategic location protected by Allied forces and producing vital wartime refined oil products during the 1940s to

---

[31] Today the remains of the one hundred-plus, 17th- and 18th-century Dutch plantations and their slave quarters on Curaçao are becoming parts of its heritage tourism. David Koren, "Een Eeuwenlange Strijd tegen Droogte en Teloorgang; Waarden en Betekenissen van het Curaçaose Plantagelandschap," *Tijdschrift voor Historische Geografie* 5, no. 3 (2020): 131–51; David Koren, "Slavernijverleden werpt Schaduw Vooruit; Werelderfgoedstatus voor Plantagesysteem West-Curaçao?" *Tijdschrift voor Historische Geografie* 5, no. 3 (2020): 152–68.

Fig. 6.43. Young family (he is smoking) heading down to the water on a white, empty beach in Aruba (Six Bits of Holland in the Caribbean, *ca. 1950*) (*NIS archive, HCASC*)

a place competing for Caribbean tourists with sun, surf, scenery, shopping, and culture.

Six Bits of Holland in the Caribbean is a visual overview of the entire Dutch Antilles and, for the first time, includes footage of the northern three islands, Sint Maarten, Saba, and Sint Eustatius (fig. 4.13). During the NIB's foreign policy oriented 1940s, these islands had no perceived wartime or colonial bragging rights to capture on film. This film is a cross between a tourist film and a travelogue, reflecting the progress that tourism had made on the different islands of the Netherlands Antilles. The ABC islands—Aruba, Bonaire, and

Curaçao (fig. 4.13)—saw much WWII-related development of airports, roads, and ports. Such infrastructure was essential to spur the tourist industry on these islands after the war. The three northern islands did not experience such development, so the tourism industry could not flourish as on the ABC island group. The film footage about these islands is more of a travelogue than about tourism.

The film footage about Curaçao in the film is a condensation of the footage from *Curaçao: The Island You Will Always Remember*. Aruba receives similar treatment: an already strong and prosperous economy based on oil refineries and a modern harbor is now hard at work adding tourism to its economic base. Shown are a couple on their honeymoon and a young family (fig. 6.43) with both the woman and young daughter in bikinis, swimwear introduced just a few years earlier. They are alone on wide expanses of white beach, ringed by turquoise water under a blue sky. Horseback riding through the open, natural landscape is another tourist pastime highlighted in the film. The third island, Bonaire, receives scant attention. Beach tourism was then quite defining for the Caribbean, and Bonaire lacked beaches. Moviegoers see no tourist activities on this island, and the film can show only possible future tourist attractions: historic Kralendijk, the capital; the seventeenth-century fort; and the large, saltwater flamingo colony. As on the other islands of the ABC group, however, wartime investments in infrastructure in Bonaire also provided some of the necessary preconditions for tourism to develop in time.

The Leeward Islands of Sint Maarten, Saba, and Sint Eustatius receive only the last three minutes of screen time in the ten-minute-long *Six Bits of Holland in the Caribbean*. The film changes from tourist film to travelogue when these islands are introduced. Gone are the tourists and the tourist attractions; it is clear that the requirements for this industry are not yet present on these islands. What takes their place are items of historical significance (the fort on Sint Eustatius that fired a cannon salvo recognizing the Stars and Stripes of an American ship for the very first time by a foreign government), social conditions (government-provided education and supplemental feeding of students on Sint Maarten), and transportation inadequacies on rugged Saba.

Conclusion

Without its foreign policy propaganda mainstay, the renamed NIS became much more like a cultural institute, although still an agency of the Dutch government. Gone was the global colonial empire—even from its letterhead map (fig. 5.7). Gone were the political urgency and activism fueled by foreign policy objectives. In their place came a quiet public diplomacy by means of cultural programming and a largely consumer-driven information agency, dispensing more standard promotional knowledge. This had always been a part of the agency's work, but it now defined it. Without the former focus on the colonies, the Netherlands itself naturally received much more attention from all the media, including film. The Dutch reconstruction of wartime wreckage and, toward the latter half of the decade, the gradual improvement of human welfare witnessed by modernization, economic growth, and increasing incomes were leitmotifs for a remodeled information and cultural agency.

Like all other programs of the NIS, the film library was also forced to adapt to these changes in the agency itself and in the country it represented. The foreign-policy-directed films were deaccessioned, as were earlier, American-made, culture-directed travelogues about the colonies and the Netherlands itself. In their place came a new and larger cohort of films mainly about the Netherlands on a greater variety of topics; new acquisitions about the Dutch overseas territories were few and far between. American audiences continued to prefer the films that devoted significant attention to the Netherlands of old. The more successful films elaborated on some topic that was already part of or tied into the general international knowledge about the Netherlands. Some films made for Dutch viewers did not do well across the Atlantic; American audiences lacked the contextual knowledge necessary to understand and enjoy them. Films made for non-Dutch viewers and those from Dutch film crews produced by American film companies fared better.

CHAPTER 7

1960s/70s: From Cultural Nationalism to Internationalism

Economic change and social upheaval in the Netherlands during the 1960s[1]

In the countries of Western Europe—such as the Netherlands—that had been occupied, looted, and economically shattered by Nazi Germany, the road to recovery and reconstruction during the immediate post-war years of the forties and early fifties was slow and arduous. The contrast between that period and the one following could not be greater. The Dutch government's brakes on wage growth were loosened, and salaries rose rapidly. The prewar export economy recovered, expanded, and added other sectors, such as electronics (Philips). With rising wages, the demand for affordable consumer goods grew rapidly, fueled for the first time by television advertising.

With full employment, a first wave of guest workers arrived from Italy and Spain. Automobile ownership grew rapidly as more and more people could afford to buy cars; highways and other automobile infrastructure had to expand to keep pace. Leisure time increased with a mandated five-day work week and a generous summer vacation allowance. Exploring other European countries by car became possible for many middle- and working-class Dutch.

In sum, unprecedented, broad-based affluence and consumerism characterized the Dutch economy during the 1960s. Several of the films distributed by the NIS during the 1960s do shed light on some of these economic changes but, overall, the film topics are a very mixed bag in which the Dutch economy takes up little space, with more attention given to the economic

---

[1]   See endnote 7:1, p. 405.

recovery and reconstruction of the fifties than the affluence of the sixties.

As in other Western democracies, the decade of the 1960s also brought more cogent social change to the Netherlands than the previous decades, not counting the German occupation. Some of this change, led by the postwar generation of students, hippies, and "provos" (playful provocateurs), was upheaving, for example, anti-Vietnam war protests and teach-ins; improvement of high school, university, and seminary teaching and education; emancipation of women; and efforts to democratize policymaking from the ground-up to give the rank-and-file a voice. Other changes were more broad based: the end of class-based entrance to preparatory high schools and higher education, the coming of age and institutionalization of watchdog and investigative journalism, the construction of high-rise apartment blocks as a solution to severe housing shortages, the breakdown of the denominational and ideological organization of society (pillarization) and the related increase of secularization, and the beginning of the environmental movement.

About these profound structural social changes—many achieved through protest, generational dissent, social action, lifestyle, and political pressure—the NIS films of the 1960s were completely silent. The so-called VPRO film school took on many of these social issues but the NIS must have regarded these films as too controversial and lacking a positive image of the country. Moreover, they were in-house films about difficult and challenging issues not readily transparent and transferable to non-Dutch viewers. The VPRO cinematography, with its journalistic style, spontaneity, and lack of voice-overs, also made preparing versions for other countries a very tall order.

The film library

The NIS-Holland film lending library swelled from 70 to 163 films during the 1960s and early 1970s. Forty-two (60%) of the films from the 1950s library continued to circulate, making more than 25 percent of the 1960s/70s collection somewhat outdated—one quality measure of any film library. Helpful again in this regard is that many of these films had much smaller audiences than in the preceding decade and, therefore, much less impact. As in the 1950s, around a third of the films found in the circulation records are not present in the archives, although the absolute number of these films increased substantially from twenty-one to sixty-one during the 1960s/70s. Most had meager attendance figures and therefore, again, little influence. But several topped the ten thousand mark: *NATO Tattoo* (n.d.), *Adventures in Perception* (1971), and *The Language of the Flowers* (1960). Fortunately, the first two are available, in whole or part, on YouTube and can therefore be part of this analysis.

Film attendance

The aggregate yearly attendance figures from 1960 to 1974 are included in fig. 4.2. Until 1964, the pattern from the mid-fifties had held: total yearly film audiences amounted to less than fifty thousand. Then in 1965—just as in 1953 with *Holland: A Modern Country*, pt. 1, *Country and People* (1950), but now more sustained and with seven films—television broadcasting greatly boosted yearly attendance to some 270,000. And on the other side of the seven-year data gap, total attendance for 1973, also pumped up by television, was sustained at the same level. This pattern is also evident from the viewership of individual titles shown on television on either side of the data gap: *Holland Today*, 48,000/46,000; *Dutch Miniatures*, 8,000/48,000; *Speaking of Glass*, 41,000/20,000; *Hold Back the Sea*, 0/41,000; *Amsterdam, City of Canals*, 41,000/0; *Vibration*, 41,000/0; *NATO Tattoo*, 41,000/0. It is highly likely then that attendance for several of the years in the data gap was also significantly boosted by the television broadcasting of NIS films. Even with the seven years of missing borrowing records, some 22 percent of the aggregate viewership in the 1960–74 period still came from logged television audiences.

Total viewership in Holland-NIS for the entire period increased by more than 250,000 and for the United States by nearly 400,000 (fig. 4.1), spurred on, it is clear, more by television broadcasting than by the increase in the number of available films or borrowing rates. Without television, the yearly attendance figures for the 1960s/70s, compared to the 1950s, would have been flat. Without television, several of the top films (*Amsterdam, City of Canals* [1957; 45,890]; *Vibration* [1951; 43,170], *NATO Tattoo* [n.d., 42,761]) would have had hardly any viewers.

Fig. 7.1 ranks the top fifty films viewed during this period by attendance. The top nine films each had their viewership greatly enhanced by television broadcasting; the top two were broadcast more than once. As a result, the decline in attendance by film on this graph is not nearly as steep as it is on the comparable graph for the 1950s (compare figs. 7.1 and 6.1); only the four-part film, *Holland: A Modern Country Full of Old-Time Charm* was shown on televi-

sion during the 1950s, compared to seven films during the 1960s/70s. More generally, viewership on the 1960s/70s graph steps down more quickly for the first seventeen films, from 113,615 to 8,578, and then declines very gradually to 3,144 for the fiftieth film. The attendance floor of ten thousand is already reached by the sixteenth film (18th for the fifties and 34th for the forties). That slow slide in attendance continues for the next 111 films and ends with only double figures at the tail end of the distribution. The top fifty films encompass 95.6 percent of the attendance from 1960 to 1974. Attendance figures, especially for the films acquired just prior to and during the 1966–72 data gap are significantly underreported; among the top fifty films in attendance, there are twenty that record attendance beginning in 1965 or 1973. Films screened during the last ten years of the NIS likely had twice the recorded attendance.

Film attendance by place

Fig. 7.2 maps the attendance at the screening locations from 1960 to 1974, the year the NIS shut its doors. The nearly nine hundred thousand moviegoers during this period were distributed over 825 screening locations throughout the service zone of Holland-NIS. More than 61 percent of these attendance locations were particular to this period, underscoring again the geographical spread of knowledge about the Netherlands and its territories to many new locations. Compared to the 1950s attendance map (fig. 6.2), note, for example, the spread of attendance in North Dakota and northern Minnesota, the decline in screening locations in southern Michigan and Ohio, and the very different distribu-

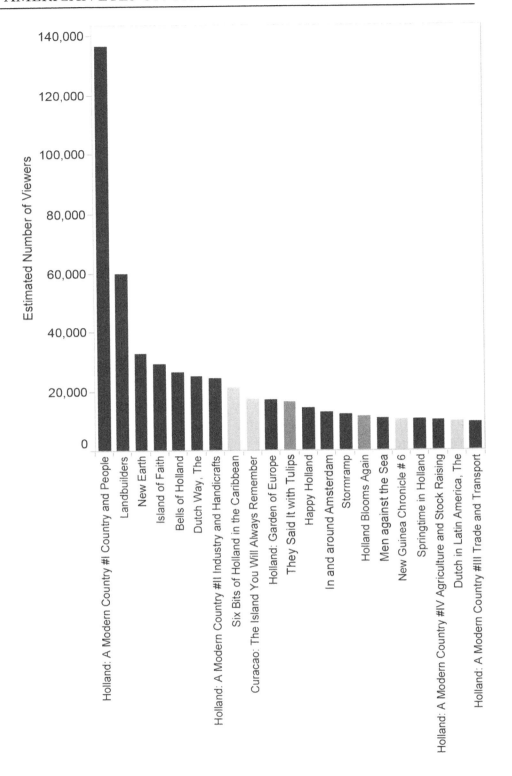

Fig. 7.1. NIS-Holland: Attendance by Film during the 1960s/70s
(top fifty films)

95.6% of total 1960s/70s attendance

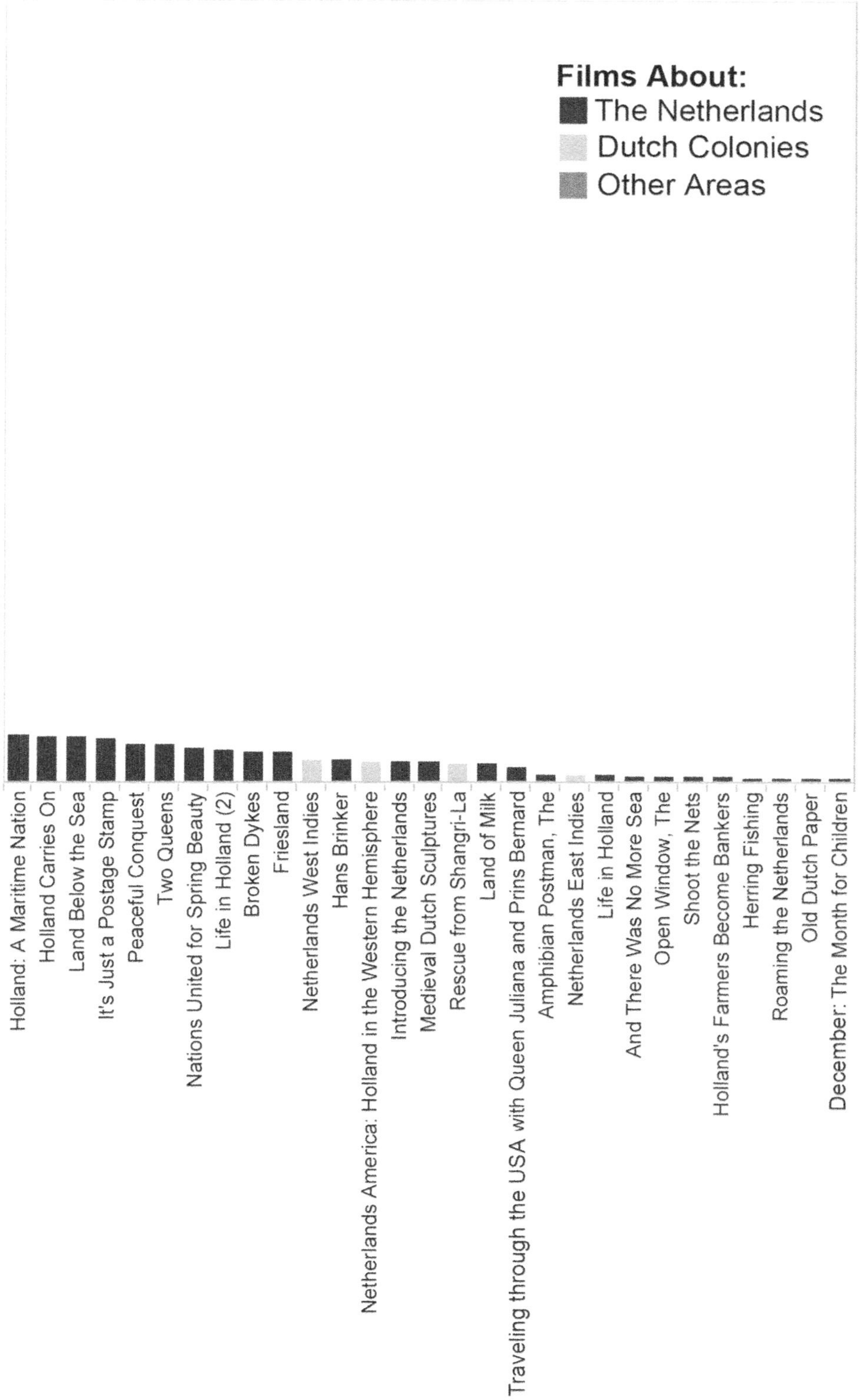

Films About:
- The Netherlands
- Dutch Colonies
- Other Areas

Holland: A Maritime Nation
Holland Carries On
Land Below the Sea
It's Just a Postage Stamp
Peaceful Conquest
Two Queens
Nations United for Spring Beauty
Life in Holland (2)
Broken Dykes
Friesland
Netherlands West Indies
Hans Brinker
Netherlands America: Holland in the Western Hemisphere
Introducing the Netherlands
Medieval Dutch Sculptures
Rescue from Shangri-La
Land of Milk
Traveling through the USA with Queen Juliana and Prins Bernard
Amphibian Postman, The
Netherlands East Indies
Life in Holland
And There Was No More Sea
Open Window, The
Shoot the Nets
Holland's Farmers Become Bankers
Herring Fishing
Roaming the Netherlands
Old Dutch Paper
December: The Month for Children

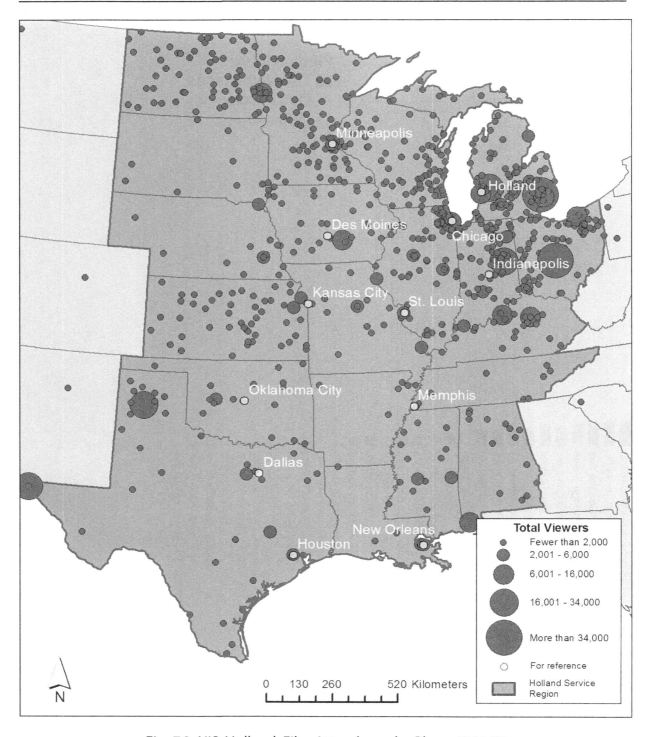

Fig. 7.2. NIS-Holland: Film Attendance by Place, 1960-74

tion of attendance in Mississippi. Again, the 1960–74 attendance substantially created a new map.

Distinctives of the new

films in the collection

With the marked growth in the size of the film library and the retention of a sizable number of earlier films, the cinematographic diversity grew apace. The most telling filmmaking change evident in the new films made and acquired in the 1960s was a focus on people in the documentary as subjects with agency. Earlier films very much looked at things (factories, crops, buildings, customs, etc.), and people, as objects with particular attributes described by the narrator. In more of the new films, information and knowledge for the viewer were given by people in the documentary doing and speaking rather than a voice-over. Viewers saw people making things at their workplaces and, sometimes, talking about what they were doing; they were asked questions off camera and gave answers on camera, making the knowledge and views shared more personal. More of these new films lacked a voice-over; those that still had one used it more sparingly and made it less authoritative and more informal.

Rather than the common encyclopedic linear structure of scenes, more new documentaries created coherence by, among other things, focusing on events, stories, and timelines and using the principal personage as the narrator. Diegetic soundscapes were no longer the exception for new films in the collection. Musical scores were more often better married to the topics and disposition of documentaries, and their variety grew to include jazz, blues, and modern classical.

Films about the Netherlands and the Dutch territories

During the 1960s/70s, the holdings of the NIS-Holland film library became even more focused on the Netherlands proper: 144 of the 163 films (88.3%) were about the country, and only 14 (8.6%) were about its overseas possessions; a "miscellaneous" category, neither about the Netherlands nor its colonies, rounded out the collection. Of the top fifty films, only four fell into the "overseas" category, each one with less than sixty-five hundred viewers. The percentage of films about the Netherlands and not about the Dutch overseas climbed steadily from only 41.8 percent during the 1940s to 71.1 percent during the 1950s, as the perceived economic, cultural, and geo-strategic value of these territories for the Netherlands diminished. At this point, I will focus entirely on the films about the Netherlands and return to those about the Dutch territories at the end of this chapter.

Thirty-nine (27.1%) of the films about the Netherlands were carried over from earlier decades, five as far back as the 1940s. But that still left more than a hundred new films available during the 1960s/70s. Many of these, however, had trifling attendance figures and, therefore, a negligible impact on the American perception of the Netherlands. For that reason, I again focused my closer analysis, in this case, on the top forty-eight films about the Netherlands in the archive that, together for this period, took in 86.6 percent (742,758) of the viewers of the films about the country. About a third of these films were carried over from the 1950s; they are scrutinized in the previous chapter. The top forty-eight films about the Netherlands from the archive is a different number, of course, than the top forty-eight from the circulation records. The films missing from the archive include twelve (49,804 viewers) with an attendance range similar to the ones analyzed for the 1950s, with a lower limit of two thousand; they were either lost from the library or simply not kept for any number of reasons.

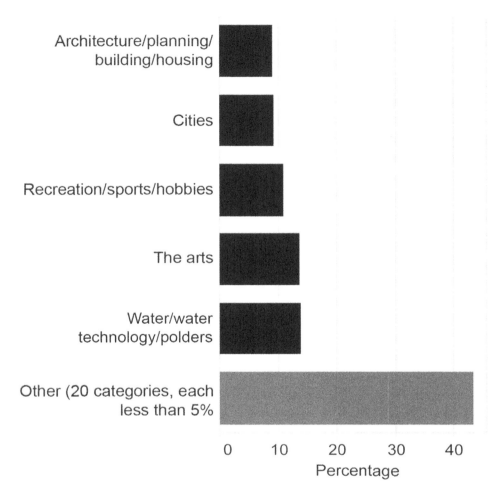

Fig. 7.3. Films about the Netherlands: percentage of
film threads by subject, 1960s/70s

608 film threads, top 44 films about the Netherlands, 726,690 viewers (84.7%)

Almost none of these films could receive a closer reading because they were not available for viewing elsewhere, and they did not come with detailed, timed descriptions of their scenes in any of the national film archives. The remaining 53,508 viewers of films about the Netherlands in the lending library were divided over eighty-four films, all with small attendance figures (less than 2,000, average of 637); nearly half of which are not in the archive. Again, low attendance meant a very minor impact on the American perception.

Topical threads in films about the Netherlands during the 1960s/70s

When the topical threads of forty-four top films about the Netherlands are identified, classified, and ranked, only five categories stand out above the 5 percent level, the smallest topical specialization of the three decades (fig. 7.3). Besides the water and water technology class, first in every decade, the other four—arts; recreation/sports/hobbies; cities; and architecture/planning/building/housing—each between 9 and 14 percent of the total, are, one by one, part of the more modern, international, and consumer-oriented Netherlands of the 1960s/70s. Gone from the top tiers are fisheries, agriculture, and folk life—parts of an older and tradition-bound Dutch life. From this distribution of topical film threads, one can see that the collective image of the Netherlands on offer for Americans had shifted once more.

Dutch place representations in the films during the 1960s/70s

Considering the Netherlands itself as a place, the film library was the most focused during the 1960s/70s on the country proper rather than on the Netherlands overseas, either as parts of its sovereign territory or its immigrant and ethnic enclaves abroad. With the NIS film collection more than doubling in holdings during the 1960s/70s to more than 160 films about the country itself, the range of places shown grew apace. But I want to focus on effective representation—places that were actually seen by a large number of moviegoers. The top thirty-five films seen during the 1960s/70s about the Netherlands encompass 82.1 percent of all the viewers in this category; the remaining films—many not in the archive—each had an average attendance of only some one thousand viewers and, therefore, much less impact on place perception.

Figs. 7.4 and 7.5 depict the same gross patterns as the maps of the 1940s and 1950s. The top thirty-five films show sixty-one different "small" places (villages, towns, cities, and polders); 70.4 percent of which are located in the three western provinces. For the third decade in a row, there are no places in the films from the provinces

of Groningen, Drenthe, and Limburg, the truly passed-over regions of the country. Adding multiple showings (fig. 7.4) to these figures again intensifies the hold of the west (81.8%), as does including the showings of all places (fig. 7.5), large and small (75.6%).

All these figures are strikingly like those of the earlier decades and lead to the conclusion that the center/periphery contrasts, as measured here by the differences in place showings between the three coastal provinces and the rest of the country, hardly budged over the thirty years of the NIB/NIS film showings. One might have expected that as the influence of American-made travelogues disappeared; as the country recovered from WWII, modernized, and became more affluent during the 1960s and 1970s; and as it grew its film industry, it would also have produced a more geographically diverse body of films. A quick survey of titles and topics of films released between 1955 and 1965 in the Hogenkamp filmography, however, again shows the same dominance of the provinces of Noord- and Zuid-Holland with place showings in the tens and twenties, and with the other provinces in single figures.[2] In sum, the Netherlands' center/periphery division held fast, also for Dutch films shown in the United States.

National films

Of the forty-eight top films about the Netherlands examined more closely, twelve introduced moviegoers to the country as a whole and its national identity (265,456 viewers, 35.7%). Commonly, Dutch national films were meant for those outside the country's borders; sometimes, they did not

---

[2] Bert Hogenkamp, *De Documentaire Film, 1945–1965. De Bloei van een Filmgenre in Nederland* (Uitgeverij 010, 2003), 283–305.

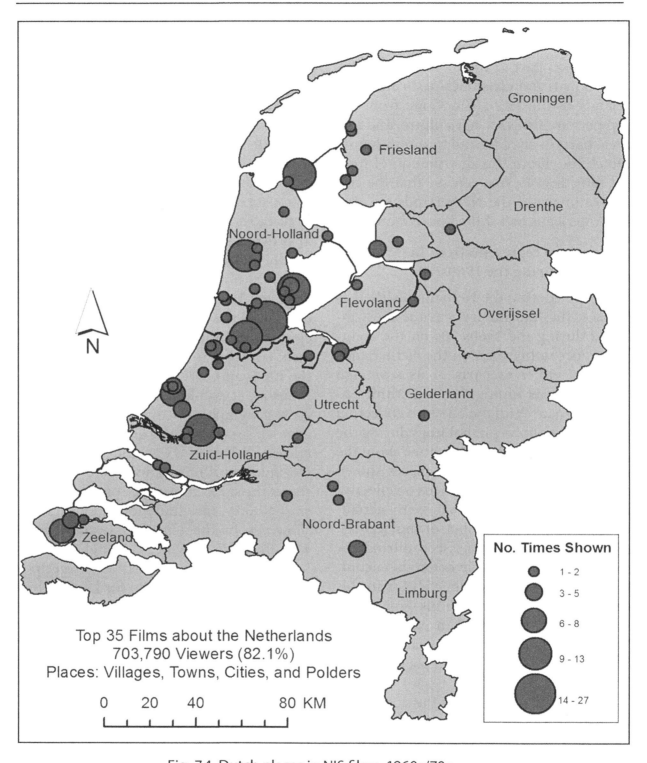

Fig. 7.4. Dutch places in NIS films, 1960s/70s

Top 35 Films about the Netherlands
703,790 Viewers (82.1%)
Places: Villages, Towns, Cities,
Polders and Regions

Percent of Places Shown

2% or less	15.01% - 25%
2.01% - 5%	More than 25%
5.01% - 15%	

0   15   30   60 KM

Fig. 7.5. Dutch places shown in NIS films by province, 1960s/70s

even have a Dutch-language version. The Dutch inhabit their national identity, but for those in other countries, except for certain generalizations, it is more of a *tabula rasa*, needing to be colored in. As in the 1940s and 1950s, many national films drew more screenings and larger audiences than the rest of the films in the lending library. They were important also because they left more of a general impression of the country as a whole.

Five of these national films were carried forward from the 1950s and extended their messaging into the 1960s and 1970s; they drew 59,771 viewers during this period, making up 22.5 percent of the viewing audience for these national films. Recall that, together, these national films from the 1950s—each in different proportions—sought to make visible both the country's "old-time charm" and its modern developments. This focus on the worthwhile past and the promising advancements of the present is, of course, a universal theme, important for any country. The national films from the 1950s that continued to attract significant numbers of borrowers in the 1960s and 1970s, as well as several new national films, continued to play on this binary pair.

But the most-viewed national film of the 1960s and 1970s, *Holland Today* (113,615), produced in 1962, accessioned in 1964, tipped this balance almost entirely in favor of modernism and the present and regarded the past approvingly only if economically useful for the present. "No matter how quaint or attractive, people must break down the ruins their ancestors left them, the wreckage of past centuries," intones the narrator at the beginning of the film. This film grabbed more than 40 percent of the viewership of the twelve nation-

al films. Commissioned by the Dutch ministry of education, culture, and science, *Holland Today* was distributed in no fewer than five languages—English, French, German, Spanish, and Portuguese (but not Dutch). With the exception of German (the largest Dutch trading partner once again), these different translations were all Western world languages; although the film was directed to the outside, it stayed largely within a Western orbit.

Holland Today was clearly meant to shape other nations' perceptions of the Netherlands. The opening credits tell the tale. They are interspersed with pairs of alternating and contrasting images and music. The traditional Dutch scenes have tuneful jazz and blues musical accompaniment, and the modern international scenes have discordant notes struck together.

Viewers are confronted with a number of binary opposites: a polder cow pasture next to windmills beside an oil storage and refinery in Rotterdam, a traditional tree-lined canal with street and row housing on both sides looking toward an old church beside a modernist edge city with high-rise buildings among wide-open green spaces, a slipway for repairing fishing boats in Urk beside a large passenger liner in Rotterdam's harbor, a painting by a seventeenth-century Dutch master beside a drip painting, and a woman in Volendam period costume beside a model in a bikini on a North Sea beach. The contrasts are clear enough, but the musical accompaniments work at cross purposes: the jarring music marks out the modern settings, but it also feeds negative reactions to them, certainly not something the director had in mind. The closing scenes reinforce the theme of *Holland Today* in the then earlier characteristic Dutch artistic documen-

Fig. 7.6. Windmill skeleton about to be razed (Holland Today, *1962*) (*NIS archive, HCASC*)

(See endnote 2:29, p. 398, regarding the resolution of these stills.)

tary style: after every sledgehammer blow and piece of falling debris, a new project comes into view—a power station, a modern wharf, a high-rise office tower—along with the same harsh musical score.

The body of the film is a synopsis of the Netherlands' modern international face. Science, knowledge, and cutting-edge technology have taken the place of hard physical labor and now drive the making of new land from water, as well as the steel, textiles, flower breeding, and electronics industries. Abstract (drip) art, a sculpture class with a nude female model, and a rehearsal for opera dancers all provide a glimpse into the modern Dutch international arts. Likewise, infrastructure and

logistics are world class: mechanized and automated cargo handling in the port of Rotterdam, Autobahn-type highways, efficient inland shipping reaching into much of Europe, and high speed-electrified railways. Speed is a distinguishing hallmark of this modernity. A camera mounted at the front of the railroad engine at the level of the rails creates a feeling of blurred swiftness; red-hot steel is rolled at much the same speed in the Hoogovens, the Dutch steel producer; and threads from hundreds of spools in a textile mill noisily speed by on their way to becoming fabric.

Traditional Dutch products, such as flowers, bulbs, cheese, gin, and Delft Blue, continue to be seen as important mainly as

Fig. 7.7. Roadside picnicking (Dutch, *bermtoerisme*) with first-time car ownership (Holland Today, *1962*) (*NIS archive, HCASC*)

exports to which modern science, manufacturing, increased scale, and marketing needed to be applied in order to diversify their offerings and improve international sales. But other relics, such as Dutch windmills, the old wooden engines for pumping water and industry, are now superseded by new technologies and need to be torn down, with a few working examples remaining intact for tourists. *Holland Today* includes clips of dilapidated skeletal windmills about to be razed (fig. 7.6). As much as this film wants to be up to date, it is far from that goal when it asserts that windmills "hardly fit the economy of today," when, for more than a century already, steam and electricity had replaced wind as the principal energy source for pumping water and for industry in the Netherlands.

Another hallmark of the Dutch modern consumer society of the 1960s is amply shown in *Holland Today*. The entire last third of the film features people recreating on weekends: sailing, hunting waterfowl, playing golf, working with homing pigeons, watching soccer (in the stadium, not on television), picnicking by the roadside on automobile trips (fig. 7.7), swimming and sunbathing at Scheveningen, and dancing at a nightclub. Worship services are included in this part of the film, but leisure and amusement receive the lion's share of attention by far. Rest, relaxation, and diversions are essential ingredients for mod-

Fig. 7.8. 1945 Dutch 7.5-cent postage stamp with the Dutch lion, entitled *The Netherlands, Rising Again* (Dutch Miniatures, *1961*) (*NIS archive, HCASC*)

ern, affluent societies, if only—as shown in the film's closing scenes—to return to the workaday world with renewed enthusiasm and resourcefulness.

Several other national films (*Dutch Miniatures*, 1961; 68,842) and *Girls of Holland*, 1966; 3,273), both new to the collection, employ integrating topics or storylines that, in addition to framing the information about the country, generate another level of interest for viewers. *Dutch Miniatures* is about a boy who lives with his family in a windmill (in the 1960s) and collects stamps; the images on the stamps recount the singular qualities and accomplishments of the Netherlands. A strong parallel is drawn between the Dutch Golden Age (modern then) and reconstruction following WWII (modern now and again). The past and the present are sharply di-

vided between the first and second half of the film. The war is regarded as the turning point at about the midpoint of the film. Zadkine's sculpture, *The Destroyed City*, located in the heart of Rotterdam, is shown from a number of vantage points amid sounds of bombs whistling down and exploding and debris clouds from their blasts lofting into the sky. People are shown waking up from their nightmare lives, and a collective determination to rebuild and modernize is awakened.

The achievements—all depicted on Dutch stamps—of the Golden Age and earlier find a counterpart in post-WWII reconstruction and modernization. That section of the film begins with the 1945, seven-and-a-half-cent stamp depicting the Dutch lion slaying the dragon, with the title *The Netherlands: Rising Again* (fig. 7.8),

Fig. 7.9. High-rise apartment blocks as a solution to severe housing shortages in the 1960s (Dutch Miniatures, *1961*) (*NIS archive, HCASC*)

a common text and visual commemorating the liberation. On one side are Hugo Grotius, the Binnenhof, Erasmus, historic monumental churches, urban canals lined with merchant houses, and Rembrandt and other Dutch masters. On the other side are a rebuilt modern merchant fleet and navy; high-rise residential and office towers (fig. 7.9); new bridges across the rivers, replacing those destroyed during the war; a modern transportation system of highways, tunnels, diesel and electric trains, and commercial aviation (not a bicycle in sight); continuing land reclamation in the former Zuiderzee, now at a larger scale and with advanced technology; and unprece-

dented industrialization. The dawning of this new Golden Age is clearly more about artifacts than the human way of life.

Released in 1966, *Girls of Holland* (3,273) was part of the film library for only a few years before the NIS closed its doors. Commissioned by the Netherlands National Tourist Office, the film was directed by Rob Houwer, a well-known Dutch filmmaker who produced most of Paul Verhoeven's Dutch films, for example, *Soldier of Orange* (1977). Verhoeven is one of the best known international Dutch film directors, with eighteen years in Hollywood. Like *Dutch Miniatures, Girls of Holland* also uses a unifying theme—Dutch young women—to tie the subject matter about the Netherlands together for its viewers. It also uses stories and human action rather than encyclopedic tableaus to draw viewers into the film. Moreover, *Girls of Holland* brings the Dutch past into the present and mixes them together much more. Stories of the careers, travels, and lives of several young women, who are actors without dialogue in this documentary film, are employed to show viewers what the Netherlands is like—modern and with-it. These storylines produce another level of interest, help to focus the audience's attention, and make viewers more receptive to absorbing knowledge about the country. The stories appear newly filmed, whereas the information about the Netherlands consists of stock footage.

Aside from the stories of these particular women in their own environment, there is also, in the opening and closing footage, a visual focus on beautiful Dutch young women in general, which, given the filmmaking of Rob Houwer, Dutch cinema, and Dutch culture at the time, can best be described as playful titillation. Attractive KLM flight attendants at Schiphol; buxom, bikini-clad young women on the beach in Scheveningen; and lovely guides on Amsterdam's tourist canal boats all pass in review as girls of Holland and open windows on familiar Dutch scenes. This visual packaging, along with some of the music, is clearly aimed at a younger demographic of potential tourists.

The lives and travels of several other young Dutch women showcase other parts of the country. On a boat moored on the Amstel River in Amsterdam, Annabelle, a young girl, paints memories of her vacation. Her paintings take viewers to the Artis (Amsterdam's zoo), and the Eftel-

ing, a theme park in Noord-Brabant that brings European fairy tales and legends to life. Later, she shows up in Spakenburg, in the costume of this fishing village, to participate in its folk dances. This footage is part of a larger segment in the film about the trading centers and fishing villages along the coast of the former Zuiderzee, now largely cut off by the Afsluitdijk from shipping lanes and fishing banks. Annabelle makes several other appearances in the film: at Madurodam, a miniature park near The Hague of 1:25 scale models of well-known Dutch buildings and other structures, and at the annual opening by the queen of parliament in the Knights Hall, part of the Binnenhof, the seat of the Dutch parliament in the center of The Hague (she loves Princess Beatrix). Scenes of her painting on the boat also create the appropriate link to bring the paintings of the Dutch masters into the film.

Jannie rides her bike to the construction site of the sluices closing off the Haringvliet estuary, part of the Delta Plan enacted after the 1953 flood that devastated especially the islands of the southwestern Netherlands. She works in a canteen that provides the construction workers with refreshments and meals. Her entrance provides an opening for the film's director to show the viewers something about present-day Zeeland, even though the Haringvliet estuary is not in this province but in Zuid-Holland. Stock footage, however, again portrays traditional Zeeland in the form of costumes worn by spectators at the age-old contest of tilting the ring (fig. 7.10).

Liesbeth is an aspiring singer who lives on one of the Wadden Islands. She travels by ferry and rail to Amsterdam for her debut performance at a cabaret in Amsterdam. On the way, she watches various

Fig. 7.10. Tilting the Ring in Zeeland (Girls of Holland, *1966*) (*NIS archive, HCASC*)

kinds of sailing races and takes in the river and canal shipping trade, eighteenth-century country estates, and the pageantry of a shooting guild in the south of the country. Liesbeth even has time to relax on a North Sea beach before her performance. Never mind that these sights and activities do not line up with her itinerary by train through Noord-Holland to Amsterdam.

Finally, there is Marion, a layout editor for a Dutch women's magazine. But more important to the film is that she works as a medieval hostess in Keukenhof, one of the world's largest flower gardens, and a principal, international Dutch tourist destination. This, once more, creates space for the film to present the Dutch flower sector—Keukenhof, flower pageants, and flower auctions.

In spite of its modern packaging, *Girls of Holland* hits most of the usual traditional notes for the Dutch tourist industry. In that respect, the film is very different from *Holland Today*. Those who saw *Girls of Holland* were likely more entertained and, therefore, may have paid more attention to the information presented. But that information is harnessed to the interests of tourism and not to any larger educational objectives. Actually, one sees little of the modern Netherlands besides tourist sites. This is brought home especially in the segment on the islands of the southwest; Janny may work at the Haringvliet construction site, but there is no segue to show and explain more of the Delta Plan. This project was not regarded as a tourist destination, unlike Zeeland's age-old costumes and games.

As with *Girls of Holland, And They Named It Holland* (6,544), released in 1968, had its recorded attendance suppressed by the 1966–72 missing data and the closing of the NIS in 1974. In the opening credits, the title of the film is given in five different languages, including Japanese, but not Dutch. The film itself has neither voice-over narration nor sound; the aerial visuals are accompanied throughout by bracing twentieth-century, modern classical music from the Dutch composer, Hendrik Andriessen, played by the Amsterdam Concertgebouw Orchestra. *And They Named It Holland* won international recognition for its visual rhetoric, remarkable because the film was constructed from outtakes of an aerial film commissioned by the Philips company.[3]

Aerial cinematography is well suited to national promotional films destined for other countries; it can readily assemble and integrate large swaths of the physical and human diversity of a country and present it in novel and often spectacular bird's-eye views for an audience. Aerial films suggest a safe objectivity and by nature steer clear of issues and topics. Because of their arresting aerial imagery with unfamiliar and interesting perspectives, most everyone likes films of this genre, and they generally draw large audiences. Together with *Sky over Holland* (1967) (not in the film library), *And They Named It Holland* belongs to a tradition of aerial documentaries (and photography) of the Netherlands, both with and without voice-over narra-

tion, of which *Holland the Movie* (2008) and *Nederland van Boven* (2012, 2014) are just two of the most recent examples.[4] The commercial availability first of fixed-wing aircraft, then helicopters, and now drones has steadily created more possibilities for aerial cinematography, especially after WWII. Comparing *And They Named It Holland* with the latest films of this genre, makes it clear that aerial cinematography has steadily become more sophisticated and high-tech.

The content of the film is divided between the pre-human (2 min.) and human landscapes (7 min.) of the country. The opening scenes show ice- and snow-covered land with open coastal water. The filmmakers attempt to represent the glacial landscapes that covered part of what became the Netherlands during its early environmental history, forgetting that, during the last ice age, both Dutch land *and* sea were ice-covered, and the channel between England and the Netherlands fell dry because of a much lower sea level. The remaining footage for the pre-human Netherlands portrays a postglacial environment of open water and ice-free land, together with some of the wildlife that this more genial environment attracted: seals, deer, horses, swans, and other waterfowl. What is disturbing here (especially today) is the loud noise of the helicopter (not heard by the viewers) causing all these animals and birds to flee in panic; the wildlife action in the film is entirely produced by helicopter rotor noise.

The remainder of the film shows human-made landscapes and artifacts with-

---

[3]   *Ariadne*, 2 Oct. 1968, 25; magazines.laddb.org/Issue/ARI/1968-10-02/edition/null/page/25 (accessed 15 June 2016).

[4]   *Holland the Movie*, DVD, 30 min., Wim Robberechts & Co. (Diegem, Belgium, 2008); *Nederland van Boven*, seasons 1 and 2, DVD, 669 min., VPRO, 2012 and 2014.

Fig. 7.11. Imagined primordial Dutch farm (And They Named It Holland, *1968*)
(*NIS archive, HCASC*)

out any historical progression. The earliest phase of the human occupation of the country is entirely speculative and, as is most often the case, focused on the low Netherlands, ignoring that the central and eastern higher parts of the country witnessed sedentary life much earlier. *And They Named It Holland* in one scene shows someone rowing a small boat into a coastal waterway; the next scene is that of a small, raised farmstead surrounded by marshes and small wet fields (fig. 7.11).

From that primordial Dutch farm, the film with dramatic music abruptly cuts to an aerial collage of diverse human settlement forms and built environments, without any attention to historical development, that is, twentieth-century Flevoland polders, medieval land reclamation, peat-mining landscapes, historic trading towns along waterways and the coast, monumental historic buildings and towers with carillons, and multicolored bulb fields. The last several minutes are devoted to transportation (infrastructure for inland shipping and automobiles, ocean passenger liners, and commercial ports), which have a decidedly more modern look.

The response by outsiders to a film such as this, without narration, must have been largely aesthetic and intellectual. Audiences outside the Netherlands, such as the American viewers of NIS films, would not have had the additional satisfaction, enjoyed by Dutch audiences, of recognizing familiar places, buildings, structures, and landscape patterns, especially from a new aerial viewpoint. American eyes would have been seeing these spectacles for the first time and, although they may have captivated and charmed them and piqued their curiosity, no identification, contextualization, or explanations were provided. For Americans, the film would have delivered a collage of intriguing visual impressions, but little more.

Bert Haanstra's *The Voice of the Water* (1966; 7,327) could certainly also have been put into the water category, along with other films added during the 1960s and 1970s, such as *Hold Back the Sea* (1961; 51,246) and *Delta Phase 1* (1962; 29,278). I placed it in the national films category because it so comprehensively covers the many associations of the Dutch and water, a key and enduring component of their national identity (also for outsiders). It is not clear when the NIS library acquired the film; it was released in 1966, just at the beginning of the data gap in the circulation records; the recorded attendance is just for 1973 to 1974, the last two years of the NIS. In the Netherlands, the film was wildly popular with nearly half-a-million viewers.[5] It was released for the international market in a number of different languages, including English. With Haanstra's reputation as a leading Dutch filmmaker, *The Voice of the Water* was distributed, of course, not only by the NIS but also by American companies. Clearly, many more Americans saw

this movie than especially the incomplete records of the NIS show.

In several ways, *The Voice of the Water* broke with the heretofore traditions in documentary filmmaking, certainly with the films in the NIB/NIS library. Documentaries, especially national films, had been mainly about things—coasts, airports, villages, housing tracts, marshes, factories, and so on; there could be people in the filmed scenes, but they were another silent constituent. This film's focus is on people, together and individually, interacting and working with and behaving in things, in this case, water, but also with items related to water—eels, ships, swimming pools, sailboats, flood-control structures. Audiences see children at swimming lessons, toddlers introduced to water (fig. 7.12), people vacationing on watercraft, Sinterklaas arriving by boat in different Dutch towns and cities and being welcomed by children and their parents, and a lifeboat crew heading out to sea in a storm to rescue those on a vessel in distress. This focus on people rather than things makes room for more emotional engagement from the audience.

People give water a voice; not only do people actually speak—which they hardly ever did in earlier documentaries—but, in speaking, they describe, interpret, and reflect on their experiences and lifeworld. A survivor of the 1953 flood recounts her experiences as her family and acquaintances tried unsuccessfully to escape the rising floodwaters in their homes and village, and an eel fisherman describes his love for the daily, place-based rhythms of his work on the water. Such voices helped break the hegemony of the authoritative, detached voice-over, also a longstanding, defining component of (Dutch) documen-

---

5   Beknopt Overzicht van het Nederlandse Filmklimaat, 24; http://www.lchr.org/a/14/oy/nfove.html (accessed 17 June 2016).

Fig. 7.12. Toddler in floating playpen and baby carriage in the water
(The Voice of the Water, *1966*) (*NIS archive, HCASC*)

taries. People speaking brought a more multivocal and emotional quality to documentary filmmaking and viewing. For audiences in other countries, this required subtitles in their own language, translating the spoken language, something that was becoming more common in documentary film. Today, audiences take speech (along with subtitles) for granted in documentary filmmaking, but at that time, this development broke new ground.

The Voice of the Water also ignored convention as related to length. Most documentary films were less than thirty minutes, suitable as shorts in theaters and lesson plans in the classroom. At ninety minutes, *The Voice of the Water* fits into the length and stature of a feature film. With such a timespan, topical threads can be much more fully developed and nuanced. Given the breadth of their subject matter and their length constraints, films about the entire country—here labeled national films—often had an encyclopedic quality with very short thematic threads of under a minute. *The Voice of the Water* has much longer topical threads of three to six minutes and longer, making mini storylines possible and immersing the audience more fully in the subject.

A good example is the more than thirteen-minute thread about competitive skûtsje sailing. Frisian cargo sailboats (skûtsjes) were once used in inland shipping; today they are raced in competitions. We meet Siep and Ulbe, two Frisian barge captains who, together with their wives, each ply the inland European

Fig. 7.13. Dutch cleaning a pleasure craft
(The Voice of the Water, *1966*) (*NIS archive, HCASC*)

shipping routes out of Dutch ports for a living. But their passion is skûtsje sailing, and we see them representing their Frisian hometowns, competing against others and each other on the Frisian lakes. We follow their races, witness the art and techniques of sailing these craft, catch the excitement and tension, see the winning boat skippered by Siep cross the finish line, and take in the presentation of the silver skûtsje trophy and the celebrations. The attention of American viewers of NIB/NIS films had been drawn to sailing as a signature Dutch activity before (plentiful water and strong winds), but not with a focus on the people, drama, and details of the sport, something that film length and this kind of cinematography made possible.

The Voice of the Water is a film about the then present-day Netherlands but not in the way other films have shown this quality. Rather than highlighting the markers of modernity—the most advanced trains, planes, automobiles, buildings, factories, and so forth—it films present-day Dutch people in a very lifelike way, engaged in, experiencing, and describing their different occupations, pastimes, events, and distinctive activities, all related directly and indirectly to water. And, although these scenes are also given a Dutch cultural expression (a woman in a swimsuit and cap scrubbing the side of a boat, see fig. 7.13), there is a universal quality to them—fishing, swimming, sailing, boating, water rescue, floods are all worldwide human activities and events. The film is less about Dutchness and more about a common humanity. American and all other non-Dutch viewers could easily relate to such a film.

In *Hans Brinker's Return* (ch. 6), an American father travels to the Netherlands with his son to introduce him to the country of his birth. In *A Country for My Son*

Fig. 7.14. Jan van Dijk rides into his high-rise residential future
(A Country for My Son, *1972*) (*NIS archive, HCASC*)

(1972; 5,166), commissioned by the national Ministry of Housing and Physical Planning, a Dutch father describes the changes required to keep the Netherlands' quality of life intact for his son in the face of a rapidly growing population. The film was released in 1972 and acquired by the NIS that same year; it circulated for only two years before the NIS was shuttered. By this time, the rapid population and economic growth of the 1960s had revealed their shadow sides in persistent housing shortages, traffic congestion, and pollution, among other issues.

As narrator in the film, the father introduces his son Jan, shown riding his bike from school and arriving home in a high-rise apartment building on the edge of a city. The father's voice narrates the entire film, and Jan himself later makes vignette appearances (fig. 7.14). There is no dialogue in the film either between the father and son or anywhere else. But the voice-over carries additional significance because the father describes what will affect his son's future wellbeing. The father as narrator and the son appearing at several points in the film serve as thin, integrating storylines that help draw the audience in.

This minor narrative is joined to a conventional documentary that stresses the necessity of government spatial and environmental planning (with public input) for the future habitability and wellbeing of the country. With stock footage, the film contrasts the pre-WWII and wartime conditions with those of the present (1970s) and argues that these new conditions require new forms of government mandates. The country is faced with such present-day intersecting issues as rapid population growth in a small country, increased industrialization, traffic, rural to urban migration, pollution, and growing affluence and leisure time. These require detailed and legally binding land use and transportation plans at the local, regional, and national levels. With a background score of modern music, especially jazz, viewers see map animations of the entire country that direct and decentralize population growth and set aside recreational zones as well as green buffer belts between cities. They see technocrats bending over plans on maps and scale models. New residential urban areas on city outskirts depicted in the film—including those in Jan's own neighborhood—invariably are the now very characteristic, postwar, large blocks of walk-up and high-rise apartments or blocks of two-story row houses with small yards. All this high density, Le Corbusier-inspired, modernist housing includes generous amounts of intervening semi-public and public open space.

American audiences of this film, much less accustomed to and often nervous about or opposed to governmental urban and regional planning, uniform urban design, and high-density residential living, would have seen the contents of *A Country for My Son* as perhaps inevitable and necessary for a small country with a very high population density, such as the Netherlands. But there would have been very little American affinity and admira-

tion for this modern, less distinctive, and more international Dutch urbanism and mandated regional planning backed with the force of law.

Mirror of Holland (2,918), released in 1950, was not added to the NIS film library until 1960; in circulation for fourteen years, the film did not even garner three thousand viewers, even though it was filmed and produced by Bert Haanstra and received accolades from the international press and awards from the industry. Perhaps this was because it was an art film, a visual poem, without narration, and with little appeal to the general public was unable to teach its viewers much about the Netherlands. *Mirror of Holland* carried the theme of the Dutch and water to a new level by filming the images of the country from moving reflections in water. This meant, of course, that Haanstra could only film the Netherlands either from along the water (city canals, country drainage channels and rivers) or in the water (lakes). Because reflections of things (buildings, cows, sailboats) beside or in water are upside down, Haanstra had to turn his camera around. The images, of course, were not static because surface water is moving in currents, waves, and ripples. And this is the essence of the film: in moving water, Dutch iconic images—canal houses (fig. 7.15), cows, sailboats, towers, swans, bridges, milk cans, windmills, and so forth—modify their true, more static forms to changing rhythms and pulses of their outlines, much like the changing reflections in a house of mirrors. Toward the end of the film, the changing contours become more and more abstract and disoriented from their originals—a sail becomes animated vertical lines and patterns, and human figures dissolve into inchoate swirls. The few who

Fig. 7.15. Canal houses reflected in adjoining water
(Mirror of Holland, *1950*) (*NIS archive, HCASC*)

appreciated avant-garde art films would not have seen *Mirror of Holland* via the NIS film library but at an art house theater or film festival; rank-and-file Americans showed little interest in the film.

For all its cutting-edge cinematographic techniques, *Mirror of Holland* conveys a rather traditional composite image of the country, in part, because filming sites had to be along waterways and water bodies, and this is where traditional Holland, that is, the low Netherlands, is found. In the central and eastern "high" Netherlands, above sea level, without the need for surface drainage channels, the built environment is usually not very close to water,

and in both the low and high Netherlands, modern developments, such as new housing developments, high-rise office towers, factories, freeways, railway lines, and new farmlands are often not located on water. Much local drainage is now carried underground, producing large tracts of land, and transport is by land rather than water. The technique of filming the country reflected in water left out a large portion of the country and focused attention on the older parts of the low Netherlands—in this film, on canal houses, bridges and church towers, milk cans ready for collection by boat, cows grazing close to a drainage ditch that lines their pasture, windmills along waterways, the older parts of villages situated on water, and willows along a channel's edge.

The NIS's national films of the fifties were mainly encyclopedic surveys with authoritative voice-overs; a number of the 1960s/70s films in this class reflect the then, more recent changes in documentary cinematography, including more playful and engaging narration, artistic interpretation, storylines, dialogue, and a greater focus on individuals and events. In the ledger measuring attention given to the Netherlands of old and the present-day, the balance shifted to the latter.

Films about Dutch places

The NIS film library in the 1960s/70s again had very few films available about Dutch places. Films about places are similar to national films but about smaller geographic units, such as regions, cities, and towns. More suitable and common for travelogues and tourist films, documentaries about places remained a challenge for filmmakers. Among the top forty-eight films about the Netherlands in the 1960s/70s, there were only five such films that together make up only some 8 percent (61,321) of the viewers. All except one, *Amsterdam, City of Canals* (1957; 45,890), rank low in the attendance registers. One, *In and around Amsterdam* (1949; 17,096), was carried over from as far back as the 1940s. The four "new" films were about the two largest cities in the country: two about Amsterdam, *Amsterdam, City of Canals* and *Amsterdam* (1959; 2,787), and two about Rotterdam, *Steady as She Goes* (1952; 3,643) and *That Most Living City* (1954; 2,329). Three of these four films had already been released in the 1950s but were not accessioned by the NIS until the 1960s and so were not up-to-date acquisitions.

The fourth, *Amsterdam*, came on board in 1959, but because the film had almost no viewers for that year, I treated it as a new film for the 1960s/70s.

The discrepancy in attendance with *Amsterdam, City of Canals*, the fifth most popular among the forty-eight films; *Steady as She Goes, Amsterdam*; and *That Most Living City*, at thirty-second, thirty-ninth, and forty-fifth, respectively, again had everything to do with television broadcasting and, indirectly, the perceived allure of Amsterdam for American and international viewers. The television station in Southfield, Michigan, broadcasted *Amsterdam, City of Canals* in 1965, and it received a Nielsen rating of forty thousand. Without that television broadcast, the film, shown in twenty-one other conventional locations, would have had the same rather small total viewership as the others. And one can be quite sure that the international reputation of Amsterdam and its canals played into the decision to air this film and not the one about Rotterdam. At the same time, the other film about Amsterdam, even though it was in color, was not chosen for a television broadcast; its total audience was as low as the others. Television skewed the geography of viewership for *Amsterdam, City of Canals*, with 90 percent or more of the audience in the Detroit, Michigan, area and the rest from small audiences in scattered locations throughout the twenty-state, Holland NIS service region.

These films gave American audiences an opportunity to take in the work of several leading filmmakers of the internationally celebrated Dutch documentary school (1945-65), such as Herman van der Horst (*Steady as She Goes* and *Amsterdam*) and Max de Haas (*Amsterdam, City of Canals*). Unlike earlier documentaries that concen-

Fig. 7.16. Barge with bagged bulk negotiates the passage under a bridge at the entrance to a canal (Amsterdam, City of Canals. Impressions by the Waterside, *1957*) (*NIS archive, HCASC*)

trated on the exterior, built environment, the two films about Amsterdam focused on people in their daily tasks—a woman washing clothes on the deck of an inland shipping barge, stevedores loading and unloading various kinds of cargo from ships in the harbor, a barrel-organ player turning the crank as his partner collects money from bystanders on the street, commuters arriving for work in central Amsterdam by ferry from across the IJ, and shoppers at Waterlooplein, inspecting and haggling over items for sale at this outdoor market.

What also sets these two films apart from standard practice in documentary films is the absence of voice-over commentary. In *Amsterdam, City of Canals*, De Haas worked only with a music soundtrack (there is virtually no soundscape or dialogue), fitted to the tempo and kinds of human pursuits in one, twenty-four-hour, filmed rhythm of the city, including evening carousel riders, dawn over the city center, hurrying commuters, the grand scale of shipbuilding, and the life on and along the canals (fig. 7.16) and in the harbor. This documentary is best remembered for its ballet of the port cranes, a typical artistic scene from the Dutch documentary school, but with little connection to the

Fig. 7.17. Ballet of the port cranes (Amsterdam, City of Canals. Impressions by the Waterside, *1957*) (*NIS archive, HCASC*)

rest of the film. With walkie-talkies, De Haas directed and orchestrated six operators' movements of their cranes (fig. 7.17).

Van der Horst, by contrast, used no music track nor hardly any dialogue but only Amsterdam's rich city soundscape—screeching gulls, pipe organs and carillons in churches (fig. 7.18), a Jewish cantor (chazzan), the buzz of people and barkers' shouts at an open-air market, the pounding of pile drivers, barrel organs on the street, warehouses, and working cranes and other machinery in the harbor. The use of sound as an independent constituent of film, again, was an essential ingredient of this Dutch documentary school.

The use of such relatively novel filmic techniques in these two documentaries of the NIS film library, as well as others, such as *Mirror of Holland* and *Steady as She Goes*, does underscore an issue about screening films in one country that are from and about another country. Films produced to promote, educate people about, and tell the story of the Netherlands in other countries, such as the blockbusters, *Holland Today* and *Holland: A Modern Country Full of Old-Time Charm*, discussed earlier, and others commissioned by tourist, trade, and multinational agencies, invariably used and relied on voice-over narration to effectively communicate their content and message.

By contrast, the films under scrutiny here were not intended, in the first place, for export to and viewing by those living in other countries but were produced primarily for the domestic market and (some) for international film festivals. Dutch viewers of such films instinctively understood their visual and acoustic rhetoric. But without voice-over narration describing and explaining what they were seeing, viewers in other countries, albeit perhaps entertained

Fig. 7.18. Carillonneur (Amsterdam, *ca. 1959*) (*NIS archive, HCASC*)

by a film's special techniques and effects, likely learned less about the country than from a film with accompanying narration. This is especially true, for example, about the section in the film *Amsterdam* about the pogroms against the Jews and the related February general strike.

If it is well done, voice-over narration can play a vital educational role to help an audience unfamiliar with the content to understand and interpret it. Film buffs may enthuse over the techniques on display, but most rank-and-file moviegoers in other countries come to a documentary to discover and learn something about another country. A voice-over helps such learning; it ties the visual to a spoken elucidat-

ing text. Alternatively, one may argue that what is shared here with another country is as much about Dutch cinematography as the subject matter of the film. Moreover, a documentary without a voice-over has the advantage of not needing narration in different common languages.

Both of these films about Amsterdam feature people of the city in the 1950s going about their daily lives in the setting of the old city and harbor dating back to the seventeenth century and earlier. The people themselves, however, do not have a voice. Viewers see little of nineteenth- and twentieth-century Amsterdam, although the workings and equipment of the harbor are up to date. We see modern people

Fig. 7.19. Tugboat captain on his way to help dock a large oceangoing freighter in the port of Rotterdam (Steady as She Goes, *1952*) (*NIS archive, HCASC*)

living and working in an age-old setting. For filmmakers, old Amsterdam continues to be the soul of the city. More than earlier documentaries, which were often quite linear and encyclopedic, these two films also have more structural coherence. *Amsterdam, City of Canals* films the rhythms of the city for a twenty-four-hour period, starting in the middle of the night. It connects the present to the past by joining filmed scenes with historical paintings of the same places and activities, for example, the interior of the Nieuwe Kerk with a seventeenth-century painting of the same scene.

Amsterdam had international importance and allure beginning already in the seventeenth century, and the city became a destination for travelers, travel writers, and tourists from the beginning of tourism; this was very much less so for Rotterdam. Whereas the two films about Amsterdam seek to capture the identity, diversity, and timeless qualities of the city, the two films about Rotterdam, *Steady as She Goes* (1952) and *That Most Living City* (1954), focus on an event—the postwar reconstruction of the city center destroyed by the German air force on May 14, 1940. Events, of course, are more time bound, and public interest in them fades as the years pass. Both films were released in the 1950s, *Steady as She Goes* already in 1952, the decade that Europe recovered from the war. They were not acquired by the NIS film library until the early 1960s, a decade of renewed prosperity as well as social upheaval in the transatlantic world. By then, the more immediate public interest in the war had begun to fade. As a result, these two films are to some extent out of place for the 1960s, something that, no doubt, is reflected in the attendance.

Steady as She Goes (1952; 3,643), produced by Herman van der Horst, in black and white, represents the best of the creative Dutch documentary school with its close-ups of idiosyncratic human activities—a pigeon fancier exercising and feeding his birds from the roof, a tugboat captain docking an ocean liner (fig. 7.19), and road builders passing brick pavers hand to hand. Human voices, machines, and other environmental sounds integral to all construction and other activities are accentuated in the film and bring its scenes to life. There is construction going on everywhere, and the focus is on industrious and determined people working to rebuild their city center. Several reappearing "characters" integrate the film: mischievous young boys playing in the construction sites; a one-legged, armed-forces veteran surveying the goings-on; and a military drum band marching through the area. The final scenes are classic Dutch documentary school; with every strike of the pile-driver's hammer, a new building rises from the ground.

Steady as She Goes does not have a structured narrative or storyline; it consists of a series of tableaus that leave impressions. It also has neither (nor needs, some would say) a voice-over nor a music track. It was commissioned by the Marshall Plan, the American initiative to help Europe re-

cover from WWII and, as such, was to be shared with other participating nations, including the United States. Clearly, the film was produced to not have a voice-over, and given its visual form, one could not be easily added. A significant portion of the meaning of this film's content was lost in its cultural transfer abroad.

By contrast, *That Most Living City* (2,329), released in 1954, is an entirely conventional documentary, information and promotion driven, with a structured visual narrative, voice-over, and music track. If a viewer was asked what they learned from this film, there would be a great deal of information to report. The storyline of a police officer showing a boy around the reconstructed city and port was added from an earlier film, *En Toch . . . Rotterdam* (1950), which had previously documented the destruction and reconstruction of the city.[6] The storyline of the film resembles *Hans Brinker's Return* (1954), in which a father, born in the Netherlands, shows his American son around Noord-Holland and engages him in a running conversation about what they are seeing together. In *That Most Living City*, too, there is no real dialogue; the policeman talking to the boy is the voice-over narration of the film. As in *Hans Brinker's Return*, this softens the authoritative voice-from-nowhere of the narrator, locates it within the film, and makes it more intimate and credible. The boys in both films are captivated by a 'Dutch' story, in *Hans Brinker's Return*, about the boy who plugged a hole in the dike with his finger, and in *That Most Living City*, about Erasmus who, on his statue

---

6   F. J. J. W. Paalman, "Cinematic Rotterdam: The Times and Ideas of a Modern City" (PhD diss., Amsterdam School for Cultural Analysis, 2010), 172–75.

Fig. 7.20. Allotment (community) gardens provided for those in apartment buildings in the rebuilt downtown a nearby plot of land for gardening and relaxation (*That Most Living City, 1954*) (*NIS archive, HCASC*)

in Rotterdam, turned a page of the book he was holding every time the clock struck.[7]

With an English, not Dutch, voice-over and commissioned by Rotterdam's information and publicity office, the film announced to the world that Rotterdam and its port were once again open for business. As background for the reconstructed city center and port, the film includes footage of the prewar downtown as well as the firestorm after the German bombardment that totally destroyed and leveled more than 650 acres of homes, business-

es, churches, schools, and hospitals. But the focus of the film and more than three quarters of its footage was on the new and modern-style city and port. The policeman takes the boy past repaired and new extended quays, cranes, and dock-worker housing. In the reconstructed downtown, they stop at the Ahoy exhibit hall that featured working, scale-model replicas of the new port's facilities for the international shipping industry and general public. The planning for the redevelopment of the area could be done from a blank slate that allowed modernist urbanism to come to full expression with its large-scale open space

[7] Chr. Van Abkoude, *Kruimeltje* (Kluitman, 1923), 18.

and parks, residential apartment blocks and office towers, allotment gardens (fig. 7.20), separate pedestrian shopping streets, and even its heliport. All this new development passes before the boy's (and viewers') eyes. The tenor of the film is not unlike that of *Holland Today*; although the Dutch did not destroy this past themselves, with the old city center gone, an opportunity for a new idealized one had presented itself.

Topical films

The move to more topical films in the lending library, over against other films about places, large and small, first seen during the 1950s, broadened during the 1960s/70s. A count based on films in the archive and on titles and information in online databases—for those films that did circulate but were not in the archive—yields some 120 topical films, three-quarters of the collection. The sky is the limit, of course, when it comes to topics and, unlike national and place-based films, multiple films about the same topic are much less likely. Of the top forty-eight films screened during the 1960s and 1970s receiving closer scrutiny in this study, thirty (62.5%) are topical films. These were seen by 417,153 moviegoers throughout the NIS's twenty-state Midwest region, more than 56 percent of the attendance of the forty-eight top films about the Netherlands. Six of these films were carried over from the 1950s, with a viewership of 63,410, with *And There Was No More Sea* making up more than half of that number. One film, *New Earth*, all the way from the forties, still generated 19,128 viewers, a testimony to its continuing appeal. The remaining twenty-three films were first screened during the 1960s/70s to 334,615 viewers.

Specialization of topical films

In chapter 6, I make a distinction between the topical documentaries about the country of interest to Dutch residents and those that appealed to non-Dutch populations outside the country. Because of their insider, cultural identity, knowledge, and interests, enough Dutch residents would be attracted to viewing documentaries about more specialized, arcane, and local topics. Americans, on the other hand, lacked the situational knowledge to appreciate and be interested in such films, and when public diplomacy agencies, such as the NIS, included those films in their offerings, they drew small audiences. Put another way, unless there was some distinctive and internationally recognized element of Dutchness in the documentary and/or for the NIS a perceived American link to the Netherlands as part of the film, the viewership of topical films was more likely to be rather trivial. This contrast persisted as a borrowing and attendance barrier for the expanded 1960s/70s film library, as it had in the 1950s.

Some additional specialized topics—many about building projects—rendered on film and part of the Holland-NIS 1960s/70s library but borrowed by very few people and therefore not part of the forty-eight films examined more closely, include:

1. the overnight move from the old to the new Schiphol in 1967 (*Schiphol International Airport in Operation*, 1971; 748);
2. the building of the Oosterschelde Bridge, then the longest in Europe (*Elements Facing Elements*, 1960; 594);
3. the construction of the market square in the municipality of Dronten, a new

town in the Flevopolder (*The Glass Square*, 1972; 917);

4. finding work after illness or injury (*Helpers on the Threshold*, 1960; 1,143); and

5. the interior life of a seriously wounded man undergoing treatment (*The Injured Man*, 1966; 435).

These films were not inferior productions compared to those with higher attendance figures; they were simply less suited for an American or international viewership. They may be regarded as acquisition misjudgments on the part of the NIS; alternatively, as with any library, there are both more general and more specialized works, and the latter will have an acceptable, more limited circulation. It does, however, need to be underscored again that some topical films could hardly develop any traction simply because they were added in the years just prior to the closing of the NIS; others had much lower attendance figures than recorded due to the six-year data gap.

With some significant exceptions, topical films that were toward the higher end of the attendance range (from 113,615 to 2,219) of the forty-eight films singled out for attention featured the more general, internationally recognized and distinctive accomplishments and unique features of the country, such as its remarkable relations with water (*Hold Back the Sea*, 1961; 51,246), its award-winning documentary filmmakers (*Speaking of Glass*, 1958; 68,236), its famous artists (*Adventures in Perception*, 1971; 17,040), and its military alliances with the United States (*NATO Tattoo*, n.d., 42,761). The popularity of such topics was reflected in the decision to broadcast some of these films on television, guaranteeing high viewership numbers.

Types of topical films

The topical films break into two principal groups: films with distinctive Dutch content and international Dutch films, the latter category made up of documentaries lacking distinctive Dutchness, as well as Dutch-made art and experimental films. More traditionally, a Dutch documentary film distributed abroad by a government agency and borrowed by a librarian or schoolteacher was expected to teach its viewers something about the world of the Dutch—their history, geography, natural environments, economy, arts, and so forth. The focus was more on distinctiveness and difference. Such was clearly the case in the 1940s and 1950s. Beginning in the 1960s, another kind of Dutch topical documentary began to surface in the NIS film library: international Dutch films. Their emphasis was more on common features that the Netherlands shared with and contributed to—together with other "advanced" countries—developments in the arts, architecture, science, technology, healthcare, and industrialization. In documentary filmmaking, too, Dutch directors and producers had demonstrated their international leadership in novel cinematography and film art. In part, the appearance of this type of documentary in the film library was due to late modernity as an international movement; the Netherlands wanted to showcase that it, too, was a modern country. The Dutchness of its modernity was considered less notable than its more international and universal qualities.

Earlier, I discussed the shifting emphasis between tradition and modernization in the national films shown in the

1950s and 1960s/70s; in these films, the interplay between Dutch particularity and Dutch commonality became quite visible. It can be argued that American and other non-Dutch viewers of Dutch documentaries would be more interested in Dutch distinctiveness, but Dutch viewers would especially want to see the international contributions of their country. In the same way, a Dutch government film library outside the Netherlands, such as the one at the NIS, would also especially want to show off the country's worldwide accomplishments. This suggests somewhat of a mismatch between the non-Dutch viewer preferences and the goals of the NIS, one that likely had some bearing on borrowing rates and attendance of particular films.

Topical films with distinctive Dutch content

Common in the earlier decades, these films showcase some notable aspects of Dutch history, technology, economy, and culture. Altogether, ten new films and seven continuing from preceding decades fit this category during the 1960s/70s, with 265,100 viewers, some 63.5 percent of the attendance of the topical films about the Netherlands and 35.7 percent of the entire viewership of all forty-eight top films about the country. These percentages are greater than the corresponding ones for the international topical films category (36.4/20.5%), only because the films with distinctive Dutch content include the Dutch and water (always a killer topic for non-Dutch audiences), with attendance figures for individual films in five figures, whereas nearly all other topical films have four-figure audiences.

Topical films about Dutch water defenses

Although hardly any films covered the same topic, the same cannot be said of films about the Dutch and water. There are no fewer than five films (three new ones) on this topic among the top forty-eight films about the Netherlands in the 1960s/70s, all in the top tier of attendance and with a total viewership of 148,730. If *The Voice of the Water* (7,327) and *Amsterdam, City of Canals* (45,890), discussed under the rubrics of national and place-based films, were added to this group, more than two hundred thousand people in NIS-Holland saw films about this, arguably, best-known feature of the country for American viewers from 1960 to 1974. Besides national films that generally already had a fair amount to show and say about water and the Netherlands, topical films about this subject were the most predominant. American viewers had ample opportunity to learn a great deal about the Dutch and water. The new films could build upon the demonstrated interest of Americans in this subject and expand their knowledge with much improved historical overviews and accounts of new technologies.

Recall that films about this topic shown during the 1950s underlined the destructive and human suffering side of water and the Dutch, especially seen in the scorched-earth strategy of the German occupiers and Allied liberators, and later, in the devastating 1953 storm flood. The narrative of the new films changed that perception quite drastically to one of greater technological control and optimism. Throughout history, the Dutch had repeatedly implemented groundbreaking innovations for managing water for safety, live-

Fig. 7.21. Student rides home from school on what was seafloor three
decades earlier (Wieringermeerpolder, drained in 1930)
(Hold Back the Sea, *1961*) (*NIS archive, HCASC*)

lihood, commerce, and defense. Together, these technologies, institutions, and laws related to water had provided increasing levels of safety and societal and economic security and wellbeing. During the twentieth century, water-related science, technologies, and management had achieved new levels of sophistication and scale. With the renewed prosperity of the 1960s, the state-of-the-art engineering works of the Delta Plan promised to protect the Dutch population of the low Netherlands for good.

Both *Hold back the Sea* (1961; 51,246) and *Dam the Delta* (1969; 16,041) provided American viewers with quite trustworthy primers on the natural and environmental history of the low Netherlands as it related to water. Both films engaged professional advisors in geology and water management. Both ably kept viewers' attention with scenes of objective hydraulic landscapes alternating with (often more light-hearted) human activities related to water. Each passing technological phase shown achieved a greater measure and larger scale of security and control: occupation mounds (Dutch, *terpen, wierden*), sluices, dikes, polders, windmills, lake drainage, steam driven pumps, dredging vessels, and the closure of sea arms and related land

Fig. 7.22. The highly indented Dutch coastline in the fifteenth century
(Hold Back the Sea, *1961*) (*NIS archive, HCASC*)

reclamation, such as the Zuiderzee project (fig. 7.21).

Hold back the Sea opens with a shot over the top of the riveted steel gate of the Hollandse IJssel flood barrier with churning water on the other side, and the narrator reads, "Behind this great steel gate lies Holland." This river storm-surge barrier was the first completed phase (1958) of the fifty-year-long Delta Works project, enacted by the Dutch parliament after the 1953 flood to protect not only the islands of the southwestern Netherlands

but also the below-sea-level lands of the province of Zuid-Holland. Then, immediately, the film looks back and, for most of its length, traces the prehistory and history of the low Netherlands related to water (fig. 7.22).[8] That visual chronicle ends with the 1953 flood, and the film returns to the

---

[8] The film covers much more of the water history of the Netherlands than the title, *Hold Back the Sea*, would suggest. Technology and practices related to inland waters and groundwater (polders, land reclamation, dredging, etc.) are also covered. The Dutch title *De Lage Landen* (The lowlands) is more fitting.

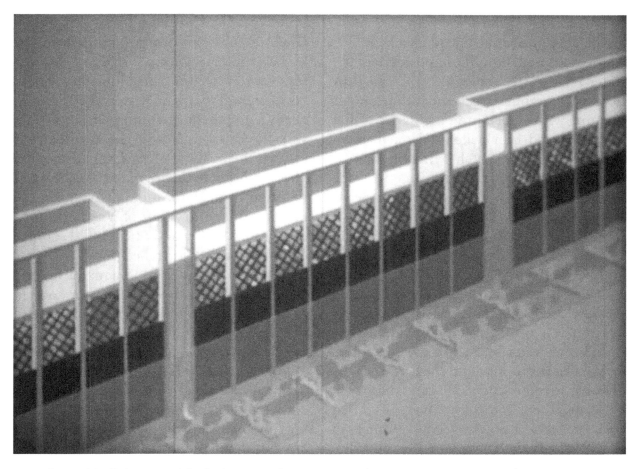

Fig. 7.23. Caissons with their gates shut create a dam across a sea arm. The gates are in black and gray, resting on the seafloor, with the line separating these two shades marking the water elevation (*Dam the Delta*, ca. 1969) (*NIS archive, HCASC*).

country's answer to this storm event: the first completed flood barrier of the Delta Works and the approved plans for damming the sea arms in the southwest of the country to shorten and make for a continuous and storm-resistant coastline. The film looks even further into the future with a map outline of a plan to build sea walls between the Wadden barrier islands on the northern perimeter of the country and change the lagoon behind them (the Wadden Sea) into a freshwater lake, like IJssel Lake. With state-of-the-art sea walls along a much shorter and hardened national coastline without any sea arms, the long-sought-after permanent security from sea flooding was thought possible. Public environmental concerns had not yet emerged in 1961 when *Hold Back the Sea* was released. Today, the promotion of such a future plan would be unthinkable; the Wadden Sea, a Unesco Heritage site, is now protected as the most important natural intertidal zone in the country. A paradigm shift about the country's relationship to water is underway, from one of battling water with increasing sophisticated technological barriers to one of working with and making room for water.[9]

9   Tracy Metz and Maartje van Den Heuvel, *Sweet and Salt. Water and the Dutch* (NAi, 2012).

Dam the Delta is an animated movie, the only one in the entire film archive.[10] As a cartoon, it simplifies and renders the water-related technologies and institutions with graphic precision and promotes learning with entertainment. It is clear that this animated film benefitted much from the advice of the Dutch Ministry of Water Management. The film covers the same history of Dutch water management technology as *Hold Back the Sea* but extends it into the know-how essential for the Delta Works—caissons and sluice complexes, both essential for the realization of this extensive regional project lasting half a century. Caissons are prefabricated hollow concrete boxes which float and can be towed over water into place next to others in a line across a sea arm; they are sunk by opening their wooden side gates and then, to secure them into place, partially filled with gravel and sand. Water continues to flow through the caissons with the tides. At a moment of zero tidal motion, all the caisson gates are simultaneously shut, closing the sea arm once and for all (fig. 7.23). The caissons form the core of the dam. Sluice and lock systems have a long history on canals and rivers; their application to seacoasts and sea arms is more recent. The sea arms closed by the Delta Plan required transport connections to the open sea for fishing, commerce, and recreation. Sluice and lock systems built into the dams were constructed as part of the project; they had to be able to withstand major storms and keep salt- from freshwater.

Delta Phase 1 (1962; 29,278), directed by Bert Haanstra, detailed the construction of one of the first dams of the Delta Works that used the caisson method to complete a sea wall between the islands of Walcheren and Noord-Beveland in Zeeland (the Veerse Gat dam). Haanstra's camera records the cooperative effort between tugboat captains and valve and heavy equipment operators who position, sink the caissons into place, and then reinforce them. Before that final closure, he pays attention to the water and land behind the soon-to-be dam, and, in particular, the fourteenth-century city of Veere. Its fishing fleet and other activities would soon be cut off from the North Sea (fig. 7.24).

In his classic style, Haanstra depicts the tidal nature of the Veere harbor, soon to be tidal no more: with every rapid strike of the city's tower bell, the ships in the harbor are shown raised at high tide and lowered at low tide. Reminiscent of Haanstra's *And There Was No More Sea*, released six years earlier about Zuiderzee fishing villages cut off from the sea by the Afsluitdijk and the lament about the impending loss of their culture, *Delta Phase 1* has a much more hopeful outlook. True, the fishing fleet has to leave for a nearby port, but Haanstra shows that the Zeeland culture behind the dike will be protected and thrive, isolation lessened, and recreational resources expanded. In contrast to the closing epitaph to a way of life in *And There Was No More Sea*, a celebration with fireworks attended by many residents, tops the final closure and completion of the dam.

Additional topical films with distinctive Dutch content

That leaves an additional twelve topical films with distinctive Dutch content (7 new, 5 from previous decades), with a total viewership of 116,373—43.9 percent of this category and 15.7 percent of the attendance of the forty-eight films about the Nether-

---

Fig. 7.24. Fourteenth-century fishing port of the city of Veere, Zeeland, eliminated by the Delta Plan (Delta Phase 1, *1962*)

lands receiving a closer reading. The earlier films are discussed in the preceding chapter; their messaging—substantially diminished—does remain a part of the kaleidoscope of imagery and information on offer during the 1960s/70s period.

Speaking of Glass (1958; 68,236) was the third most-viewed NIS film during the 1960s/70s, behind two national films, *Holland Today* and *Dutch Miniatures*. This film's popularity, in general, stemmed from its world-class director, Bert Haanstra, and in particular, rested on the coattails of its more famous cousin, *Glass*, which won an Oscar in 1960 in the documentary short-subject category. *Glass* was the shorter (10 min.), more poetic version,

and *Speaking of Glass* was the informational and narration-driven, longer version (27 min.). Like other top films of the 1960s/70s, its attendance was significantly boosted by a television broadcast in the Detroit region, and an additional seventy-one other places throughout the NIS-Holland region screened the film.

Speaking of Glass showcases the Dutch glass industry—the handicraft of designing and blowing glass (fig. 7.25) at Royal Leerdam in the city of the same name, as well as the factory production of bottles and jars at the United Glass Works in Schiedam. Royal Leerdam, especially, has had a worldwide reputation for quality glasswork already since the eighteenth

Fig. 7.25. Glassblowers in Leerdam leave the furnace with precise amounts of molten glass on the end of their blowpipes, which they then roll and blow to form a bowl; others add the stem and base with molten glass (*Speaking of Glass, 1958*) (*NIS archive, HCASC*).

century. The film documents the entire glass and glass products production chain, from charging the furnace with sand, crystal chips, and other ingredients to the final packaging of glassware for shipment. It details the craftsmanship of the glass blower rolling and shaping a mold into a goblet and of the engraver fashioning cut-glass vases. It also shows the highly automated, mass production of consumer glass products.

How does *Speaking of Glass*, not *Panta Rhei*, both Haanstra films, feature Dutch content? The film's interior factory imagery provides viewers with no real clue that they are looking at Dutch scenes. The answer lies in the English-language voiceover, absent in *Panta Rhei*, that guides and contextualizes Americans' viewing experience. When, for example, they hear and see that Royal Leerdam glassware is shipped all over the world, Dutch glassware takes a place beside other world-class Dutch exports such as cheese and tulips.

Such was also the case with the industry promotional film about the Dutch tree and ornamental shrub nursery sector, *The Magic Square* (1965; 2,521), made

Fig. 7.26. Pruning and tying blue spruce saplings near Boskoop
(*The Magic Square, ca. 1965*) (*NIS archive, HCASC*)

in cooperation with Plant Propaganda [a pun] Holland in Boskoop in the province of Zuid-Holland. The tree nurseries in Boskoop go back to the fifteenth century; today, it is the largest contiguous area of tree and ornamental plant nurseries in the world. Through accumulated skills in grafting and propagation, its nurseries continue to produce new varieties of plants found elsewhere in the world and market their nursery trees and shrubs internationally (fig. 7.26). The Netherlands is the number-one exporter in the world of live trees, plants, bulbs, roots, and flowers.[11]

The Magic Square, with its rather implausible title, directs attention to the four essential sides of the nursery industry: climate, soil, skills, and science. At the very beginning of the film, harp and percussion music (no video) are a lead-in to the voice-over naming each of these ingredients in turn. Colored squares then appear on the screen to serve as the source for the opening credits and then reappear at the end. This artistic packaging surrounds what is an entirely conventional encyclopedic documentary consisting of a sequence of separate linear visual threads in real time with a voice-over. Scenes of Dutch residential gardens and urban parks with flowering trees and shrubs are used to make the point

[11]   Netherlands Ministry of Foreign Affairs, *Holland Compared, Facts and Figures*, 2nd ed. (Netherlands Enterprise Agency, 2017). 80.

that the plants in such settings have come not from nature but from nurseries that, by means of grafting, have produced suitable and attractive varieties from plants all over the world, such as azaleas, rhododendrons, and junipers. *The Magic Square* next turns its attention to the Boskoop region whose nurseries have produced much of the plant stock for such environments in the Netherlands and abroad. The film shows sales representatives from abroad in Boskoop ordering nursery stock.

The film then returns to each of the necessary four sides of the "magic square"—sufficient moisture without extremes (climate); soils rich in humus, well-aired and drained (soils); cutting, grafting, and propagating expertise in the local workforce (skills); and new ways of making varieties by such methods as hand pollination and injections with nutrients (science)—and finds they are present in Boskoop and several other Dutch locales. Before returning to the gardens and parks dependent on such plants propagated in nurseries, *The Magic Square* shows the specialized kinds of containers and packaging required to ship such nursery stock abroad by boat and plane.

The Netherlands as a land of horticulture has been well-established in the perception of those outside the country. Bulb cultivation but also, as here, nurseries, as well as truck gardening and landscape services are strongly associated with the Dutch. Events such as Keukenhof, one of the world's largest annual flower gardens near Lisse, and Floriade, an international flower and garden show held every decade in a different location in the Netherlands, continue to nourish that perception. The same association has also come to apply to

Dutch Americans and Canadians, that is, truck farming in the urban shadows of, for example, New York, Chicago, and Grand Rapids, Michigan, often on drained muck soils,[12] as well as their disproportional participation in the landscaping, nursery, and greenhouse sectors of Dutch American and Dutch Canadian urban North America.

Holland: Terra Fertilis (1967; 2,287), a more general film for consumers around the world about Dutch farming, farm output, and food processing uses an entirely different visual language and cinematography than *The Magic Square*. Here, once again, the artistic film editing techniques of the Dutch documentary school are used to create a fast-paced, kaleidoscopic, entertaining, and humoristic visual overview of the Dutch agricultural sector. In this case, visual poetry is not an end in itself but very much related to conveying subject matter. That *Terra Fertilis* has no voice over is quite understandable; its visual rhythm and pace made writing a script unfeasible. Without it, the film is much less didactic; the visuals, soundscape, and background music create significance and meaning. *Terra Fertilis* occupies an interesting place on the span between Dutch particularism and international modernism but, like other documentaries from the film library during this period, it clearly tips the balance in

[12]   *Dutch Muck—and Much More: Dutch Americans in Farming, Religion, Art, and Economy*, ed. Earl Wm. Kennedy, Donald A. Luidens, and David Zwart (Van Raalte Press, 2019), includes two pertinent chapters: Robert Swierenga, "Dutch on the Muck: Celery Cropping in Michigan and Elsewhere," 15–64, and Ken Bult, "Onion Set Farming in South Holland, Illinois," 65–74. See also, Albert VanderMey, *And the Swamp Flourished: The Bittersweet Story of Holland Marsh* (VanderHeide Publishing, 1994).

Fig. 7.27. Holstein Friesians loaded onto a KLM cargo plane for export
(Holland: Terra Fertilis, *1967*) (*NIS archive, HCASC*)

favor of the latter. The Dutch agricultural sector is shown as up-to-date, technologically advanced, and export oriented. The final scenes show a dual-trailer truck crossing the Dutch-German border with farm products and a KLM cargo plane crew member wearing a full Holstein Friesian cow-head mask giving the thumbs-up for take-off, carrying these once Dutch but now global cows (fig. 7.27).

Terra Fertilis is cleverly framed into sections by a most unlikely Dutch (originally, Frisian) traditional pastime and sport—pole vaulting across a water course. In Frisian, it is called *fierljeppen* (lit. "leaping far") in Dutch, *polsstokspringen*. To transition into different sections of the film,

a young man pole vaults across a drainage canal into the opening credits and title, a landscape of greenhouses, boxes of picked cherries, and a Dutch flower auction. At the end of the film, he lands on the other side of the canal and is showered by all the food and other farm products that have been featured in the film. The social turbulence of the 1960s as related to the women's liberation movement is also on display in the movie. The pilot in the duster plane is a young woman; she buzzes and laughs at a young man walking through the fields, spraying the same crops with a hand-held unit.

The subject matter of *Terra Fertilis* is cut up into very short scenes (5–10 seconds), and scenes with entirely different content are often juxtaposed (tomatoes going up a conveyor belt and the queen of the flower parade with floats waving to the onlookers; buyers at a flower auction and a woman piloting a crop-duster plane). Other juxtapositions of scenes depict foreshortened food processing (cows and then milk poured into a glass; blossoms, then ripe apples on a tree, followed by apple juice filling a glass). Included is the classic visual rhetoric of the Dutch documentary school: every slap against the side of a cow by an interested buyer takes the viewer to a scene of his farmstead, and when fruit is picked, the moment the fruit is separated from the stem is accompanied by a distinctive non-diegetic sound. Other scenes are outright zany, for instance, round Alkmaar cheeses portrayed as bowling balls, with gin and milk bottles as pins.

Overall, *Terra Fertilis* projects a modern, productive, and technologically advanced image of Dutch agriculture (automated greenhouses, vacuum egg-lifters, milking machines, duster planes, combines, and automated crop handling). Especially funny are the scenes of the greenhouse grower drinking coffee, reading the newspaper, and falling asleep while the smart greenhouse goes about regulating temperature, sunlight, and water by opening and closing shades, louvers, and sprinklers. The internationally well-known agricultural export sectors such as flowers, bulbs, and cheeses receive plenty of attention (but not nursery stock) but so do other parts of standard Dutch agriculture—poultry, grains, pork, fish, and fruit— then more related to domestic consumption and, therefore, less well known outside the country. Again, it is not only what is im-

portant and unique about the Netherlands' relations with other countries (where do American flower bulbs come from?) but also what is important to Dutch people themselves. American viewers' knowledge about the Netherlands was more fully developed by awareness of both of these aspects of Dutch agriculture.

Rembrandt, Painter of Man (1957; 4,762), directed by Bert Haanstra, is another topical film with distinctive Dutch content, although the themes of Rembrandt's paintings, especially those that capture Biblical events, are often very universal, something the title of this film clearly brings out. At the same time, many of his portraits, group portraits, and paintings of historical events and landscapes are of Dutch scenes and Dutch people, and taken together, his works carry a seventeenth-century Dutchness. *Rembrandt Painter of Man* surveys the work of one of the most outstanding representatives of Dutch Golden Age painting.

During the seventeenth century, Dutch painting broke with the older Catholic and monarchist art traditions, both in subject matter and style. The range of subject matter and genres greatly increased—especially everyday scenes—and the styles became more realistic. A distinctive Dutch-art tradition developed with a very large output of paintings with which the names of such artists as Rembrandt Van Rijn, Johannes Vermeer, Frans Hals, Judith Leyster, and Peter de Hooch are associated. Today, Dutch Golden Age painting continues to be admired as one of the most significant Dutch cultural achievements and exports, just like "land below the sea," a key building stone in the perception of the country by those living elsewhere.

Fig. 7.28. Last self-portrait of Rembrandt (at age 63)
(Rembrandt, Painter of Man, *1957*) (*NIS archive, HCASC*)

In *Rembrandt, Painter of Man*, moviegoers are introduced to Rembrandt's life through his paintings. The visual side of the film is made up entirely of camera zooms, pans, and stills of details and entire canvases, something non-Dutch viewers especially would have liked, somewhat like going to a gallery to look at a painting in detail. The film is book ended by Rembrandt's first and last self-portraits (fig. 7.28) and features many other self-portraits to document the changing stages and vicissitudes in his life. At the end, each self-portrait dissolves into the succeeding one.

The voice-over is indispensable for viewing the film; it connects the content, themes, and moods not only of Rembrandt's biblical paintings but also his other commissioned works to the changing circumstances and emotional and spiritual states in Rembrandt's life—his marriages, the early deaths of his wives and children, and his up-and-down financial circumstances. The film was produced from the outset for an international market, with an English-language voice-over in addition to the Dutch-language version.

The Dutch have, some would say, an obsession for skating on natural ice, which of course, is no match for Rembrandt as a cultural marker. Yet the Eleven Cities Tour (Elfstedentocht) is part of a popular pastime and sport that has been associated with the Netherlands for centuries. First held in 1909, the Eleven Cities Tour is a skating race as well as a noncompetitive tour of nearly 200 km on canals, rivers, and lakes that join eleven historical cities in the province of Friesland. Both professional skaters and the general public may participate. It is held only when the natural ice all along the route is 15 cm (5.9 inches) thick; therefore, depending on the weather (which in mid-latitude maritime climates is often quite changeable and mild), the tour has been held at times in consecutive years but also with a twenty-year hiatus. When the conditions are right, skating fever strikes, and a national holiday mood floods the country. Schools close; people take time off work, and everyone heads for the nearest waterway to put their skates on. The race was last held in 1997.

Golden Age painters, such as Hendrick Averkamp, produced iconic Dutch scenes of winter landscapes with skaters having fun.[13] These and later literary works, such as *Hans Brinker, or the Silver Skates*, by American writer Mary Mapes Dodge, fixed this facet of Dutch identity abroad.[14] And, although American viewers might not have heard of the Eleven Cities Tour, they could readily fit it into their perception of the Netherlands.

The documentary, *The Eleven-Towns Tour* (*Elfstedentocht*) (1963; 3,743), is a part and further elaboration of this aspect of Dutch identity as seen from abroad. It did, however, require some adjustment to this predominant earlier image of the country as a fun-filled winter skating paradise—the tour has always been a marathon, requiring great physical exertion and stamina. Moreover, this newsreel is of the 1963 tour, the twelfth running of the event, arguably the most brutal at zero degrees Fahrenheit, with much colder wind chills; strong, icy, northeast winds; drifting and blowing snow on the course; and uneven ice throughout (fig. 7.29). Only sixty-nine of the ten thousand contestants finished the tour, which became known as "the hell of 1963."[15]

The winter weather and surface conditions were punishing not only for those who took part but also for the news crews covering the race; they could not reach many of the filming locations, with the result that the reporting was quite spotty. Although the resulting ten-minute newsreel with English-language voice-over does show these difficult conditions, it also sets a distinctly confident tone: the music remains upbeat throughout and the voice-over cheerful, conversational, and positive. The visual rhetoric is heroic: crowds of bystanders cheering the leading skaters as they enter the towns and have their tickets stamped, proof of a completed leg, and these same skaters, especially Reinier Paping, the eventual winner, overcoming the grueling environment through sheer grit.[16]

---

[13] Peter J. Robinson, "Ice and Snow Paintings of Little Ice Age Winters," *Weather* 60, no. 2 (Feb. 2005): 37–41.

[14] Mary Mapes Dodge, *Hans Brinker, or The Silver Skates* (Dover, 2003).

[15] In December 2009, a feature-length, Dutch drama film, *De Hel van 1963*, directed by Steven de Jong, was released in theaters.

[16] The extreme hardships endured by the skaters during the 1963 tour did come to light fifty years later—for the Dutch public at least—in an installment of the television program *Andere Tijden Sport*, which in order to accurately reconstruct the event, relied not only on the scant 1963 foot-

Fig. 7.29. Leading skaters entering Hindelopen during the 1963 tour
(The Eleven-Towns Tour, *1963*) (*NIS archive, HCASC*)

The first minute of the film introduces non-Dutch viewers to recreation on natural ice in the Netherlands with stock footage of pairs skating, ice yachting, and sleigh racing before the newsreel itself covers this less-well-known Dutch skating event and pastime. The film also modernizes, solidifies and adds another facet to the earlier positive perception abroad of the Netherlands as a skating people and country, here, especially, the competitive and endurance side. That image has been only further strengthened since the 1960s with the continuing dominance of the Dutch in speed skating at the Olympics. That accomplishment, however, is only very indirectly related today to the abundance of water or the Dutch affection for natural ice but, instead, to the state-of-the-art indoor racing rinks, skating equipment, and coaching. Today, the Netherlands as skating land has become a rich and multilayered international image.

Juliana: Queen of the Netherlands, 1948–1973 (1973; 2,229) is at once one of the best directed and produced documentaries in the NIB/NIS film library and also

_____

age and news coverage but also on images from photojournalists and interviews with the leaders themselves. *Andere Tijden Sport*, "Elfstedentocht: de Wedstrijd van 1963," NOS, 16 Jan. 2013. It is available in Dutch on YouTube.

one of the less suitable documentaries for an American or Dutch American audience. It was produced by the Dutch Broadcast Foundation (NOS), in Dutch, for television, in four parts, together, an hour-and-a-half long, on the silver anniversary of Queen Juliana's reign. The cinematography and direction of this documentary have a modern look and feel, with some qualities of the journalistic VPRO school. There is a modest role for the voice-over, with much of the information for the audience provided by the spoken words of those featured in the film. The shots are of relatively short duration, holding the audience's attention. The film uses old photos and film footage integrated into the topics covered. It has full diegetic sound accompanying what the audience sees, and the music, including songs, is carefully chosen to fit and enhance the content and meaning of particular scenes.

Juliana: Queen of the Netherlands, 1948–1973 is a retrospective of the first twenty-five years of the reign of Queen Juliana, consisting largely of informal and candid interviews (the first for the royal family) with the queen, her husband Prince Bernhard, their grown children, and political leaders, as well as the Dutch public. Jan Van Hillo, the film's director, narrator, and interviewer, is largely off camera, with only a minor role as commentator—the focus is entirely on those he interviews and films. There are questions and answers about, for example, the significance of this silver anniversary, memories of the abdication by Queen Wilhelmina and the inauguration of her daughter Queen Juliana, the nature and weight of the queen's tasks, state visits, and the perception of the queen by other members of the royal family and the Dutch public.

Answers from the royals to these different questions provide the unifying thread of the film and are the occasion for segueing to archival footage and photos to show the actual event talked about or to other scenes shot for the film to show examples of what those interviewed had said. In the section devoted to the inauguration, for instance, Queen Juliana, her husband Prince Bernhard, their children, and prime minister Willem Drees all describe their memories and the significance of the ceremonies. Archival footage is interspersed throughout these interviews—the abdication by Queen Wilhelmina, the procession to the Nieuwe Kerk in Amsterdam in the golden coach, and there the oath of allegiance to the constitution by the queen before members of parliament. *Juliana: Queen of the Netherlands* is the first intimate portrait of the queen and her family for the Dutch people.

It is a Dutch-language film made for the Dutch citizenry. Films made for domestic viewing are for insider, resident citizens who embody the culture, grew up and were educated in the country, participate in its daily life and traditions, and more or less know its history. Such films are often highly particular, carry an implicit and nuanced understanding, and do not need to explain the obvious. Understandably, an English-language version of the film was never made; it would have required an extensive English-language voice-over to set the stage and explain the content for the various scenes as well as hampering subtitles for the many spoken words. Moreover, such a voice-over along with subtitles would shed light on particulars perhaps known to and of interest to Dutch residents but not to those looking at the Dutch royal family from another country—minuti-

Fig. 7.30. Queen Juliana greets school children at the Royal Palace of Amsterdam (Juliana: Queen of the Netherlands, 1948-1973, *1973*) (*NIS archive, HCASC*).

ae, such as Prince Bernhard never singing the first stanza of the national anthem in public; jesting popular songs, sung as part of the musical score, about prime minister Willem Drees and the nation; excerpts from the queen's Christmas radio broadcasts to the nation; and briefings for the queen at the palace from parliamentary leaders about the formation of the government and cabinet.

There are other, more accessible scenes in the film that the American public, often still enamored of royalty, would enjoy—those of the queen, her children, and grandchildren together at the at the Paleis Soestdijk and on the ski slopes in Lech, Austria, and the queen hosting an open house at the Royal Palace of Amsterdam for school children (fig. 7.30), as well as the archival footage of the inauguration. But overall, this film has too many pro-

prietary country particulars to generate a broader appeal for the film outside Dutch borders. That is why its viewership is small and largely restricted to a few Dutch American enclaves.

Juliana: Queen of the Netherlands was added to the film library in 1973, the year of its release, just one year before the NIS ceased operation,[17] which is certainly one factor accounting for its low viewership. Equally important in this regard, however, is that, without an English-language voice-over and subtitles, the film was shut out of almost all of its potential market. Which

---

17 The NIS library includes only one reel of the first two parts of this nearly 90-minute-long documentary. I assume that, for the film to circulate, there had to have been two reels and that the other one went missing. The Dutch national archive at the Netherlands Institute for Sound and Vision has a detailed scene-by-scene description of the entire four-part film.

also explains its low viewership. Even among Dutch Americans, very few could understand and read, let alone speak, Dutch anymore during the 1970s. And for those who could, the film is short on the explanations a voice-over would provide for satisfactory viewing enjoyment and learning. Even with an extended period of circulation, its total American viewership would have remained low. In the Netherlands, the film was shown on television and, understandably, drew enormous audiences. It was about the history and reign of their queen and her family, and interviews with the queen and members of her family about a wide range of topics created a more personal portrait of the Dutch royals.

The art and experimental films discussed in the next section all lacked Dutchness except for the art film *An Army of Hewn Stone* (1957; 2,219). With sculptures, wartime poetry, and mournful music, it tells the story of the horrors of the German occupation of the Netherlands during WWII, the Dutch resistance to it, and the liberation from this yoke by the Allies. The film is a fifteen-minute visual poem; for each of the filmed sculptures, the voice-over consists of fragments of suitable wartime resistance poetry by Dutch writers.[18] As poetry, it is preoccupied with symbolism and meaning and understandably furnishes no facts about the featured sculptures or the poetry—the names of the sculptors, sculptures, writers, and poems are not identified nor are the locations and sites of the sculptures. As with all art and poetry, an explication of the visual and textual rhetoric and of the background of the artists would significantly enhance the viewing experience.

In the decade following the end of the war, many communities in the Netherlands commissioned sculptors to fashion public art in prominent places to commemorate the war experience. Director Theo Van Haren Noman creatively filmed a number of these sculptures, which, when matched with wartime poetry, tell the story of invasion, occupation, and liberation in the symbolic and emotive language of art. The film opens with the camera panning across the North Sea dunes to a single cross and the spoken words:

> I can't forget that single grave wreathed by no single flower that leafed.
> God giveth, God taketh away again.
> Man has become a beast.

Among the sculptures included in the film are a Dutch soldier looking up at the sky at invading enemy aircraft, a human figure without a heart and outstretched hands to the skies railing against the destruction of the center of Rotterdam, a woman with her dead child in her arms, a dockworker in Amsterdam striking against the deportation of the city's Jews, a Jewish mother and child on their way to an extermination camp, a resistance fighter before a firing squad, an emaciated young girl in the hunger winter, a woman determined to break her chains that keep her from freedom (fig. 7.31), and a British commando coming on shore in Vlissingen, Zeeland.

The Dutch version of *An Army of Hewn Stone* was released in 1957; the NIS acquired the English version in 1963. The Dutch and English versions of the film are identical except for the English translations of the poem fragments. The film was commissioned by the ministry of education, art, and science, a Dutch government agency eager to showcase Dutch culture

---

18   Hogenkamp, *De Documentaire Film*, 113–15.

Fig. 7.31. Statue of a chained woman by Fred Carasso, in Sprang-Capelle, Noord-Brabant (*An Army of Hewn Stone, 1957*) (*NIS archive, HCASC*)

abroad. In both 1973 and 1974, nearly a thousand people altogether saw the film in nine different locations throughout the NIS service region; the 1966 to 1972 data gap masks the total viewership, but a figure of ten thousand is not unreasonable.

An Army of Hewn Stone was produced as an in-house Dutch film. In the Netherlands, it made the rounds as an art film short in theaters as well in special showings. It met and reflected the needs and emotions of the Dutch people who had experienced and witnessed the savagery of the German occupation and the exhilaration of the liberation. The sculptures together with their accompanying poetry

touched raw nerves and provided an outlet for intense feelings. American viewers were outsiders looking in, lacking the impassioned personal memories and feelings about WWII. With the blunt measure of attendance, we do not know, of course, how American viewers reacted to this or any other film borrowed for viewing. But without any explanation, rank-and-file American viewers would find it hard to understand and appreciate the allusions and symbolism that are the essence of the film. Even without the same level of interest and much more limited knowledge and experience than Dutch viewers, seeing these images of oppression and death and hearing the poetic laments, American audiences would reflect on the advantages of not having been occupied by an enemy invader, on the role that the United States played, and the American loss of life in bringing this nightmare to an end. Still, *An Army of Hewn Stone* is an example of a Dutch film that, even in an English version, could not easily cross the Atlantic.

International Dutch films

The international Dutch documentaries, discussed below, have little apparent "Dutch" content. The films enjoyed a total NIS viewership of 152,050, that is, 20.5 percent of the attendance of the forty-eight, Holland-NIS films about the Netherlands during the 1960s/70s. These films fall into two, more-or-less distinct groups: (1) more conventional topical international films, and (2) experimental, art, and introspective films.

Like all cultural goods, particular films cannot be unambiguously classified; they possess other qualities that fall outside of the assigned class. Although classification is necessary and useful to draw important distinctions, at the same time, it may obscure other features of certain films. For example, not all Dutch art films lack Dutch particularity, case in point: *An Army of Hewn Stone*. Or a documentary, such as *Interlude by Candlelight*, that shows the artist making his dolls and casting them in a puppet-theater presentation, can be both an information-driven film and an art film. Or *Application*, a documentary about aging, may be viewed not only as an international topical film but also as a reflective and introspective art film. I will discuss these particular films together with others that comprise these categories.

International topical films

I will first take a closer look at the topical international films. Some of these reported on Dutch contributions to endeavors common to many nations, for example, in sports, art, science, military defense, and entertainment. Their focus was not on Dutch distinctives but on the Netherlands working and making progress on such, more-universal trends and issues. This class of films was very much related to a rising internationalism, modernism, and placelessness in Dutch society—and other Western societies— in the 1960s/70s.[19] Modern art, design, architecture, factory assembly lines, transportation systems, and scientific research all looked and functioned very much the same around the world. There might be a Dutch touch or setting, but it would be entirely superficial. The Netherlands wished to be seen as a modern, future-focused, and internationally oriented country. To achieve that goal, the country-bound traditions and markers had to get out of the way. Such films are often favored by foreign affairs officials because they demonstrate that their country is keeping up with, contributing to, or leading on issues of interest to all nations. The Dutch Ministry of Education, Art, and Science had a budget to place such films into the distribution system of other countries as shorts accompanying feature films, in their film libraries, and at their film festivals.[20]

There are ten films in this category among the forty-eight films receiving close scrutiny; they drew 39,334 viewers—18.8

[19] James C. Kennedy, "Vlucht naar Voren op Buitenlands Terrein," in *Nieuw Babylon in Aanbouw. Nederland in de Jaren Zestig* (Boom, 1995), 50–77.

[20] Hogenkamp, *De Documentaire Film*, 203.

Fig. 7.32. Students at a school for the deaf in the Netherlands feel the vibration of an airplane passing overhead by holding one hand over their throat and chest while waving with the other (Vibration, *1951*) (*NIS archive, HCASC*).

percent of the attendance of the forty-eight top films. None of these films was in the lending library before 1960, and there were no topical films in this category in the film library before 1960.

Vibration (1951; 43,170) was shown on television in the Detroit area in 1965, not because it covered an important "Dutch" achievement but because program managers regarded this (rather outdated) film on the training of deaf-mute children to be of interest to a general audience.[21] The children at a school for the deaf in the Netherlands are shown associating their physi-cal sensation of particular vibrations with specific commands, pitches, notes, words, phrases, and machines (fig. 7.32). This was a curriculum to replace sign language for educating deaf children.

Vibration was screened in only three other places to a total of 397 viewers. The black and white film was released in 1951 but not accessioned by Holland-NIS until 1965. *Vibration* is the unmodified Dutch film, with opening captions in Dutch, with sound and dialogue, but without a voice-over; knowledge of Dutch was not needed to understand the information presented in the film. St. Michielsgestel, the Nether-

21   Ibid., 176–78.

lands, is identified in the opening captions as the place of this school for deaf children. It is an important science film but tells its viewers little to nothing about the Netherlands except perhaps that the school is located there. An argument can be made, as with some other films in this category, that this is a more international film in which diverse contributions to tackling common issues are front and center and cultural context takes more of a backseat. The Netherlands was reporting to the international community on its progress training deaf children; in that vein, the film was shown to the International Scientific Film Association Festival in 1951.[22]

In the early 1960s, the Dutch building industry and its workers commissioned a film about that sector's work and accomplishments. It is an award-winning film and selected by film historian Bert Hogenkamp and the NRC newspaper as one of the notable films of the Dutch documentary school. It was distributed in English as *The Building Game* (1963; 4,367) and screened in seventeen widely scattered locations in Holland-NIS.[23] Given this industry's business and practical interests, one would have expected it to be technology and statistics driven, with lots of Dutch content. Instead, the director used the commission to make a visual ode to the exterior forms and patterns of new buildings and construction workers, one that employed all the cinematographic techniques of the Dutch documentary school. With only music and the occasional sound of construction work and equipment, but with-

out voice-over narration, the film communicates no distinctive Dutch content. The film is rather placeless, and the newly built residential environment consists of uniform, walk-up apartment blocks separated from each other by extensive open spaces, an international, modernist style found in most other Western European countries.

The film received a rather curious and unsuitable English title, *The Building Game* (Dutch, *Bouwspelement*; French, *Jeu de Construction*; and German, *Bauspiel*). In no way does the film describe the practices, routines, or customs of the Dutch building industry. Rather, it alternates between scenes of construction workers at their trade (fig. 7.33), with close-ups of their faces, often accompanied by marching music, and poetic scenes of the forms and textures of what they have built. Their skill in making apartment buildings, roads, and bridges is praised, and viewers see their completed infrastructure and residences put to use. *The Building Game* is replete with all the visual effects for which Dutch documentary filmmaking had become internationally famous—multiple exposures, reflections, animation, rapid zooming in and out, and contrived synchronization of sound/music and image (as the music speeds up, images of buildings move by faster and faster). During the last minute of the film, a fish-eye lens—a new tool—is used; construction workers look at flowing, nonrectilinear forms of their buildings. *The Building Game* shows American viewers avant-garde filming as well as a state-of-the-art building industry with skilled and dedicated construction workers. Once again, Dutch distinctiveness (except for the pile drivers) is downplayed and underscored is Dutch participation in what must have been a very similar building industry

---

[22] The very little information the British Film Institute provides for this film does include this significant tidbit.

[23] Hogenkamp, *De Documentaire Film*, 206.

Fig. 7.33. Construction workers hoisting a prefab building component into place
(The Building Game, *1963*) (*NIS archive, HCASC*)

throughout Western Europe. What is most Dutch about this film is the cinematography of the Dutch documentary school.

NATO Tattoo (1958–65; 42,761) is a film about the military musical and marching spectacle held yearly from 1958 to 1969 on the market square in front of the province of Gelderland government building in the capital city of Arnhem. These became increasingly popular and were broadcast on television not only in the Netherlands but also in other NATO countries. This tattoo was discontinued in 1969 due to antimilitary protests and related increased security concerns and costs. The viewing geography of *NATO Tattoo* is much like that of *Vibration*, with a television broadcast in the Detroit area in 1965 to an es-

timated forty-one thousand viewers and film screenings in six additional locations to a total of 1,761 viewers.[24] In the prologue of some of the films of these tattoos, audiences do learn about the location of Arnhem and see shots of the destruction of the city during WWII, but the films are almost entirely about the tattoo itself on the market square—the marching, formations, music, uniforms, and flags of the military bands from different NATO countries (fig. 7.34). There was a Dutch audience in the stands, but it was an international specta-

---

24 This film is not in the NIB/NIS archive. Its first NIS screening was a television broadcast in 1965, but the year of the tattoo in the film shown to American audiences cannot be determined. Only film fragments of these tattoos are available online.

Fig. 7.34. NATO Tattoo on the market square in Arnhem, the Netherlands.[25]

cle. The military bands of NATO-member countries joined together in an intergovernmental military alliance and mutual defense pact.

Everything or Something (1960; 7,469) is an international Dutch film about an approach to achieving versatile physical conditioning for the Dutch public. The Dutch National Sports Federation helped produce the film, which reflects its ambitions and interests. Rather than personal exercise programs at or close to home that required little time or equipment, such as the world famous Royal Canadian Air Force Plans for different age levels that was developed at this time, *Everything or Something* pro-

posed that everyday Dutch people take up one or more international, Olympic-like sports at an amateur level to achieve a measurable overall fitness.

Everything or Something is relatively fast paced, in black and white, with short scenes, a jazzy musical score adapted to what is being shown, and an engaging narrator. Shown are cross-country, swimming, diving, pole vaulting, basketball, weightlifting, baseball, wrestling, javelin, boxing, and others. The first part of the film shows professional, world-class Dutch athletes competing in these sports. Then the film cuts to ordinary Dutch workers at their job and sport—a train engineer runs track, a machine operator boxes (fig. 7.35), a cabinet maker plays soccer, a farmer speed skates, a construction worker lifts weights, a student plays baseball, and an office secretary faces opponents in judo.

[25] HHA140411 NATO Taptoe, YouTube. This is a presentation with slides by an historian about the history of the Arnhem military tattoo at Molenplaats Sonsbeek, a museum in Arnhem. Fig. 7.34 is one of these slides.

Fig. 7.35. Machine operator in the boxing ring
(Everything or Something, *1960*) (*NIS archive, HCASC*)

This sheds light on the title: professional athletes achieve nearly "everything" in a sport, and hobbyists achieve an important "something"—fitness and enjoyment.

The advantages of fitness from participation in sports are shown in several humorous vignettes, including a housewife successfully sprinting from the far end of her home to the kitchen to stop milk on the stove from boiling over and athletic shoppers winning the race to the sale tables when the store's door open. At the end, officials from the Dutch Sports Federation are shown administering proficiency tests and awarding certificates for different sports to individuals from various age groups. The film was a clear winning gambit for sports organizations serving to recruit people into their sports and, at the same time, help improve the physical conditioning of the Dutch. At the same time, this program could not serve as any kind of blanket solution to better the fitness of the Dutch populace; many would have had little interest in taking up a sport. It is curious that cycling is not one of the Olympic sports featured in the film; the widespread use of bicycles by the entire Dutch population in all facets of daily life would qualify every Dutch person as fit.

The voice-over in *Everything or Something* hardly makes any reference to the Netherlands, although classic Dutch urban and woodland landscapes are part of

Fig. 7.36. Spinning plates act (Circus Elleboog, *1951*) (*NIS archive, HCASC*)

the outdoor setting for some of the physical conditioning and sports shown, and viewers hear some background conversation in Dutch among the participants. It is instructive that the narration was also in English for the original production; the film was clearly intended for international distribution. *Everything or Something* shows the Dutch participating in sports that are recognized and shared throughout the world; there is little or no Dutchness in the film. It telegraphs to outsiders that the Netherlands is a modern, science-based country and can hold its own in the international community.

Circus Elleboog (1951; 5,852) is a film about a circus troupe of children from Amsterdam with the same name. It was started in 1949 as an initiative for post-WWII youth in the city to join a circus and continues to the present day.[26] It was named Circus Elleboog (Circus elbow) to make a witty association with Circus Knie (Circus knee), the famous circus of Switzerland. Without any historical background to this circus, the film shows only a series of the

26 The Dutch television history program, *Andere Tijden*, devoted a program to Circus Elleboog, first broadcast 8 Dec. 2015; a selection from the 1951 film is part of the program npogeschiedenis.nl (accessed 8 Aug. 2016).

Fig. 7.37. Only the applicant and the driver are left in the tram as it approaches the retirement home at the end of the line (Application, *1964*) (*NIS archive, HCASC*).

troupe's acts in front of an audience, such as tightrope walking, various balancing acts, spinning plates (fig. 7.36), clowns, and horse acts (children in horse costumes). The film is from 1951 but was not accessioned, strangely, by the NIS until the late 1960s. It is in black and white and largely silent except for the introductions by the ringmaster (in Dutch) and has no voice-over.

Only if American viewers realized that the film was borrowed from the NIS might they know that it was a Dutch film; otherwise, they would not know where it was filmed because only the interior scenes of the circus acts are shown. And, again, there is nothing distinctively Dutch about

the acts; they are part and parcel of the standard repertoire of circuses the world over. That is not to say that *Circus Elleboog* was not an enjoyable film; judging by the audience response to the circus in the film itself, it was, especially for children who could identify with these child performers and relate the film to their own visit to a circus and to what they already knew about circuses. As with other films in this class, *Circus Elleboog* had a certain universal appeal. But it did not help Americans get to know the Netherlands any better.

Another film that explores transnational issues is *Application* (1964; 4,115). Well known Dutch filmmaker Rob Houwer explores the subject of aging as it relates to independence, caregiving, and memory. The film has a soundscape, musical score, and storyline but no dialogue or narration. An elderly woman takes the tram from downtown (Amsterdam) to the loop at the end of the line (fig. 7.37), right next to a retirement home at the outer edge of the city. She has come to make an application for an apartment. The film cuts back and forth between her journey on the tram and routine scenes and activities that are possibly in store for her at the senior living facility—old men playing billiards, a woman with a cane and her assistant slowly walking down a long corridor, and a group of women knitting. When she leaves the tram and walks to the front entrance, all of the residents look down on her from their flats, signaling the loss of privacy in such a facility.

At the interview, the woman is taken aback by the standard impersonal questions designed to measure her eligibility; her answers make it clear that she is perfectly able to continue to live independently, look after herself, and keep in contact with her friends where she lives now. The questions and her answers also bring back memories: her work as a guide on sightseeing canal boats, horse riding along a North Sea beach, and enjoying the seaside with her friends as a young girl. She returns downtown on the tram.

This is a film more about aging than it is about the Netherlands. Unless a moviegoer is familiar with Amsterdam, there is little to nothing to suggest that it is set in the Netherlands, let alone in Amsterdam. Its backdrop and human activities are very generic and would not be out of place in most European countries, but the setting does not really enter into the subject matter of the film. The film reveals little about the particulars of the Dutch care for the aged. *Application* is a Dutch filmmaker's visual story about the humanity of aging and senior care, predictably employing its Dutch milieu, much as a Japanese filmmaker would employ his or her own country's milieu.

The next four films in this category shine a light on Dutch artists and their creations. *Interlude by Candlelight* (1959; 4,207), also known as *Harry's Dolls*, has an English voice-over, which makes it very clear in the beginning that the film is about the Dutch sculptor and dollmaker Harry van Tussenbroek (1879–1963).[27] In the first part of the film, viewers see the artist collecting materials for his creations, such as driftwood and bird skeletal remains along the coast and in the dunes; at times, these natural landscapes look distinctively Dutch, at other times not Dutch at all. Next, we see Tussenbroek at home, outside making his puppets from these and other remnants and discarded materials such as fabrics and jewelry.

In the second part, the artist becomes the puppeteer bringing his dolls to life; they interact, menace, and dance during the midnight interlude in rather macabre, frightening, and otherworldly ways (fig. 7.38). This part has no voice-over; interpretations are left to the viewers. The puppet performance ends when some of the marionettes disappear into enveloping flames. At the end of the film, the narrator returns and describes the puppet performance as a cosmological struggle between the sun and the moon that was both won and lost.

American viewers of *Interlude by Candlelight* did become familiar with the work of a particular Dutch artist, someone

---

27 Hogenkamp, *De Documentaire Film*, 205.

Fig. 7.38. Recycle-art marionette in Tussenbroek's puppet show
(Interlude by Candlelight, *1959*) (*NIS archive, HCASC*)

whose work was totally different from what they likely already knew about the Dutch masters and their legacy. At the same time, Van Tussenbroek's art had little to no content and very little background that can be described as country specific. His recycle-art, doll sculptures and puppetry could have been created and performed anywhere.

Unlike Tussenbroek, Dutch graphic artist M. C. Escher (1898–1972) already had an international following, which began to increase near the end of his life. By commissioning a film on his work as part of a series on then modern Dutch artists, the Dutch foreign ministry had hoped to expand international appreciation of his

work. The result was *Adventures in Perception* (1971; 17,040), released a year before his death and part of the NIS film library for only a few years before it closed down.[28] Yet, this award-winning film garnered twelfth place among the 160-plus films screened during the period and was shown in sixteen places with relatively large audiences.

Like Tussenbroek, the subject matter of Escher's art, albeit with exceptions, was not drawn from or applied to Dutch life. He was a one-of-a-kind artist who connected mathematics and art, creating two-

[28] Ibid., 265. *Adventures in Perception* is not in the NIB/NIS film archive but on YouTube.

Fig. 7.39. Artwork, *Day and Night*, M. C. Escher (Adventures in Perception, *1971*)

and three-dimensional geometric artwork with woodcuts, lithographs, and mezzotints. His work explored properties such as perspective, mirroring, proportions, stellation, tessellation, and metamorphosis. Much of the film is a minute exploration—set to electronic and experimental music—of a number of his works; the camera zeroes in and out and slowly pans a number of his prints to reveal fine detail and components as well as its gestalt and, where appropriate, metamorphosis. There is narration only in the middle part of this twenty-minute film; the voice-over reveals biographical details of Escher's life and extensively uses his own words in translation. Escher worked at a boundary between art and science. The particularity of his home country did not carry much weight; rather, more abstract and universal traits carried the day, and American viewers—judging

by the viewership—were apparently very interested in the novelty of this Dutch artist's work.

In *Day and Night* (fig. 7.39), one of his more well-known works, Escher *does* apply his craft—especially tessellation and metamorphosis—to the Dutch landscape. The camera very slowly pans over this artwork's Dutch river landscapes, complete with walled river towns, river commerce, windmills, river dikes, canals, tree-lined roads, checkerboard fields, and water birds flying overhead. The flat day and night landscapes are mirror images; fields metamorphose upward into tessellated shapes of water birds, and white birds fly into the night landscape and black birds into the day landscape. Here, together, are both a meticulous rendition of a real landscape and geometric abstractions and illusions that suggest movement, cycles, and transformations.

Fig. 7.40. Dutch artist Lou Strik (1921–2001) dusts his woodcut with talcum powder to see that everything has been properly cut (Graphic Art, Its History and Technique, *1963*) (*NIS archive, HCASC*).

Escher is also recognized as one important figure in the Dutch-made film, *Graphic Art, Its History and Technique* (1963; 7,441). It is both an instructional and a historical film. The techniques of woodcuts (relief printing), engraving (intaglio), mezzotint, and lithography are each demonstrated step-by-step by practicing graphic artists who show both the making of the master with special tools and the printing methods using each template. Following the demonstration of each technique, the film highlights the influential historical masters who used these methods, as well as examples of their artwork.

Produced in black and white, with a jazz musical score, as well as period music for scenes of historical works of art, the film came with Dutch, English, and Spanish voice-overs.

What is this film doing in the NIS library and among the top-twenty films shown during the 1960s/70s? It does not show Dutch scenery as a backdrop, only interiors of ateliers and close-ups and slow pans of representative artwork. Like other Dutch international films, *Graphic Art, Its History and Technique* is part of the library because Dutch contributors to the international history of graphic art take their place in the film alongside those from other countries (also shown in the film)—China, Japan, Germany (Durer, Hopfer), France (Claude, Daumier, Doré), Great Britain (Bewick), Italy (Canaletto, Piranesi), and the United States (Pasqua). Dutch and Flemish contributors to this larger history include: Maurits Escher, Lucas Van Leyden, Frans Masereel, Samuel de Mesquita, Lou Strik (fig. 7.40), Rembrandt Van Rijn, and Hercules Seghers. Again, the focus of the film is not on difference and uniqueness but on one common and longstanding international undertaking in the arts in which the Dutch also have had and continue to have a prominent place.

The film *A Wall* (1968; 2,912) is not an art film within the meaning of aesthetic or experimental, such as *Panta Rhei* (1951) or *Promise of Heaven* (1961), discussed under the next heading, but rather in the sense of creative practice and artistic freedom.[29] It is another one of a number of such films available from the NIS marking out a distinguishing feature of the film library during the 1960s/70s. The Dutch government subsidized such films and was eager to showcase them abroad as proof of a modern, Dutch film industry and modern, international (not Dutch) art.

A Wall is about the planning and making of an artwork, a 4.5 by 10 meter wall of steel filled with cutouts of colored glass for the lobby in the new headquarters of the Bank of the Netherlands in Amsterdam. The film is in color with an unusual voice-over from Jules Chapon, the artist himself, putting into words in Dutch-accented English his creative thoughts and explanation of the development and con-struction of his artwork. It has no dialogue; the soundscape is related to the making of this artwork by the artist and many others—cutting out shapes in scrap steel plates with blowtorches, grinding and sandblasting the plates, and firing and cutting glass to fit into the cutouts. *A Wall* has a modern musical score of drums, xylophones, and other percussion instruments.

There are few if any Dutch markers in this film because most of the footage is shot in indoor workspaces. Chapon's voice-over does provide some geographical context: the studio for the full-size mockup (fig. 7.41) of the art wall is in an empty building in Haarlem, his home city, and the installation of this very large piece is in Amsterdam. But that is about it for any explicit Dutch particularity. In the introduction, a car drives past seemingly endless uniform apartment blocks in the rain; this visual, further enforced with the slapping of windshield wipers and heavy percussion music, represents, for Chapon, a dystopian world without call or opportunity for civic engagement or creativity. This footage, actually of the garden city Osdorp, near Amsterdam, does not need to be identified because it stands for all such urban habitats around the world. The making of this art wall as a type of public art, bringing the contributions of many individuals' crafts and skills together, is seen, in contrast to the earlier placeless and anonymous urban world, as an example of civic engagement and imagination. Though set in the Netherlands, *A Wall* is not about the Netherlands. By means of this film, a Dutch artist and a Dutch film director make universal statements about creativity, civic engagement, and the habitat for humanity.

---

[29] Hogenkamp, *De Documentaire Film*, 264–65.

Fig. 7.41. Jules Chapon in his studio opening the cutouts in the full-scale mockup of his art wall (A Wall, *1968*) (*NIS archive, HCASC*)

Art and experimental films

Art and experimental films serve niche markets. Their focus is on some combination of aesthetics, symbolic communication, and introspection together with unusual subject matter and visual rhetoric. Like other visual arts, such films are often favored national exports—their meaning may be equivocal and contested, but they are unlikely to provoke political or social controversy. Only three NIS films met these defining criteria and attracted 12,715 viewers (just 1.7 percent of the attendance of the top 48 films about the Netherlands during this period). Each film drew less than five thousand people, which, given their market, is understandable.

Pan (1963; 4,164) reprises the ancient tale of the Greek nature god Pan charming creatures with his flute.[30] Produced by Herman van der Horst, a leader in the Dutch documentary school, the film is in black and white, without voice-over, dialogue, or music. As with many films belonging to this movement, the soundscape was a central element, and in this production, it greatly enlivens the visual rhetoric; the calls of many different water birds, such as ducks, spoonbills, gulls, herons, and swans, dominate the soundscape. Much of the film may be seen as an early (1963), short-subject nature film, unwit-

[30] Ibid., 202–4.

Fig. 7.42. Camouflaged by water plants, a boy plays his pan flute and enjoys observing enchanted nature (Pan, *1963*) (*NIS archive, HCASC*).

tingly introducing American viewers to one of the most common natural settings of the Netherlands—fresh and saltwater wetlands and their wildlife. For Dutch viewers, such landscapes are the furniture of their culture.

In the film, a boy rows his boat into a wetland through the reeds and disturbs, frightens, and angers the water birds as they go about their normal activities. He leaves the boat, camouflages himself, and hides among the water plants. In this way, he is able to observe the natural behavior of the wildlife close at hand. When he begins to play his pan flute, birds, insects, and fish become captivated and excited and start participating in a variety of different ac-

tivities, including mating rituals (fig. 7.42). A more harmonious relationship between people and nature is established.

Again, there are no Dutch markers whatsoever in the film, and there is no voice-over to contextualize the content—for example, the wetland as a quintessential Dutch landscape. The boy reprises the role of Pan, a universal myth, without giving it Dutch content for non-Dutch audiences. For Americans, this was not really a film about the Netherlands but one directed by a Dutch filmmaker who was making cutting-edge experimental films. Such Dutch cultural exports also have a place in public diplomacy.

Fig. 7.43. Shadows of tree trunks moving across the forest floor
(Panta Rhei, *1951*) (*NIS archive, HCASC*)

Bert Haanstra's early experimental film, *Panta Rhei, All Things Flow* (1951; 2,706), was also completely focused on the natural world but in a more elemental and abstract fashion, as in the Greek philosopher Heraclitus's famous aphorism, the title of the film. It is entirely centered on flows and changing forms in nature. It makes use of time-lapse filming and shows flows and mutating forms—for example, shadows of trees moving across the forest floor (fig. 7.43), patterns of water currents moving up a beach, a lake surface with minuscule moving wave forms, rapidly developing cloud formations, the arrangements of sunlight reflections from waves running up a beach, and liquid water changing into ice crystals.

Panta Rhei has no soundscape, storyline, dialogue, or voice-over; there is only a modern musical score by Max Vredenburg, a much-celebrated Dutch composer. Watching the film is not a knowledge-based learning experience but an aesthetic and poetic one. It is another example of a much earlier film (1951) not added to the film library until the late 1960s, likely because, by that time, Haanstra was a world-famous Dutch filmmaker, and a number of his other later and more well-known films were already part of the collection. With its title in the original production in ancient Greek, Dutch, German, English, and French, *Panta Rhei* was clearly intended for international distribution. To be sure, its filmed cloudscapes,

Fig. 7.44. Two of the seventy-two stained-glass windows in the sixteenth-century Sint Jan Church, in Gouda, the Netherlands (Promise of Heaven, *1961*) (*NIS archive, HCASC*)

woodlands, heathlands, beaches, and lakes and rivers were Dutch, but with its focus on more abstract visual flows and forms in nature, even Dutch viewers would be hard pressed to recognize them. This again underscores the less particular and more universal themes of films in this group of international Dutch films. American audiences likely went to see this film because it was made by Haanstra, a world-renowned Dutch filmmaker and in this way took in his universal visual poem about the natural world.

Promise of Heaven (1961; 3,613) is a ten-minute experimental and artistic film about light and stained glass.[31] It was released in 1961 but not acquired by the NIS until the late 1960s. The film consists of three very distinct parts, each with its own signature music. The film is in color without a voice-over and no sound other than the musical scores. Because the scenes are of daytime church interiors (the first and third parts) and nighttime cities (the second part), there is no identifiable Dutchness in the film, even though it is filmed in the Netherlands by Dutch director Frans Dupont. Other than the film com-

---

31   Ibid., 264.

ing from the NIS, viewers would not know that *Promise of Heaven* was a Dutch film; the opening credits roll the title in four languages—Dutch, English, German, and French—with the credits below the titles in the corresponding language. Without a voice-over, venues remain unidentified.

The opening and closing parts of the film are of daylight streaming through stained-glass windows into church interiors, and the middle part is of energetic artificial lights illuminating and messaging downtown at night. A sharp contrast is drawn between the preferred calm light in the churches, filtered, diffused and projected by stained glass windows (the promise of heaven), and the cacophony of artificial city lights at night. Accompanied by classical organ music, the first section shows the daylighting of the sixteenth-century Sint Janskerk, in Gouda, by its world-famous, seventy-two stained-glass windows.

Viewers see close-ups of the windows themselves (fig. 7.44) and the dappled colors and patterns from the windows moving across the walls, floors, and columns of this monumental church. The second section shifts abruptly from this natural, serene, and holistic light to an artificial, light-animated, and frenetic urban night scene of store window displays, street-lights, colored and moving neon signs, and car lights. At the end, the camera moves rapidly and blurs all these sources of human-made, night light into a single pattern. Supporting and enhancing this feverish scene is the electronic jazz of Tom Dissevelt, a Dutch originator of the genre. The last section of the film returns the viewer to the serene natural daylight of the first section but here enhanced by modern, stained-glass art in the windows of sever-al contemporary Dutch church interiors. Organ music again accompanies the light streaming through the stained-glass windows, but now it is the modern music of the French composer Messiaen.

Films about the Netherlands overseas

Surprisingly, unlike the 1950s, thirteen of the sixteen NIS films (23,902 of 33,221 viewers) about the Dutch overseas territories shown during the 1960s/70s were new films; only three carried over from the 1950s—*Medical Care of the Native Population*, New Guinea Chronicle, no. 6 (1954–62; 16,807), *Six Bits of Holland in the Caribbean* (1950; 23,107), and *Curaçao: The Island You will Always Remember* (1950; 18,575). Seven of these newly acquired films, however, had attendance figures at or below one thousand, very much dampening their impact on the American perception of the Dutch territories.

It is important to be reminded how much the place of the Dutch colonies/territories in the film library had eroded since the 1940s. In that decade, there were more films about the colonies (28) than about the Netherlands (23). And these documentaries, altogether, drew a larger viewership (609,482) than films about the home country (596,338). Compare that to the 33,221 viewership of films about the Dutch territories during the 1960s/70s against the background of nearly nine hundred thousand total viewers (less than 4%). This is one of the most significant changes in the film library during its three-decades-long life and speaks to the foreign policy reasons that led to the founding of the NIB in 1942 and to decolonization in the subsequent decades.

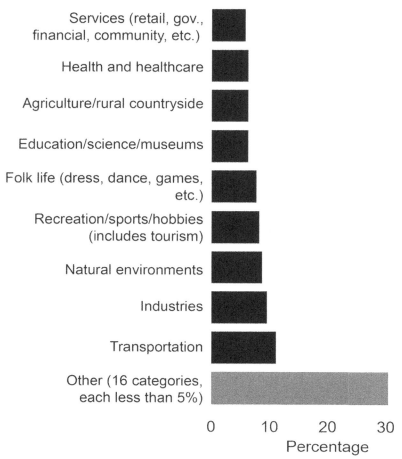

Fig. 7.45. Films about the Dutch Territories, 1960s/70s:
percentage of film threads by subject

208 film threads, top 9 films about the Dutch Territories, 28,906 viewers (87%)

Topical threads in films about the Dutch territories the 1960s and 1970s

When the contents of the better attended films about the Dutch territories overseas were classified and tabulated for this period (fig. 7.45), several subjects, for the first time, reached the 5 percent threshold I had reserved for leading topics—education/science/museums, health and health care, and services (retail, govt., financial, community); two other former leading subjects fell below that threshold for the first time—cities and the military.

In all, nine subject areas exceeded the threshold, ranging from 5.8 percent to 11.1 percent of the topical threads; sixteen others came in below 5 percent.

Some of the trends in leading topics, noted earlier in the changes from the 1940s to the 1950s, continued; others were reversed. The share for some topics increased still further (fig. 4.19). Threads related to industries grew further from 5.3 percent in the 1950s to 9.6 percent in the 1960s/70s, recreation and tourism from 6.2 percent to 8.2 percent, and services from 4.4 percent to 5.8 percent. Attention to natural environments declined slightly, from 9.7 percent to 8.7 percent, as did transportation, from 13.3 percent to 11.1 percent, but both maintained the higher levels attained during the 1950s when compared to the 1940s. These increases and retentions reflected global economic developments related to post-WWII consumer societies. The sharp decline in several other leading subjects from the 1940s to the 1950s were checked during the 1960s and 1970s: agriculture/rural countryside, from 14.7 percent to 5.3 to 6.3 percent; folk life, from 12.7 percent to 7.1 percent to 7.7 percent; and church/religion, from 8.6 percent to 1.8 to 3.4 percent (fig. 4.20). These later upturns were steered by three new films about Dutch-led comprehensive development programs in Dutch New Guinea. Unlike the films about the Dutch colonies in the Western Hemisphere in the 1950s, these films focused more on the rural folkways of New Guinea's indigenous peoples. The attention paid to natural resources (from 7.2% to 4.4% to 3.4%) and cities (from 7.9% to 6.2% to 2.9%), however, continued to slip.

Dutch New Guinea and the Dutch Caribbean

On the basis of both geography and content, the films added to the NIS library about the Netherlands overseas from 1960 to 1974 fall into two clear divisions. The first consists of seven government-commissioned films about very specific and planned development programs in a single territory, part of the island of New Guinea, and the last remaining Dutch possession in the former Dutch East Indies. Five of these are English versions of films in the twenty-three-part New Guinea Chronicle

series, first produced with Dutch voice-overs from the 1950s to the early 1960s.[32] Because Dutch New Guinea was ceded to Indonesia in 1962, all these films were pulled from the NIS library in that year; this was the last year American audiences in general could see Dutch-made films about Dutch territories in Southeast Asia. With no more than three years of circulation and greatly reduced American interest, the viewership and impact of these eight films was predictably quite limited. When the viewership of these films is added to that of the 1960/74 viewership (6,210) of the film about this region added during the 1950s, *The Medical Care of the Native Population*, no. 6, New Guinea Chronicle (1956; 16,807), a total of 18,598 Americans in the Holland-NIS region watched these documentaries about Dutch New Guinea.

These films document the effort of the Netherlands to politically integrate and centralize New Guinea and ramp up the civilizing mission in education, policing, health care, economic welfare, and business and community organization—all in preparation for the approaching eventual independence of the territory. The Dutch government was investing $25 million yearly in development programs for that area. By 1958 more than six thousand medical doctors, missionaries, nurses, engineers, teachers, and other experts had been sent to New Guinea.[33] Like many films in the 1940s, those in the New Guinea Chronicle series from the 1950s and early 1960s were propaganda films meant to again influence the foreign policy of the United States, a key player in determining the final politi-

[32] See endnote 7:32, p. 406.

[33] Dutch national film archives, the Netherlands Institute for Sound and Vision (beeldengeluid.nl), s.v. *Report from Netherlands New Guinea*, film notes.

cal status of the territory. The Dutch want-ed an independent nation with close links to the Netherlands—the country that was paving the way to its nationhood.

The entire series was meant to show the United States and other world powers that, in every respect, the Dutch were lay-ing the groundwork for an independent western New Guinea. The Dutch govern-ment did not want this territory to become part of Indonesia, something that its gov-ernment had been demanding all along. The Dutch foreign policy objective was an independent western New Guinea with strong connections to the Netherlands, serving as a settlement region especially for Eurasians from Indonesia. In spite of all its intensive development programs and its film propaganda, this policy—again—failed; the Dutch government in 1962 bowed to international pressure and the threat of an invasion from Indonesia and agreed to cede control of Dutch New Guin-ea to Indonesia.[34]

The second and smaller group of films about the Netherlands overseas is made up of five new films: *Wij Surinamers* (1961; 3,570), *Te Aworò* (1964; 3,502), *Faja Lob-bi* (1960; 2,738), *ABC* (n.d., 973), and *Blue Peter* (1958; 731). When the attendance from these documentaries is added to the 1960/74 attendance of the two films carried over from the 1950s, *Six Bits of Holland in the Caribbean* (1950; 23,107) and *Curaçao, The Island You Will Always Remember* (1950; 18,575), the total viewership of these films from NIS-Holland about the Dutch Caribbean during the 1960s/70s comes to 14,619. This group of films is far more diverse both geographically and topically

than the films about Dutch New Guinea. The films all deal with the highly scattered, different Dutch territories in the Caribbean and Suriname on the north coast of South America. The Dutch West Indies consist of two island subgroups in the Caribbean's Lesser Antilles: one, Aruba, Bonaire, and Curaçao (the ABC islands), off the coast of Venezuela, and the other, Sint Maarten, Saba, and Sint Eustatius, all east of Puerto Rico (fig. 4.13).

Whereas the films about Dutch New Guinea are about very specific, Dutch-gov-ernment development initiatives for the path to independence, for example, in ed-ucation, health care, policing, and gover-nance, these new films about the Dutch Caribbean are general surveys of the peo-ple and cultures of these territories and their potential for economic development, including mining, industries, and tourism. Moreover, unlike the government-con-trolled films about New Guinea, these doc-umentaries are from more independent filmmakers, for example, Herman van der Horst (*Faja Lobbi*) and John Fernhout (*Blue Peter*). American viewers had the op-portunity to take in the distinctive quali-ties of the Dutch documentary film school embodied by these directors, now applied to the Dutch overseas territories. Perhaps more so than with such films about the Netherlands itself, the question of where these films are found on a continuum be-tween education and art is telling. More-over, is the greater part of the Dutchness projected by the NIS to American audi-ences through these films the "ownership," the cinematography, or the personality of these overseas territories?

I will take a more close-up look at the top three films in each of these groups. They had the highest attendance figures

[34]   C. L. M. Penders, *The West New Guinea Debacle. Dutch Decolonization and Indonesia 1945–1962* (University of Hawaii Press, 2002).

Fig. 7.46. Learning and recording native languages and training indigenous teachers in the Baliem Valley of Dutch New Guinea. The tablecloth (*tafelkleed*, lit. table rug) is a Dutch cultural artifact, commonly called a Smyrna or Persian tablecloth, made of plush wool. Retro today, these were widely used in the Netherlands during the late nineteenth and first half of the twentieth century (The People of Shangri-La, *1958*) (*NIS archive, HCASC*).

and follow-on greater influence on the American perception of the Netherlands overseas. The attendance of these six, new-to-the-library films ranged from 4,875 to 1,355, from thirtieth to eighty-second in the ranking of films screened during the 1960s and 1970s. These are low numbers and rankings, reflecting much-diminished interest and attendance thresholds than for earlier films about the Dutch territories for Americans, compared to films about the Netherlands itself.

Films about Dutch New Guinea

Each of the three new films about Dutch New Guinea selected for a closer reading is from the New Guinea Chronicle Series; these, plus the 1960/74 view-ership of *The Medical Care of the Native Population*, no. 6, make up 86 percent of the American viewership of the documentaries about Dutch New Guinea. *The People of Shangri-La* details the kinds of initial contacts the Dutch-led civil service, together with the embryonic national Papuan police and Dutch missionaries made with village groupings in the upper Beliem River valley of the New Guinea Highlands. These expeditions included programs of assistance (for example, injections against disease); the establishment of relationships of genuine interest, trust, and friendship with Papuan villagers; and pacification agreements with civic authorities to protect campongs from attacks from their neighbors with corresponding promises

Fig. 7.47. Male villagers welcome the motor launch of the Dutch medical team to their kampong by wobbling their legs (Polyclinic in the Wilderness, *1957*) (*NIS archive, HCASC*).

from village leaders to refrain from striking other compounds; warfare was a normal and long-standing cultural practice. Areas of peace, order, and trust emerged around civil service and mission posts.

Without constant strife and with mutual trust, work by civil authorities and missionaries on other development goals could begin. The film shows staff at a mission post implementing agricultural improvements to raise living standards by introducing new crops (cabbage, beans, tomatoes, strawberries), fencing crop fields to keep out pigs, bringing in other livestock such as chickens and goats (dairy), and demonstrating the marketing of farm products by various forms of payment (salt, shells, beads). Audiences also see efforts to implement other development goals such as learning and recording regional languages and training indigenous teachers

to give instruction in these languages (fig. 7.46) as part of establishing formal education throughout Dutch New Guinea.

Even though these development initiatives have a strong Western and Dutch flavor (including an attempt to teach a young Papuan to ride a Dutch bicycle), a broad civilizing mission is brought into play. The contrast between the sight of living conditions in the villages—cultivating soil with a digging stick and bare hands, felling trees with stone axes, cutting off parts of fingers as a sign of mourning—and the development objectives outlined in the film must have seemed entirely appropriate and necessary to American and other Western viewers.

Polyclinic in the Wilderness (1957; 4,874) documents the journey upriver from the southwest coast of New Guinea by a Dutch-led medical team, first in a motor launch and then, farther inland, in canoes. The goal of the expedition was to administer penicillin injections to the entire indigenous population of the region against framboesia (yaws), an infection of the skin, bones, and joints caused by bacteria. Because it is spread by contact, the entire population of every village along the river's course had to be treated. Although the film is about a medical mission and the need to convince everyone to participate (including those who were hiding from the team), it is the folkways and material culture of these native Papuans—many of whom had never had contact with the world outside—that makes this documentary very memorable. Viewers see male villagers on the river's bank wobble their legs as a sign of welcome and friendship (fig. 7.47), homes on stilts and in trees, burned-out villages, raised platforms for reposing and honoring the dead, human skulls used as pillows, and villagers using their own teeth and stone axes as tools.

The film gave American viewers an entirely altruistic picture of development in West Papua. In the face of significant hardship, Dutch physicians, assisted by native medical assistants and translators, were systematically eradicating a debilitating disease. Papuans were fellow human beings in the orbit of Dutch sovereignty, and the Netherlands had assumed an ethical responsibility for their welfare.

Report from the Netherlands New Guinea (1958) presents an overview of how the Netherlands was, in the words of the film, "building a bridge between the centuries," leading Dutch New Guinea into modern and independent nationhood that would be economically self-supporting. Most of the film focuses on indigenous

Papuans and depicts the Dutch not as administrators or businessmen but, again, as school teachers, missionaries, doctors, nurses, nuns, and technical instructors. The first and shorter part depicts Papuan native folkways. They were people from the Stone Age who lived by simple hunting, gathering, and farming and, while engaged in perpetual deadly violence against their neighbors, blended their rituals, festivals, music, and art with Christian rituals, such as the Catholic mass. The second and longer part shows Papuans (now in Western clothing) with a wide variety of modern—mainly technical—skills being supervised by Dutch instructors, learning in a classroom with an indigenous teacher, felling trees in a modern logging operation, operating a winch and hauling in nets on an offshore fishing boat (fig. 7.48), using sewing machines to make clothing, spraying a crop with pesticides, bulldozing roads, and building housing tracts.

Report from Netherlands New Guinea (1958; 1,355) was a special English-language compilation film intended for the United States about the diverse development programs carried out by the Dutch government; there may well not be a Dutch version. It is instructive that the Dutch national film archives, the Netherlands Institute for Sound and Vision, lists this film by its English title and has only an English-language film in its collection; all other films from this series in the archive are Dutch-language versions. The documentation of this film lists the Dutch government of Netherlands New Guinea as holding the rights for showing this film in the United States.

Fig. 7.48. Dutch fishermen training Papuans to operate a modern fishing trawler (Report from the Netherlands New Guinea, *1958*) (*NIS archive, HCASC*)

Films about the Dutch Caribbean and Suriname

The top three films set in the Dutch territories of the Western Hemisphere are much different films—thematically and cinematographically—from the films about bringing Dutch-led improvements to the lives of the people of New Guinea, as discussed above. Together, they make up 67.1 percent of the 1960/74 American viewers of films about the Dutch Caribbean and Suriname. Two of the films, *Faja Lobbi* (1960; 2,738) and *Wij Surinamers* (We, the people of Suriname) (1961; 3,570), are about Suriname, then also called Dutch Guiana, a territory on the northern coast of South America, governed and exploited by the Dutch since the seventeenth century (fig. 4.13). They were the first films exclusively about Suriname distributed by the NIS since *Dutch Guiana* (1942; 40,268), an American-made newsreel shown during the 1940s. Both films focused attention on the human mosaic of this territory. The third film with the title, *Te Aworò* (1964; 3,502)—a popular greeting in Papiamento meaning "See you soon," or "Good-bye,"—has as its subject the economic potential of the islands of Netherlands Antilles in the Caribbean. All in all, the interest in these films among Americans would be expected to be higher than those about West Papua, not so much because of their Dutchness, but because they were about areas in the economic backyard of the United States. In fact, the viewership for the West Papua/Dutch Guinea films was considerably higher (18,598) than for those about the Dutch Caribbean and Suriname (14,619).

American viewers would be hard pressed to identify the first film, *Faja Lobbi*, as a film about a then Dutch territory, Suriname. The film has no voice-over, which was less problematic for Dutch residents but much more important as context for American viewers unfamiliar with the history of the Dutch overseas. It also lacks a musical score and dialogue, but it is endowed with a rich soundscape. For those American viewers who could read Dutch, the translation of *Faja Lobbi*, the creole title—*Vurige Liefde* (Fervent love)—and the Dutch subtitle— *Een Impressie van Suriname* (An impression of Suriname)—as well as the opening credits would confirm that *Faja Lobbi* was a Dutch-made film about a largely unknown and fascinating part of the world, somewhat like the earlier travelogue films, but now in color and with much more creative and illuminating cinematography. For everyone else, only the fact that it was borrowed from the NIS tied it to that country in any way.

Nevertheless, *Faja Lobbi* is a wonderful, award-winning, anthropological portrait of Suriname in the 1950s, with a focus on its ethnic and religious diversity. With this film, American viewers could enjoy another fine creation of the internationally renowned Dutch documentary school.[35] Filmmaker Herman van der Horst was one of its leading exponents. The soundscape of the film—a feature of particular interest to the Dutch documentary school—is a vibrant, rich, and integral component throughout the film. Different sounds and voices together make for a changing soundscape: water and transportation by canoe on water; rainforest and water wildlife; flutes, drums and guitars; call and response, as well as religious singing; everyday speech,

as well as cries of market vendors in Paramaribo in many different languages (hardly any Dutch); and calls to prayer by a muezzin. The singing and the instrumental music shown and heard in the film are both part of the soundscape and at times serve as an integrating musical score. The foremost example of this occurs during the last twenty minutes of the film—sequences of call and response singing of a maroon man in Paramaribo playing a guitar repeatedly alternate with the camera zooming in and panning scenes of the urban and industrial landscapes and their diverse peoples.

The first two-thirds of *Faja Lobbi* present an unhurried look at the daily round of work and leisure in Native American and maroon villages (formerly, Bush Negroes) inland along the Marowijne River, the border between Suriname and French Guiana. Viewers see canoeists navigating rapids, women pounding cassava and threshing and winnowing rice, and men and boys spearfishing on the river and hunting wildlife living high in the canopy of the rainforest with bow and arrow. The special leisure activities during the extended hours of darkness in these villages, lit only by fires, receive much attention. The soundscape of the nighttime river and rainforest combines with the playing of instruments, especially drums and woodwinds, and with singing, costumed dancing, and chanting.

The last twenty minutes of this nearly seventy-minute-long film take the viewers from the Marowijne River to Paramaribo, the capital of the territory. Native Americans, Indo-Surinamese, Maroons, Javanese, Chinese, Creoles, and Lebanese (no Dutch) mingle in the city's market places (fig. 7.49) where store signage is shown in several languages (including Dutch).

---

[35] Hogenkamp (*Documentaire Film, 1945–1965*, 145) reports an attendance of 374,000 in the Netherlands for *Faja Lobbi*, whereas the American attendance by way of the NIS-Holland was 2,738 for the two years that it circulated (1973–74).

Fig. 7.49. Paramaribo's ethnic diversity on display in its open-air market
(Faja Lobbi, *1960*) (*NIS archive, HCASC*)

Religion complements these ethnicities; viewers see and hear worship services in Christian churches, Hindu temples, and mosques. Toward the end of the film, Van der Horst returns to his preferred settings, the setting of much of the film–the Surinamese forests and rivers–and cinematographically draws naturalistic parallels between the many equally different colorful and intricate tropical flowers and the headdresses worn by maroon women.

Earlier films about the then Dutch colonies in the Western Hemisphere were either the 1940s foreign policy-driven films focused on the (wartime) strategic resources these areas provided or films defending the Dutch colonial project by pointing to

its help in bringing about a multicultural/ethnic Kingdom of the Netherlands. During the 1950s, NIS films presented these territories as tropical vacation destinations of sun, beaches, and natural landscapes, with Dutch culture as an added attraction. *Faja Lobbi*, an ethnographic documentary, made no such claims. Nor, unlike the films in the New Guinea Chronicle shown during the 1960s/70s, did it include anything having to do with the history of Dutch-led policies and initiatives for its colonial territory.

There is really nothing in the film that informs the viewer that Suriname is a part of the Netherlands or even that it is about a place called Suriname. Given the objectives of the NIS, it is difficult to understand why this film was acquired. It is silent on how Suriname's different ethnic groupings came to the territory and their place and livelihood. There are two very brief shots in Paramaribo that in quick succession zoom in on the Dutch Surinamese flag and on a statue of Queen Juliana with the Dutch flag. But few viewers would recognize these symbols of Dutch sovereignty. *Faja Lobbi* was released in 1969, five years before Suriname became an independent nation and, by that time, the Dutch government had taken a hands-off approach to its territory.

The lack of clarity of *Faja Lobbi* about Suriname's Dutch connections and particularity about the country itself are largely due to the kind of film the director, Herman Van der Horst, decided to make. When the lack of a voice-over is added to these qualities, it is clear that *Faja Lobbi* is an audiovisual impression and interpretation operating on emotional and artistic levels. Its purpose was not to inform and explain but to paint a canvas.

By contrast, the other two films in this group—*Wij Surinamers* (We, the people of Suriname) and *Te Aworò*—are much more information driven and didactic. Both are the work of Dutch filmmaker Peter Creutzberg who, like some other Dutch filmmakers, shot travel documentaries about faraway places.[36] Before television began making inroads, these directors often traveled with their films to showings in the Netherlands and there provided commentary about their travel and living experiences while filming in such locations. This model for travelogue showings continues to the present day.

The takeaway from *Wij Surinamers*, already apparent in the title, is oneness amid many differences.[37] School children, and children in general, as the future of the country, represent and see that oneness throughout the film, in the classroom, on class trips, in their neighborhoods, and in sports and civic organizations. When a Creole teacher in a public elementary school calls on a student and asks in Dutch: "What kinds of people live in Suriname?" She answers—after prompts from several other students—"Ordinary people." The teacher and the class agree and, with that reminder, proceed to compile a list of the many ethnic and national groupings that make up the country. On a class trip in the countryside, with notebooks at the ready, the students pass by and learn about a Hindu planting rite, a mosque, lemon orchards, coffee and cacao plantations, mechanized wetland rice production, and cassava harvesting, each represented as the livelihood of a different ethnic group. *Wij Surinamers* was commissioned by the Foundation for Cultural Cooperation between the Netherlands, Indonesia, Suriname, and the Dutch Antilles (Sticusa), which explains its focus on cultural diversity. It was prepared especially for showing in Suriname itself to help foster a conversation about its own identity.[38]

---

36 Ibid., 145–47.

37 The Holland NIS copy of *Wij Surinamers* has a 1.4-minute animated map spliced in at the very beginning of the reel, unrelated to the film, with a Spanish language voice-over, showing the location of Suriname in the Western Hemisphere and a country map of its vegetation and changing economic geography. No source is provided and, unless the film was borrowed by Spanish-speaking audiences (doubtful), it is difficult to understand why this short introduction was added. It does give American viewers a geographic context.

38 Peter Creutzberg, a biology-trained filmmaker, led a film production unit in Suriname that released a

Fig. 7.50. A Surinamese boy crosses out the Dutch word *"neger"* as a caption
for a stick figure with a black face and begins to replace it with "Surinamer."
In the following frames, a Surinamese Hindustani boy adds an "s" to
the name (Wij Surinamers, *1961*) (*NIS archive, HCASC*).

Through this lens of education for both children and adults, the primary economy of Suriname—traditional and modern—passes in review; the audience sees people of different ethnicities working in specific livelihoods. Filmgoers see mechanized wetland rice seeding and harvesting by Dutch farmers as well as hand planting, scything, and flailing rice by Hindustani farmers. Large-scale, export-oriented bauxite mining, together with alumina production and logging as the resource for plywood factories, round out the picture of Suriname's economy. Each of these modern sectors employs an ethnically diverse workforce. Toward the end of the documentary, several neighborhood boys of diverse ethnic backgrounds draw and label stick figures with faces of the different ethnicities on a wooden fence. One of the boys crosses out the name "*neger*" (in Dutch, "black") and replaces it with "Surinamer," and another adds an "s" to the name (fig. 7.50).

---

large number of films about the territory (Hogenkamp, *De Documentaire Film*, 145–47); Albert Helman, *Cultureel Mozaïek van Suriname* (De Walburg Press, 1977), 411. On the role of Sticusa, in Suriname, see Bob Christiaan Molenberg, "Chance, Change and Sticusa, On the Nature of Cultural Cooperation between Sticusa and Suriname" (master's thesis, Utrecht University, 2017).

The government and the material culture of the ethnic Dutch have a low profile in the film, reflecting that, except for the Dutch language, Suriname in the 1960s was very much a non-Dutch place, demographically (general population and workforce) and culturally. The mission hospital and medical aviation are shown as directed by the Dutch but staffed by people of diverse ethnicities. The film does show the Dutch minority as the elite. A young maroon father presents gifts to the Dutch nurse and doctor who delivered their baby, and a maroon woman head-carries a hamper of washed laundry to the back door of the home of a Dutch woman in Western dress and speaks deferentially with her.

Like other Dutch documentaries of that time, *Wij Surinamers* has a very full and highly differentiated soundscape of human voices, livelihood activities, and background sounds from urban, village, and natural settings. In addition, a musical score of Caribbean genres accompanies different subject threads. In the transition between threads, the film also, again, incorporates a cinematographic touch of the artistry of the Dutch documentary school. Commonly, a voice-over steers the transitions in a documentary, in addition to cuts, fade-ins, and fade-outs from one thread or subject to the next. Without a voice-over, it is more challenging to create such continuity. Creutzberg cleverly creates transitions from unrelated actions or events inserted in the closing scene for one topic and the opening scene of the next. The immediate transition from a segment about Amerindian women in a village making and firing clay pottery to the next largely unrelated segment about bauxite mining is created by two, quick successive scenes of pouring water: one, a closing scene showing the woman, after firing a pot, pouring water from a pottery jug for a drink; the other, an opening scene, set in a bauxite mine excavation, of an Amerindian worker from the same village, pouring water from a thermos on a break. Another transition: after Hindustani farmers thresh their rice with oxen and by hand, the closing scene is of throwing the threshed rice into the air to separate it from the chaff; in the next opening scene for commercial logging, that same rice falls onto the dinner plates of maroon loggers enjoying a rice-based meal on their boat pulling rafts of logs.

Without voice-over narration or subtitles for the spoken languages, *Wij Surinamers* was unable to provide American audiences with very much context or explanatory depth for what they saw on the screen. The audience does, however, receive first impressions of Suriname and enjoy captivating, individual visual accounts, but placing them into a more coherent framework for understanding Suriname is out of reach and not something one can ask of a film like this. Given the nature of this film, it falls short as material from the NIS in educating Americans about Dutch history and the place of the Netherlands in the world, let alone about Dutchness. It is a more modern version of a travelogue that, except for some Dutch cinematographic touches, could have been produced by documentary filmmakers from any country. But the dominant idea in this film of oneness in diversity can come through to any audience without reference to the Dutch.

Te Aworò relocates the geographical focus from Suriname to the other six Dutch territories (fig. 4.13) in the Western Hemisphere, that is, the islands of the Dutch Antilles in the Caribbean Sea, principally Curaçao and Aruba. It is a more entertaining update for Americans of *Six Bits of Holland in the Caribbean*, distributed by the NIS in the United States in the 1950s. If *Faja Lobbi* and *Wij Surinamers* gave attention to that territory's people and their cultural diversity, also as related to livelihood and modernization, *Te Aworò* is centered on Dutch-initiated development ambitions in trade, tourism, and industry on the Dutch Antilles.

The difference between these two films is embodied entirely in their titles: *Wij Surinamers* points to the territory's residents and their sought-after solidarity, and *Te Aworò* points to visitors (tourists, outside investors). That difference came not only from the requirements of the RVD, the agency commissioning the film, but also from the distinctive WWII and postwar features of the Netherlands Antilles compared to Suriname. The southern Dutch Antilles (Aruba, Bonaire, and Curaçao) during the war took on geostrategic importance in defense and resource security and processing, as well as shipping. All the islands of the Dutch Antilles in the post WWII decades became increasingly important as Caribbean sun and beach tourist destinations for Americans and Europeans by air and cruise ship. Suriname did attract some wartime attention (bauxite mining and alumina production), but its mainland location in South America, its greater distance from the United States, and its perceived less suitable climate and coastline were all seen as drawbacks for tourism.

Sometimes *Te Aworò* uses voice-over but other times (dubbed) speech and dialogue. The musical score is modern, eclectic, and upbeat, with a fully supporting soundscape. But it has a weak storyline: two Dutch salesmen/investors, each car-

rying a case with an architectural model inside, deplane at Curaçao International Airport and straightaway taxi to a hotel to meet with island public officials and businesspeople. One has a model of a chemical plant, the other of a resort. Each group makes a pitch to the potential investors about the advantages of locating their businesses on the islands. For the chemical plant, these include resources in South and Central America, markets in North America and Europe (the Common Market), the Panama Canal, and suitable local ports for shipping. For the resort, affluent nearby tourists, beaches, sun, cruise ships, and direct airline connections are among the obvious draws.

This six-minute introductory storyline sets the stage for these two investors to be shown around the islands to see these site advantages for their development of the Dutch Antilles. They are largely off-camera as the film surveys the assets of the islands with voice-over and sound. The investor focused on the chemical industries takes in Curaçao's harbor with its shipping, loading, bunkering, and repair facilities; he visits Curaçao and Aruba's oil refineries, petrochemical plants, the phosphate mine and fertilizer processing facility, and factories in the tax-free industrial zone. He becomes familiar with the necessary secondary amenities for successful industries, such as educational and training facilities at all levels, remote access to the New York Stock Exchange, telecommunications, automation, workforce, water supply, health care, representative government, and infrastructure.

On this last item, one very telling scene is of a surveyor/engineer imagining a sky bridge (superimposed on the landscape shown in the film) across St. Anna

Fig. 7.51. Tourists disembarking from a cruise ship in Curaçao for duty-free shopping (Te Aworò, *1964*) (*NIS archive, HCASC*)

Bay, the entrance to Curaçao's Schottegat port. The only existing bridge across this entrance then was a swing bridge on pontoons, a chokepoint where ocean-going vessels were given priority to get into the port and motorized and foot traffic across the inlet—joining two parts of the main city, Willemstad—had to wait. In the film, just before the engineer dreams about the sky bridge, there are scenes of ship traffic competing with motorized, bicycle, and foot traffic on the bridge. In 1974, ten years after *Te Aworò* was released, the Queen Juliana Bridge, high enough for almost all ocean-going ships to pass under, was opened for motorized traffic.

Later, the two investors/developers are reunited at a resort in Aruba, and at that point, the focus of the film switches to a survey of the tourist economy on the islands, a topic of more direct interest to American audiences. Visitors arriving by air and cruise ships (fig. 7.51) find every kind of tourist attraction: welcoming steel bands, duty-free shopping, markets, casinos, night clubs, Dutch architecture, ethnic dancing, beaches, snorkeling, and natural scenery. In the eyes and imagination of the investors, "empty" coastal sites are transformed into resort developments and are shown in outline on the screen.

As with other earlier film surveys of the Dutch Antilles, the three northern islands—Sint Maarten, Saba, and Sint Eustatius—receive much less attention, in this case, a mere six minutes of this long, fifty-three-minute documentary. Even the main players—the two investors—do not show up on these islands; they are shown putting down their slide viewers in Aruba after this short section of the film ends. It consists mainly of a compilation of stock footage for each island and focuses entirely on tourism and its limited infrastructure—airports and landing strips, landing piers for tourist ships, and roads—all necessary for the sun, beach and nature vacations these islands have to offer. With their "visit" to the northern Dutch Antilles at an end, the two investors return to the airport in Aruba for their return flights to Curaçao and the Netherlands but not before once more singing the praises about the locational advantages of the Dutch Antilles for investments.

To make its content more engaging, *Te Aworò* is, at times, fueled by a comedic line, a kind of zaniness. That line does not come through the voice-over, as is sometimes the case, but through the storyline of the two developers at the beginning of the film. The investor looking for opportunities to site a chemical plant is more of a typical, proper businessman, but the resort developer is a colorful character wearing horned-rimmed sunglasses, with a large cigar or pipe in his mouth. For the presentations to the developers, a broadcaster-type host and hostess place icons (of ships, the sun, factories) onto a flannel board map of the Atlantic world; it looks like a parody at a grade school level—quite funny and entertaining. At other times, the lighter moments come from the film's editing; a

thirty-second scene about health care on Curaçao, for example, consists of a montage of close-up head shots of five young boys in rapid succession sticking out their tongues, saying "ah" for a doctor.

For American viewers, *Te Aworò* brought a larger dose of Dutchness than the films about Suriname. The Dutch history of these islands and the then current Dutch economic and cultural interests were more transparent. Viewers received a definite message that these islands were Dutch. The voice-over and English dialogue contributed substantially to a better understanding of the material presented. That several of these Dutch islands were home to modern export industries was likely surprising new knowledge for most viewers, as was their high standard of living. For a growing American tourist industry in the 1960s, not only was the Caribbean in their backyard a warm destination vacation of sun-drenched islands with bays, beaches, and pristine landscapes but also the different cultural flavors—British, French, Dutch, Carib, Jamaican, Hispanic—further enhanced the appeal of the islands. *Te Aworò* helped make the Dutch Caribbean strand more visible to Americans.

The films about the Dutch territories overseas distributed from 1960 to 1974 mark the end of the extensive efforts by the NIS to justify Dutch colonial rule to the American public. Already by 1962, the most undisguised defense of the Dutch civilizing mission—the New Guinea Chronicle series—was removed from the lending library. New Guinea became part of Indonesia in that year, and these films no longer served any public diplomacy purpose.

The films chosen by the NIS to showcase Suriname (Dutch Guiana) made no reference to its colonial status, its history of slavery and Dutch colonial policy for this territory, or its Dutchness. Rather, the films' directors were on a mission to catalog and celebrate Suriname's anthropological, cultural, and religious diversity. They painted a picture of a present-day ideal of a multicultural Kingdom of the Netherlands without referencing its three hundred-year history of subjugation, slavery, plantations, and dependency. Suriname became an independent nation in 1975, one year after the NIS had shut its doors.

In the films of the 1960s and 1970s, the Dutch Antilles for American viewers morphed from strategic colonies in the earlier films to largely self-governing tourist, resource, and tariff-free islands with distinctive Dutch touches and connections to patria. Unlike other former Dutch territories, they willingly remained part of the Netherlands and erstwhile colonial dependence turned into advantageous mutual interdependence.

Close

The NIS film library during the 1960s and 1970s became much more dated, with about one-third of its circulating films produced in earlier decades; it was not keeping up with suitable new releases. Forty-two films carried over from the 1950s collection, and sixteen (30%) of the top forty-eight films accessioned during the 1960s/70s have release dates from the 1950s. The most consequential films that reported on the social and economic changes sweeping the Netherlands during the turbulent and affluent sixties were not added to the library because they were regarded as too controversial and not suitable as promotional material; in addition, their dialogue-driven, journalistic cinematography was more challenging to convert into versions in other languages.

Although the closing of the NIS in 1974 ended the Dutch government's official program of film diplomacy, it did not dampen either the American interest in Dutch films and other Dutch visual media or the desire of Dutch filmmakers, the government, and the public to share, market, and make available their films in the United States. What, if anything, took the place of the NIS to distribute Dutch films in America and internationally over the next four or five decades? More generally, what is the place of the NIB/NIS program of film diplomacy in the larger history of American exposure to and consumption of Dutch visual media?

CHAPTER 8

Historical Survey of Dutch Visual Media in America

NIB/NIS films, together with other visual media about the Netherlands in the United States

Some American eyes have been on the Netherlands from the beginning. Original paintings, drawings, and maps for most income levels, as well as prints of any subject from engraved plates with customary Dutch subject matter and Dutch styles were accessible to segments of the public in today's Downstate New York and northern New Jersey throughout the New Netherland era (1609–64) and the British colonial period (1664–1776). These visual media have remained mainstays to the present-day for Americans everywhere to see the Netherlands—via art and other books about the country, popular and scholarly magazines and newspapers, and museum exhibits and other expositions—

without having to travel there. Continuous innovation in reproduction and printing has resulted in improved resolution and color; transmission and acquisition has gone from slow—cartage, retail sales, and the postal system—to fast and instantaneous—wire services, satellite, and the internet.

Other visual media and their technologies came later: magic lanterns, photographs, films, slide projectors, and videos—each, first in analog and then in digital format. Each phase expanded the suite of visual media and made them more widely available, until the "pictorial turn,"[1] that is, the widespread dominance of visual culture in all aspects of society beginning at the end of the twentieth century. There are

---

[1] The term comes from W. J. T. Mitchell, "The Pictorial Turn," *Art Forum*, no. 5 (1992): 89–94.

Fig. 8.1. Jan Daimen's country house and orchard near Sloterdijk (part of Amsterdam today), Claes Jansz. Visscher (II), between 1596 and 1630 (Rijksmuseum; *Wikimedia Commons*)

banks of digital photos and videos for any place in the Netherlands on the internet today, and visuals accompany most other search results on Dutch topics (Wikipedia, Tripadvisor, Google Maps, Wikimedia Commons, etc.). It is helpful to place the films of the NIB/NIS program of public diplomacy into this encompassing history of visual media about the Netherlands and its overseas territories in the United States. The growing availability and dominance of visual media has steadily created more scope for disseminating information and knowledge for promotion and propaganda campaigns. Next to the United Kingdom, the Netherlands is among the relatively small number of countries that from the beginning have enjoyed a high level of con-

tinuing interest and longstanding, positive visual attention from those who lived in what became the United States.

I will begin with a discussion of the availability of art with Dutch subject matter—broadly considered to include paintings, sketches, drawings, maps, and their prints—available to those living in the area of the United States from the New Netherland era to the present day. This is followed by an examination of photographs about the Netherlands and its overseas territories in American, Dutch, and Dutch American newspapers and magazines read and seen by the American public and Dutch immigrants and their descendants. Next up are documentary and educational films about the Netherlands and its overseas territories

Fig. 8.2. View of the coconut-tree-lined Tijgersgracht, Batavia, now Jakarta, Dutch East Indies, 1682. Atlas van der Hagen, Koninklijk Bibliotheek, The Hague (public domain). "In the mid-17th century, the Tijgersgracht was deemed the most attractive of the fifteen city center canals in Batavia. The canal was lined with the houses and buildings of the city's most prominent families."

available to Americans alongside and later than the NIB/NIS films distributed in the United States by the Dutch government, the focus of this study. And then there are feature (fiction) films, the Goliath of cinema. I discuss the interest in and availability of VHS cassettes and DVDs of Dutch feature films for more recent immigrants, those of Dutch ancestry, and Americans in general. Finally, consideration is given to how the pictorial turn and the internet have revolutionized access to Dutch art, photographs, and films for all Americans everywhere and for people worldwide.

Dutch immigrants to the United States and their visual media about the Netherlands

In the New Netherland period, Dutch immigrants, as shown by the wills and legal inventories of their goods,[2] brought with them and also later bought inexpensive paintings and prints of different kinds

2 Mary Black, "Early Colonial Painting of the New York Province," in *Remembrance of Patria. Dutch Arts and Culture in Colonial America, 1609–1776*, ed. Roderic H. Blackburn and Ruth Piwonka (Albany Institute of History and Art, 1988), 213–14.

of Dutch subject matter—landscapes, daily life in the Netherlands (genre paintings) (fig. 8.1[3]), still lives, the Dutch East Indies (fig. 8.2) and other exotic locales, Biblical and mythological stories, and family portraits. Their seventeenth-century homeland was awash with paintings and prints; most households covered the walls of every (small) room in their homes and workplaces with art. Two-thirds of homes in Delft had pictures on the walls.[4]

> John Evelyn [British travel writer] wrote, "Pictures are very common here [in the Netherlands], there being scarce an ordinary tradesman whose house is not decorated with them." The figures given to us by historical documents confirm the travelers' amazement. In the middle of the seventeenth century, some Dutch homes had thirty to fifty paintings per room, rooms which, it should be noted, were not all that spacious.[5]

It is important to remember that, until the widespread use of photography during the second half of the nineteenth century, the only way people could see other environments, people, and events with all of their human activities and particu-

larities was by means of paintings, drawings, and prints from engravings, either as stand-alone images or as plates and other reproductions in books.

No longer largely under the control of the church and the aristocracy for commissions and subject matter, art was lifted by the rising power, income, and tastes of the Dutch urban bourgeoisie. This broadened art to embrace any subject and the art market to include much of the general population. These changes fueled dramatic growth in demand for paintings and prints and, by extension, for painters and engravers (1 per every 3,000 people). Artwork and prints were produced for most income levels, and the resulting high demand for new and used pieces led to extensive and profitable retailing by art dealers. The Dutch passion for art expressed, as well as deepened, their love for their country.[6]

New Netherland received only a small number of colonists (from 7,000–8,000), many of whom were not Dutch but hailed from neighboring European countries, either already living in the Dutch Republic or recruited from their own countries as soldiers and sailors. After their tours of duty, some decided to remain in the colony. Farmers, merchants, and Dutch West Indies Company (WIC) officials were more likely to be Dutch colonists.[7] The Dutch immigrants and their descendants in New Netherland and, after 1664, in these areas

[3] Except for fig. 8.5, the specific artwork and drawings shown in this section on seventeenth- and eighteenth-century America (figs. 8.1–8.4) have not been found in inventories of American households nor produced in New Netherland or, later, in the Middle Colonies. They are examples of the *types* of prints and subject matter—largely produced in the Netherlands—Dutch Americans and others in this region collected and displayed in their homes, workplaces, schools, and churches.

[4] "A Brief Overview of the Dutch Art Market in the Seventeenth Century, the Abundance of Paintings," *Essential Vermeer 3.0*. www.essentialvermeer.com/dutch-painters/dutch_art/ecnmcs_dtchart.html.

[5] Ibid.

[6] Ibid.; Madlyn Millner Kahr, "Dutch Culture and Art," in *Dutch Painting in the Seventeenth Century* (Harper and Row, 1978; reprinted with corrections, 1982), 8–27; John Michael Montias, *Vermeer and his Milieu: A Web of Social History* (Princeton University Press, 1989).

[7] Jaap Jacobs, "Population and Immigration," in *The Colony of New Netherland; A Dutch Settlement in Seventeenth-Century America* (Cornell University Press, 2009), 12–61.

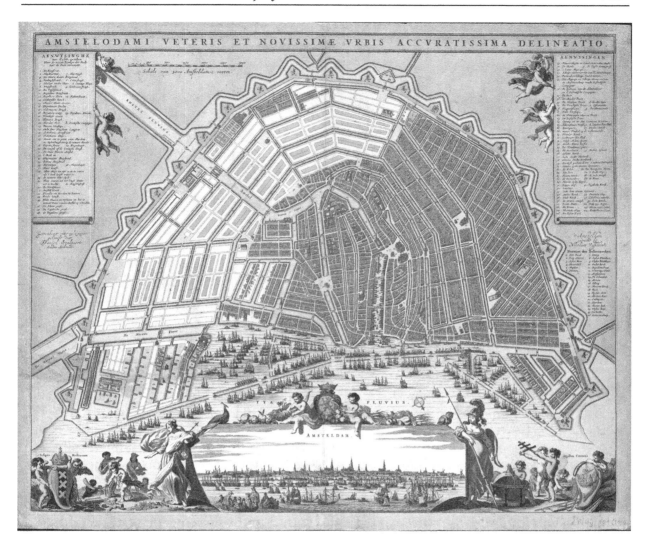

Fig. 8.3. Map of Amsterdam in 1662, with a panorama below. The expansion of the three-ring canal plan is partially realized. North is at the bottom of the page (*Daniel Stalpaert, 1662. University of Amsterdam Library*) (*Wikimedia Commons*).

under British colonial rule, carried their passion for acquiring, displaying, and enjoying artwork with them to the New World and either passed it and the paintings and prints on to their descendants or sold their collections to art dealers.

The Dutch were world leaders in cartography at this time,[8] and engravings and their prints could be made of any noteworthy subject. Those with explicit Dutchness would include maps of Dutch cities (fig. 8.3), regions, the entire country, and the colonies; drawings were made as part of travel diaries, written during and after Dutch voyages of exploration and trade (fig. 8.4); and there were images of char-

8   Cornelis Koeman, Günter Schilder, M. van Egmond, Peter van der Krogt, Kees Zandvliet, *The History of Cartography*, vol. 3: *Cartography in the*

European Renaissance (pt. 2: "Low Countries"), ed. David Woodward (University of Chicago Press, 2007), 1246–1462.

Fig. 8.4. *Sugar Plantation* on Sint Eustatius from the travel diary of Joannes Veltkamp, 1759-64, Nederlands Scheepvaart Museum, Amsterdam, no. A. 1710 (03). The print shows the cutting of the sugarcane on the right, the horse-powered sugar mill in the center, the distillery on the left, and a vegetable garden and tree fruit for the plantation's own food requirements in the foreground.

acteristic Dutch daily life (fig. 8.1). Besides paintings and prints produced in the Netherlands, resident painters in the Middle Colonies began to develop their own style and subject matter, shaped mainly by Dutch and British content and styles.

During the British colonial period, hobby painters and limners, copying from European prints, painted and sold—not only to those of Dutch American ancestry but also to a wider public—canvasses of Dutch scenes, portraits, and other familiar Dutch content (biblical figures and stories) (fig. 8.5).[9] Such Dutch and Dutch-in-spired paintings and prints graced homes in Dutch American settlements and farmsteads, as well as their Dutch Reformed churches and day schools, which all held on to the Dutch language, folkways, and Reformed religious practices throughout the British colonial period.[10]

In the seventeenth-century Netherlands and its colonies, this taste for art was an example of visual media enjoyed by a broad public in daily life. These prints and paintings of Dutch and Dutch-colonial

[9] Black, "Early Colonial Painting," 208–55, details about *Adoration of the Magi*, 254; Mary Black, "Remembrances of the Dutch Homeland in Early New York Provincial Painting," ed. Roderic Blackburn and Nancy Kelly (Albany Institute of History and Art, 1987), 119–29.

[10] Henk Aay, "Present from the Beginning: Reformed Dutch Day Schools in North America, 1638–2019," in *Dutch Reformed Education: Immigrant Legacies in North America* (Van Raalte Press, 2020), 5–16.

Fig. 8.5. *Adoration of the Magi*, unidentified limner, Albany, ca. 1740, Albany Institute of History and Art, 1940.600.84. This scripture painting is related to an illustration in a Dutch Bible. It is one of a number of New York paintings of biblical stories related to Dutch sources. Dutch upper classes favored such paintings in the seventeenth century.

landscapes, maps, and daily life served decorative, aesthetic, patriotic, and topophilic ends. They were part of a taken-for-granted and desirable domesticity. Three hundred years later, the NIB/NIS films were also viewed, likewise, not only by the wealthy and highly educated elite but also by the public in general. But unlike the NIB/NIS films, the seventeenth-century paintings and prints were not in any overt way educational or entertaining or even part of a promotional program; their messaging reinforced a Dutchness already fully present.

They were not meant to promote and help outsiders understand the Netherlands. In New Netherland and later the Middle Colonies, these Dutch paintings and prints served to quietly remind Dutch Americans of their identity and heritage as they also added aesthetic enjoyment to their lives. But given the steadily growing population, ethnic diversity, and interaction, they must have also quietly communicated Dutchness to non-Dutch residents.

During the century following the founding of the United States, visual attention to the Netherlands by Americans by means of paintings and prints waned. By then, it had been more than a hundred years and three or four generations since the British takeover of New Netherland. Lacking a steady stream of new immigrants from the Netherlands, Dutch heritage—including its visual media—was steadily eroded by inevitable de-ethnicization—the hollowing out of Dutch identity, preferences, and practices through neglect and through immigration of non-Dutch residents into what had heretofore been solidly Dutch American communities. This led to intermarriage, assimilation, and a loss or blending of traditions. At the same time, the shared commitment to the new republic increasingly provided a growing common cultural identity. In the world of art, for example, the first decidedly American movement—the nineteenth century Hudson River School—was largely coterminous with the Dutch American culture region of the state of New York.

The middle of the nineteenth century witnessed the beginning of a second and much larger wave of Dutch immigration than that to New Netherland (1609–64) and their descendants during the ensuing British colonial period (1664–1776). From 1840 to 1940, more than two hundred thousand Dutch immigrants came to the United States, settling primarily in the Midwest,[11] with concentrations in West Michigan, the Chicago region, and central and northwestern Iowa.

There has been little to no research on Dutch-themed prints and original artwork taken along in trunks and baggage by Dutch immigrants during this period. We can be sure that, alongside framed family photos and photo albums, wall-art mementoes were also included in what emigrants took with them. But few nineteenth- and twentieth-century Dutch immigrants had the cultural passion and obsession for art—not to mention the means—that merchants, traders, WIC officials, and the middle class from the western part of the country had in New Netherland during the art mania of the Dutch Golden Age. Many nineteenth-century immigrants were farm laborers and small farmers from peripheral Dutch regions looking for farmland in the Dutch communities of the Midwest; they were less likely to have wall art on display in their homes in the Netherlands and, understandably, even more unlikely—given the restrictions on and the cost of luggage—to include such items in their trunks. A sizable percentage of these earlier Dutch immigrants were seceders from the Reformed state church. Oppressed and marginalized by the civil authorities, many left the Netherlands for, among other reasons, religious freedom. Their experiences had left them with very negative perceptions of the country they had left; prints about their country or home area would have been very unlikely choices for their trunks and suitcases. Moreover, their religious focus compelled them to take along the Statenbijbel (the Dutch authorized version of the Bible) and theological texts; their cultural abstinence, pietism, and otherworldliness would have led them to avoid most art.

As more urban, middle class, educated, and culturally engaged Dutch people became part of the immigrant stream in the twentieth century, their interest, ownership, and enjoyment of the wall art in their homes must surely have been trans-

11   Hans Krabbendam, *Freedom on the Horizon: Dutch Immigration to America, 1840–1940* (Eerdmans, 2009), app. 1, 361–62.

Fig. 8.6. *View of Haarlem with Bleaching Grounds*, Jacob van Ruisdael, ca. 1670-75, Royal Cabinet of Paintings, Mauritshuis, The Hague (*public domain*)

ferred at least in part to their newly adopted land; without frames and glass, canvases and prints take up little to no room. They could afford to take more household effects and include some of their favorite

wall art—some Dutch scenes would have had pride of place and served as a constant reminder of their heritage.[12] Many

---

[12] My parents immigrated to Canada in 1957 and took at least five framed pieces with them, including a

first- and second-generation immigrants, especially after WWII, could afford to return to the Netherlands both to visit relatives and friends and reconnect and learn more about their country of origin. Dutch-themed—usually place-based—art was often included with what they brought back, strengthening their affective bond with patria.

Dutch wall art was handed down through the family generations in Dutch American communities, but it steadily lost its appreciation as Americanization eroded ties to the Netherlands. Eventually, much was tossed out, donated to thrift shops and local museums, or sold to art dealers if it had value.[13] Unless museums exhibited this Dutch wall art, it could not wield much influence on the broader American public perception of the Netherlands.

Dutch art from Dutch, American, and Dutch-immigrant artists in museums and galleries in the United States

Until the second half of the nineteenth century, when public art galleries were founded in the United States to showcase valued art to the general public, viewing and appreciating art remained the preserve of the moneyed, educated, and leadership classes. Dutch art had achieved an enviable international reputation, and Dutch paintings by recognized masters had become highly desirable. Wealthy collectors acquired original Dutch canvases, and their social circles and the wider public within their communities would be given periodic opportunities to view these private collections. When public galleries and museums opened—first in larger Eastern Seaboard cities and gradually elsewhere as inland American urban places grew and matured—Dutch art of the Golden Age (fig. 8.6), the nineteenth-century Hague School (fig. 8.7), and the American art movement that was part of the "Holland Mania" period (figs. 1.1 and 8.8) found their way into art museum exhibits. This last art school was especially significant because it brought together American artists and Dutch subject matter; from the late nineteenth to the early twentieth century, American painters regularly visited the Netherlands and used Dutch picturesque subject matter to express antimodernist and pro social-reform sentiments.[14] The renderings of the Netherlands by these three groups of painters profoundly shaped the preferred American perceptions of the country.

In addition to these American artists, professional (as well as hobbyist) painters, of course, also arose from within Dutch-immigrant ranks.[15] These career artists had two homelands; they had spent time as painters in both countries and painted both Dutch and American subject matter. In their choice and treatment of Dutch subject matter, the work of some of these painters resembles that of the Holland Mania period. Like the American artists working in the Netherlands, they were influenced to some degree by the Hague School (fig. 8.7). John Henry

---

print of the St. Bavo Church in Haarlem (not far from Hillegom where they were born and raised), a watercolor of the Veluwe, a recreation area not that far from Driebergen and Zeist where they lived until they emigrated, and a print of the Nieuwmarkt in Amsterdam.

[13]   The Holland Museum in Holland, Michigan, has a sizable collection of donated Dutch wall art; other museums and historical societies in Dutch American centers have also received such donations.

[14]   Annette Stott, ed., *Dutch Utopia, American Artists in Holland, 1880–1914* (Telfair Books, 2009).

[15]   See endnote 8:15, p. 406.

Fig. 8.7. The trekvliet shipping canal near Rijswijk, known as the *View near the Geest Bridge*, Jan Hendrik Weissenbruch, 1868, Rijksmuseum (*public domain*)

VanderPoel (1857–1911), Cornelis Adriaan Zwaan (1882–1964), and Chris Stoffel Overvoorde (1934–2019) are examples of such Dutch-immigrant artists.

VanderPoel immigrated at age ten and is best known for his career as a drawing instructor at the Art Institute of Chicago. He founded the art colony in Rijsoord near Dordrecht where he and other—mainly American—nonresident artists painted picturesque, premodern rural scenes of the village and its surroundings (fig. 8.9).[16] Zwaan immigrated to Chicago in 1909 with his wife Alida. He is best known for his portraiture, especially one of Queen Juliana. He frequently traveled between Laren, the artist colony—his home base in

the Netherlands—and various cities in the United States to paint portraits of prominent citizens. His Dutch genre paintings are romanticized premodern domestic scenes (fig. 8.10).[17]

Overvoorde immigrated to Grand Rapids, Michigan, from the Rotterdam area in 1957 at age twenty-three. His emigration also marked an about-face in his career—from shipyard metal worker and diesel mechanic to professional artist and art teacher. He served as a faculty member in Calvin University's Art Department for more than thirty years. Overvoorde is best known today for his landscapes, although his career-spanning work to give visual

---

16 Nella Kennedy, "John Henry VanderPoel—Who?" in *Dutch Muck and More: Dutch Americans in Farming, Religion, Art, and Astronomy* (Van Raalte Press, 2019), 275–302.

17 Nella Kennedy, "Cornelis Christiaan Zwaan (1882–1964): Betwixt Laren and Detroit," in *Dutch American Arts and Letters in Historical Perspective*, ed. Robert P. Swierenga, Jacob E. Nyenhuis, and Nella Kennedy (Van Raalte Press, 2008), 1–12.

Fig. 8.8. *Two Women near the River Waal*, Wilhelmina Douglas Hawley, 1894. Collection of William van Dongen, Utrecht, the Netherlands (*public domain*)

Fig. 8.9. *Shelling Peas*, Rijsoord, John Henry VanderPoel, ca. 1888 (*Wikimedia Commons. No higher resolution available.*)

Fig. 8.10. *De Naailes* (the sewing lesson), Cornelis Adriaan Zwaan, n.d. (*Holland Museum*)

form to the history of Dutch America(ns) and its colleges and churches is equally noteworthy.[18] Overvoorde did not turn to

landscape painting until he returned to the Netherlands on a sabbatical leave after more than twenty years and rediscovered the polder landscapes of his youth. He developed a singular and striking aesthetic language for capturing his perceptions of these Dutch landscapes (fig. 8.11) and painted many landscapes based on this aesthetic. In time, he transferred this landscape vision to Michigan, as well as Alberta, Canada, where he and his wife Greta

[18] For example, Overvoorde painted fifteen canvasses (36" x 48") of the personal histories of the notables after whom the dormitories of Calvin College were named so that the students in residence would learn and be reminded of their lives and contributions. The paintings are mounted in the lobbies of the residence halls. Chris Stoffel Overvoorde and Ann Saigeon, *Stories of Faith: Fifteen Heroes of Calvin College and the Christian Reformed Church* (Calvin College, 1993).

Fig. 8.11. *Near Alblasserwaard*, Chris Stoffel Overvoorde, 2004 (*author's collection*)

spent many summers toward the end of his career. The introduction to an Overvoorde exhibit at the Willock and Sax Gallery in Banff, Alberta, captures his perspective well: "The artist revels in the open space of Western Canada; it is his homecoming, imprinted as he is by the famous Dutch landscape of his youth, intensely cultivated, flat like water, and the floor of a vast, cloud-filled sky."[19]

Overvoorde had no truck with the earlier painters associated with Holland Mania. He painted his landscapes from a distance in broad lines and bright colors as enduring amalgams of natural and hu-

man-made places; they are at once both modern and ageless. Although humanized by pastures, crops, drainage canals, fields, hedgerows, orchards, tree lines, and cows, the constituents of Overvoorde's Dutch landscapes are still all part of the natural world. His is a rural landscape view of the Netherlands.[20]

The works of these four different groups of career artists discussed here, each producing Dutch subject matter—those from the seventeenth century's

[19] https://www.willockandsaxgallery.com.

[20] Chris Stoffel Overvoorde, *Passing the Colors. Engaging Visual Culture in the 21st Century* (Eerdmans, 2002). In this partly biographical account, Overvoorde describes his journey as an artist and introduces readers to his oeuvre.

Golden Age, the Hague School, Holland Mania, and Dutch immigrants—were periodically exhibited around the country at national, regional, and local art galleries and museums. These venues were open to the public but drew only a tiny sliver of the population—those with access (geographic and economic) and those interested in Dutch art rather than a broader curiosity about the country. The working and middle classes of small-town and rural America were largely shut out of public art by some combination of geography, interest, and price. At the same time, art was no longer regarded by the public as a medium for learning about the world—the Netherlands in this case. Once photography became widespread, art was viewed more for appreciating and understanding aesthetics, emotions, symbolism, subjectivity, and allusiveness.

Photos and films about the Netherlands and its colonies for the American public[21]

The rise of the new visual media of photography and film greatly broadened the Dutch visual subject matter on offer to the American public and enhanced its accessibility—both geographic and economic. During the first half of the twentieth century, compact cameras, flashbulbs, wire photos, and photographs reproduced on printing presses all made photos a regular part of newspapers and magazines. They also made possible new types of publications—illustrated news magazines such as *Life* and pictorial scientific journals such as *National Geographic* and later *Smithsonian*. As with art labels and audio guides in a museum, captions for photos and related writing in the body of an article join visual content to text; they produce a different and enhanced combination for knowledge, understanding, and enjoyment than a visual medium by itself.[22]

Similarly, discoveries, innovations, and continuing developments during the late nineteenth and early twentieth centuries in motion-picture cameras, projectors, celluloid film, and synchronized sound brought movie theaters to every town and city and into classrooms, libraries, churches, and homes. Sending moving images by radio waves to television receiver sets in homes completed the process of making films into a mass medium. Photos and films were now as close as the daily newspaper, the television in the living room, magazine subscriptions, newsstands, and nearby movie theaters. Films with intertitles, subtitles, voice-overs, soundscape, and dialogue—all now-expected components of the film viewing experience—combined seeing, reading, and listening to produce a still greater level of immersive enjoyment, engagement, and understanding.

The viewing experience of photographs and film is, of course, different. A thirty-second film thread composed of several shots of a place and/or subject with a voice-over and/or dialogue provides a more immersive viewing experience than photographs, each with a caption as part of

---

21   The location, identity, and particulars of different Dutch places in photos and films—both small—a living room in the town of Zoutelande, Zeeland—and large—a satellite image of the Rhine-Meuse delta—are hardly ever apparent to either an international or a Dutch viewership from the image(s) alone. It takes captions, additional text in an article or book, voice-overs, and sometimes maps to locate, situate, and learn about the place of a photo or a scene in a film.

22   Helpful here, John Bateman, *Text and Image: A Critical Introduction to the Visual/Verbal Divide* (Routledge, 2014).

an accompanying article. The knowledge on offer or gained, albeit processed differently, may not be all that dissimilar.

The issue of what about the subject country (the Netherlands) would be of interest to an international (in this case, an American) readership was very relevant not only to the directors of the NIB/NIS but also to the editors of American newspapers with major international desks and foreign correspondents, such as the *New York Times*, as well as American magazines with much international content, such as *National Geographic* and *Life Magazine*. All countries publish newspapers and illustrated newsmagazines in their own language with both domestic and international stories. All such media make decisions about which international stories to run and with what detail, based on their perceived national and political interests and that of their readership; they must meet a bar for what counts as relevant and engaging international knowledge in a specific country. Many Dutch topics, issues, and stories in the Dutch media, including its documentary films and photojournalism, may be of great interest to a Dutch audience but are far too specialized, in-house, and granular for an American or international audience (see ch. 6 and fig. 8.12). Some NIS/NIB films with low viewership numbers were not suited for American audiences for these reasons.

Photos of the Netherlands in the Dutch American and Dutch press read by immigrants and their descendants

Before discussing the availability of photographs about the Netherlands and its territories for the American public in general, I will focus first on the small but still significant Dutch American sliver of the population (1.08%, more than 3.5 million in 2019[23]). Dutch American eyes are, of course, a subset of all American eyes on the Netherlands. They shared media for Dutch photographs available to all Americans but, in addition, some also consumed the products of the Dutch American—as well as, to a lesser extent, the Dutch—press in the form of ethnic newspapers, magazines, and journals. The larger American public, by and large, of course, did not read what was on offer from the Dutch American press. As Americanized generations followed their Dutch-immigrant forebears, the use they made of these publications naturally diminished. If the first several, nonimmigrant generations of Dutch Americans had an interest in their heritage, they would read English-language sources, and later, during the second half of the twentieth century, they would subscribe to Dutch heritage magazines and/or visit the Netherlands in person.

Dutch-language newspapers and magazines

The yearly arrival of Dutch immigrants, beginning in the 1840s, led to a steadily growing number of Dutch speakers and readers in the Dutch settlement zones and centers and throughout the country. The editors and owners of Dutch American newspapers and magazines, unlike

---

[23] United States Census, American Community Survey, People Reporting Ancestry, 2019, 1-year estimates. The reported percentage of Dutch Americans in the US population has been falling because (1) Dutch immigration has fallen off since the 1970s, whereas the total population of the United States increased more than 63% from 1970 to 2020, and (2) with increasing generational distance from their immigrant cohort and with more interethnic marriages, fewer self-identify as Dutch American.

their more mainline American newspaper counterparts, clearly did not need to be concerned about the interest of their readers in Dutch and Dutch American news. Dutch immigrants would read any and all such news if it came in their own language. For Dutch-immigrant families—much more so than for the general American public—that interest must have included Dutch visual representations; photos and sketches of Dutch scenes, places, societal events, and daily life must have been welcomed and appreciated, given the enduring emotional attachment of immigrants to their home country. Until the mid-1960s, however, with a few exceptions, Dutch-language newspapers and magazines read by Dutch immigrants did not or could not easily meet their readers' interest in Dutch visual media. This timing underscores that the NIB/NIS films available from 1943 to 1973 were, in fact, the first Dutch visual media widely accessible to Dutch Americans well before Dutch-language newspapers began to include photographs. About 12 percent (336,434) of the films' viewers in the twenty-state Holland service area were Dutch Americans.

Place-based, Dutch-language newspapers in the United States such as Holland's *De Grondwet* (1871–1938), Orange City's *De Volksvriend* (1874–1951), and others focused on matters and events—civil, ecclesiastical, and political—in the settlement area; they also reported news by correspondents from other Dutch American centers and newspapers in the home country itself; the reporting about the Netherlands often reflected the Dutch regional origins of the residents.[24] Their circulation

was largely confined to a local area, with smaller numbers delivered to other Dutch settlement zones. A sampling by decade of *De Grondwet* and *De Volksvriend* on delpher.nl (a Dutch website that provides fulltext, Dutch-language, digitized newspapers, among other historical print media) shows that, until well after WWII, Dutch American newspapers were entirely in Dutch and just text—only advertisements included visuals. Although non-Dutch interests—political, land development, and business—also reached out to influence and market to Dutch Americans via their own newspapers, the reporting itself stayed in a largely closed ethnic circuit, much like the Dutch wall art discussed earlier.

In smaller numbers, Netherlands-born American settlers also subscribed to newspapers from the Netherlands, again, often those from their own home region and province. Jacob Van Hinte's sources in the Netherlands during the 1920s reported noteworthy American subscriptions to *De Bildtsche Courant* (from the region of het Bildt in Friesland), *De Graafschapper* (from Gelderland), the *Franeker Courant* (Friesland), and the *Leeuwarder Nieuwsblad* (Friesland), but there were certainly other Dutch newspapers with subscriptions in the United States, especially from regions of high emigration.[25] A sampling on delpher.nl of the *Leeuwarder Nieuwsblad* and *De Graafschapper* shows, again, that these local and regional Dutch newspapers lacked any documentary photography. Dutch immigrants also subscribed to Christian magazines from the Netherlands. Because of their subject material, these again were, by and large, without

---

[24] See endnote 8:24, p. 407.

[25] Van Hinte, *Netherlanders in America* (Baker Book House, 1985), 1001–2.

any illustrations. One, however, listed by Van Hinte, was an exception—*De Spiegel* (1906–69), a Christian, illustrated weekly news magazine for the entire family.[26]

Illustrated news magazines date from the middle of the nineteenth century. Publishers realized that they could sell many more copies and reach a broader demographic if every issue of their paper included wood engravings, sketches, and artwork. By the beginning of the twentieth century, photographs had replaced wood engravings. More than written reporting, photographs give proof, underline actuality, speed up comprehension, and create interest as well as emotional attachment. The illustrated news magazines were meant to provide diversion as well as information; they focused on illustrated human interest stories and news both in the country and from other nations near and far—reporting judged to be appealing and appropriately interpreted for their readership (fig. 8.12). Like most other Dutch institutions in the first half of the twentieth century, the illustrated press in the Netherlands developed along worldviews and religious affiliations. *De Spiegel* was the most successful illustrated news magazine for the Protestant (Reformed) demographic; the Catholic population was served by *De Katholieke Illustratie*, and more secular Dutch were drawn to magazines like *Panorama* and *De Wereldkroniek*.

Reformed Protestants made up the largest percentage of the roughly quarter million Dutch immigrants to the United States from 1840 to 1940.[27] Some likely subscribed to *De Spiegel* in the Nether-lands and continued to receive it in their adopted country; others subscribed in response to notices and ads for the magazine in the Dutch American press, such as this review—including the address of the publisher and subscription cost of two dollars per year.

> It indeed is a "mirror" of the most important events of the world and of Christendom. . . . It is especially welcome to us because it gives a great deal of views and news from the Reformed circles of the Netherlands. Pictures referring to actors and actresses are kept out. Beautiful views of the realm of nature and art are given as well as of political and ecclesiastical life.[28]

It is also quite likely that *De Spiegel* was shared within extended families, friendship networks, and church communities. That the library of Calvin University and Calvin Theological Seminary in Grand Rapids, Michigan (founded by Dutch Reformed immigrants in 1876), carries a nearly complete run of *De Spiegel* is one measure of its one-time standing in this part of the Dutch American immigrant community.

In its choice of subject matter and prescription of morals, *De Spiegel* reflected the changing worldview and conduct of the Protestant Dutch middle class—and many Reformed Dutch Americans—during the magazine's sixty-three-year history. Events, actions, liturgies, debates, ministers, organizations, conferences, and

---

26 Ibid. The subtitle of *De Spiegel* changed from *Week Illustratie voor het Christelijk Gezin* to *Christelijk Nationaal Weekblad*.

27 Krabbendam, *Freedom on the Horizon*, app. 1, 361–62.

28 Henry Beets, "*De Spiegel*," *The Banner* (27 Oct. 1910), 683, quoted in Jacques Dane, "'Opdat Wij de Hand Gods in Alles Mogen Merken': De Eerste Vijftien Jaargangen van *De Spiegel* (1906–21)" in *Anderhalve Eeuw Protestantse Pers*, ed. G. Harinck and D. Th. Kuiper (Meinema, 1999), 99.

Fig. 8.12. Format of the illustrated press, with pictures, captions, and text on each page. This page from *De Spiegel* of May 29, 1937 (*courtesy Zomer & Keuning*) reports on the nineteenth national convention of the societies of Reformed young women, held in the city of Zwolle. *Clockwise, from top left*: one of the venues of the closing mass gathering with more than ten thousand participants, the leaders of the association address the convention, a lunch venue, making keepsake pictures, headshots of the convention speakers, opening theatrical presentation (*Reproduced in Piet Terlouw,* Dit was De Spiegel; Een Boeiend Beeld uit ruim 60 Jaren Christelijk-Nationaal Weekbladnieuws, 1906-1969, *[Zomer & Keuning, 1975], 73*).

Het strandbeeld te Scheveningen uit onzen tijd.

Fig. 8.13. Scheveningen, NL, North Sea beach scene, 1929 (De Spiegel, *31 May 1929, 434; courtesy Zomer & Keuning; reproduced in Terlouw,* Dit was De Spiegel, *49*)

anniversaries—all related to the church— had pride of place in the illustrated press's formula of pictures and text together (fig. 8.12). The news of other organizations within the Protestant pillar of Dutch society—in education, political parties, the press and radio, tourism and travel, and labor associations—also received regular photographic attention.

As the above review from the *Banner* makes clear, the opposition of *De Spiegel* to "worldly amusements," such as dance, movies, and gambling, helped build and enforce a Dutch (American) Protestant public morality into the 1950s. Dutch beach resorts also had their moral hazards—living beyond one's means and indecency—but unlike worldly amusements,

they could also be a source of responsible enjoyment of God's creation with family and friends—beach evangelism and churches in resort communities were there to counter the immoral side of seaside recreation (fig. 8.13).[29]

But *De Spiegel* was not entirely about church and Christian organizations, evangelism and acts of mercy, regular columns by ministers and other religious leaders, and Christian fiction in installments. National and international news headlines also had their place in every issue. The weekly format allowed for more "settled" news rather than the news in progress of the dailies; its pictures provided supple-

29 Dane, "de Hand Gods," 88–89.

Tienduizend mensen door het ijzige water verjaagd!

Donderdagmorgen 14 januari jl. werd Nederland opnieuw opgeschrikt door berichten over een dijkbreuk. Nu niet op een van onze Zuid-hollandse of Zeeuwse eilanden, maar even ten noorden van Amsterdam. Uur na uur steeg het water, dat de noordelijke IJ-polder binnenstroomde, terwijl de sneeuwvlagen door de lucht joegen. Van een paniek was er gelukkig geen sprake, maar duizenden inwoners van Tuindorp Oostzaan zagen toch wel met angst en beving het grimmige ijskoude water stijgen.
In allerijl werden hulpploegen opgeroepen, zodat met de evacuatie een begin gemaakt kon worden. Op deze pagina de eerste opnamen uit het rampgebied. In De Spiegel van volgende week komt nog een grote reportage met een algemeen overzicht van de ramp en vele vraaggesprekken, die onze verslaggevers met de slachtoffers hielden.

Terwijl de sneeuwjacht onverminderd voortduurde moesten de bewoners van Tuindorp Oostzaan hals over kop een goed heenkomen zoeken voor het snel wassende water. Oude mensen beleefden de schrik van hun leven, maar sterke jonge armen droegen hen dwars door het ijskoude water naar droger gebied. ◄

Dolgelukkig dat ook haar poesje gered was, keek deze kleuter rond. Met beide armen houdt zij haar vriendje in een handdoek gerold tegen zich aangeklemd. Gelukkig vielen er bij deze overstromingsramp geen mensenlevens te betreuren. ►

Alles wat vaarbaar was, werd ingezet in de hulpverlening en wie nog op eigen benen de boten of vletten kon bereiken, strompelde moeizaam door het water, dat tot een hoogte van 1.60 m steeg. ◄

Alleen met een tasje, waarin haar goud en geldswaardige papieren geborgen zijn, moest ook deze vrouw haar huis verlaten. Tienduizend bewoners van Oostzaan werden verzocht het Tuindorp te verlaten. 's Nachts mocht iemand het gebied niet betreden en direct werd er een girorekening geopend om de gevolgen van de overstroming te kunnen lenigen (nr. 768 t.n.v. Watersnood, Amsterdam). ►

Onvermoeid was de politie bezig de evacué's uit het rampgebied te halen. Naast deze politiemannen waren ook de B.B., het Rode Kruis en de U.V.V. in touw om te helpen wat er te helpen viel. ◄

de Spiegel

Fig. 8.14. *De Spiegel*'s reporting on the January 14, 1960, flood caused by a dike break in Tuindorp Oostzaan, part of Amsterdam North. The headline notes that ten thousand people were ordered to leave their homes. The photos show neighbors and emergency services helping to evacuate the elderly and others who needed assistance (De Spiegel, *23 Jan. 1960, 30; courtesy Zomer & Keuning; reproduced in Terlouw*, Dit was De Spiegel, 144).

SPAKENBURG

Fig. 8.15. Spakenburg woman adjusting oil lamp (Goed Nieuws *[July 1966], 1; Dutch Tourism Board*)

Fig. 8.16. The translated title of this photo is "Spring in the Betuwe." It shows flowering fruit trees and the face of a traditional regional farmstead. The Betuwe is a region in the southern Netherlands between the arms of the Rhine River, known for its fruit orchards and for their beauty when they are in bloom (De Krant, [May 1987], 4).

mentary information to the daily news reporting of important issues and events. In these news categories, the illustrated press, including *De Spiegel*, was known for highlighting more sensational happenings, such as natural and human-made disasters (fig. 8.14). *De Spiegel* would often put such events into a metaphysical frame. Especially in its formative years, *De Spiegel* gave its subscribers surplus value, interpreting its illustrated secular news through Bible stories and theological lenses, including seeing the hand of God in everything—his judgment, idolatry, sin and forgiveness, and Christian virtues.[30]

The era of place-based, Dutch-language newspapers and their unique journalism in the United States came to a definite end not long after WWII; the late nineteenth and early twentieth centuries had been their heyday. Along with other reporting, they transcribed local news into Dutch to keep immigrants up to date. Their publications, however, became unviable due to Americanization and fewer Dutch speakers; they were superseded by English-language papers for everyone in the community. Dutch-language newspapers that catered to regional and national populations of new and established Dutch immigrants took their place. The center of

30   Ibid., 91–96.

Fig. 8.17. An illustrated article about guidebooks for bicycle vacations in the Netherlands (Windmill Herald, *Christmas issue [1990], 4; Vanderheide Publishing*)

Herald

the Windmill

Your Dutch-language bi-weekly newspaper with English supplement $1.00   September 7, 1990   Volume 33 Issue 667

In dit nummer o.a.   Read about:

Werkgeversbond haalt uit naar kabinet
Burgerslachtoffers Ned.-Indie herdacht
Protest group gave Ontario an election issue
1848: cautionary change in Dutch system

Fig. 8.18. Characteristic front page of the *Windmill Herald*, traditional architecture and visitors enjoying refreshments along the quay facing the former fishing—now recreational—harbor of Marken. It also gives headlines for some Dutch- and English-language articles inside (Windmill Herald *[7 Sept. 1990], 1; Vanderheide Publishing*).

gravity of the Dutch press in North America shifted to Canada, a reflection of its considerably larger post-WWII Dutch immigration wave, and the American market was served from Canada by *Holland News/Goed Nieuws/The Windmill Herald* (1954–2012), with several Canadian and an American edition, and *Maandblad de Krant* (1969–) for both Canada and the United States. Several other Dutch-language newspapers were launched for immigrants in Canada, including *Calvinist Contact/Christian Courier* (1949–) and *De Nederlandse Courant* (1953–2018) for readers in Ontario.[31] Compared to their predecessors, these new-generation, Dutch-language newspapers read by immigrants in the United States were less sectarian and devoted most of their reporting to news and stories from the Netherlands with smaller amounts of Dutch American/Canadian content. In time, the *Windmill Herald* added an English-language section, but *De Krant* remained an exclusively Dutch-language paper. The two competed for subscribers in the North American market until 2012 when the *Windmill Herald* ceased publication, leaving *De Krant* the only Dutch-language newspaper on the continent.

Routine news photography became part of mainline American newspapers well before WWII but not until much later for this new crop of Dutch-language, North American newspapers. In 1966 *Goed Nieuws* for the first time began to regularly place a single, stand-alone, atmospheric photograph of the Netherlands on its front page, with titles and topics such as "Winter in Holland," "City Hall in Veere," and "Spakenburg" (fig. 8.15). These were postcard-style photos chosen to evoke emotion, nostalgia, memories, and longing; they were unrelated to any news or stories in the paper and easier to obtain than news photographs. In time, such stock photos and drawings were also interspersed throughout issues of *De Krant* (fig. 8.16). Over time, the number of story-related photos also began to grow and became standard issue in the North American, Dutch-language newspapers. Unlike the wistful picturesque photos, these were prosaic and functional, helping to make reporting visible, actual, eye-catching, and more interesting (fig. 8.17). Immigrant families now had regular access to photographs of all manner of scenes of Dutch life, people, events, and activities. In time, the *Windmill Herald* and *De Krant* used both a picturesque, color postcard view on the front cover or immediately inside (8.18) and diverse news-related photography—including color—throughout every issue.

After nearly 150 years, more than twenty-five newspapers, and with only *De Krant* left, the newspaper era of the Dutch press in North America is ending, along with their Dutch photographs. The fall in the number of Dutch immigrants in the population; the low immigration rate since the 1960s, without much prospect for an uptick any time soon; the near fluency in English of more recent Dutch immigrants; Dutch news sites on the internet; changes in the way news is consumed; and the availability of different subscriptions to digital versions of visual, media-rich Dutch newspapers in the Netherlands, such as *NRC De Week*, all make the future of North American Dutch-language newspapers very problematic. Stories and news from the Netherlands have been the mainstay

---

[31] In 2018 *De Nederlandse Courant* was folded into *Maandblad de Krant* as a separate section.

of the post-WWII Dutch newspapers, but this content is now available online. Dutch American and Dutch Canadian news and stories of all kinds, past and present, from across the country or continent, is their unique beat, but this is not enough and/or does not have sufficiently broad interest to support such newspapers.

English-language, Dutch-heritage magazines

A more recent development and the next stage of the Dutch American press after newspapers are English-language heritage magazines and journals. Books and journal articles in different fields of study produced a growing body of literature on Dutch America. With the establishment of several archives and research institutes focused on Dutch America, even more critical mass developed to support magazines (and books) that had an exclusive focus on Dutch America, namely, the Holland Society of New York (1885–); Heritage Hall, Calvin University (1961–); the New Netherland Institute, New York State Library and Archives (1983–); and the A. C. Van Raalte Institute, Hope College (1994–). Examples include *De Halve Maen: Journal of the Holland Society of New York* (1922–),[32] a scholarly journal written by experts that publishes research on the New Netherland Dutch and their legacies; *Origins: Historical Magazine of the Heritage Hall Archives* (1983–),[33] a magazine with contributions by amateur, local, and professional histori-

ans on the nineteenth- and twentieth-century wave of Dutch immigration and settlement, including church history; and *Dutch, the Magazine about the Netherlands and Its People at Home and Abroad* (2011–), a popular magazine written by professional writers, columnists, and journalists on both the Dutch in North America and the Netherlands itself, with primary attention paid to the latter. These magazines connect those who identify as Dutch North Americans to all aspects of their history and legacy on the continent and to the country they or their forebears left behind; they are also of interest to some Americans in general, curious about this strand of American history and its relationship to broader historical developments. *De Halve Maen* and *Origins* publish original research that adds to the body of knowledge about the history of Dutch America. *Dutch, the Magazine* reprises accepted knowledge in engaging, creative, and accessible pieces for a general readership on all aspects of the Netherlands'—and to a lesser extent Dutch American—history and culture; its rubrics include "place," "typically Dutch," "travel," "history," "people," "cooking," "literature," and "art."

Now normal, expected, and more common and prominent, photographs are an essential and regular part of all three magazines. This is especially apparent in *Dutch, the Magazine*, launched more recently and given over to more general articles. First impressions come from its many, high quality, large, color photographs, some extending across two pages. They are integral to every article, often with or without very brief captions; the pictures not tied into the text make their own contribution to the articles. Text and visual media are equally important, and a first look at

---

[32] *De Halve Maen* has used several different subtitles; this is the current one.

[33] Heritage Hall holds the archives of the Christian Reformed Church in North America, Calvin Theological Seminary, and Calvin University, as well as Dutch immigration records, including letters, family histories, and ship passenger manifests. The subtitle of *Origins* has changed over time.

Fig. 8.19. Street market in the center of Arcen, province of Limburg. Opening of a six-page, ten-picture article about the village and its surroundings that covers its history, sights, village center, and (white) asparagus cultivation, marketing, cuisine, and culture (*Sonia Motisca, "Arcen, Asparagus village on the Maas River,"* Dutch, the Magazine, *May/June 2018*)

an issue usually is skimming its photos before deciding which article to read first, a la *National Geographic* (fig. 8.19). *De Halve Maen* and *Origins*, by contrast, include fewer and smaller pictures, ones in the former now in color, and those in the latter in black and white. The text has greater control with visual media in the form of maps, portraits, documents, family paintings, and photos more directly related to the writing. Because Dutch America and not the Netherlands is the subject matter of these two magazines, their photographs are principally scenes in the United States, not the Netherlands, and therefore, outside this study's focus on Americans' access to and perceptions of images of the Netherlands. Only when Dutch antecedents are relevant to a Dutch American topic do readers come across photos from the Netherlands, primarily of ancestral villages, churches, farmsteads, homes, families, and communities (fig. 8.20).

Fig. 8.20. Wierum, Friesland, Dutch childhood village of Meindert De Jong, award-winning
American writer of children's and juvenile literature. From Richard H. Harms'
photo essay, "Meindert De Jong," *Origins* 26, no. 1 (2008), 17
(*Heritage Hall, David De Jong Collection, box 5, folder 10*)

Subscriptions to these English-language magazines/journals (not *De Halve Maen*) and North American, Dutch-language newspapers and their visual media were and are concentrated in the immigrant and second generations. Since the 1960s, the immigrant cohort has steadily fallen from more than 118,000 to an estimated 82,000 in 2019, as more older immigrants pass away than new immigrants take their place, a trend that will only accelerate with much reduced annual Dutch immigration.[34] Interaction of recent generations with the immigrant cohort is key to passing on and reinforcing ethnic knowledge and practices in general and with more recent immigrants in helping to keep ethnicity up to date.

These magazines, therefore, are also one of the vanishing ethnic markers among some of the more intellectually curious Dutch Americans of the first few generations still in contact with their immigrant ancestors. Because they still largely self-identify as Dutch American, some remain interested to learn their family stories and genealogies and the encompassing history of their nationality in the United States and in the country of their forebears; the magazines help to satisfy and develop these interests. The curiosity about their pasts and their ancestral homeland may be more enduring for some Dutch Americans than for other ethnic groups whose traits have fallen away more rapidly with Americanization. Ethnic traits in the first three generations of Protestant Dutch

[34] United States Census, American Community Survey, Foreign-born populations, 1-Year Estimates, Detailed Tables 2019; Gibson, Campbell and Jung, Kay, table 3, "World Regions and Country or Area of Birth of the Foreign-Born Population: 1960–2000" in *The Foreign-Born Population of the United States: 1850–2000* (Novinka Books, 2007), 12–13, and appendices.

Fig. 8.21. Stranded by floodwaters on the second story, residents are evacuated by a rowboat in the Dutch town of 's-Gravendeel, southwest of Dordrecht in the province of Zuid-Holland. (New York Times *[4 Feb. 1953]*, 10).

Americans have been more persistent than in some other American ethnic groups because, like German Lutheran immigrants, they carried their own family of Reformed Dutch denominations with them and founded others in the United States. These ethnic churches and their own Reformed day schools kept children and grandchildren more tied into the subculture when it came to marriage, church, and place.[35]

Because of ethnic intermarriage and lack of any remaining ethnic markers and practices, later-generation ethnics[36] usually

[35] James D. Bratt, *Dutch Calvinism in Modern America: A History of a Conservative Subculture* (Eerdmans, 1984). Michael Douma, *How Dutch Americans Stayed Dutch: An Historical Perspective on Ethnic Identities* (Amsterdam University Press,

2014). A moving and insightful memoir of growing up in a Dutch American urban subculture in the 1950s is Jane Griffioen, *London Street: A Memoir* (Resource Publications, 2020).

[36] The term refers to fourth and later generations of ethnic Americans; the fourth generation is the first without direct contact with its immigrant ancestors. The term is used and expounded upon in Herbert J. Gans, "The Coming Darkness of Late-Generation European American Ethnicity," *Ethnic and Racial Studies* 37, no, 5 (2013): 757–65; see also Richard D. Alba, "The Twilight of Ethnicity among Americans of European Ancestry: The Case of Italians," *Ethnic and Racial Studies* 8, no. 1 (1985): 134–58.

do not claim any ethnicity or self-identify with multiple ethnicities. With such ethnic attrition, subscribers to these magazines from these later generations are likely few and far between—hobbyists, genealogists, academics, specialists, and leaders of ethnic organizations and tourism.

Photos about the Netherlands and its territories for the American public

New York Times and Life Magazine

Later-generation Dutch ethnics and the larger American public paid little to no attention to publications of the Dutch American press and its visual media but, rather, learned about the Netherlands, like everyone else, from national dailies and magazines like *Life* and *National Geographic*. National dailies that carried international news, such as the *New York Times*, were available throughout the country from newsstands, libraries, and paperboys and girls; increasingly, they included photos related to major headlines and feature articles, and occasionally, as might be expected, the Netherlands and its colonies were in their international spotlight. During the entire first week of February, for example, the North Sea storm of January 31, 1953, and the resulting flooding in southeastern England, southwestern Netherlands, and coastal Belgium were on the front page of the *New York Times*—the United States newspaper of record—with more detailed reporting inside the paper every day. Photographs accompanied much of the reporting (fig. 8.21). American readers could not only read about but also see this disaster—an altogether different cognitive modality.

Illustrated news magazines such as *Life Magazine* privileged the visual even

more; pictures took the lead, and captions and text situated the photos. *Life* became a weekly American photographic news magazine in 1936 and continued as such until 1972 when it became an occasional and then—until 2000—a monthly publication. Its weekly circulation soon reached well into the millions. More than nineteen hundred issues were published, and with an average of ninety pages per issue, ultimately more than 170,000 pages total (about half in advertising). Google Books scanned the entire run of the weekly *Life* into searchable PDFs and made them available online, which allows ready identification of its photo essays about the Netherlands and its colonies/territories.[37] The run of *Life* as a weekly roughly corresponded to that of the NIB/NIS film library.

For American eyes, there were thirty-two, short (3–4 pages) photo essays in *Life Magazine* from 1936 to 1972, either entirely or partially about the Netherlands and its territories. Most were about the country itself, and the majority (15) appeared during the 1940s and the 1950s (13). The topics covered war and the military (10), the Dutch royal family (7), the arts (5), floods (3) (fig. 8.22), and the Dutch colonies/territories (6) (fig. 8.23). These Dutch photo news stories reflected the interests and tastes of the American public.

National Geographic Magazine

National Geographic[38] was launched as a monthly by the National Geographic

---

37   See endnote 8:37, p. 407.

38   Because this is a study about the NIB/NIS, and I am placing the distribution of its films in the United States into the context of other Dutch visual media available to Americans, the photos from *National Geographic* that I reproduce in this section fall within the years the NIB/NIS films were distributed.

Fig. 8.22. The former island of Walcheren, Zeeland, was flooded by the Allies in October 1944 to drive out the German defenders. It remained flooded for more than a year. Here, the Huysman farming family of Brigdamme, north of Middelburg, the capital of Zeeland, stands on the catwalk outside their home at low tide. At high tide, there was two feet of water in their living room and kitchen. The inset (© George Rodger, photographer/Magnum Photos) shows Maria Huysman (*catwalk, center*) in the costume of Walcheren, on one of two Dutch covers of *Life*, with the title "Dutch Girl." Anne Frank was featured on the Aug. 18, 1958 cover ("Flooded Dutch Island," *Life* [19 March 1945], 75-83, George Rodger, photographer).

Society in Washington, DC, in 1888 and, beginning in 1905, changed from a scholarly magazine entirely made up of text to one that combined high-quality photographs with text. It became best known for its photographs and, as a result, steadily increased its circulation with a much broader readership. What began as a magazine for exploration, travel, and geography for scholars became a magazine that covered world cultures, science, environment, geography, and history in understandable and interesting ways through accessible writing and engrossing photography. By the 1980s, its circulation stood at around twelve million; in 2015 *National Geograph-*

Fig. 8.23. Indonesia expelled Dutch citizens and seized their property in retaliation for the Dutch government refusing to negotiate on ceding its colony, Dutch New Guinea. The photo shows part of a group of women from a retirement home near Jakarta about to board a ship that would take them to the Netherlands. They were born in Indonesia, widows of Dutch men, and had never left the country ("The Poignant Figures of a Modern Exodus," *Life* [6 Jan. 1958], 8-13. James Burke, photographer).

ic was available in nearly forty languages, with a circulation of nearly seven million. American readers and viewers made up half of that number.[39]

Subscribers to *National Geographic* have access to its archive; this includes high-resolution digital copies of every issue from the very beginning of the magazine. Most important for my purposes, not only the articles but also the photographs are tagged for different countries, places, and topics. For any of these rubrics, metadata are provided for the number of articles and photographs, the month and year of the is-

sues in which these photos were published, keywords, and a frequency distribution by decade. When one enters "Netherlands" into the search engine and filters for photos, 538 thumbnail photos come up as part of an index—thirty per page—with, next to each thumbnail, the tags "year," "issue," and "photo" on the first line and primary descriptor "Netherlands," and secondary descriptor—often for a place and/or topic—on the second line. The primary descriptor could be "Netherlands," "Netherlands Indies," or "Netherlands Antilles."[40] For comparison, "France" yields 2,614 photos and "Greece" 1,103.

39 Paul Farhi, "National Geographic Gives Fox Control of Media Assets in $725 Million Deal," *The Washington Post*, 9 Sept. 2014.

40 See endnote 8:40, p. 407.

With millions of American eyes on *National Geographic* every month and therefore also its fairly consistent coverage of the Netherlands and its colonies and territories, the magazine was and remains a principal source of American public knowledge about the country. Though not a Netherlands-only source, such as the NIB/NIS film library, the magazine—in addition to home subscriptions—is cataloged, bound, shelved, and available in many school and public libraries. It has remained a ready, ongoing, and trusted reference and source for student essays and projects to the present day, a role that films could not match. Back issues can continue to shape international knowledge once the current issue has had its impact and is "retired." Not until videotape for the home market became available in the late 1970s could "films" be used in this way.

Photographs of the Dutch colonies/territories

Of the 516 *National Geographic* "Dutch" photos identified using the magazine's archive, 35.1 percent (134) were of the Dutch colonies and territories. From the 1920s to the 1940s, there were nearly as many photos about the colonies—especially the Dutch East Indies—as the Netherlands itself (figs. 8.24, 8.25), somewhat mirroring this split for the NIB films screened during the 1940s. *National Geographic*—given its origins—was interested, especially then, like the NIB, in environmental and ethnographic portraits of non-Western lands, and these colonies fit the bill. This spate of photos about the Dutch colonies in *National Geographic* for the American public parallels the culture-directed films about the Dutch colonies produced by American travelogue filmmakers of the

1920s and 1930s and distributed by the NIB during the 1940s. The Dutch stamp on these islands and territories was hardly visible. With Indonesian independence in 1949, the loss of Dutch New Guinea to Indonesia in 1962, and statehood for Suriname in 1975, the number of photos about the Dutch colonies plummeted—they continued to appear, of course, but under different country names—and the magazine was left with only the six islands of the Dutch Antilles. Even these territories disappeared from *National Geographic* beginning in the 1980s and have not been seen there since (fig. 8.24).

The geography of the photographs of the Dutch colonies/territories is reasonably representative. With several exceptions, the constituent areas are all included. There are thirty-seven photos (25.4%) from the Netherlands Antilles and Suriname in the Western Hemisphere (fig. 4.13). The southern three islands of the Lesser Antilles in the Caribbean (the ABC group—Aruba, Bonaire, Curaçao) and the northern three (the SSS group—Saba, Sint Eustatius, Sint Maarten) each have between five and eight photos. For the NIB/NIS films, the SSS group was largely a footnote. By contrast, there was only one photo of Suriname, whereas several NIB/NIS films gave considerably greater—some, exclusive—attention to this territory.

The ninety-seven photographs of the sprawling Dutch East Indies (fig. 4.12) in *National Geographic* until 1949 (Dutch New Guinea until 1962) are focused on several major islands and archipelagos—the economic center, Java (33); Bali (22); and the Maluku (Moluccas) Islands (20), long known as the Spice Islands. Relatively small Bali (fig. 8.26), immediately east of Java, one of the Lesser Sundas, received

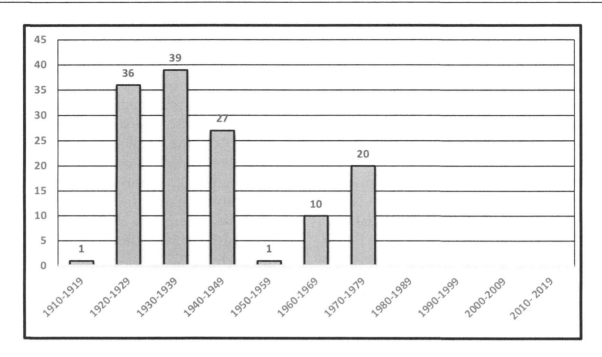

Fig. 8.24. Number of photographs about the Dutch colonies/territories per decade in *National Geographic* from 1910 to 2019 (*National Geographic Archive*)

Fig. 8.25. In Bali, rainwater from higher elevations is penned in flooded, staircase, rice fields, producing three crops a year; the darker grey fields in the photo have been plowed by water buffalo and are ready for transplanting rice seedlings. This caption is a paraphrase from the one in the magazine (*National Geographic Archive; Maynard Owen Williams, "Bali and Points East,"* National Geographic *(March 1939), 313-52; photo p. 330. Finlay photograph by Amos Burg; Amos Burg photographs, Org. Lot 450, Oregon Historical Society Research Library*).

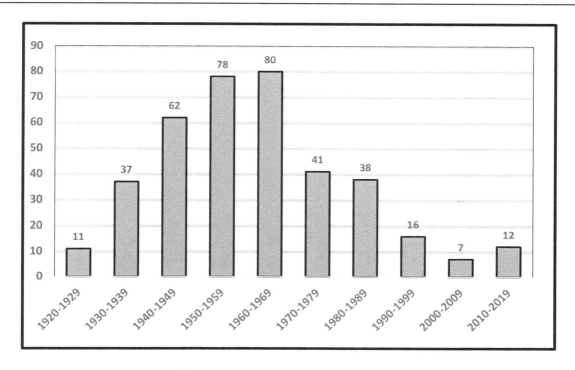

Fig. 8.26. Number of photographs about the Netherlands per decade in *National Geographic* from 1920 to 2019 (*National Geographic Archive*)

outsize photographic attention because of visits by anthropologists and documentary filmmakers in the 1930s. In the West, their work helped establish an image of the island as a sensuous paradise, which brought tourists there already during Dutch colonial rule. Other islands receive sparse visual attention, that is, the rest of the Lesser Sundas (9)—almost all of the Island of Flores—Sumatra (5), Celebes (Sulawesi) (5), and Dutch New Guinea (3). There are no photos of Kalimantan (part of the island of Borneo), the largest coterminous land area of the Dutch East Indies (now Indonesia).

Like the *National Geographic* photos about the Dutch East Indies, the NIB/NIS films also gave much attention to Java, with adjoining Bali, along with Sumatra. The NIS focus on outlying Dutch New Guinea provides the largest difference; it acquired nine of the films of the Dutch-govern-ment-sponsored New Guinea Chronicle series, each about different Dutch development programs for this vast area. The few *National Geographic* photos of this area were rather desultory. Other outlying areas from Java—the colonial center of the Dutch East Indies—the Lesser Sundas, and the Maluku (Moluccas) Islands, unlike the photos from *National Geographic*, received no attention from the NIB/NIS films.

Photographs about the Netherlands

The distribution of photographs of the Netherlands itself in *National Geographic* by decade for a century approximates a bell-shaped histogram (fig. 8.26). The number of photos ramps up quickly over the first thirty years, peaks and levels off during the fifties and sixties, plummets sharply during the seventies, and then continues to decline gradually over the last

Fig. 8.27. Spakenburg women in traditional costume watch a fishing boat enter the harbor; their costumes include the starched "shoulder boards" that suggest a wooden yoke a milkmaid would wear. From the fifteenth century, Spakenburg was a fishing town on the Zuiderzee with direct access to the North Sea fishing grounds, especially herring. With the building of the enclosure dam in 1932, the town lost access to the high seas, and the former North Sea arm became a freshwater lake (IJssel Lake) with very limited opportunities remaining for commercial fishing (flounder, eel). This caption is a paraphrase of the text accompanying the photograph in the magazine (*National Geographic Archive; Gilbert M Grosvenor, "Helping Holland Rebuild her Land,"* National Geographic *(Sept. 1954), 365-413, photo p. 384; photographer, Gilbert Grosvenor*).

four decades to return to the low numbers of the 1920s. This frequency pattern surprised me. I expected an overall horizontal graph line with rises and dips for individual decades. How might the coverage of an individual country over time by an international magazine such as *National Geographic* be characterized and explained by

a bell-shaped frequency curve? One possible framework would consist of three stages. The first sees a rapidly growing number of articles—or parts of more general articles—over time, as the country is "discovered." The second describes a plateauing of content as available new and reused subject matter can no longer match the growth

Fig. 8.28. After WWII, the Netherlands experienced a severe housing shortage. This photograph is of the new town of Emmeloord, now the administrative center of the municipality of the Noordoostpolder in IJssel Lake. The German occupation had paused the settlement of this polder, already dry in 1942. In the foreground, the concrete foundations and scaffolding poles for new housing are in place. In the background are what are still called "Austrian" houses; the Netherlands bought and disassembled eight hundred houses in Austria and then reassembled them in select Dutch centers, including Emmeloord. This caption is a paraphrase from the text accompanying the photograph in the magazine (*National Geographic Archive; Sydney Clark, "Mid-Century Holland Builds her Future," National Geographic (Dec. 1950), 747-78, photo p. 766; photographer, Fenno Jacobs from Black Star*).

rate in published material. This is followed in the third stage by a gradual decline in attention as material thought to be of interest to an international readership is exhausted.

These three stages may be applied to the changes in the frequency and content of the photos about the Netherlands over the century. For the first fifty years (1920–69), the photography in *National Geographic* regularly reprised for new readers the distinctive stock images of the old Nether-

lands many Americans had already come to cherish: greenhouse flower growing and flower auctions using the descending-price clock, regional and place-based traditional costumes for different villages and regions (fig. 8.27), bulb cultivation amidst carpets of single-colored flowers, narrow houses lined along picturesque canals, women mending nets in fishing villages, and porters moving cheese balls on barrows to the weigh scale. Some 25 percent of the photos of the first fifty years fall into this

Place	Times Shown	Place	Times Shown
Amsterdam	57	Brielle	3
Rotterdam	45	Hindelopen	3
Alkmaar	13	Schiphol	3
The Hague	14	Spakenburg	3
Aalsmeer	12	Westerbork	3
Neeltje Jans	11	Wijster	3
Scheveningen	10	Afsluitdijk	2
Marken	7	Balk	2
Haringvlietdam	6	Den Oever	2
Hillegom	6	Groningen	2
Middelburg	6	Keukenhof	2
Veere	6	Medemblik	2
Volendam	6	Naarden	2
Delft	5	Nijmegen	2
Hoorn	5	Noordwijkerhout	2
Lisse	5	Nuenen	2
Staphorst	5	Spaarndam	2
Urk	5	Vlissingen	2
Eindhoven	4	Zaandam	2
Utrecht	4		

Fig. 8.29. List of the number of times places (villages, towns, cities, infrastructure projects) in the Netherlands are shown more than once in photographs in *National Geographic*, 1900-2019 (*National Geographic Archive*)

category. A second group during this period were photos about WWII—defense preparations during the late 1930s, the war's destruction, and the liberation, reconstruction, and economic revival of the country (fig. 8.28). A final principal group of photos during these fifty years recorded the many different activities related to water defenses and reclamation projects, including the monumental Zuiderzee Works begun in 1924 and completed in 1967; the 1953 flood, its aftermath and recovery; and the answer to this recurring flood threat—the Delta Works—begun in 1954, but not completed until 1997. These three, broad topical foci helped spur a growing number of articles, accompanied by related photos. By the 1950s and 1960s—the second stage—stories and photos based on these three subject areas peaked and leveled off; there was not enough new material suitable for a non-Dutch readership to continue the growth rate. It is instructive that the photo subjects of the Netherlands in *National Geographic* during this period comport well with those of the films circulated by the NIB/NIS from 1943 to 1974.

By the end of the 1960s and the beginning of stage three, these three subject areas had lost a lot of their steam, and additional rubrics—social change and modernization, as with the NIS—did not generate as much international interest and copy. The American and international love affair with the nineteenth century and the older Netherlands had either largely ended—at least for knowledgeable magazines—or been updated with modern habits—skating, for example.

WWII and postwar reconstruction were in the rearview mirror; the economy had recovered and expanded, bringing broad affluence and consumerism to the country. The Zuiderzee Works was largely complete, and the Delta Works was now in full swing. The Netherlands looked increasingly like other modern Western European countries—affluent, consumerist, and technology driven. Similarities replaced differences, although the latter had received more attention from the international media. The topic of social change fit less well into the *raison d'être* of *National Geographic* and was also less photographable. A more pervasive modern look at the country was reflected in its photographs beginning in the 1970s. Together, all these changes led to a steady decline in articles and photos about the Netherlands in *National Geographic* during the last fifty years, approaching the relatively low level of attention it had received in the 1920s.

A country's identity requires regular refreshment and reinforcement, but *National Geographic* had laid down an enduring set of images of the Netherlands for over a century. Another bell curve of interest is doubtful; a more steady, flat level of international attention is now more likely. The identity of a country is, however, never static. Much will depend on exigencies and accomplishments that receive international attention and reconfigure the personali-

ty traits of the country during the next half century.

Fig. 8.29 lists the number of times Dutch cities, towns, villages, and infrastructure projects (all point features) are shown in the photos of *National Geographic*. Understandably, as seen in fig. 4.21, which lists the number of times Netherlands places are shown in the NIB/NIS films, the principal economic centers of Rotterdam (45) and the capital, Amsterdam (57), both again head the list. As the premier cultural center, Amsterdam could stand in for the entire country on many fronts, both traditional and modern. Many of the other places quite high up on this list—and in fig. 4.21—have photos that cater largely only to American—and other outsider—traditional perceptions of the Netherlands: Alkmaar (13)—cheese market; Aalsmeer (12)—flowers; Hillegom (6) and Lisse (5)—bulb growing; Scheveningen (10), Marken (7), Veere (6), Volendam (6), Staphorst (5), Urk (5), and Spakenburg (3)—traditional fishing villages and local traditional attire; and Middelburg (6), Delft (5), Hoorn (5), and Vlissingen (2)—markets and historic centers. Without all these different touristic and stereotypic assets, these places would not have had their photos in *National Geographic*. Several other places with a high number of photos are directly tied to the Delta Works, such as Neeltje Jans (11), the artificial island created at the center of the Oosterschelde barrier, and the Haringvliet Dam (6), the barrier across the estuary of the Rhine and Meuse with that name.

When the ninety places are mapped (fig. 8.30), along with the number of times their photos make an appearance in *National Geographic* (including those shown only once), a familiar pattern emerges. The

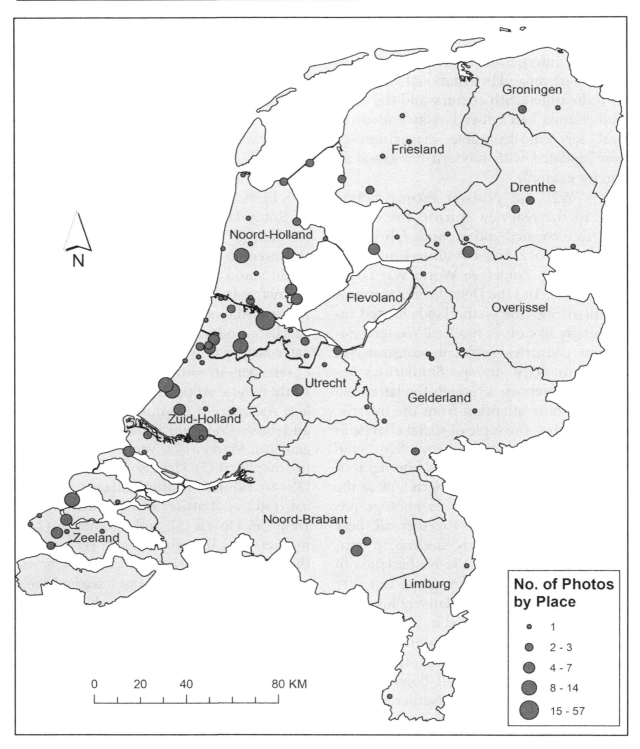

Fig. 8.30. Location and number of times places (villages, towns, cities, infrastructure projects) in the Netherlands are shown in photographs in *National Geographic*, 1900-2019 (*National Geographic Archive*)

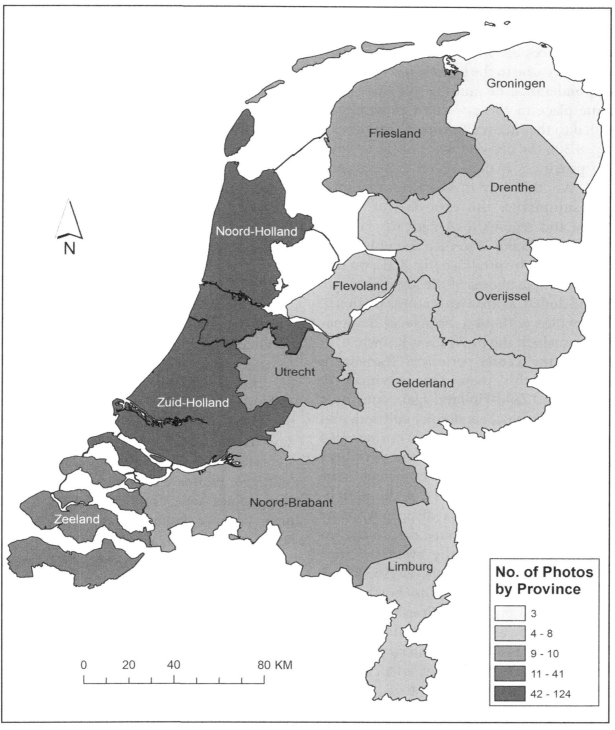

Fig. 8.31. Number of photos of places by province in the Netherlands (villages, towns, cities, infrastructure projects, and regions) shown in *National Geographic*, 1900-2019 (*National Geographic Archive*)

greatest density of photographed places is in the western coastal provinces; fifty-nine of the places are in these three provinces and thirty-one in the other nine. When the preponderance of multiple photos of the same place in these western provinces is added to the mix with proportional circles (fig. 8.30), the pre-eminence of these western provinces is made even more prominent. Another way to visualize, measure, and summarize the exposure of Dutch places and regions to Americans via *National Geographic* is to map the number of photographs by province (fig. 8.31); on this map, multiple photos of the same place are also included, as are area features (regions), and photos without a clear local designation for which the province is known.

In the center-periphery framework shown by this map, the provinces of Noord- and Zuid-Holland again constitute the demographic, economic, cultural, and political core of the country; it corners 69.0 percent of the photos and the periphery (the other ten provinces) 31.0 percent. The province of Zeeland—part of the periphery—nevertheless, has a disproportionate 11.7 percent of the photos, due to the internationally newsworthy events of wartime flooding, the calamitous 1953 flood, and the Delta Works. The north-south central tier of provinces (Friesland, Flevoland, Utrecht, and Noord-Brabant) drew 10.2 percent, and the five eastern provinces with a border on Germany, 9.1 percent of the *National Geographic* photos.

The geographic distribution of Netherlands places shown both in the NIB/NIS films and the *National Geographic* photographs is fundamentally the same. The films have a 31-year run and the photos a 119-year run. The center-periphery ratio of the photos (69:31) is more pronounced than that of the films (61:39). I explained this pattern at the end of chapter 4 in reference to the places shown in the NIB/NIS films program during the lifetime of its political and cultural diplomacy, and it applies here as well. Those making decisions about film acquisitions for the NIS/NIB and those deciding on stories and photos for *National Geographic* were of different nationalities and worked for very different kinds of organizations. This Dutch national core and periphery also clearly shapes its international visual media.

Photobooks

Photobooks—print or digital—are another medium that give an exclusive or dominant place to photos to convey appearance, content, explanation, and meaning. They should not be grouped with tourist books and guides, which also highlight the visual. A photobook—especially today—is not a book of photos, just like an atlas is not a book of maps. Photobooks not only give photos a special place, but they also include text, graphics, statistics, and maps. Nor are they necessarily coffee table books, meant for display and browsing and often given to either a superficial treatment or the aesthetics of a topic or place. Rather, they can be and have become multimedia books, led by photographs that have been chosen, shot, and compiled by experts and can offer a very comprehensive and scholarly treatment of topics and places. Photobooks are almost always oversize books that allow the photos and their details to stand out. There are photobooks for every conceivable topic and so also for places, from neighborhoods to continents; some topics, however (government), are less suited to photobooks than others (land use).

Fig. 8.36. Island ribbons, formerly used to dry dredged peat in what are now the
Loosdrechtse Lakes, Noord-Holland; note the cottages
(Karel Tomeï, *NLXL, Made in Holland*, 262–63).

Nearly every Dutch city, town, region, and province has been the subject at one time or another of one or more photobooks, and it seems there is a new one for the entire country nearly every year. Besides general photo surveys of Dutch places large and small, there are thematic, national photobooks of (from my professional library) occupation mounds (*terpen* in Frisian, or *wierden* in Dutch), landscapes, water infrastructure, megalithic tombs (Dutch-*hunebedden*), country estates, and castles. Nearly all photobooks are in-house, with Dutch captions and text.

They are authored with a particularity required and appreciated by residents of the place under the microscope and by Dutch inhabitants interested in learning more about—and visiting—other places in their own country.

As with documentary films, only Dutch topics and places with international standing and allure are the subject of photobooks in either English or in Dutch and English together; these are available from international and online booksellers. I have collected and use a number of them: the varied and distinctive looks of Dutch landscapes (fig. 8.36);[41] the dike, one of the most important inventions of the Netherlands;[42] Dutch landscapes as video art;[43] polders as the fundamental land use unit in the low Netherlands;[44] and water management in the Netherlands.[45]

Films about the Netherlands and its territories for the American public

The NIB/NIS films as part of the American Ecosystem for Producing and Distributing Nontheatrical Films, 1920s–1970s

In the previous chapters, I did not place the circulation of the NIB/NIS films into the ecosystem of nontheatrical film production and distribution in the United States. This created the impression, perhaps, that the 2,292 different places throughout the twenty-state, Holland service area that screened NIB/NIS films consisted of unique "Dutchophile" audiences. With very few exceptions, however, this was not at all the case. The churches, schools, libraries, army bases, and civic organizations that showed these films were part of the growing market for nontheatrical, educational, training, and industrial documentary films produced and distributed by hundreds of commercial filmmaking companies. The Shive Elementary School in Vernon, Texas, for example, showed the NIB film, *Holland and the Zuyder Zee*, in February 1947 to 220 students (NIB/NIS film database), but it could well have shown a film on an entirely different subject, borrowed/rented from another film distribution company or film lending library, in the following month. The curricula, programs, and interests of the borrower organizations, in general, were quite diverse; they would either use the catalogs of the various nontheatrical film production/distribution companies to pick their films or borrow films that had been acquired by the film library of their school district.

From the late 1920s—with the standard gauge of 16 mm film, its cameras, and projectors—to the early 1980s—with the adoption of video tape—there were essentially two film production and distribution systems in the United States (and throughout the world)—35 mm theatrical fiction films produced by major studios, such as Warner Bros, Paramount, Universal, and Columbia, and shown in movie theaters, and 16 mm nontheatrical, nonfiction films, produced by hundreds of companies that produced, rented, and sold academic, training, guidance, in-

41   Karel Tomeï, *NLXL, Made in Holland* (Scriptum, 2017).

42   Eric Jan Pleister and Kees van der Veeken, *Dutch Dikes* (NAi, 2014).

43   Maartje van den Heuvel and Tracy Metz, *Nature and Artifice; New Dutch Landscape in Photography and Video Art* (NAi, 2008).

44   Clemens M. Steenbergen, Wouter Reh, Steffen Nijhuis, and Michiel Pouderoijen, *The Polder Atlas of the Netherlands* (THOTH, 2009).

45   Martin and Marijke Kers, *Holland, Land of Water* (Terra, 1998).

dustry, and advertising films for schools (kindergarten to university), companies, governments, and the armed forces. One area where these two systems intersected was significant for NIB/NIS films: several categories of nontheatrical films, notably, international films, films about American life and culture, and newsreels, were regularly shown in theaters as shorts before the feature film. Given the popularity of movie theaters in this era, any NIB/NIS films shown as shorts in theaters would have had their viewership boosted many times over their nontheatrical showings. There are no viewership records in the NIB/NIS archive that document theatrical showings of its films, but there are estimates of audiences for NIS films shown by particular television stations.

It is estimated that during this era, one hundred thousand different educational films alone were produced, many with funds made available by federal legislation.[46] Compared to 35 mm movie cameras, the 16 mm versions were considerably cheaper, lighter weight, and more versatile for movie making. This helped produce films more quickly, with smaller budgets and more affordable prices for consumers in education, business, and government. Albeit not nearly as profitable as movie-house films, rental and sales plans offered reasonable returns for producers and distributors. For screening, the 16 mm

projectors, too, were less expensive and ran on the regular voltage found in homes, classrooms, and libraries (fig. 8.32).

Frequent users of particular films would likely buy them outright; for single, occasional, or periodic viewings, films were rented. The United States Post Office (USPS) and United Parcel Service (UPS) delivered to any address in the country the—now vintage—heavy, cardboard, film-reel, shipping boxes that had reinforced corners, straps, a frame for a label and was sized for the number of feet of film (fig. 8.32). This gave small centers and remote locations equal access to nontheatrical films.

The NIB/NIS film libraries joined this expansive 16 mm film production and distribution system and benefitted from the established American familiarity, interest, and use of nonfiction film throughout society, particularly in education. Nearly 70 percent of the viewership of all the NIB/NIS films were students (from grade school to university); in the United States, these documentaries functioned especially as films for education. The same cinematographic and technical development arc for the NIB/NIS documentaries—from silent films to color films with full soundscape and dialogue—also summarized the development of American nontheatrical film.

When, during the 1970s and 1980s, videotape, video players, and television monitors took the place of 16 mm movie cameras, films, projectors, and screens, many nontheatrical 16 mm film titles, considered outdated and with little demand, were never transferred to videotape by the production and distribution companies and eventually removed from film catalogs. With the advent of videotape, 16 mm

---

46 Geoff Alexander, *Films You Saw in School, A Critical Review of 1,153 Classroom Educational Films (1958–1985) in 74 Subject Categories* (McFarland and Co., 2014), 5. This, and its companion volume, Geoff Alexander, *Academic Films for the Classroom: A History* (McFarland and Co., 2010), are the definitive works about nontheatrical educational films in the United States. Especially in the subject categories of social studies, geography, and history, there was a large crossover between academic classroom films and more general documentaries.

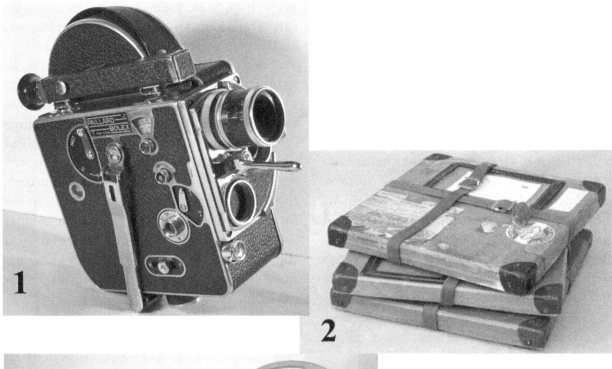

Fig. 8.32. Essential components for nontheatrical 16 mm film production and consumption, 1920s–1980s: (1) 16 mm movie cameras: Paillard Bolex H16 deluxe 16 mm movie camera from 1953 (*vintagebolex.uk*), (2) film-reel shipping boxes (*laurelleaffarm.com*), and (3) 16 mm sound movie projector: Bell & Howell Filmosound 535T (*flickr.com*)

films, owned and stored—often poorly—by users, were gradually shown less often and, as a result, the quality of their fragile film stock deteriorated. Eventually, throughout the country, much of the stock of 16 mm films was trashed. Many titles became hard, if not impossible, to find.[47]

---

[47]   Alexander, *Academic Films for the Classroom*, 194–97.

Only recently has the historical value of these 16 mm films been recognized, and from that has grown the need to locate, preserve, archive, digitize, and make them available again for viewing and study.[48] In 2001 Geoff Alexander, who would later author the two book-length overviews of academic 16 mm films,[49] founded the Academic Film Archive of North America (AFA), which provides know-how and encourages film aficionados and educators in local communities to identify, buy, collect, archive, digitize, and show nontheatrical 16 mm films. Micro cinemas showing amateur, art, and other low-budget films are starting to program such recovered educational films into their offerings. The other avenue for a broad public to see such films is, of course, the internet. The AFA on its website includes an opening page for viewing nearly four hundred uploaded films (afana.org); for each film, there is bibliographic information and a brief annotation. The Internet Archive (archive.org) also has a section on educational films, and Rick Prelinger, professor of film and digital media at UCLA and collector and specialist in educational, industrial, and advertising films, is one of its archivists, with more than eighty-five hundred of his collected films available here.[50] YouTube also includes academic educational films, and at least ten of the NIB/NIS films are found there as well.

The digitization of the Holland NIB/NIS film archive—the first stage in the research for this book—should be seen as part of these much broader, global efforts to recover, preserve, and focus scholarly attention on 16 mm nontheatrical films. In 2022 the digitized NIB/NIS films, along with the entire NIB/NIS archive, were moved from the Holland Museum to the Hope College Archives and Special Collections.[51] Now, an important next step would be to upload these either to the archives website or, better, to other sites that are consolidation points for archiving and viewing such films. Because this is a collection of Dutch documentaries, shown in the United States, the Netherlands Institute for Sound and Vision, tasked with archiving and making Dutch films available to the public, would be another logical place. Many of the NIB/NIS films produced in the Netherlands and the Dutch territories are already archived here and, where the institute holds the rights, may be viewed online. The Internet Archive and the AFA website are other suitable places for archiving and showing the NIB/NIS film collection.

The NIB/NIS films: breaking the hold of American-made films about the Netherlands and its overseas territories

It has been argued that the best and most internationally useful documenta-

48 For an introduction to a special international issue of *Film History* on nontheatrical and small-gauge, 16 mm films that provides an overview of the sources, uses, and some of the findings of the scholarly study of such films, consult Dan Streible, Martina Roepke, and Anke Mebold, "Introduction: Nontheatrical Film," *Film History* 19, no. 4 (2007): 339–43.

49 Ibid., and Alexander, *Films You Saw in School*. The world of educational films is divided by those devoted to preserving its 16 mm predecessors into "academic" and "guidance" films. Guidance films promoted acceptable social behavior; academic films transmitted knowledge in the fields of science, history, social studies, geography, and literature.

50 He founded the Prelinger Archives, a collection of sixty thousand, nontheatrical, education, industry, and advertising films.

51 Formerly, the Joint Archives of Holland, https://hope.edu/library/archives-special-collections.

ries about any country meant for outsiders are those shot, directed, and produced in the country by its own filmmakers. This may be debated, but in practice, powerful, wealthy, and advanced outsiders have been more influential—especially early on in the film industry—in capturing other countries on film for audiences in their own country and, to a lesser extent, for international viewers. During the first half of the twentieth century, most documentary films about other countries available in the United States for education, libraries, the military, and civic and religious organizations were made by American commercial film companies that sent crews all over the world. Their efforts to export these films abroad, however, were stymied by import duties, red tape, worldwide rights, the cost of making their voice-overs available in other languages, and their lack of marketing experience in other countries.[52] Beginning in 1953, the United States Information Agency (USIA), the public diplomacy—others would say, propaganda—division of the State Department, made many films in and about other nations that were shown not only in the country in question but also abroad more generally. They promoted American values in the context of the Cold War; for example, the film, *Himalayan Awakening*—now available on YouTube—describes the background of modern Nepal and its current achievements, made possible with help from the United States and India. At the time, however, these USIA films could be shown only to international, not American, audiences.[53]

The *Educational Film Catalogs/Guides* of the H. W. Wilson Company reveal the split between American- and Dutch-made films about the Netherlands. They show which non-American-made films about the Netherlands were acquired by American film companies, and they help in keeping track of the films about the Netherlands and its territories that were available from both American sources and the NIB/NIS. The Wilson film guide was the most widely used and respected nontheatrical film catalog in the United States from 1936 to the early 1960s.[54] Education was clearly the largest market for the films listed—as it was for those of the NIB/NIS—but the introductions in these guides stressed their relevance and value for all nontheatrical users, including churches, industries, social agencies, clubs, and libraries. It is also important to note that the producers and distributors were not just film companies but also industries, product associations, colleges and universities, and federal and state agencies.

I took a close look at two of the Wilson film guides: the 1945, 5th ed. (3,540 films, 490 pages), and the 1953, 11th ed. (11,000 films, 1037 pages). Both are complete guides, replacing all the previous volumes and annual supplements, and both use the Dewey Decimal System. It is important to remember that, in any national

---

52   Robert W. Wagner, "The International Educational Film," *Audio Visual Communication Review* 6, no. 1 (Winter 1958): 51.

53   Richard Dyer MacCann, *The People's Films: A Political History of the U.S. Government Motion Pictures* (Hastings House, 1973).

54   These catalogs were divided into two parts: (1) an alphabetical subject classification of the films and, (2) an annotated bibliography, along with other relevant information for each film at first cataloged by the Dewey Decimal System and later organized alphabetically by title. The annotations also recommended an appropriate age and grade level, referenced an evaluation, and supplied the names of the film production companies, authorized and other distributors, and their prices for sales and rentals. The films receiving this detailed treatment were approved by a team of collaborators.

Fig. 8.33. Extract from a list of films under Dewey Decimal heading, "914.92, the Netherlands," available for rent or purchase. The Netherlands Information Bureau is abbreviated as "Netherlands I bur" (Educational Film Guide, 1945 Edition, *compiled by Dorothy E. Cook and Eva Rahbek-Smith [H. W. Wilson Co., 1945], 381, archive. org).*

catalog, such as the Wilson Guides, films about other countries make up only a small percentage of the total number of films. As a rough estimate, in the 1945 film guide, the Dewey Decimal geography and travel category (910–919.9)—leaving out American places—yields only about 13 percent of the films. Of course, films about historical biography and events in other countries, not part of this category, would raise this percentage somewhat. Overall, however, documentaries about other countries make up only a small part of the total number of films on offer in a national film catalog.

Besides the NIB, the 1945 film guide, in its directory of producers and distribu-

tors, lists nine other national information bureaus—Australia, Canada, Czechoslovakia, Great Britain, India, New Zealand, Norway, the Philippines, and Poland—operating in the United States at that time, producing and distributing their own and other films. As occupied countries and/or Allied nations during WWII, they all shared many of the same objectives and operational strategies in the United States as the NIB.

The 1945 film guide lists twenty-one films about the Netherlands and its colonies, eight about the Netherlands itself (fig. 8.33 is an extract from that list), and thirteen about the colonies (11 about the

Dutch East Indies and 2 about the West Indies, including Suriname (Dutch Guiana). The 1940s NIB circulation records make clear that thirteen of these twenty-one films were also part of the NIB film lending library, most toward the upper end of its 1940s viewership list; the NIB acquired from American film companies eight of these films found in the Wilson Guide—as well as a number of others—for its collection during the 1940s.

Except for the foreign-policy-directed films, the NIB is seldom listed as a distributor for these films in the film guide. This may have had to do with the fees charged to production and distribution companies for listing each of their films. Of these twenty-one films in the film guide about the Netherlands and its colonies, sixteen are culture-directed travelogue and ethnographic films produced by American production companies. The other five are foreign-policy-directed documentaries that were made, directed, and produced by Dutch filmmakers, agencies, and firms: *Fishermen in Exile* (1944), *High Stakes in the East* (1942), *Netherlands America: Holland in the Western Hemisphere* (1942), *The Dutch Tradition* (1944), and *New Earth* (ca. 1943). Each of these films is linked in the film guide to the NIB as a distributor and/or producer.

The use made of this widely consulted film guide by the NIB to list films it made and distributed is significant on several levels. First, having these Dutch foreign policy films listed in the guide with not only the NIB but also a number of others as distributors—*High Stakes in the East* had six—multiplied the viewership and impact of these films many times, something the NIB could never have achieved on its own. This, again, underscores that the circula-

tion figures from the NIB's lending library for its own films that were also listed in other catalogs greatly undercounted their total national viewership.

Second, once more, it raises the question of why the NIB found it necessary to acquire a group of American travelogues from the 1920s and 1930s (films that painted nostalgic, premodern pictures of the Netherlands and scenes of exotic customs, artifacts, and physical settings in the Dutch colonies) when they were widely available and could be rented from a number of distributors throughout the United States. Why reinforce these tropes even more and this time with the authority of an agency of the Dutch government? Did it have to do with the NIB not renting but lending its films at no charge (just postage) and thereby enlarging their market? Or was the NIB shut out of films in the Netherlands and the Dutch East Indies because these lands were occupied, respectively, by Germany and Japan? Alternatively, was the NIB held back by the considerable cost of translating the script and redoing the voice-over in Dutch productions from Dutch to English?[55] Although the cost for such translations, when necessary, may have been justified for foreign-policy-directed films—the main task of the NIB during the 1940s was foreign relations—culture-directed films were not given the same financial priority.

That the NIB included in its film library thirteen films about the Netherlands and its colonies that were also listed in the 1945 Wilson *Educational Film Guide* does not, of course, in any way, support a conclusion that the NIB went by the listings of the catalog to acquire its culture-directed

55 In 1958 R. Wagner estimated a cost of $500 ($4,585 today) to translate ten minutes of film; Wagner "The International Educational Film," 51.

films. First, there were eight films in this catalog not available from the NIB. Second—and much more impactful—there were forty-two films in the fifty-five-strong NIB film library during the 1940s that were not part of the film guide listing for 1945. Some may have appeared in later updates, but it is clear that the NIB made a telling and independent contribution—backed by its circulation numbers—to the dissemination of information about the Netherlands and its colonies to a broad American public. It accomplished this by both listing films that it produced in the film guide and having available in its lending library a large number of its own films—not listed elsewhere—on diverse topics and places. One may argue that it should have tried to list more of its films in general film catalogs and involve additional distributors for a still greater overall impact, but the NIB/NIS during the 1940s, as an agency of the Dutch government, did position itself in and took advantage of the American distribution system for nontheatrical films.

By the time of the release of the 1953 Wilson film guide, the earlier NIB foreign-policy-directed and produced films were gone from both the guide and the NIS, now repurposed exclusively into an information and cultural agency. Gone also were the documentaries about the former Dutch East Indies (now Indonesia) (although they remained a fixture in the film guide for some time) because many had little specific Dutch content and could be placed under another geographic rubric. The film guide now no longer listed all the distributors, only the main source (the authorized distributor) for each film,[56]

and the NIS was not listed as a main source for films at the back of the 1953 film guide, even though it held fifteen of the twenty-one films listed in the guide about the Netherlands proper in its lending library (fig. 8.34 is an extract from that list). Only one of the eleven films about the former Dutch East Indies and three of the five films about the then current West Indies in the Wilson film guide remained part of the circulating NIS films. Until 1962 additional supplements to the guide did not list the NIS among its main sources for particular films. Since only the film production companies and authorized—not all—distributors were listed in the 1950s and into the 1960s, and the NIS was no longer producing its own films, it was shut out from marketing a selection of its own films to the American public via the film guide, but other distributors for these same films in the guide could still meet that demand.

Nearly all the films in the 1953 film guide about the Netherlands and its former and then current territories were produced and distributed by American film companies. Again, the marketing reach of the film guide was far greater than that of the NIS as, presumably, were the follow-on circulation and audience figures compared to the NIS resulting from the rentals of these films via the guide. As in the 1940s, however, the NIS in the 1950s, again, independently marketed sixty additional films about the Netherlands and its territories that were not listed in the film guide. Many

---

56 Users of the guide were instructed to contact the "main source" for information about other distrib-

utors of a particular film. If the NIS was included as a distributor for a film company (main source), some of its films could still be circulated independent of its own catalog marketing and mailing lists. The circulation resulting from such marketing, however, would still show up in the audience numbers for these NIS films and, therefore, is included in the database for this study.

HOLLAND, GARDEN OF EUROPE. Filmsof
  Nations 1950 14½min sd color $125, rent
  $4.50   914.92
  jh-sh-c-ad
  Produced by the Netherlands Information
Bureau. English narration
       Stresses the theme of Holland as the
'garden of Europe.' Also shows modern cities
and typical Dutch countryside with canals and
windmills

IN AND AROUND AMSTERDAM. FilmsofNa-
  tions 1948 10min sd b&w $30, rent $1.50;
  color $85 rent $3   914.92
  jh-sh-ad
       Presents the charming old and the pro-
gressive new in a city that was already famous
in the 15th century, and which because of its
canals has been called the "Venice of the
North." Shows not only the historical buildings,
the canals, the seventeenth century Rembrandt
house and the busy streets of a modern capital,
but also interesting points outside Amsterdam
—the famous cheese market at Alkmaar, and
Bunschoten, a quaint fishing village where
traditional costumes are worn
       EFLA evaluation card No. 576

Fig. 8.34. Extract from a list of films about the Netherlands available
for rent and purchase for 1953 (Educational Film Guide, *11th ed., ed.
Frederic A. Krahn [H. W. Wilson Co., 1953], 886*) (*archive.org*)

of them could also have been purchased for rentals by for-profit, American film production and distribution companies, but unlike the NIS, their acquisitions had to produce adequate revenue, and adding more specialized films, such as *It's Just a Postage Stamp*, would fall short of that requirement. As a nonprofit promotional agency of the Dutch government, the NIS used different acquisition criteria and could continue to lend films with a small total viewership, which was avoided by American, for-profit film companies, and though the NIS had its share of duds, they did not affect the bottom line. That did not

mean that the NIS was free from financial constraints; its budget had to be approved yearly by the Dutch parliament, and even though the NIS regularly had to do with less and either cut back or eliminate some of its services, there were no revenues generated from its film collection. The film library sent out films until the NIS closed in 1974.

The place and role of American producers/distributors and the NIB/NIS with respect to the body of nontheatrical films about the Netherlands and its colonies/territories available in the United States changed dramatically over time. In the

1940s, a large majority of the culture-directed films, especially those with higher attendance numbers, were distributed by both American firms and the NIB. These were documentaries filmed, directed, and produced by American companies; there was considerable overlap in film offerings between the NIB and American distributors. The Dutch, foreign-policy-directed films of the 1940s were produced by several agencies of the Dutch government, including the NIB; they were marketed both by the NIB and American distributors lined up by the NIB. Except for a group of culture-directed films available exclusively from the NIB, American distributors and the NIB played equally significant roles in marketing Dutch films.

Beginning in the 1950s and increasingly during the 1960s/70s, the contributions of Dutch filmmakers, directors, and producers to the NIB film library and to the films on offer by American film companies grew markedly. Dutch-made films comprised a growing share of the body of films about the Netherlands and its territories available for rent and loan in the United States. Joint ventures between Dutch film crews and directors and American film production companies became more common in the 1950s. For example, *Peaceful Conquest* (1950) was directed by Dutch filmmaker Herman van der Horst and produced by Multifilm in Haarlem, the Netherlands. It was then adapted for American viewers by Maurice T. Groen of DPM Productions in New York City.

In order to have a full-fledged and economically viable nontheatrical film industry, a very small country, such as the Netherlands, with its own language and an internationally oriented economy, needed to produce films in world languages—English, French, German, and Spanish were the most common then—and market them internationally, such as promotional films commissioned by different agencies of the Dutch government (e.g., *Holland: A Modern Country Full of Old-Time Charm*, 1952), industrial films from different economic sectors (e.g., *Land of Milk*, 1953, from the Dutch Dairy Bureau), and films from independent filmmakers with support from public and private funds (e.g., Bert Haanstra, *And There Was No More Sea*, 1955). Because few documentary films at that time had dialogue, only a different voice-over in another language and translated credits and title were needed. Those judged able to generate reasonable returns because of their synoptic and educational qualities were bought and rented out by American as well other foreign distributors, for example, *Netherlands: Past and Present* (1960).[57] Except for some carryovers from the 1950s, the NIS film library of 163 titles in the 1960s/70s consisted almost entirely of documentaries made by Dutch companies, crews, directors, producers, and marketers. The lion's share of these films was not available from American film production and distribution companies.

The shuttering of the NIS in 1974 largely removed these and other future Dutch-made films from the American nontheatrical/educational film circuit. When that market changed over to VHS in the late 1980s and then to DVD in the midaughts, the collaboration of Dutch experts and filmmakers with American film

---

[57] This film is listed in the Wilson *Educational Film Guide: 1961 Annual Supplement* (H. W. Wilson Co., 1961), 36. It was not in the NIS film library, although it was produced by the Netherlands Government Information Service.

companies, however, continued to produce new nontheatrical films about the Netherlands for world markets.[58]

Home viewing Dutch films by immigrants, Dutch Americans, and the American public from videocassettes, DVDs, and satellite TV[59]

The NIB/NIS film library included documentary films from the 1920s to the 1970s and spanned most of the era of 16 mm nontheatrical film production. When the NIS shut its doors in 1974, the film industry throughout the world was expanding viewing beyond movie houses to videotape for the home and small group markets. By the mid-1980s, the price of VCRs and videocassettes had come down to a level at which most Americans could buy, rent, or borrow both feature and nontheatrical films for home viewing. Twenty years later, this versatile technology for viewing films—with or without video projectors—at home, work, school, or in other group settings was upended again, this time by digital video optical discs (DVDs) and their players/recorders. In addition to their compactness, DVDs could also be played on computers and carry channels for subtitles in different languages. Today, we are in the middle of the transition to streaming services and video sharing over the internet, another delivery technology that is dramatically cutting into DVD sales and rentals. Brick-and-mortar video stores are gone, and some films are no longer marketed as DVDs.

As in other countries, much of the body of well-known earlier 35 mm theatrical Dutch fiction films and some 16 mm nontheatrical films were rendered as VHS tapes and cassettes, later as DVDs, and marketed for sale and rent, giving many Dutch residents and the Dutch overseas an opportunity to see these films for the first time. Very few Dutch feature films have had theatrical runs in the United States.[60] New Dutch feature films and all other kinds of new documentary films were marketed in the Netherlands (after their theater and television runs) as videocassettes and later, DVDs; they were sold, rented, and borrowed by a broad Dutch public from video stores, libraries, and online retailers. Videocassettes and DVDs launched a new era of consumption of visual media worldwide.

As in all countries, the portability and convenience of these physical media and their viewing technology also facilitated the spread and marketing of Dutch films abroad, including the Dutch diaspora, especially when paired with subtitles in world languages. For the first time, especially post-WWII Dutch immigrants—but also Dutch Americans more generally—had an opportunity to obtain and watch on their televisions at home VHS tapes and, later, DVDs, of Dutch feature and documentary films (not to mention homemade films from family and friends in the Netherlands). At first, Dutch immigrants relied on their contacts there to obtain films they had heard about. Much like the immigrant generation reading Dutch novels and nonfiction, watching Dutch movies remained a pastime for later arrivals;[61] videocassettes

58   A recent example is *The Netherlands*, episode 1, *Europe from Above*, National Geographic, 2019.

59   See endnote 8:54, p. 408.

60   Thomas H. Guback, *The International Film Industry: Western Europe and America since 1945* (Indiana University Press, 1969), 85 (table 1).

61   For me, the pleasure of hearing and understanding the spoken Dutch is as strong as having my eyes on

and DVDs would be shared via friendship and institutional (e.g., church) networks.

For viewers to watch videocassettes acquired from the Netherlands, their players have to be compatible with the European PAL system, one of three television technical standards used in different regions of the world. North America uses a different standard (NTSC) than Europe, so therefore, European videocassettes and DVDs cannot project to televisions from American players. Although the regional coding did present a technical hurdle to viewing Dutch films, this barrier was surmounted. Before long, "region free" or dual-region players became available; clever users could also program a player or a DVD itself to be "region free."

It is impossible to know the extent to which Dutch films have been viewed by immigrants, but a 2009–13 survey shows 140,000 people in the United States were speaking Dutch at home at that time, so Dutch-language videos must have been a part of their subculture's use of the language.[62] Dutch films are generally not dubbed into English or any other language; the audio language track is in Dutch, and the subtitles for the North American market are mainly in English.

An additional source for Dutch immigrants, but not for the American public, available twenty-four hours a day, and with a large diversity of offerings, is the television channel BVN, with the name today (translated as): "the Best of NPO" (the public broadcasting company of the Netherlands).[63] It is a free television service established in 1996 for Dutch speakers (immigrants, expats, tourists) residing permanently or temporarily outside the Netherlands and the Flemish, Dutch-speaking region of northern Belgium. At first, the initials (translated) stood for "the Best of the Netherlands," but when the Flemish region joined the channel, it became "the Best of Flanders and the Netherlands." In 2021 the Flemish region withdrew from the channel and it, once more, broadcasted programming only from the Netherlands.

In several European countries with a lot of Dutch tourists and seasonal residents, BVN is part of the cable offerings that pull their signal from satellites. For the United States and the rest of the world, until the summer of 2021, BVN was delivered by different satellites in geostationary orbits over specific world regions. Reception at home required a dish on the roof and a receiver unit hooked to a television. Today, the satellite service around the world has been greatly cut back, and BVN for many viewers—including those in North America—is now delivered as a free streaming service over the internet, something which makes it far more economical and accessible. Dutch residents are not able to receive it unless they have an IP (Internet Protocol) address outside the country. BVN broadcasts existing programs mainly from the Dutch public broadcasting network, for instance, sports, news, talk shows, movies, documentaries, drama series, and children's programming.

At the passing of the foreign-born cohort, the ethnic practice of reading Dutch-language newspapers, novels, and

---

the Netherlands in these films. The current common practice of including subtitles in the spoken language of the film adds yet another level of understanding and Dutchness.

[62] United States Census, Community Survey, 2009–13, table 1. Detailed Languages Spoken at Home and Ability to Speak English for the Population 5 Years and Over for the United States.

[63] www.bvn.tv.

nonfiction, as well as watching Dutch movies and television, vanishes. Succeeding generations do not learn the language and lack the imprint of Dutch culture and emotional ties to the country. Dutch immigrants cannot give away their Dutch-language books, videocassettes, and DVDs; there is no place for them, and selling them online offers little prospect. Americans of Dutch ancestry might well be more interested than most to see a subtitled Dutch movie because it relates to their heritage, but it is no longer an ethnic disposition.

Dutch feature (fiction) films in the United States

Dutch feature films, like all fiction films, are enjoyed, for most viewers, for the stories they tell.[64] Set in the Netherlands and its territories, in whole or in part, they tell an imagined story—albeit sometimes based on actual events and persons—about Dutch characters in a Dutch physical and cultural setting. They are, of course, also able to show American and other non-Dutch viewers plenty about what is distinctive and different about the country and foster an acquaintanceship with the nation but without the overt education of a documentary. That which sets the country apart may not make much of an impression when the storyline is what holds the attention of the viewer. At the same time, an unfamiliar and intriguing setting and culture may act as a drawing card and help account for the growing popularity of international feature films.

Until the arrival of online shopping in the mid-1990s, the opportunity for the American public and Dutch Americans to rent, borrow, and buy Dutch feature films remained quite limited. Except for sporadic offerings of award-winning films (e.g., *Antonia* [Antonia's line], 1995; *Karakter* [Character], 1997; *Spoorloos* [The vanishing], 1988) in the foreign films section at the local Blockbuster, there was no consistent retail presence of Dutch feature films in brick-and-mortar video stores. Unlike Hispanic, Chinese, and Vietnamese neighborhoods, video stores in the Dutch American residential areas of Grand Rapids and Holland, Michigan; Pella and Orange City, Iowa; and Sheboygan, Wisconsin, had no special section of Dutch feature films. These later generations of Dutch Americans had long been fully assimilated, no longer used Dutch, and resembled Americans at large in their movie tastes. As with everything else, the internet would soon change the retailing and later the transmission of Dutch feature films abroad.

The internet, online retailing, the globalization of the film industry, and the growing worldwide interest in foreign films all helped establish a growing international market for many Dutch feature films, past and present. With its small national market and the resulting need for the Dutch government to subsidize film production, the direct export of films and selling their international rights so that they could be distributed in foreign markets made eminent sense, economically and culturally. For much of the history of Dutch cinema, public funding was based on the artistic and cultural qualities of a film project, resulting in more literary-type films, seen by selective audiences (e.g., *De Aanslag*

---

[64] Dutch-language feature films in the United States, with or without subtitles, have received little to no study. But see: Leo Groenweghe, "Videos of Dutch Language Movies in the U.S.," *D.I.S. Magazine* (Sept. 2001), 7–10.

[*The Assault*], 1986),[65] whereas most Dutch moviegoers enjoyed Dutch-subtitled Hollywood films. Beginning in this century, the merits for funding and tax credit support were broadened to also include the commercial and entertainment potential for a film scenario. This led to rapid growth in the production of Dutch feature films, with selective appropriations of the Hollywood model. Such films have a much larger international market potential.[66]

Increasingly, feature films were released as VHS tapes and DVDs, with English subtitles for international releases. Surprisingly, Dutch-made feature films now sold in the Dutch market regularly include English subtitles. Today, even after a decade of steep decline in DVD sales,[67] many Dutch feature films are still available with English subtitles either included at the initial or international release or added to earlier releases. For example, all the yearly winners of the Golden Calf (the Dutch Oscar) for the best, long feature film from 1981 to 2004 were released with English subtitles.[68] In addition, most DVDs of Dutch feature films—not all—are marketed in North America with the

NTSC technical format required by players here, whereas the Netherlands—as well as the rest of Europe—uses the PAL format. All-region DVD players, however, have become an affordable option.

By the turn of the century, internet shopping dramatically improved access to Dutch feature films. It opened up profitable online sales by American and Dutch shopping outlets of English-subtitled Dutch feature films and some documentaries. Because demand for these and other international films was very small at brick-and-mortar video stores, online sites could be profitable by aggregating demand and marketing with pictorial catalogs and links to additional information about their films. Gone were the days of expensive, local special orders.

The internet soon provided information in English under the entry "Dutch films"; Wikipedia, IMDb, *Paste Magazine*, and many other sites provide descriptions, synopses, evaluations, and ratings of Dutch feature films in English. For buying Dutch films with English subtitles on DVD in the United States, the place to begin is Amazon (US).[69] I am continually surprised by the breadth of its inventory of Dutch films; it provides product details about subtitles, languages, and technical standards (PAL and/or NTSC) that are important for American buyers. Even arthouse feature films, for example, those of celebrated Dutch director Alex van Warmerdam, are available with English subtitles, some in NTSC, others in PAL or in multiple formats. If Amazon does not carry a desired

65 *De Aanslag* was the first Dutch feature film to win an Oscar for best foreign film. It is based on a novel of the same title by Harry Mullisch, well-known Dutch literary writer.

66 Jaap Kooijman, "Contemporary Dutch Cinema and Hollywood," in *Four Centuries of Dutch-American Relations* (SUNY, 2009), 1060–61.

67 Sarah Whitten, "The Death of the DVD: Why Sales Dropped more than 86% in 13 years," *CNBC Newsletters*, 8 Nov. 2019. https://www.cnbc.com/2019/11/08.

68 For its twenty-five-year anniversary in 2005, the Netherlands Film Festival issued a boxed set of the Golden Calf winners for best feature film from 1981 to 2004, each with English subtitles. *Kalverliefde, Gouden Kalfwinnaars, Beste Speelfilm, 1981–2004* (A-Film Distribution, 2005).

69 Putting "Dutch films" in the search bar on Amazon (USA) misses most of the feature films available. A better strategy is to search "Dutch films" on the internet and then go to Amazon with specific titles of interest (Dutch or English).

title, ordering it from a Dutch online site that delivers to American addresses, such as megamoviestore.com, is the best option.[70] There are fewer and fewer Dutch feature films with English subtitles that for a variety of reasons have not been imported into the United States.

Dutch documentary films in the United States after the NIS

From 1943 to 1974, Dutch public diplomacy had made more than two hundred documentaries about the Netherlands and its overseas territories available at no or little cost to all corners of the United States. During the four decades after the NIS was shuttered by the Dutch government, the market economy and modern mass consumption, aided by technological innovations, rather than the state, slowly made increasing numbers of Dutch feature films with English subtitles available to the American public for purchase, to the point where, today, the lion's share of these films can be purchased online as DVDs in the United States and the Netherlands. The availability of films about the Netherlands in the United States swung from documentaries only to feature (fiction) films only—from education to storytelling. Dutch documentaries largely went away.

Stages in viewing of documentaries about the Netherlands/Dutch territories by American and Dutch audiences

Because this study's focus is on Dutch documentary films in the United States, it is worthwhile to sketch its larger history. Think of Venn diagrams for three periods representing documentaries about the Netherlands/Dutch territories available and of interest to two groups (sets): American and Dutch viewers (fig. 8.35). Before the NIB began distributing films in 1943, these two groups did not share any documentaries (fig. 8.35a). American audiences were watching a small number of educational films and theatrical shorts about the Netherlands and its territories, all made by American filmmakers; much larger Dutch audiences were enjoying a greater number of Dutch-made documentaries in their theaters and other group settings (cf. the relative size of the sets). A country will, of course, produce and flock to more documentaries about itself as a matter of national education, interest, and devotion.

The NIB/NIS's public diplomacy in the United States made available by mail more than two hundred Dutch-made films to more than six million Americans from 1943 to 1974; most of these films also circulated in the Netherlands (fig. 8.35b), except—likely—the foreign-policy-directed films the Dutch government in exile had produced during the 1940s. This gray area of overlap—the union—of these two sets of viewers contains the documentaries about the Netherlands/Dutch territories that were marketed to and seen by both Dutch and American viewers; it represents the films that were imported by the NIB/NIS and is much larger than the number of cir-

---

[70] For nearly twenty years, bol.com, an Amazon-type, online marketplace, the largest in the Netherlands, with the most extensive selection of Dutch films, delivered to American addresses. Recently, it restricted delivery to Dutch and Belgian addresses as does Amazon (NL). For Dutch speakers, bol.com is still the best site to browse Dutch film titles.

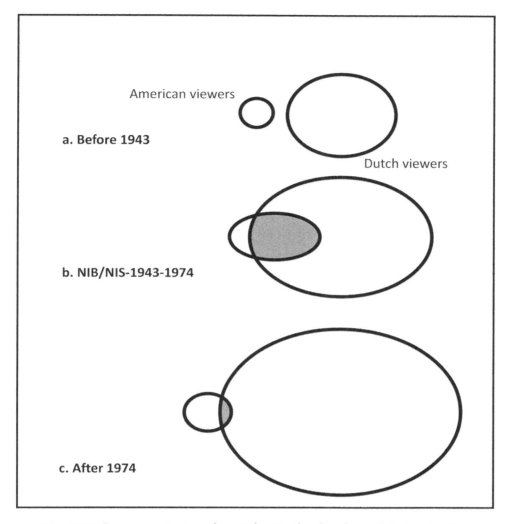

American viewers

a. Before 1943

Dutch viewers

b. NIB/NIS-1943-1974

c. After 1974

Fig. 8.35. Documentaries about the Netherlands and its territories with Dutch and American audiences

culating American-made films about the Netherlands and its territories (travelogues for education and theater shorts).

During the time of the NIB/NIS, this area of crossover documentaries was larger than it had ever been. Promotional films produced for the Dutch government information services, such as the four-part series, *Holland: A Modern Country Full of Old-Time Charm* (1952), would generally be released in several languages, including Dutch. It was not, however, uncommon to produce promotional films in several oth-

er world languages but not Dutch; *Holland Today* (1962), the NIS film with the highest attendance during the 1960s/70s, is an example. Such films were not crossover films. During much of the lifetime of the NIB/NIS, cultural, political, and educational factors played a larger role in the international distribution of documentary films than commerce with its more straightforward profit motive. Were it not for the NIB/NIS program of public diplomacy, very few of these films would have been imported or made their way into the United States.

Those films selected and distributed by the NIB/NIS made up only a small percentage of the Dutch national viewership of Dutch-made films screened (the remaining white area for "Dutch viewers" on fig. 8.35b). The output of its film industry had grown and the national viewership along with it, as is clear from the growing size of this area. These documentaries were seen only in the country; they were passed over by the NIB/NIS either because the producer or distributor had not or would not add an English voice-over or the Dutch government's information services, including the NIB/NIS, regarded them as specialized topical or local films, not suitable for or of interest to non-Dutch viewers. They assumed insider knowledge of local, regional, and national issues and participation in Dutch society, history, and culture, for example, *Uit en Thuis* (1954), about the national Dutch youth hostel organization; *Van een Eiland en Schapen* (1948), sheep farming on the island of Texel; and *Uitbreiding Ouder-Amstel* (1965), preparing the ground for urban expansion of the town).[71]

On fig. 8.35c, for the period after 1974 until the present-day, the area of overlap of American and Dutch viewers watching the same documentaries has shrunk significantly, even though Dutch documentary film production ramped up and grew in popularity during this entire period.[72] Commercial, for-profit marketing took the place of public diplomacy for the distribution of documentaries to institutions and individuals abroad while government information agencies backed away from making and commissioning promotional films for non-Dutch viewers. By the market's calculus, there were inadequate returns in the export of most Dutch documentaries. Today, very few reach an international audience.[73] One reason continues to be the understandable aforementioned topical specialization and particularism of Dutch—and other—documentaries, something already evident and noted for some of the NIS films but now with a different and higher bar—most films are intended, understandably, for Dutch—not international—audiences. Many relate to and reflect on in-house personages, events, and issues already familiar to their viewers and lack interest and/or adequate context for non-Dutch viewers. Most Dutch-made films in fig. 8.35c would not be considered for export outside the Netherland's borders. A look at some recent titles provides examples: people who never leave their parental home (*Nestblijvers*, 2008), a young Dutch boxer with much potential (*De Zwijgende Bokser*, 2012), and the tension between franchisees and head offices in Dutch retailing (*Woede in de Winkelstraat*, 2014).

Other Dutch documentaries tackle issues found the world over but now with Dutch stories, experiences, and experts (e.g., loneliness, multiculturalism, obesity, bullying, secondhand clothing, climate change—actual examples from FilmVandaag.nl). Unless they identify unique Dutch manifestations and answers to such social problems, these films would also stay put in the Netherlands.

Another reason for the shrinking number of Dutch documentaries market-

---

71　These examples are from the filmography of Bert Hogenkamp, *De Documentaire Film, 1945–1965. De Bloei van een Filmgenre in Nederland* (Uitgeverij 010, 2003), 288, 291, 301.

72　See endnote 8:67, p. 408.

73　Dutch speakers abroad, of course, have been able to order any available videocassette or DVD online in the Netherlands for delivery in the US.

ed in the United States is, I believe, related to the changing cinematography of non-fiction films. For much of the lifespan of the NIB/NIS documentaries, their voice-overs provided the information and made sense and interpreted what Americans saw on the screen; in time, the soundscape became more fully developed, but the films did not include dialogue. The original voice-over could readily be translated and perhaps tailored and expanded and then revoiced in a different language for a different national viewership. Spectators could effortlessly look and listen simultaneously and more passively; viewer engagement, however, was dampened by a know-it-all narrator.

In the period after the NIB/NIS, and for documentaries everywhere, monologue and dialogue by those featured in the film increasingly shared and then took the place of the voice-over in communicating information, opinions, and meaning about what was on the screen and the topic of the film. Speaking to the camera and using dialogue made documentaries much more realistic and multivocal. But what could once be more easily transposed from one language and culture to another at a modest cost became more challenging—and costly—with subtitles. For viewers, these needed to be read on the screen while eyes were also on the visual presentation and ears were hearing another language. Such documentaries appealed less to the general public and more to those already quite conversant with the Netherlands. A recent film, *Veearts Maaike* (2019), about a woman veterinarian serving dairy farmers in the province of Groningen, is a good example. In documentaries that include subtitles for an intermittent voice-over as

well as for on-screen speech, hearing both forms of speech in another language and keeping track of subtitles and visuals is seen by some as distracting and diminishes understanding and enjoyment and, by extension, a film's marketability.

Producers and distributors consistently made decisions not to ready Dutch-made documentaries with such perceived handicaps for export by adding English—and other language—subtitles and voice-overs because their considerable costs would not make them profitable in the international market. The results are clear in fig. 8.35c there are hardly any Dutch-made documentaries about the Netherlands/Dutch territories available in the United States also enjoyed by Dutch viewers.

The vanishing Dutch-made documentary in America

To prove this point, I surveyed the listing of Dutch-made documentary films on FilmVandaag.nl. It is the most exhaustive online database—albeit in Dutch—for everything related to films in the Netherlands, not only for Dutch productions but also for all films available to Dutch viewers: film news and reviews; listings of types of films; films currently and shortly playing in theaters, on television and video-on-demand (VOD) online; and film titles on DVD (including Blu-ray) for sale. With the shift to subscription streaming services in the 2010s, online—rather than physical—media are the default viewing options on the site.

FilmVandaag includes a chronological inventory of nearly seven hundred, Dutch-made documentary films (not documentary series) from 1928 to 2021. Each listing includes a synopsis, as well as the year, length, and director, and a link to the

IMDb film database for further information. Especially important for my purposes, the listing includes the ability to check if there is a DVD or VOD for each title. Several, but not many, NIB/NIS films are included in this database; the inventory is much more complete for the past thirty years.

Missing from the FilmVandaag database are Dutch-made documentaries intended first and foremost for audiences abroad rather than in the country. During the lifetime of the NIB/NIS, these films were usually promotional, encyclopedic overviews of the country, foreign policy apologia, and more focused looks at specific aspects of the Netherlands, used for international and, to a lesser extent, domestic promotion. The NIB/NIS library included a significant number of such documentaries. They were produced or commissioned by government entities and economic interests, for instance, the NIB itself (*Fishermen in Exile*, 1944); the National Information Service (*Holland Today*, 1962); different government departments, for example, the Ministry of Welfare, Health and Culture (*Pan*, 1963); and organizations representing economic sectors, like the Dutch Building Industry and Construction Workers (*The Building Game*, 1963). The Dutch government and business advertisers have largely quit producing these kinds of promotional films, making room for more independent, commercial filmmakers to tackle such topics in a more nuanced and critical manner; the documentary, *Hollandse Nieuwe/Raw Herring* (2012) is a good example.

I surveyed 671 Dutch-made documentaries in the FilmVandaag listing from after the NIS was shuttered in 1974 to 2021. Of these, 59 percent were about the Netherlands/Dutch territories, and 41 percent

were not. From the synopses of this first group of films—the one relevant for the issues discussed in this study—I applied selection criteria for crossover films learned from my analysis of the NIB/NIS films. These include a country-wide orientation, particular topics (WWII), internationally well-known personages (Rembrandt) and places (Amsterdam), the nostalgic "old" Netherlands with its traditional ways of life, works of civil engineering and water management, and the colonial past. Of the nearly four hundred films about the Netherlands/Dutch territories, I chose fifty-seven that I judged met one or more of these criteria and then checked if these were available as DVDs with English subtitles in either the United States (amazon.com) and/or the Netherlands (bol.com). I was very surprised to learn that, of those fifty-seven candidate documentaries, only thirteen—just 2 percent of all documentaries about the Netherlands/Dutch territories and 23 percent of those meeting my standards—are available on DVD with English subtitles. Of these, six are retailed in the United States, seven in the Netherlands,[74] and three in both countries. Those available in the United States would generate the largest sales by far, and largely predictable, they are about Anne Frank (2), Rembrandt, the Rijksmuseum, the unique Dutch light that made the Netherlands seventeenth-century paintings famous, and the management of foxes in the country. Not many Americans would order the English-subtitled films online from the Netherlands for delivery in the United States; they too are about Dutch subjects but further removed

---

[74] For several of these DVDs available in the Netherlands, it is unclear whether there is an entire English subtitle track; they contain several spoken and subtitled languages.

from American interests, such as retailing, the royal family, an Amsterdam neighborhood, colonial Indonesia (2), amusement parks, and veterinary services.[75]

Examples among the more than forty documentaries that met my criteria for crossover films but were not marketed internationally with English subtitles are: *Wild Zwijn* (Wild boar), 2013, an examination of the relations between people and wild boars in the Netherlands; *Snelweg NL* (Highway NL), 2019, a survey of the Dutch highway system and its infrastructure; and *Sprekend Nederland* (Typical Netherlands), 2018, a look at Dutch public multiculturalism. Today, Dutch documentaries, like others, are not made into DVDs but, after their theatrical run, enter the national streaming circuits. American viewers are typically shut out of such subscription and pay-per-view services by their geolocated IP (internet protocol) addresses and lack of English subtitles.

Given national interests, experiences, schooling, enculturation, and (historical) memory—embodied locally, regionally, and on a country-wide basis—only a small percentage of a country's documentary films about itself will be viewed beyond its borders—likely more by its geographic neighbors than by those further removed. Understandably, the lion's share of the body of documentary films about and made in a country is walled off by *its* nationality and language.

The size, distribution, and contents of this "small" percentage of crossover films does, however, matter a great deal. The NIB/NIS program of public diplomacy with film—the number of films, lending rather than renting and selling,

institutional borrowing, group viewing, films produced for the American public and other foreign markets, the widespread viewing geography, and the broad social and economic cross section of audiences—was a one-off. Closing the NIS removed its currently circulating and the country's future documentaries from this kind of easy and wide distribution and attention from a broad American public.

What took the place of the NIB/NIS film library were consumer purchases in the United States and the Netherlands by American institutions and individuals, first of videocassettes and then DVDs with English subtitles, considered both appropriate for and profitable in the international market. What is clear from my survey of the Dutch-made documentaries listed by FilmVandaag is that commerce alone is able to deliver only the most unambiguous crossover Dutch documentaries to the American public, leaving other suitable documentaries stranded. Beginning in the 2010s, even such films are today less likely to be made into physical media. They and other in-house productions might reach international film festivals, expos, and Dutch diplomatic missions and there acquaint, inform, and entertain film intelligentsia and aficionados the world over about Dutch documentaries, directors, and Dutch cinematography, but they never reach the education markets and home viewing public in other countries. Experts in visual culture agree that something more than the market is needed to disseminate a country's documentaries abroad more widely.[76]

---

[75] See endnote 8:70, p. 409.

[76] A report from the European Audiovisual Observatory notes that European films "suffer from a somewhat weak circulation outside their country of origin" and surveys regulations (quotas and

The market delivered many fewer Dutch-made documentaries about the Netherlands and its territories to the American public than public diplomacy had. If directors would consider international viewers when planning certain film projects, more crossover films would be produced and marketed abroad. An outsider's perspective is required to put visual content, voice-overs, and dialogue into films that those outside the Netherlands and its territories would like to see to better understand different aspects of the country; this includes, but is certainly not the same as, the tourist's view. Nor does such a perspective come only from directors and film companies from other countries or internationally oriented organizations, such as National Geographic. The commissions given to top Dutch directors by the Dutch government, cities, and industries to produce films for international audiences demonstrate that resident directors can take such a vantage point, albeit with some restrictions by the commission on the filmmaker's freedom of expression in terms of a film's purpose and viewpoints. The three-part series by Dutch director Max de Haas, *Holland: A Modern Country Full of Old-Time Charm*, produced in 1952, commissioned by the Dutch Economic Information Service and part of the NIS film library, shows the merits of taking an outsider's point of view for international audiences. The upending of DVD sales and the flowering of the pictorial turn expressed in VOD and video sharing over the internet over the course of the last decade has opened new opportunities—and restrictions—for the worldwide distribution of Dutch-made documentaries, as well as for other Dutch visual media.

The pictorial turn: the growing (and shrinking) global availability of Dutch visual media

My brother-in-law immigrated to Toronto, Canada, in 1952, in his twenties, after serving in the Dutch army in what had become Indonesia. During the last several years of his life—he died in 2020—when he was confined to his home, he regularly FaceTimed on his laptop with friends from his youth back in his hometown of Winschoten, Groningen, and with his Dutch army buddies scattered throughout the Netherlands and abroad. His laptop screen could show not just his friend's face but also his comfortable chair, table, furnishings, living room setting, and even the street view from the large (Dutch) window of his apartment—these were visits, not just calls. He and his friends could show each other items of mutual interest (photos) and turn the camera to bring other things and people into the frame.

This is part of the amazing growth of video and its transmission through the internet in all aspects of society over the last thirty years, including medical imaging and telemedicine, real estate, online education, social media, building security, body cams, criminal and civil courts, smart bombs, drone surveillance and strikes, and how-to videos, among many other applications. The modern world has shifted from a dominance of and reliance on text to the primacy of the visual. The internet makes real-time video and playback of stored video—new and old, professional and amateur— possible from anywhere on

prominence obligations) in European countries to improve the access of films to television and VOD distribution systems. *Mapping of National Rules for the Promotion of European Works in Europe* (Audiovisual Observatory, Strasbourg, 2019), 1.

Earth. This pictorial turn has profoundly affected both the display and transmission of Dutch visual culture.

Dutch art is just a few clicks away

Dutch wall art carried to North America by Dutch immigrants, Dutch scenes captured by American and Dutch American painters, and Dutch art on exhibit in American museums all delivered a limited number of works and viewers to select urban markets of the country. By contrast, the internet has allowed art museums worldwide to put their works—including Dutch art—online. For example, Rijksmuseum, the Dutch national museum in Amsterdam, in a groundbreaking move, placed seven hundred thousand, high-resolution works of art online in 2012. It created "Rijksstudio," an application in English to help online visitors navigate and search this massive collection by artist, type of object, period, place, materials used, and art technique. A virtual visitor can zoom in on any piece of art, download it, order a poster, listen to an explanatory audio fragment, and display their choice on a high-resolution screen. One can also curate a personally themed collection of artwork.[77] Most prominent national and regional art museums now have some or much of their collection online, including exhibit labels in English, the ability to zoom in on details, and search engines to find specific pieces, artists, and genres. Museums also use their websites to post videos—mainly in English as a second language to their national language—introducing their collection, facilities, exhibits, programming, and offering comments by experts about the highlights of the collections and special exhibits. These are designed not only to bring local people to their museum but also to encourage international tourists to include it in their itinerary.

The 2020–21 pandemic restrictions further accelerated the digitization of collections and the development of virtual tours, audio stories, online conferences and discussions, and other innovations—also in English—to provide the museum experience in visitors' homes. The access to these online collections and digital programs is free, with donations and memberships strongly encouraged. For example, the Mauritshuis, in The Hague, with a collection of Dutch Golden Age paintings, provides Second Canvass, an app that contains gigapixel images[78] of its collection and the museum galleries, making it possible to zoom in on the smallest details; a number of its paintings can be viewed as infrared images making visible the changes the artist had made to the canvas. This app includes audio stories and exhibit labels for thirty-six of its masterpieces.[79]

Similarly, the Van Gogh Museum in Amsterdam has extensive online programming that can bring nearly everything the museum has to offer into the homes of those interested: trek through the galleries on one's own and linger at and zoom in on favorite pieces; watch videos about the artist, the collection, and a 4K virtual tour on the museum's YouTube channel; listen to podcasts on Spotify about Van Gogh's letters; research the properties, exhibit label, provenance, and literature for a particular painting in the online collection; and

---

[77] https://www.rijksmuseum.nl/en/rijksstudio; Ann Randall, "A Virtual Visit to the Rijksmuseum," *Dutch, the Magazine* (March/April 2023), 12–13.

[78] One thousand times the information captured by a one-megapixel digital camera.

[79] https://www.mauritshuis.nl/en/explore/the-collection/virtueel-mauritshuis/.

take in slide shows about different aspects of Van Gogh's life and legacy.[80] The collections of all the principal art museums in the Netherlands and other collections of Dutch art around the world are now available online in English to everyone at home, at work, and in education, along with related information and explanatory material. When considering American eyes—or those of any other nationality—on these works of art, it is again necessary to distinguish between those that, beside their artistic qualities, convey and represent some characteristics of Dutch life, culture, history, and geography and those that do not (international and abstract Dutch art and Dutch art of non-Dutch subjects and places). Both are valuable, but the former can more directly help make Americans better informed about the Netherlands itself.

These multimedia online services and programs on the digital platforms of Dutch art museums represent a staggeringly large potential American—and global—market of people, schools, colleges and universities enjoying and learning about Dutch art and, by extension, the Netherlands, compared to in-person visits. Rather than a reduction in digital offerings once in-person visits and international travel resumed (after Covid restrictions), museum critics argued for their expansion: "With cheaper and rougher digital tools—just do it on your iPhone, for goodness' sake— every exhibition should become a Zoom classroom, a podcast lecture, a Twitter thread."[81] Robust, in-person, visitor num-

bers will be needed to finance museums' virtual platforms; online advertising of a museum's virtual services will also drive up visits and donations to its website. Holland.com is an important website for information about the Netherlands as a tourist destination, including its art museums.[82]

In-person visits and online services are, at least in part, related. There is little justification for the claim that parallel online museum services will drive down in-person visits. In fact, visiting a museum's website— for example, the site of the Rijksmuseum— can build interest for a future in-person visit, with a rise in income or as part of international travel. In addition, a virtual visit may follow an in-person visit when a person wants to relive and review their experience, learn more about and show others what they saw, take in artwork they did not have time to see, or revisit pieces that really stood out. And for the many Americans who will never have the opportunity to visit a Dutch art museum or a Dutch art exhibit in person, there is the option of a virtual visit, which in its own way and with the continuing development of technology, can offer an equally rich, informative, and multifaceted viewing and learning experience.

Dutch photos galore

When their *National Geographic* arrives in the mail, Americans try to find time—before next month's issue—to leaf through it. And there is a reasonable likelihood that, in any given year, there will be an opportunity to learn from the text and photos something about the Netherlands and its territories in that magazine. Occasions for enjoying and learning from visual

80 https://www.vangoghmuseum.nl/en/visit/enjoy-the-museum-from-home.

81 Jason Farago, "Reimagining Museums. After Enormous Challenges, 10 Ways They can Survive and Thrive in the Post-Pandemic World," *New York Times*, Museums, 23 May 2021, national edition.

82 Holland.com is the official website for the Netherlands as a tourist destination; it is managed by the Netherlands Board of Tourism and Conventions.

Fig. 8.37. Photo of Hegebeintem, Friesland, NL (one of 63), included in an excursion guide about terps (occupation mounds) that I prepared for students. The terp has largely been dug away to sell its fertile soil, and only the approach road to the church and a few houses at the top of the terp remain. The flooded field on the right becomes a skating rink during freezing spells (*Uberprutser, CC BY-SA 4.0 via Wikimedia Commons*).

media about what sets the country apart still come to the American public principally as magazines in the mail, movies in the classroom, exhibitions at an art museum, assignments in formal education, and Dutch news from newspapers in print and on the internet, including the online English-language, Dutch nltimes.nl. People either choose or are assigned these opportunities and these visual media—as part of written accounts or by themselves—and they normally come as curated, directed, edited, and themed stories, reports, exhibits, and films. Not so for the hundreds of millions of photos about the Netherlands and its territories available by way of Google, Bing, Wiki, and so forth, and global and Dutch for-profit and public-image banks and archives.

The most common route—today entirely a reflex action—for Americans to ac-

cess Dutch pictures is googling the name of a place (Utrecht), person (Antonie van Leeuwenhoek), history (Dutch Golden Age), or topic (Friesian Holstein) on the internet as a targeted information search that is part of any number of encompassing projects and everyday activities—leisure or work-related tasks, travel planning, professional writing, or working on course and subject assignments in higher education, just to name a few. All human enterprises, at times, may need and benefit from a quick online search to provide information, clarification, or understanding. Such daily queries are the instantaneous, handier, and more fulsome internet versions of the earlier print encyclopedias. Visual media are an integral part of the search results.

For a good part of my career in higher education, I was tasked, among other

Fig. 8.38. In 1933 the Steenstraat, the principal shopping street of the city of Arnhem, Gelderland, celebrated its 300th anniversary. The street is decorated on both sides on the second story, with white candles topped with a flame (not for Christmas but for the anniversary). Notice the tram rails, the mixing of car and bicycle traffic (in 1933), and the pedestrians along the storefronts (*Netherlands National Archives, photo collection Spaarnestad*).

responsibilities, with programming related to the Netherlands, including courses and talks about Dutch topics for American students in both the United States and the Netherlands, screening of Dutch fiction and documentary films, and month-long geography excursions with field guides in the Netherlands for American students. Visual media are indispensable for teaching these programs effectively; photos for lectures and excursion guides came from a wide variety of sources. For the past twenty years, internet photos, especially Wikimedia Commons, however, were at the ready

and filled a lot of visual gaps in journals and books (fig. 8.37).

If Americans cannot find a photo for the Dutch topic, person, or place they are looking for among the more than sixty-five million images in Wikimedia Commons, there are global for-profit "microstock" photo companies—such as Shutterstock, 123RF, iStock (Getty Images), and others—with hundreds of millions of royalty-free, searchable images, including many Dutch photos. Hollandse-hoogte.nl and other Dutch websites sell tens of millions of general Dutch images and, for specific catego-

Fig. 8.39. Teahouse, Druten, Gelderland, 1976, a national monument located on the outside of the dike of the river Waal. The towering structure appearing behind the house on the other side of the dike is a crane for ship repair (*Ton van der Wal, photo collection of the Cultural Heritage Agency of the Netherlands, CC BY-SA 4.0; https://creativecommons.org/licenses/by-sa/4.0, via Wikimedia Commons*).

ries, Buiten-Beeld.nl sells nature photography, and aerophotostock.com specializes in Dutch aerial photos.[83] In addition to microstock photo companies, Dutch public (government) photo archives are open for searches, that is, the National Archives of the Netherlands (fig. 8.38), the Cultural Heritage Agency of the Netherlands (fig. 8.39), the Amsterdam City Archives, and other provincial and municipal archives. The National Archives holds more than

fifteen million largely historical photos, searchable and filtered by collection, key word, theme, location, and person. Many are downloadable; others require permission. The Cultural Heritage Agency of the Netherlands recently transferred its more than half-a-million photos to Wikimedia Commons, making them fully accessible. Dutch microstock companies and government photo archives generally allow for searches in English; most of the captions and other metadata, however, are in Dutch.

Even though hundreds of millions of Dutch photos from microstock companies and public archives for any place, topic, historical period, or person are today just a few clicks away, the American public is further removed from such images than a google search. Unless people are working on a Dutch project, interest, or travel, these vast Dutch photo resources are unlikely to be viewed and shape the American perception of the country more broadly. One does not need a subscription to access microstock sites, and their images can be searched, browsed, enjoyed, and studied for themselves—even with watermarks. These companies' raison d'être, however, is not to make their photo collections available to the public but to sell subscriptions to businesses and individuals to use photos for their publications, research, advertising, and websites. For that reason, very few consumers will venture on to these sites unless they are looking for usable photos. The world is awash with Dutch photos, but that has not led to a rush by the American public to see them.

The American public *will*, however, be interested, respond, and be educated by curated photos about the Netherlands and its overseas territories found in print and digital photobooks, coffee table books, visual stories, photo atlases, and magazines and newspapers, as well as photo exhibits and museums. Beside original photographs shot for especially for a book or exhibit, photo archives and microstock companies are also sources of photos for such curated works.

From DVDs to streaming: Dutch video-on-demand, geoblocking, and subtitles

From 2011 to 2018, revenue from subscription streaming—by far the most-used type of VOD service in the United States—soared to $12.8 billion. During the same period, DVD sales revenue, after peaking at $16 billion in 2005, fell from $6 billion to $2 billion.[84] Since 2018, both in the United States and around the world, even more subscription VOD (SVOD) services have entered the market, and VOD will dominate home, small-group, and especially educational film viewing, advancing the eventual demise of the DVD market.

It is hard to know precisely how VOD will impact the availability and viewership of Dutch films in the United States as fewer titles are released in DVD format. Several conditions, however, are already apparent. Many VOD services that include films produced in and about a country are, for the most part, located within that country. Without a subscription to an Internet Protocol television service (IPTV) in the United States, such as Apollo Group TV that includes Dutch channels and streaming platforms among its international offerings, people living outside the Netherlands will be geoblocked from subscribing to Dutch streaming services. Dutch immigrants and expatriates face formidable barriers, and the larger American public is shut out of Dutch SVODs and Dutch content in IPTV altogether by the lack of English subtitles. Residents of the United States need a geolocated IP address in the Netherlands to be able to subscribe directly to Dutch streaming services such as Videoland, Pathé Thuis, Cinetree, NPO Start & Plus, and others, but sometimes they *can* use a VPN (virtual

[84] Whitten, "The Death of the DVD." The many types and qualities of streaming are discussed in Hendrik Storstein Spilker and Terje Colbjørnsen, "The Dimensions of Streaming: Toward a Typology of an Evolving Concept," *Media, Culture & Society* 40, nos. 7–8 (2020): 1210–25.

private network) to hide their IP address and gain access. Monthly fees for both the VPN and the Dutch streaming services, however, would be a significant barrier for many Dutch speakers in the United States, although the VPN can be used for multiple SVODs and has other benefits, like privacy and security.

Such an extra step is entirely moot for all other Americans: although Dutch streaming services add Dutch subtitles to their non-Dutch content, they generally do not add English or any other language subtitles to their Dutch-language programming. Their subscribers, after all, are in the Netherlands and, presumably, speak and understand Dutch. Unless they change their business model, Dutch streaming services cannot facilitate the international distribution of Dutch films and, by extension, knowledge about the Netherlands. Much more of the content carried by the Dutch streaming services—except NPO Start, NPO Plus, and Videoland—is not Dutch but American; they have acquired Dutch rights for this material, and allowing non-Dutch viewers to subscribe would violate these rights.

Also in the Netherlands are the largely American-owned, international SVOD streaming services already available in many other countries. Some—Netflix, Amazon Prime, Acorn TV, Disney⁺, Apple TV—focus on feature films, drama series, and documentaries; others—Kanopy, Curiosity Stream, MagellanTV, and National Geographic—specialize in documentary films. Their films are normally streamed in their original spoken language, and subtitles are made available in several languages. A documentary's narration may sometimes be revoiced in a world language. It is important to note that the slight difference in what is on offer from these international streaming services by country is not because of the presence of films about or produced in that country but because of different restrictions on the rights to some programs.

This first group of international streaming services—mainly with fiction films but some documentaries—it was thought, would carry Dutch films to the American public, given the decline of DVDs. But in November 2021, Netflix offered just four Dutch fiction films, one sitcom (*Toon*, 2017), and no documentaries. Three of the features are about WWII (*The Forgotten Battle*, 2020; *The Resistance Banker*, 2018; and *Riphagen*, 2016); the fourth, *Layla M.*, 2016, is about a Muslim teen in Amsterdam. With hundreds of English-subtitled Dutch films currently available on DVD, there clearly is not yet a tipping point between physical and streaming media, even when including other international streaming companies besides Netflix.

There are actually very few Dutch feature films offered by these services, and I doubt, given their international focus, selection standards, and business model, that they will become the standard for Dutch producers to market their films internationally and the American public to find and enjoy Dutch feature films. Some new Dutch films do regularly show up— and then disappear—but the body of noteworthy Dutch cinema since WWII and a more representative selection and updates to current feature films, worthy of international attention, will not come to these sites. For now, DVDs will continue to be produced for Dutch feature films because their sales are higher than documentaries. These physical media, however, will eventually become unavailable for Dutch feature films.

The second group, international documentary streaming services, does not fare much better. They carry hardly any films produced or directed by filmmakers in the countries themselves; rather, SVOD services either produce their own films or license documentaries by American and international producers and organizations. When searching "Netherlands," "Holland," and "Dutch" on magellantv.com., the only films that turn up are about Vermeer, Van Gogh, and Rembrandt, all from non-Dutch filmmakers; old and new Dutch masters have received enduring international interest and these offerings continue this successful formula. A similar search on curiositystream.com brings up films and series about the Dutch-born courtesan and spy Mata Hari, the Dutch architect Rem Koolhaas, the food industry, the tulip speculation bubble, and deltas of the world. These documentaries are more international in scope; each film has Dutch content but combines it with material from other parts of the world.

To preserve and expand international interest in Dutch films and get ready for a time without DVDs, Dutch public broadcasters, film museums, and the country's film and television industry need to fund and develop viable streaming platforms that allow non-Dutch viewers onto their sites. From the provider's point of view, streaming, unlike physical media, has the advantage of global distribution from a single national location linked to servers elsewhere, even when, as with Netflix, there are regional and national versions. With streaming VOD on the way to becoming the dominant distribution system

for national film and television industries with the technical capacity to transmit video globally, there is less benefit to selling international streaming rights. It may still be more profitable to sell international rights to a hoped-for Dutch hit, such as *The Forgotten Battle*, to an American or other international platform for a limited period. Overall, however, keeping international streaming rights to Dutch films and television in-house is a more productive way forward. It will, I believe, result in greater sustained economic benefits to the Dutch film and television industry, more effective soft-power Dutch diplomacy (like the NIS), and more American and other eyes on the Netherlands.

Today, American and other international viewers are shut out of the Dutch SVODs that carry much of the Dutch content—such as Videoland, NPO plus, and NLZIET—by both the absence of subtitles and the geoblocking of subscriptions. Their permissions for showing non-Dutch content apply only to Dutch residents, making it illegal, under such arrangements, for Dutch SVODs to market beyond their national borders.

Dutch SVODs already came on the scene during the mid-2010s. The recent rise of other national streaming services, such as BritBox in 2017 (United Kingdom), Joyn in 2019 (Germany), and Salto in 2020 (France), is also instructive for SVODS streaming national content outside their country.[85] National SVODs have come on the scene to counter the increasing cultural dominance of the American ones, such as Netflix and Disney⁺—number one and three in the Netherlands.[86] National

---

[85]   www.joyn.de; www.salto.fr; www.britbox.com.

[86]   trending.nl, "film en televisie," 15 Dec. 2021.

SVODs are business enterprises, but they also make accessible to their residents their own country-specific body of film and video media; they meet and cultivate people's interest in, loyalty to, and pride in their country and help form shared experience and knowledge. Like the Dutch SVODs, Joyn and Salto are also available only to German and French residents, respectively, unless people also subscribe to a VPN, and even then, they still receive the service only in the language of the country. These platforms are not able to share French and German film content with the rest of the world. For such a culturally and diplomatically worthwhile goal, a different kind of VOD service will be required, one with both public and private investment.

BritBox has followed a decidedly different path—one of sharing and profiting from making British film culture available to countries around the world, something the Netherlands should embrace, albeit with a different configuration. BritBox was able to export British film culture, especially initially, by virtue of a geographically extensive, English-speaking world, both as a primary and secondary language, and an earned reputation for high-quality British films and television. The front pages of the site invite everyone to "Indulge your inner Brit," something, apparently, all human beings have.[87] BritBox first shared and exported its film culture not with their own but with the American public (2017). Other English-speaking countries, members of the Commonwealth, soon followed: Canada (2018), United Kingdom (2019), Australia (2020), and South Africa (2021). These were obvious choices, given their use of English, the contribution of Great Brit-

ain to the derivation of their own cultures, and their fondness for and familiarity with Great Britain. No subtitles in other languages are needed. It would be like Dutch SVODs branching out to the Dutch West Indies and Suriname.

BritBox in 2023 is available in the United States, the United Kingdom, Australia, Canada, South Africa, Sweden, Finland, Denmark, and Norway.[88] Like all multinational SVODs, BritBox creates closed national markets for its streaming service; the content varies somewhat from country to country, and only residents of the country are able to subscribe. The additional countries BritBox is eyeing are not yet identified, but many will lack the bonds to Great Britain and the English-language facility of the earlier expansions. British programming, together with national and other non-British programming, will be needed to create the demand required for a profitable BritBox SVOD in these countries. Even with some receptive English in these markets, much of the content will need subtitles in their native language or in a larger more common lingua franca.

For more than a century, and throughout the 35 mm, videocassette, DVD, and (now) the streaming eras, the global dominance of movie and television exports from the American film industry has carried American entertainment, culture, and influence to all parts of the world. At the same time, and on a much smaller scale, other countries with well-developed film industries and a movie-going public have also marketed and shared in other ways their films with their neighbors, region, and the world by means of (some)

---

[87] www.britbox.com/about.

[88] https://help.britbox.com; "BritBox Expands to Nordics in Landmark Streaming Deal," *CityAM* (14 Dec. 2021).

theatrical and television showings, diplomatic missions (the NIB/NIS), cultural institutes, museums, world fairs, and (later) the export of physical media for home and nontheatrical viewing (videocassettes and DVDs).

Currently, the formal and legal organization of SVODs is by nation state, preventing them from exporting their content; those outside their boundaries are either blocked from receiving their services or unable to use them in their own language, as with international IPTV. Today, only if national SVODS establish their own SVODs in other countries can their film culture, broadly speaking, really be shared across their borders. The large, American international SVODs, such as Netflix, Apple+, and now BritBox, have been able to set up and profitably operate their own country-specific SVODs, making American and British content, together with other film media, available in outside national markets. One would think that Spain or another Spanish-speaking country could also successfully run SVODs in the twenty-one Hispanic countries around the world. But this is not an option for such countries as the Netherlands, Sweden, Canada, Greece, the Philippines, and Australia, with fewer compatible outside markets, less well-known cultures, and a more modest film and television output. Given that the worldwide distribution of films via DVD is ending, how will national SVODs need to be reconfigured to market, share, and profit from exporting their film culture internationally?

There is no single answer to this question because there really are no good examples yet, and different configurations and their successes and failures will need evaluation. Several things, however, are clear: with DVDs going away, streaming films beyond national borders will become an increasingly important issue for a country's film industry and its public diplomacy; with streaming without boundaries, countries and their film production companies can more easily retain and benefit from international streaming rights for their films; a country's domestic SVODs need to be kept separate from its international one, the former have multi-country, the latter, only in-country content; and both public and private investment is required for a country's international SVOD.

Here is one suggestion for an international SVOD configuration for the Netherlands and similar countries that builds on these requirements. Launch an SVOD joint venture ("Dutchbox"), available only to non-Dutch subscribers, with investments from Dutch film companies and Dutch institutions funded in part by the state and other levels of government, for instance, public broadcasting, the Eye Filmmuseum, and the Institute for Sound and Vision. For new Dutch feature films and suitable documentaries, after their theatrical run, followed by a contractual international SVOD run (e.g., Netflix, Curiosity Stream), have Dutchbox claim and retain their international streaming rights. In time, acquire, recover, and assemble for Dutchbox international (streaming) rights to the body of Dutch feature films (e.g., *Soldaat van Oranje*) and documentaries (e.g., *Alleman*) from the beginning of the Dutch film industry—including documentaries from the NIB/NIS collection—to the near present.

Monetize Dutchbox programming with competitive rentals, purchases, subscriptions, government subsidies, and advertising. Revenue would come, not from long-term subscriptions and a loyal customer base—such as Netflix supplying most of one's entertainment needs and wants on a continuing basis—but from short-term (months) subscriptions and one-time rentals, with constant customer turnover. "Enjoy and explore Dutch films for a month or two" could provide the tagline for the online front page for English-speaking countries. Provide subtitles for documentaries designed and suited for international viewing and for all Dutch feature films on such a site in world languages (English, Spanish, and Chinese) and neighboring languages (German, French, and Italian). Earn revenue and strengthen the brand, as many SVODs now do, from original Dutchbox films and programming (documentaries, feature films, film series, talk shows); with the rapid growth of streaming companies the world over, SVODs are always on the lookout for more and different content to give them a leg up. Make deals to include Dutchbox as channels and offerings on platforms in other international and different countries' SVODs. Finally, be patient; give Dutchbox time to build out, and become known internationally.

There are likely other configurations for an internationally oriented Dutch SVOD based on the coming realities related to streaming. Even with a market of several billion people (save for the Dutch themselves), Dutchbox might still not make it. Much will depend on the initial content at roll out, quality, and promotion (hook) of the site; it must be state-of-the-art, user-friendly in multiple languages, up-to-date, and appealing. It needs trailers and links to other information about the films and other content on the site, quality streaming servers in multiple locations, and frequent introductions of new content.

Together, these might well set a success marker for a nation streaming its films and film culture to the rest of the world without the wherewithal and markets to roll out SVODs in many different countries in the manner of Britbox and Netflix.

The consequences of not having some kind of Dutch international SVOD in the near future are three-fold: (1) many new Dutch films, especially suitable documentaries prepared for international audiences, will never be streamed outside the Netherlands; (2) new releases and oldies that are streamed internationally will be hard to find, scattered among any number of platforms and with uncertain residence periods; and (3) much of the corpus of Dutch films dating back to the 1950s made available with subtitles in DVD will not be transferred to streaming and will disappear from international viewing. Together, these would set back immensely the worldwide enjoyment and influence of Dutch cinema and, by extension, knowledge of the Netherlands.

Coming full circle: The NIB/NIS film library and the history of Dutch visual media in the United States

Before the beginning of mass visual media in the late nineteenth century, Dutch paintings, drawings, and prints were mostly in private hands; they hardly circulated and were viewed by others only via local social networks. Notable pieces were available to a very small public in national museums. Things began to change with the arrival of photography and film and with museums becoming more widespread and accessible.

It is best to picture the overall availability and consumption of Dutch visual media in the United States from the late nineteenth to the early twenty-first century as a slightly upward-sloping line. In any place—more in cities and towns—a sporadic Dutch news photo or photo spread would show up in the daily newspaper and magazines at home or at the library; a nearby city museum would include some Dutch canvasses in its permanent collection or would hold a special themed temporary exhibit of Dutch paintings; an illustrated novel or a social studies textbook would incorporate some Dutch scenes; or an American educational film about the Netherlands would be shown in a college geography class. This was the baseline formed by everyday Americans and Dutch Americans routinely interacting with Dutch visual media for over a century; the consumption rate rose slightly over time as population, education, and income increased, and media circulated more widely. Dutch immigrants and Dutch Americans consumed Dutch visual culture at higher rates.

That slowly rising baseline registered two spikes—one from the Dutch NIB/NIS films distributed from 1943 to 1974, the subject of this study, and the other, at the start of the twenty-first century, the global adoption of the internet in every area of society, in this case, in commerce and visual media. The first spike was temporary, the second, permanent, and not yet played out. Each, in its own way, altered the more customary pattern of Americans' interaction with Dutch visual media: the first by adding another Dutch visual medium—film—the second, much more transformative, by potentially making not only all the types but also much of the body of works of Dutch visual media available to the American public all the time.

The NIB/NIS film program, the first spike above the baseline, added Dutch documentary films and made them widely available for three decades. It was much different from the customary American interaction by individuals with Dutch visual media. This diplomacy had agency and was corporate and systematic, targeting schools, army posts, civic organizations, and churches who, in turn, selected the film(s) and scheduled and presided over the screenings for groups of people, with a possible introduction and a Q & A session afterward. The NIB/NIS added this promotional program above the baseline in the 1940s to persuade the American public to take the side of Dutch foreign policy and throughout the entire 1943–74 period to educate Americans about the Netherlands and its territories during a time of world war, reconstruction, and renewed prosperity. Movie houses were not at all new, but film then still had a marked appeal, and group viewing outside of theaters remained special. The film experience was more impressive and broad based than the older Dutch visual media.

From 1943 to 1974, the films distributed by the NIB/NIS with Dutch public funding brought about the largest-ever availability and viewership of Dutch documentaries in the United States. This Dutch-government program operated film libraries and kept borrowing records, but when the NIS closed its doors, these and all other records and holdings were archived for its Midwest service region only. This made it possible for the first time to survey and analyze the content of and response to Dutch film media distributed in the United States, which is the focus of this study. The heretofore diffuse sources of Dutch visual media and their use by individuals had precluded such research.

Dutch film diplomacy began in the 1940s with American-made, culture-directed films about the Netherlands, which outperformed all others, and the NIB was quickly confronted with the deep-seated and longstanding American perception of the country, brought to the surface by these films. I detail and discuss, especially in chapter 4, this preferred, romantic imagery Americans held about the Netherlands of old. It may be argued that the NIB played into these positive perceptions to press its foreign policy objectives in the 1940s. The reception of Dutch-made NIB/NIS films over the next two decades played out, in part, against this traditional/modern pairing, and it may be seen as a campaign to extend the American admiration and approval of the premodern Dutch republic with its legacies and looks to the struggles and modernization of the then present-day country. In the process, millions of American viewers did learn a great deal about the Netherlands from the more-than 150 promotional and independent films—the country's WWII suffering and destruction, postwar reconstruction, and follow-on economic recovery and prosperity during the 1960s. They were also introduced to some of the Netherlands' master filmmakers, members of the widely acclaimed Dutch documentary school. Whether these earlier, long-held American perceptions helped or hindered a transfer of affection remains an open question. At a minimum, they created a readiness and an interest among Americans to attend film screenings about a country they viewed quite positively. More realistically, some up-to-date aspects of the country (water

defenses) lined up better with public preconceptions and preferences, others, less so (modern high-rise apartment buildings and planned cities).

The circulation of the NIB/NIS films about the Dutch colonies/territories was surprisingly robust; about half the titles and viewership during the 1940s belonged to this category, followed by a marked decline in both measures in the following decades. These did not benefit from the Holland Mania period or other American expressions of fondness for the Netherlands itself. Rather, these came, in one group of such films, from a general curiosity about exotic lands and peoples, long common in Western countries. For the first time, this fascination could be met, not with maps, paintings, sketches, and written accounts, but with moving pictures. The islands and territories depicted may have been under Dutch colonial rule, but the Dutch footprint was nowhere to be seen. They could have been French, British, or independent territories, and the documentaries would have been much the same. These American-made travelogues in the NIB/NIS film library were portrayals of the lifeworld of indigenous peoples in these areas, albeit filmed by outsiders. Americans who borrowed these films from the NIB learned about these places from an unlikely source.

Unlike the culture-directed films about the Netherlands' overseas colonies/territories that circulated in the United States, more for their intrinsic value, the other group had clear extrinsic values for American audiences. They underlined the geostrategic, trade, and resource advantages of the colonies (Dutch East and West Indies) for prosecuting the war as part of a defense of Dutch colonialism and, after the war, sang the praises of the emerging tourist potential of the Dutch West Indies in the United States' backyard. Americans were surprised and pleased to learn about Dutch territories nearby.

The closure of the NIS in 1974 led to the complete disappearance of these and future Dutch documentaries in the United States and to a fallback to the baseline of Americans' interaction with Dutch visual media for the next three decades. During this time, the production and scope of documentaries grew remarkably in the Netherlands as everywhere else. Their ability to educate Americans about the country and its territories, however, went unrealized.

The second spike, from the beginning of this century, opened up by the internet, transformed the availability of Dutch art and photographs in the United States from sporadic to permanent and from selected locations to everyplace. Online DVD sales supplied the American market with English-subtitled Dutch feature films, but Dutch documentaries still remained missing. The second spike is still unspooling; the internet—at the expense of DVDs—is changing how people watch films. It will slowly choke off the current production of DVDs of Dutch feature films with English subtitles. Streaming has the capacity to bring Dutch documentaries and feature films to households all over the world, all the time, provided an SVOD can be configured to be profitable and affordable. If less- and unprofitable film media, such as documentaries, are bundled with other genres (feature films, television series, news) in a Dutch SVOD with private and public investors, then all types of Dutch film media can be shared with the United States and the rest of the world. With the

NIB/NIS film diplomacy, the Netherlands punched above its weight, and it can do so again.

APPENDIX

Viewership of Holland-NIB/NIS Films

Title	1940s	1950s	1960/70s	Total	Circu-lation
ABC*	0	0	973	973	1962-65
A Bit of Life in Java	10,768	0	0	10,768	1944-49
A Country for My Son	0	0	5,166	5,166	1973-74
A Day at the Zuiderzee	0	0	1,781	1,781	1973-74
A Garden Granary*	12,828	0	0	12,828	1943-49
A Procession of Giants*	0	0	21	21	1973
A Wall	0	0	2,912	2,912	1973-74
A Way to the World	0	0	784	784	1973-74
Adventures in Perception	0	0	17,040	17,040	1973-74
Amphibian Postman	0	1,510	376	1,886	1954-61
Amsterdam	0	50	2,737	2,787	1959-74
Amsterdam City of Canals	0	0	45,890	45,890	1962-74
Amsterdam Concerto	0	0	1,797	1,797	1973
An Army of Hewn Stone	0	0	2,219	2,219	1963-74

*Not in archive

An East Indian Island	41,984	0	0	41,984	1943-49
And There Was No More Sea	0	1,187	33,037	34,224	1959-74
And They Named It Holland	0	0	6,544	6,544	1973-74
Application	0	0	4,115	4,115	1973-74
Around the Pacific	540	0	0	540	1945
Bali, Paradise Isle	9,249	0	0	9,249	1943-49
Baliem Valley	0	0	752	752	1961-62
Basic Mechanisms in Neurophysiology	0	0	1,493	1,493	1974
Battak of Sumatra	6,510	0	0	6,510	1944-48
Bells of Holland	0	26,365	210	26,575	1951-63
*Big City Blues**	0	0	2,813	2,813	1973-74
Big Four	0	258	0	258	1952
Birds' Paradise, Wadden Sea	0	0	751	751	1973
Bloemententoonstelling Lisse	0	376	0	376	1956
Blue Peter	0	0	731	731	1963-73
Breakers	3,762	0	0	3,762	1944-48
*Breda**	0	0	130	130	1962-63
Broken Dykes	20,178	5,448	288	25,914	1947-62
Building Game	0	0	4,367	4,367	1973-74
Celebes and Komodo	13,276	0	0	13,276	1944-48
Ceremonies on Bali	33,763	0	0	33,763	1943-49
Children of Holland	0	228	0	228	1952
Circus Elleboog	0	0	5,852	5,852	1973-74
*Costumes and Customs of Holland**	0	50	2,357	2,407	1959-74
Curacao	0	17,401	1,174	18,575	1951-74
Dam the Delta	0	0	16,041	16,041	1973-74
*De Grond Waarop Wij Leven**	0	0	2	2	1963-64
*De Nederlandse Heide**	0	376	0	376	1956
*December: The Month for Children**	0	553	5,378	5,931	1959-74
Delta Phase I	0	0	29,278	29,278	1963-74
*Docks in the Rotterdam Seaway**	0	0	1	1	1964
*Dry Docks at Rotterdam**	0	0	516	516	1961-63
Dutch East Indies	11,860	0	0	11,860	1943-49
Dutch Guyana	40,268	0	0	40,268	1943-48
Dutch in Latin America	6,004	9,606	0	15,610	1948-55

Dutch Miniatures	0	0	68,842	68,842	1961-74
Dutch Next Door	25,225	0	0	25,225	1945-48
Dutch Tradition	75,419	0	0	75,419	1943-49
Dutch Way	0	25,119	4,404	29,523	1950-65
Dynamic Amsterdam	0	0	420	420	1973
Educating the Native Population	0	0	376	376	1962
Elements Facing Elements	0	0	594	594	1973-74
Eleven-Towns Tour	0	0	3,743	3,743	1964-74
Emeralds along the Equator	509	0	0	509	1944-49
Empire in Exile	4,806	0	0	4,806	1944-48
Erasmus, Voice of Reason	0	0	1,761	1,761	1965-73
European Holiday*	0	25	0	25	1958
Everything or Something	0	0	7,469	7,469	1973-74
Eye Spot, Buy Spot*	0	501	676	1,177	1959-62
Faja Lobbi	0	0	2,738	2,738	1973-74
Fanfare*	0	0	1,176	1,176	1960-61
Fishermen in Exile	16,110	0	0	16,110	1945-49
For Better Living	0	0	140	140	1963
Friesland	31,214	5,329	190	36,733	1946-63
Gateway for Giants	0	0	1,445	1,445	1973-74
Gateway to Europe	0	0	435	435	1964-73
Gateway to Germany	16,408	0	0	16,408	1945-49
Girls of Holland	0	0	3,273	3,273	1973-74
Glass Square	0	0	917	917	1973-74
Glimpses of Holland*	0	90	6,005	6,095	1959-75
Glimpses of Picturesque Java	50,380	0		50,380	1943-49
Golden Age*	0	0	30	30	1974
Graphic Art, Its History and Technique	0	0	7,441	7,441	1973-74
H. M. Queen Juliana's Visit*	0	375	0	375	1950s
Hans Brinker*	0	1,007	0	1,007	1950s
Hans Brinker's Return	0	2,986	2,688	5,674	1955-65
Happy Holland	0	14,432	9,630	24,062	1954-64
Helpers on the Threshold	0	0	1,143	1,143	1973-74
Herring Fishing	0	784	2,701	3,485	1956-64
High Stakes in the East	40,734	0	0	40,734	1943-48

Hold Back the Sea	0	0	51,246	51,246	1963-74
Holland*	0	90	1,507	1,597	1956-74
Holland and Its Cities*	228	0	0	228	1949
Holland and the Dutch	27,569	0	0	27,569	1944-49
Holland and the Zuyder Zee	72,865	0	0	72,865	1945-48
Holland Blooms Again	32,843	11,547	0	44,390	1947-55
Holland Carries On	52,143	8,192	0	60,335	1945-56
Holland Sailing	0	0	376	376	1962
Holland Today	0	0	113,615	113,615	1964-74
Holland: A Maritime Nation*	0	8,417	0	8,417	1950-55
Holland: A Modern Country, pt. 1	0	136,799	4,701	141,500	1950-65
Holland: A Modern Country, pt. 2	0	24,232	947	25,179	1952-63
Holland: A Modern Country, pt. 3	0	9,339	145	9,484	1952-60
Holland: A Modern Country, pt. 4	0	10,005	546	10,551	1952-62
Holland: Flower Center of Europe*	0	50	1,520	1,570	1959-65
Holland: Garden of Europe	0	17,027	3,515	20,542	1950-63
Holland: Its Cities and Industries*	60	0	0	60	1945
Holland: Its Cities and Provinces*	5,104	0	0	5,104	1946-49
Holland: Land of Tulips*	0	0	3,287	3,287	1960-65
Holland: Terra Fertilis	0	0	2,287	2,287	1973-74
Holland's Bricks	0	0	1,443	1,443	1963-74
Holland's Farmers Became Bankers	0	942	0	942	1954-57
Holland's Safety Valve*	0	0	1,807	1,807	1964-74
Holland's Visor*	0	0	608	608	1973-74
House *	0	0	4,286	4,286	1973-74
Impoldering van de Zuider Zee*	0	376	0	376	1956
In and around Amsterdam	900	13,052	3,144	17,096	1949-65
Injured Man	0	0	435	435	1966
Interlude by Candlelight	0	0	4,207	4,207	1973-74
Into the Wind's Eye	0	0	228	228	1974
Introducing the Netherlands*	0	3,663	8,475	12,138	1950-65
Island of Faith	0	29,336	0	29,336	1950-57
Island of Yesterday	3,393	0	0	3,393	1944-49
It's Just a Postage Stamp	0	7,961	120	8,081	1957-62
Java and Sumatra*	0	228	0	228	1950

Juliana: Koningin der Nederlanden	0	0	2,229	2,229	1973-74
Keukenhof*	0	0	155	155	1974
Land below the Sea	0	8,119	33,594	41,713	1951-65
Land of Milk	0	3,263	8,578	11,841	1954-65
Land of Tulips*	0	0	42	42	1961
Landbuilders	97,483	59,879	0	157,362	1943-59
Language of the Flowers	0	0	10,616	10,616	1960-74
Lekko	0	0	1,145	1,145	1973-74
Life in Holland	0	1,307	0	1,307	1954
Life in Holland: A Short Story	0	5,672	1,018	6,690	1951-62
Limburg*	0	0	300	300	1974
Limburg and Noord Brabant*	0	0	185	185	1973
Little Dutch Tulip Girl	14,917	0	0	14,917	1944-49
Macassar	21,368	0	0	21,368	1943-48
Magic Square	0	0	2,521	2,521	1965-74
Magnificent Tulip*	0	0	1,007	1,007	1960-65
Malays of Sumatra	7,774	0	0	7,774	1944-49
Medical Care of the Native Population	0	10,597	6,210	16,807	1957-62
Mediaeval Dutch Sculpture	0	3,600	2,232	5,832	1952-74
Men against the Sea*	0	10,682	30	10,712	1953-61
Met Koningin Juliana en Prins Berhard op Reis door de V.S.	0	2,207	125	2,332	1953-61
Mirror of Holland	0	0	2,918	2,918	1960-74
Nations United for Spring Beauty	0	6,019	133	6,152	1953-63
Nato Tattoo*	0	0	42,761	42,761	1965-74
Netherlands America	52,163	3,900	0	56,063	1943-52
Netherlands East Indies	21,731	1,474	0	23,205	1947-50
Netherlands Molen*	0	376	0	376	1956
Netherlands West Indies*	0	4,190	0	4,190	1950-56
Netherlands, The, and Its People	6,121	0	0	6,121	1946-49
New City, New Land	0	0	752	752	1961
New Earth	78,098	32,646	19,128	129,872	1943-65
New Village on a New Land*	0	0	1,002	1,002	1961-73
Nias and Sumatra	30,932	0	0	30,932	1943-48
Old Dutch Paper	0	584	0	584	1952-53

One Million Homes*	0	0	280	280	1964-73
Open Window*	0	1,098	4,987	6,085	1957-74
Operation Mud*	0	0	200	200	1973
Outside the Borders	1,661	0	0	1,661	1946-48
Overijssel*	0	0	190	190	1962-63
Paintings of Co Westerik	0	0	491	491	1973-74
Pan	0	0	4,164	4,164	1973-74
Panta Rhei	0	0	2,706	2,706	1973-74
Peaceful Conquest	0	6,962	766	7,728	1952-63
People of Shangri-La	0	0	3,551	3,551	1960-62
Peoples of Java*	492	0	0	492	1945
Peoples of the Indies	43,519	0	0	43,519	1945-49
Piet Takes a Barge Trip*	0	50	3,981	4,031	1956-64
Polyclinic in the Wilderness	0	0	4,875	4,875	1960-62
Portrait Painting in Holland*	0	0	1,632	1,632	1961-65
Praise the Sea	0	0	1,073	1,073	1973-74
Primitief Nieuw Guinea	0	0	1,011	1,011	1961-62
Princess Beatrix's 18th Birthday	0	0	230	230	1960
Princess Beatrix's Visit to US	0	0	1,839	1,839	1960-64
Promise of Heaven	0	0	3,613	3,613	1973-74
Quaint Old Holland	30,173	0	0	30,173	1943-49
Queen Juliana in Her Kingdom*	0	0	730	730	1961-63
Reclamation of the Zuider Zee*	0	0	61	61	1964
Rembrandt Painter of Man	0	0	4,762	4,762	1960-74
Rembrandt's Etching*	0	0	436	436	1962-65
Report, Netherlands New Guinea	0	0	1,355	1,355	1962
Rescue from Shangri-La	13,924	3,521	0	17,445	1946-54
Rhapsody for Happy People*	0	0	751	751	1973-74
Roaming the Netherlands	69,704	631	0	70,335	1944-52
Romance of Rubber	8,886	50	0	8,936	1944-51
Rotterdam Europoort*	0	0	210	210	1962-63
Sailing	0	0	522	522	1973-74
Saint Nicholas in Holland*	0	50	1,103	1,153	1959-74
Scheveningen*	0	0	110	110	1962
Schiphol*	0	0	748	748	1973

Seven Provinces*	0	0	471	471	1964-65
Shoot the Nets	0	1,097	962	2,059	1953-74
Short Seven*	0	0	115	115	1973
Silver Wedding Anniversary*	0	0	1,059	1,059	1963
Six Bits of Holland in the Caribbean	0	21,176	1,931	23,107	1950-64
Slochteren on the Line	0	0	228	228	1974
Speaking of Glass	0	0	68,236	68,236	1963-74
Spoils of Conquest	22,811	0	0	22,811	1943-49
Springtime in Holland	0	10,358	13,347	23,705	1954-75
St. John's Church Windows*	0	0	42	42	1962
Steady as She Goes	0	0	3,643	3,643	1963-74
Steamboat to Holland	0	0	4,894	4,894	1964-74
Stormramp	0	12,371	1,560	13,931	1953-63
Sunday on Grande Jatte*	0	0	2,042	2,042	1973-74
Taming the Tide*	0	0	2,766	2,766	1962-74
Te Aworó	0	0	3,502	3,502	1973-74
That Most Living City	0	65	2,264	2,329	1959-65
There is a Telephone Call for You*	0	0	1,266	1,266	1973-74
There is Music in Amsterdam	0	0	1,402	1,402	1973-74
They Said It with Tulips	56,364	16,502	0	72,866	1946-58
Third Tuesday in September*	0	0	3,328	3,328	1963-74
This Changing World*	6,212	0	0	6,212	1944-49
Toradja	12,288	0	0	12,288	1944-49
Touch*	0	0	912	912	1974-74
Tour of Inspection	0	0	468	468	1961-62
Tulip Fields*	0	0	190	190	1962-63
Tulip Time in Holland*	235	0	0	235	1946
Tulip Time Slides*	0	3,364	0	3,364	1950s
Tulips, Windmills, and Wooden Shoes*	270	0	0	270	1947
Twenty Hours a Day	0	398	150	548	1954-65
Two Queens	9,560	6,899	0	16,459	1949-54
Vibration	0	0	43,170	43,170	1963-74
Vincent van Gogh	0	0	270	270	1973
Vlaardingen	0	0	416	416	1963-64
Voice of the Water	0	0	7,327	7,327	1973-74

Watersnood 1953	0	376	0	376	1953-56
We, the People of Suriname	0	0	3,570	3,570	1965-74
With a Cool Head and a Warm Heart	0	0	1,029	1,029	1973-74
Zuyder Zee	7,382	0	30	7,412	1944-74
Holland-NIB/NIS Total Viewership	**1,280,968**	**634,795**	**887,856**	**2,803,619**	**1943-74**

Notes

2:5 I am following David Snyder's account—based on archival sources—of the establishment, work, and outlook of the RVD and NIB. David J. Snyder, "The Problem of Power in Modern Diplomacy: The Netherlands Information Bureau in World War II and the Early Cold War," in *The United States and Public Diplomacy. New Directions in Cultural and International History*, ed. Kenneth A. Osgood and Brian C. Etheridge (Martinus Nijhoff Publishers, 2010), 57–80. Also helpful, Snyder, "Dutch Cultural Policy"; Roholl, "To Put Holland on the Map," 4–12; and Bert Van der Zwan, "De Regerings Voorlichtingsdienst te London (RVD), 1940–1945," in *Het Londens Archief: Het Ministerie van Buitenlandse Zaken tijdens de Tweede Wereld Oorlog*, ed. Bert Van der Zwan (Boom, 2003), 37–45.

2:6 The Dutch television program, *Andere Tijden*, included a program on Holland, Michigan, in which Jerome Heldring, former director of the NIS in New York City, gave an account of the choice of Holland, Michigan, as the NIB regional center for the midsection of the country and the related appointment of Willard Wichers as its director. "Holland, Michigan, Andere Tijden," http://www.geschiedenis24.nl/andere-tijden/afleveringen/2005-2006/Holland-Michigan.html (accessed 9 Mar. 2016). Even with the exhaustive archives of Willard Wichers at the Holland [Michigan] Museum and the NIB/NIS in the HSASC, neither a definitive biography of Wichers nor a history of the (Holland) NIB/NIS has been written. Wichers, Willard C., Papers, HMA; NIS, HCASC. Biographical summaries, sketches, and tributes of Wichers are found in: David Snyder, "The Netherlands Information Service Collection: An Introduction," *Historia Actual Online* 8 (Fall 2005): 203; Elton J. Bruins, "Willard Wichers, Founder, Director: The Netherlands Museum, 1937–1986," in *The Netherlands Museum, Holland, Michigan, 1937–1987*, comp. Elton J. Bruins (1987), 55–59; Elton Bruins, "Tributes to the Memory of W. C. Wichers," Elton J. Bruins collection (H88-0019), HCASC.

2:11 Snyder, "Dutch Cultural Policy," 978–79. Unlike the NIS, the British Information Services (BIS) lasted until the end of the 20th century. Moreover, it never shifted into predominately culture-directed diplomacy as had the NIS. The BIS continued to provide commentary in the American press in response to articles, editorials, films, and books critical of Britain and the British position and role in current events in places such as Rhodesia and Northern Ireland. See https://wikispooks.com/wiki/British_Information_Services (accessed 8 Mar. 2016). Once Indonesian independence had become a reality, the Netherlands, unlike Britain, did not have sufficient international presence, resources, and gravitas for the American press to take much notice of the country and for an agency such as the NIS to be able to step in to challenge and "correct" American viewpoints.

2:16 David Snyder provides a comprehensive overview of the contents of the NIS archive of the Holland, Michigan, NIB/NIS branch; Snyder, "The Netherlands Information Service Collection," 201–9. For documentation, throughout, I used the finding system and detailed container list for the NIS archive in place at the Holland Museum, 2011–14. This is the only archive of the NIB/NIS; similar materials from New York and the other branches were returned to the Netherlands where, apparently, they were substantially culled. In 2022 the VRI became the owner of the NIS archive.

2:23 There is an extensive body of literature on propaganda films; helpful are: James Combs and Sara T. Combs, *Film Propaganda and American Politics: An Analysis and Filmography*, 2nd ed. (Routledge, 2014); Ralph Donald, *Hollywood Enlists! Propaganda Films of World War II* (Rowman and Littlefield, 2017); Jo Fox, *Film Propaganda in Britain and Nazi Germany: World War II Cinema* (Bloomsbury Academic, 2013); and Martin J. Manning and Clarence R. Wyatt, eds., *Encyclopedia of Media and Propaganda in Wartime America*, 2 vols. (ABC-CLIO, 2010).

2:29 Stills were cut from the digitized renditions (MP4s) of the 16 mm films. They were often of inferior quality because the film stock was from forty to eighty years old and, as a result, had taken on a sepia color; moreover, over their lifetime, the films had been run through countless different projectors in varying states of disrepair.

Once selected, the stills were imported into Photoshop Elements for enhancement, but even with this, their quality sometimes remained compromised, especially so with the stills from the films of the 1930s and 1940s. Nevertheless, even with their visual shortcomings, the stills, together with their captions, do communicate some aspect of the content, themes, and composition of a film and are an essential component of this study. The discussion of each film selected for a closer reading is accompanied by a still with a caption. The Holland Museum Archives (HMA) in Holland, Michigan, has given this author the right to incorporate still images captured from the films in its NIS archive.

3:3   Unless otherwise noted, the 16 mm films, along with their digitized renderings, are part of the NIS holdings, formerly held by the HMA. In this study, I am including only those films listed in the film-showing reports and used to produce the activity reports sent by the Holland branch office to the director of the NIB/NIS in New York. The film library included other titles not included in these reports. In 2011 the work to digitize these two hundred-plus, 16 mm films was begun, funded by the Meijer Chair in Dutch Language and Culture at Calvin College, the Netherland America Foundation, and the Holland Museum. The films were screened at Calvin College with a 16 mm projector, captured with a professional camcorder, and rendered as MP4 files. The project was completed in July 2013. Several films could not be digi-

tized because they were too damaged to run through a projector. The digitized films became part of the NIB/NIS archive, of which the HCASC assumed custody in 2021.

3:8   In 1920 the National Union of Christian Schools (NUCS) brought together the Christian schools founded by Dutch Reformed immigrants and their descendants beginning in the late nineteenth century. Such schools were present in the Dutch educational system, and Dutch Americans replicated them in their adopted land. During the lifespan of the NIB/NIS, these Christian schools were overwhelmingly Dutch American in leadership, teaching staff, and students. For the history of these Christian schools, consult Harro W. Van Brummelen, *Telling the Next Generation, Educational Development in North American Calvinist Christian Schools* (University Press of America, 1986); Henk Aay, "Present from the Beginning: Reformed Dutch Day Schools in North America, 1638–2019," in *Dutch Reformed Education: Immigrant Legacies in North America*, ed. Donald A. Luidens, Donald J. Bruggink, and Herman J. De Vries Jr. (Van Raalte Press, 2020), 3–37.

3:10 Aggregate attendance figures for every film title were derived from the database of borrowing records for each year and for the decades of the NIB/NIS of the 1940s, 1950s and 1960s/70s. When these were arranged in rank order, there were a number of unknown film titles with very low attendance figures at the bottom of the lists. Many of these appeared to be the result of record-keeping shortcuts and errors by borrowers, NIB/NIS staff, and possibly, the students who created the database from the borrowing records. These titles were not found either in the film archive or in any online film databases. When there were reasonable matches with the title of a known film, the data for the films were combined. For example, for the list of films shown during the 1950s, *West Indies* (964) is not part of the archive and not found in any published or online filmography, so it was combined with the known film *Netherlands West Indies* (3,226). Similarly, *A Maritime Country* was joined with the known title *Holland: A Maritime Nation*, and *Holland: Its Land and People* was combined with *Holland: A Modern Country*, pt. 1, *Country and People*. Where there were no reasonable matches, these unidentified films were kept in the database. Because of their small attendance, their impact, as well as their effect on the overall analysis, was minimal. In any event, since they were not found, their contents could not be appraised.

3:13 As with any identification methodology, some operational rules were adopted. If a place could be unambiguously identified from the film but was not mentioned by name in the voice over, it was included in the inventory. If a place was mentioned by name but without much visual attention, it still became part of the inventory of Dutch places American audiences heard about and viewed in the films. Of course, places are always nested: the Netherlands itself is a place containing all of its places. Smaller places nest within larger ones and so on: from regions and rivers to towns to districts to individual buildings and to their interior and exterior spaces. I drew a (somewhat arbitrary) line at the scale of villages, towns, and cities: places within these units were not included in the inventory. For example, there are a number of films in the collection that showcase the city of Amsterdam, but I did not include sites and districts of all kinds within that city and certainly not sites in the interior of buildings. There are other films of interior spaces only (e.g., *Rembrandt Painter of Man*) that also were not counted as Dutch places seen by American viewers. And there are films (e.g., *The Building Game*) that show no clearly identifiable places, even though many different sites are shown.

4:2 In 2008 the NRC Handelsblad, the Netherlands Institute for Sound and Vision, and Tijdsbeeld Media released a collection of three boxed DVD sets about the history of the Dutch documentary film: *Tijdsbeeld Nederland, Hoogtepunten uit de Nederlandse Documentaire Film, 1945–1977*. The first boxed set is about the Dutch documentary school: pt. 1, *Hollandse Documentaire School, 1945–1963*. It contains eleven classic films belonging to this genre chosen by documentary film historian Bert Hogenkamp and the NRC newspaper. The moviemakers listed here are the directors of these films. The NIB/NIS film collection includes ten of these documentaries if we allow Haanstra's longer and more conventional *Speaking of Glass* to count for the shorter, Oscar-winning, film/poem version, *Glass*.

4:7 The total number of viewers in the 1940s from the circulation data was expressed as a percentage of the population of the states that made up the Midwest service region from the 1950 US census. That percentage was then applied to the population of the states that were part of the East and West Coast service regions, respectively, in order to make reasonable estimates of their total viewership of the NIB films. I made the same calculations first from the 1950s and then from the 1960s/70s circulation data to estimate the viewership in the other two service regions during those two periods, using the 1960 and 1970 US censuses, respectively. "Historical Population Change Data (1910–2020)" at census.gov.

4:11 Throughout this study, where a percentage is given for the number of viewers reported from a specific group—in this example, the total number of viewers of all the NIB/NIS films screened from 1943 to 1974 as enumerated in the circulation data— it is the percentage of this larger group that the graph or map is based on. Or, in another case, the percentage might be of the total possible number of viewers of films about the Dutch colonies during the 1940s as reported in the circulation data. The higher the percentage, the more accurately it represents the entire group. In fig. 4.9, the number of viewers of the top fifty films represent nearly 80 percent of the total number of viewers of all NIB/NIS films. In almost all cases,

the films with very small attendance figures and related marginal cultural impact were not included in surveys, follow-on analyses, and results reported by graphs or maps.

4:12 The total number of film titles from the circulation records has been somewhat challenging to pin down. After reconciling different spellings and word order for the same film title from the NIB/NIS film-showing reports, there are 227 film titles in the database. Some titles, however, appear to be shortened versions of full titles or Dutch-language versions of English ones. When such films are combined, the number is reduced to 218. This issue applies particularly to a number of films with small attendance figures and is difficult to resolve because most of these titles are not in the Holland Museum NIB/NIS film archive nor in the online film databases in the Netherlands, United Kingdom, or United States. For comparative statistical purposes, I have continued to use 227 for the number of films.

5:9 The first is Doc. K. Sternberg, *Rescue from Shangri-La*, London Film (1947; 17,445). Although the film is about WWII and set in the Dutch East Indies, it is not in any way related to Dutch foreign policy or to the Dutch colonies. The film describes the rescue of American C-47 plane crash survivors by an American air force unit in Dutch (Papua) New Guinea (part of the Dutch East Indies) in 1945. It was produced by the film unit of the Netherlands Indies Government Information Service. The film was meant especially for American audiences and marketed by other distributors besides the NIB. Its production may be seen as another example of Dutch public diplomacy reaching out to the United States, its ally and friend. The second is *A Garden Granary* (n.d.). This film remains a mystery; it was borrowed from the Holland-NIB from 1943 to 1946 and viewed by 12,828 moviegoers. It is neither in the NIB/NIS film archive nor listed in any of the national film databases regularly consulted for this project. The film cannot be classified from its title.

5:24 I have not been able to view the original film for *Landbuilders: Walcheren*. The British Film Institute collection includes the title *Landbuilders* with 1935 as production/release year and Adrian van der Horst listed under the production company heading. This suggests that an English-language version of *Walcheren* was possibly already available for repackaging into a Dutch war-propaganda film. The Dutch film archives, the Netherlands Institute for Sound and Vision, has the Dutch-language film *Walcheren* (but only the first part) but not *Landbuilders* in its collection and designates *Walcheren* as the predecessor of *Landbuilders*. It lists Adrian van der Horst as the director, with 1932 as the production/release year. The opening credits of the copy held by Holland-NIB include certification by the British Board of Film Censors (n.d.) for a film with the title *Landbuilders*; this indicates that this propaganda film may have been produced in the United Kingdom. The narrator cer-

tainly speaks with a British accent. The opening credits also list the Netherlands Government Information Bureau, and not the NIB, as an agency cooperating in the production of the film. This suggests that the RVD (the larger national Dutch umbrella government information service, established immediately in London after the Dutch surrender to Germany) was involved in its production. The Dutch film archives (the Netherlands Institute for Sound and Vision) also lists the RVD as the producer. This points to a release of the film during the very first year of the war, before the NIB became operational.

5:38 Fitting the key components of the tourist landscape all together onto a poster makes the relationships among them problematic. Polder dikes were not the locus of railway lines; they were not straight but very irregular in outline. More direct, separate, and stronger embankments were needed. The windmill is incorrectly visually associated with the dike's seepage ditch (water seeping through or underneath the dike is evacuated by this feature); the mill, rather, lifted water that flowed in drainage channels to the edge of the polder by gravity, up and over to the other side of the polder dike into a receiving waterway (the ring canal) and out to sea.

5:44 Hogenkamp, *De Nederlandse Documentaire Film, 1920–1940*, 131–49 (filmography). Hogenkamp underscores that his list of 1920–40 films is very provisional and that many are no longer available or complete. Most reflect the aims and interests of very specific Dutch organizations and businesses (e.g., the New Malthusian League, the Construction Workers League, the Gazelle Bicycle Factory); these would have been wholly unsuited to the purposes of the NIB. I focused on those titles listed in the filmography as part of the repository of the RVD (the Rijksvoorlichtingsdienst). This was the government agency that disseminated information both at home and abroad. I also paid attention to any films commissioned by the Association of the Netherlands Abroad (Nederland in den Vreemde) and by the Association for Tourism (Algemene Vereniging van Vreemdelingenverkeer). Together, these represent the kinds of films the NIB might have wanted to have in its lending library, assuming it had access to them during the German occupation and that they could be converted from 35 to 16 mm film. Like the NIB, these organizations were in the business of representing the Netherlands abroad. I have not viewed and studied these films themselves. Where available, I have only reviewed the scene-by-scene, timed descriptions from the Netherlands Institute for Sound and Vision archive as an indication of their potential value to the NIB.

6:6   For example, for the film, *The Dutch Way*, the producer was Maurice T. Groen for DPM Productions, New York City, and part of the Films of the Nations (FON) series. Film material shot by Dutch moviemakers was used by Groen for this and other films about the Netherlands he produced for DPM Productions. *Land below the Sea* was a Walter Smith production,

made by the Caltex Oil Companies; the closing credits report that it was one in a series of films made in the interest of international understanding. Even with the revival of Dutch filmmaking and the availability of Dutch-made films, the NIS had to depend on American companies to produce Dutch-made films for the American market. Although I regard the use of American-made travelogues about the Netherlands and its colonies by the NIB during the 1940s as a serious setback for American understanding of the country, the same cannot be said for American-acquired/produced documentaries from footage often filmed by Dutch directors and camera crews during the 1950s.

6:7   The Dutch title is *Holland: Een Modern Land met Oud Glorie* (Holland: A modern country with long-standing glory). The English title uses the word "charm" instead of "glory," a telling change. For the Dutch public, "glory" was meant to evoke Dutch nationalism, Dutch pride, whereas "old-time charm," directed to viewers in other countries, was a much different phrase, one that focused on what was visually pleasing and historically interesting in the Dutch past. In addition, using "Holland" in the title, rather than the official name, "the Netherlands," was also reaching out to the older and more well-known traditional aspects of especially the western parts of the country.

In January 2009, the Dutch television channel Geschiedenis 24, as part of its series *In Europa+1950*, aired two parts of the film, one about agriculture and the other about transport and trade. Until recently, these parts could still be viewed via the archive of its programs. The program reported that the film was not a big success on the Dutch movie-theater circuit. The film does provide a historical source for how government authorities wanted people, both within and outside of the country, to view the Netherlands.

6:9   This film series was the first and only NIS documentary to be broadcast on television during the 1950s, and altogether, there were sixteen broadcasts of its parts by eight different television stations, the first and introductory part, seven times, and each of the three others parts, three times. Viewership based on Nielsen ratings was provided for only one broadcast. Because viewership for television programs varies so widely depending on the program and the market area (from 6,000 to 100,000 in the NIB/NIS circulation records), I did not assign estimates of viewership to these broadcasts. No matter what the viewership of these broadcasts was, however, it is clear that television catapulted these NIS films to the top four shown in the 1950s. They do not appear in the Wilson *Educational Film Guide*, the most widely used nontheatrical film catalog in the United States; the viewership came entirely from the NIS. This series had the largest impact on American perceptions of the Netherlands during this decade as measured by NIS film attendance.

6:14   The story about a boy, the hero of Haarlem, who, with his finger, plugged a leaking dike and waited until help arrived, has its more direct origin as a separate story in Mary Mapes Dodge, *Hans Brinker, or The Silver Skates: A Story of Life in Holland* (1865); Dodge, *Hans Brinker, or The Silver Skates* (Dover, 2003). This same story was already found in many different American school textbooks and based on one in *Harper's Magazine* in 1850, which in turn had borrowed it from the just-published British magazine *Sharpe's London*. That magazine had translated it without attribution from the French author Eugénie Foa. She had written a story in 1848, not about a boy plugging a hole in a dike with his finger but, rather, about the son of a lock keeper blocking with his hand—not finger—spouting water from a hole in the gate of a lock in a canal. And Foa's story was not original either; earlier versions circulated during the first decades of nineteenth-century France. Because it was thought that children in the United States would not understand the operation of a lock, a dike was chosen for the American version of the story. Peter van der Krogt, "Het Onmogelijke Verhaal van Hans Brinker of de Held van Haarlem," *Geografie* 31, no. 5 (May 2022): 42–43.

6:16   There are at least three statues of Hans Brinker in the Netherlands: one shown in this film, in Spaarndam, a suitable location for Mary Mapes Dodge's "Hero of Haarlem," a part of her novel, *Hans Brinker, or the Silver Skates*; another, in Harlingen, Friesland; and the best known, on the faux tourist dike at the entrance to the miniature village of Madurodam in The Hague. These statues have given the broader Dutch public, as well as international tourists, more reason to accept Hans Brinker as an historical Dutch figure and this American folktale as an historical event. This is all the more remarkable because the long history of flood protection in the Netherlands has always been a highly cooperative effort, with people from different communities and water boards patrolling dikes during storms, as well as inspecting and repairing them. Dodge's Hans Brinker is a quintessential American hero, the lone individual who single handedly saves his community.

6:17 FilmVandaag.nl currently lists and summarizes nearly 700 Dutch-made documentary films; not many treat places and regions. Two examples of recent films about Dutch places not in the travelogue mold are *Weemoed en Wildernis* (melancholy and wilderness) and *De Nieuwe Wildernis* (the new wilderness). The first is a film about Tiengemeten, an island in the delta in the southwest of the country. It was originally reclaimed from the sea and made into an agricultural landscape; recently, it was transformed yet again into a wetland. The second is a film about the Oostvaardersplassen, a nature and wildlife preserve that developed rather spontaneously with the creation of the Flevo polders during the 1960s; today, it is sandwiched between two large new and planned cities—Lelystad and Almere.

6:29 The Holland-NIS film from this series is a 16 mm print with English-language narration. The Netherlands Institute for Sound and Vision, which holds the rights to the New Guinea Chronicle series, does include the Dutch but not the English-language films. The English versions and titles are not found in any of the online film databases. There were many other films made by Dutch filmmakers in New Guinea in the years after Indonesian independence from 1949 until 1963, when the area became part of Indonesia. The Institute for Sound and Vision lists more than 2,500 entries under Nieuw Guinea. The Dutch government invested heavily in the development of the region and sought to make it a showcase of enlightened colonialism for its own population and for the international community; this included publicity by means of documentary films.

7:1 There is an extensive literature on the Netherlands during the 1960s, both academic and popular. A very helpful, eight-part, popular television series is *Ondersteboven: Nederland in de Jaren 60*, VPRO/NTR, 2016; a companion book for the series is Petra Boers and Rebecca Wilson, *Ondersteboven: Jouw Nederland in de Jaren 60* (Walburg Pers, 2015). More scholarly accounts of this period include: James C. Kennedy, *Building New Babylon: Cultural Change in the Netherlands during the 1960s* (PhD dissertation, University of Iowa, 1995); Geert Buelens, *De Jaren Zestig. Een Cultuurgeschiedenis* (Ambo/Anthos, 2018); Frans Messing, *De Nederlandse Economie, 1945–1980. Herstel, Groei, Stagnatie*

(Unieboek, 1981); and Hans Righart, *De Eindeloze Jaren Zestig. Geschiedenis van een Generatieconflict* (De Arbeiderspers, 1995).

7:10 This English title, *Dam the Delta*, also does not match the contents of the film. The first level of confusion is in the phrase "the delta." When Dutch and other writers refer to the delta, as in the Delta Plan or the Delta Works, they mean the island archipelago at the outlets of the Schelde, Maas, and Rhine Rivers in the southwest corner of the country. But people also speak of the Netherlands as a delta land; this refers to the fact that, not only the southwestern corner but also the entire low Netherlands from north to south is a delta environment. The Dutch title of the film, *Nederland Deltaland* (Netherlands delta land), references that more general delta setting. The second mix-up comes with the verb "dam." Dams, in this case, are sea walls (dikes) built in the estuaries between coastal islands or in sea arms to prevent storm surge and flooding farther inland. This film, however, is not only about sea dikes but about all the water management technologies and institutions developed over the centuries (listed on pp. 150 and 151).

7:32 These are the titles of the New Guinea documentaries acquired and distributed by the NIS during 1960/74 in descending order of viewership, including the release year for the Dutch-language films, viewership, and years shown: *Polyclinic in the Wilderness*, New Guinea Chronicle, no. 12 (1957; 4,875), 1960–62; *The People of Shangri-La*, New Guinea Chronicle, no. 15 (1958; 3,551), 1960–62; *Report from Netherlands New Guinea* (1958; 1,355), 1962; *Primitief Nieuw Guinea* (1956; 1,011), 1961–62; *Baliem, Mysterious Heart of New Guinea*, New Guinea Chronicle, no. 7 (1956; 752), 1961–62; *Tour of Inspection through South New Guinea*, New Guinea Chronicle, no. 5 (1955; 468), 1961–62; *Educating the Native Population*, New Guinea Chronicle, no. 8 (1956; 376), 1962.

8:15 The destination region of the immigrant artists (US, CA, S. Afr., Aust.) and their career timespan had considerable influence on the character of their artwork. For Dutch-immigrant artists in Australia, for example, see Nien Schwarz, "Dutch Artists in Australia: Artiesten in Australie van Nederlandse Oorsprong," in *The Dutch Down Under, 1606–2006*, coordinating author, Nonja Peters (University of Western Australia Press, 2006), 398–415. Substantial Dutch immigration to Australia did not begin until after WWII and remained strong throughout the rest of the century. Its Dutch-immigrant artists, therefore, were not influenced by or part of the earlier nostalgic American "Holland Mania" movement, nor did they spend time in Dutch art colonies. Their modern art did not use Dutch settings or visual language but, rather, engaged issues brought on by immigration to this continent bordering Southeast Asia—the journey, identity, worldly goods (all of one's possessions in one trunk), Western dispositions, and Asian refugees. Dutch immigration to Canada also first began in earnest after WWII and remained strong until the early 1960s. Canadian artist Rosemary Sloot, daughter in a Dutch immigrant family, created a series of twenty-one canvases layering objects, documents, photographs, and images from the Netherlands and Canada into a personal story of the two worlds of an immigrant. Rosemary Sloot, *Immigrant. From Postwar Netherlands to Canada in 21 Paintings* (Mokeham, 2022).

8:24 Jacob van Hinte devoted a section of his magisterial study of Dutch emigration and settlement in the United States to a survey and analysis of the Dutch American press; he listed 19 newspapers and magazines. Jacob van Hinte, *Netherlanders in America: A Study of Emigration and Settlement in the 19th and 20th Centuries in the United States of America*, ed. Robert P. Swierenga, trans. Adriaan de Wit (Baker Book House, 1985), 914–42. See also Henry S. Lucas, "Press and Politics," in *Netherlanders in America* (University of Michigan Press, 1955), 529–41; Conrad Bult, "Dutch-American Newspapers: Their History and Role," in *The Dutch in America: Immigration, Settlement, and Cultural Change*, ed. Robert P. Swierenga (Rutgers University Press, 1985), 273–93; Tom Bijvoet, "The Dutch Press in North America," in *Hiding in Plain Sight: Reflections on the Dutch Presence in Canada and the USA, 1609 to Today* (Mokeham, 2022), 88–92.

8:37 Submitting searchable words to this database produces fully cited thumbnails of *Life* covers, as well an extract from the text containing the high-

lighted word. I used the English-language name of the country (Netherlands, France, Greece), not their adjectival forms (Dutch, French, Greek), which were not useful. I did not enter any other Dutch place names or subjects because an American magazine would invariably identify for its readers the country that was the subject of its news and stories. *Netherlands* was present on 207 pages of *Life*, a small fraction of 1% of all its pages. *France* was found on 306 pages and *Greece* on 226 pages. These results are very crude measures of the coverage by an American magazine of other countries during a specific period, in this case, from 1936 to 1972. When *Netherlands* was present on several successive pages, multipage photo essays about the Netherlands itself as subject were easily identified. References to the Netherlands in other articles are not unimportant for extending Americans' knowledge of the country, but they will lack the depth of topical news and articles about the country and are unlikely to include Dutch photos. The frequency distribution of the word "Netherlands" in *Life Magazine* from 1936 to 1972, in broad measure, follows that of its photo essays about the country: 57.0% from the 1940s, 21.3% from the 1950s, and 8.2% from the 1960s.

8:40 This looked very promising and straightforward, but once the thumbnail pictures were opened to the page in the magazine, things became more complicated. The same picture(s) was used for different topics; not uncommonly, there was more than one picture per page, and the thumbnail was regularly part of a photo spread in which not all the photos were thumbnails in the index. I went through each of the 538 thumbnails, eliminated duplicates and those not of the Netherlands or its colonies/territories, for example, Dutch royalty at the memorial in Washington, DC, to President John F. Kennedy. I added others that were part of photo spreads but not included as thumbnails. I identified 516 photos—382 about the Netherlands and 134 about the Dutch colonies and territories. My survey likely missed some; one would need to review every issue with articles about the Netherlands and its colonies/territories and every thematic issue that might have some Dutch content. The *National Geographic* photo index is for photos only; additional visual material, such as maps or other graphical representations of information, for which *National Geographic* is well known, is not included. I created a database for these photos that includes the place of the photo and/or the province for Dutch places and the place and/or the larger region (island or island chain) for the colonial/territorial photos. I was not able to identify the place or the province for a small number of photos taken in the Netherlands. I also added the topic and year of publication for each photo to the database.

8:54 There is some information available about marketing, sales, and viewership of Dutch feature and documentary films abroad. IMDb, the largest internet movie database, does provide for many Dutch films international release dates at film festivals or on the internet (streaming) in different countries; ratings by US viewers; theatrical attendance and box office receipts in the Netherlands; as well as the names of distributors, their region (worldwide or specific countries) and film format (theatrical, television, video [VHS, DVD, Blu-ray]). There is no data, however, at IMDb for theatrical attendance and video (VHS, DVD) sales for Dutch films in the United States or any other country. This section is also based on my experience finding Dutch feature and documentary films with English subtitles to teach short courses on Dutch fiction films, lead off-campus programs in the Netherlands for Calvin University, and organize Dutch dinner and Dutch movie nights for friends at home. "Dutch Films" are neither necessarily about or set in the Netherlands and its territories nor do they need to be made by Dutch filmmakers. This study looks at a subset of Dutch films: those about the Netherlands and its territories.

8:67 As a Dutch American academic, born in the Netherlands, with teaching and research responsibilities related to Dutch topics, I try to keep up with the release of new Dutch movies, including documentary films. Some are very suitable for showing to an American or Dutch American audience interested in learning more about the Netherlands but without any knowledge of the Dutch language. These days, I expect to find English subtitles and the correct region code for viewing such films in the US on DVDs, yet I am regularly surprised and disappointed to learn that they are lacking.

Today, English subtitles may be available for some titles and can be downloaded and added to the DVD with the right software by someone familiar with such programs. Such individual efforts, however, do not help promote a more widespread availability of such films outside the Netherlands. Several examples of Dutch documentaries and documentary series deserving but lacking DVDs with English subtitles for an international audience are: a wilderness area that developed spontaneously on the former lakebed of IJssel Lake laid dry by drainage (*De Nieuwe Wildernis*, 2013), a 13-part film series about the Dutch Golden Age (*De Gouden Eeuw*, 2013), a 7-part series about the history of major floods in the Netherlands (*Nederland in Zeven Overstromingen*, 2014), and a 20-part series about many aspects of the Netherlands viewed from the air creating very instructive geographical patterns (*Nederland van Boven*, 2012–14). Each of these documentaries would be of interest to international audiences and contribute substantially to a better understanding of the country abroad. Yet marketers have made the calculation that not enough viewers outside Dutch borders would be interested in purchasing them.

A different business model for the international distribution of documentaries is needed and currently under trial-and-error construction: VOD, delivering rentals and purchases of films over the internet to take the place of DVD sales, and regional coding. Subscription streaming services are now beginning to market Dutch feature (fiction) films internationally by adding subtitle tracks to their offerings, for example, *De Twaalf van Oldenheim* (2017) on Amazon Prime, and *The Forgotten Battle* (*De Slag om de Schelde*) (2020) on Netflix. The streaming of documentaries, in contrast to fiction films, however, remains largely restricted to national territories by the IP addresses of subscribers.

8:70 This exercise is, of course, a one-time snapshot and does not account for all the Dutch documentaries that were at one time released with English subtitles and marketed in the US and the Netherlands but are no longer for sale. Given a national documentary film industry and international marketing, I think the results would have been much the same a decade ago. As in book publishing, film titles become unavailable and are no longer reissued; one must chase down films in the online used film market (ebay.com; marktplaats.nl) and in brick-and-mortar and online film libraries and museums (YouTube; Netherlands Institute for Sound and Vision; Eye Filmmuseum). VOD could make international viewing of country-specific documentaries more widespread; subtitles in a variety of world languages would be needed and the geographic viewing restrictions imposed by streaming services relaxed.

8:78 Stock photo companies emerged in the early twentieth century as the use of film photography in society steadily advanced. These firms bought commonly used, generic photos and/ or their rights and then sold them to companies and individuals to be used for different purposes (advertising, magazines, personal use). This was far cheaper for businesses than hiring professional photographers to set up and shoot desired scenes. Digital photography and the internet have revolutionized this industry; today, for-profit, microstock companies make hundreds of millions of royalty-free images universally accessible and affordable. Previously, these images were the private property of film-stock photo companies and their clients. But now, rather than selling film negatives to customers for hundreds of dollars apiece, many photographers upload digital images to microstock companies who, in turn, sell them to customers for less than a dollar apiece, or with a subscription, for less than twenty cents each. Both photographers and microstock companies profit from these sales. A subscription is not needed to browse the collections whose images do contain watermarks. But paying customers can affordably publish these images either on paper or online.

Index of Films

These film titles are referenced and/or discussed in the text. Where available, Dutch titles are also included.

* Films in the Holland NIB/NIS film archive

** Films in the Holland NIB/NIS circulation records but not the archive

INDEX

Made in the USA
Middletown, DE
19 September 2024

60671076R00245